COLIN HARVEY'S
EVERTON
SECRETS

Presented by JOHN KEITH

COLIN HARVEY'S

EVERTON
SECRETS

Presented by JOHN KEITH

Sport Media
A Trinity Mirror Business

Acknowledgements

With thanks to all those whose help and assistance was invaluable in the research, preparation and writing of this book. We are especially grateful to that master of Everton statistics Gavin Buckland, to Jack Enright and Alan Green of the BBC, Dave Ball, Ged Rea, Jim Greenwood, Peter Robinson, Dave Horridge, Mike Ellis, Colin Wood, the late Chris James and BBC Radio Merseyside.

Colin Harvey and John Keith

Published in Great Britain in 2005 by:
Trinity Mirror Sport Media,
PO Box 48, Old Hall Street,
Liverpool L69 3EB

Executive Editor: KEN ROGERS
Art Editor: RICK COOKE
Editorial Assistant: JAMES CLEARY

ISBN 0-9546871-6-7

Printed and finished by Scotprint, Haddington, Scotland

Contents

Foreword

by Kevin Ratcliffe

I had the privilege of captaining Everton through the most golden era in their history, that wonderful period under Howard Kendall during the 1980s, yet one man rarely receives the credit for his massive contribution to those years when we tasted glory at home and abroad.

That man is Colin Harvey. I don't think it is any co-incidence that the transformation in our fortunes in the so-called winter of discontent in 1983 happened after Colin had been promoted by Howard to first-team coach.

Colin has several overriding qualities. He is modest and self-effacing to a fault. But he is also a winner and a perfectionist, personifying the club motto *Nil Satis Nisi Optimum*, which loosely translates as 'nothing but the best'.

Nothing but the best has ever been good enough for Colin the football man, a trait honed during his days as one of the finest players in Goodison's galaxy of stars. The legend of the Ball-Harvey-Kendall midfield trio will pass down the generations of Evertonians.

My own career benefited enormously from Colin's coaching abilities at every level from youth team upwards. He was probably the biggest influence on my career. When he stepped up to take the first team his impact was instant. He cut out sloppiness and things changed dramatically. On the training ground he showed you how things could be done and what he wanted you to do.

From the time I started training as a youngster under Colin's charge I was struck by the fact that he never asked you to do anything he couldn't do himself. For those players who could take it, he gave them a mental toughness crucial if you're going to develop and perform at the top level. Every player had the utmost respect for him. Colin was relentless in ensuring you did the right thing and he would bring us back in the afternoons if need be. His determination to be a winner was clear because we'd continue a particular session until his side came out on top!

His partnership with Howard was perfect. They were totally different characters and dovetailed superbly. Howard flamboyant and Colin quietly but clinically efficient.

When Colin was thrust into the job of Everton manager his task was daunting to say the least. Some players were nearing the end of their careers and even experienced managers find it difficult to replace and re-build.

Yet Colin did a respectable job, helping the club to 4th, 8th and 6th in his three full seasons, which would have secured two campaigns of European football but for the post-Heysel ban on English clubs.

Colin has never been one to sing his own praises. This book captures the remarkable breadth of his contribution to Everton Football Club, his passion and devotion to the cause. It is a story that provides its own tribute to Colin Harvey, one of the greatest Evertonians of them all.

Being covered in champagne in the changing rooms at Burnden Park, Bolton after my winning goal in the 1966 FA Cup semi-final against Manchester United. It was the start of a long night!

Chapter One

A Golden Vision

Colin Harvey saw his chance and let fly with his left foot. The ball sped towards the Manchester United net as Harry Gregg dived and flung out his left hand, intent on diverting the shot around the post. The Irishman might even have succeeded had fate not intervened cruelly for United and joyously for Harvey and Everton. At the fateful moment, the ball bounced on the quagmire pitch, deceived Gregg and hit the net just inside his left upright. There were 12 minutes left of the 1966 FA Cup semi-final, agonising, nail-biting minutes for the fans, many of whom had arrived in Bolton the night before to ensure their entry into Burnden Park. Yet none of Goodison's travelling faithful was more ecstatic than 21-year-old Harvey when the final whistle sounded that April afternoon, a few weeks after the Pope and the Archbishop of Canterbury met officially for the first time in 400 years.

It had not been quite as long since Everton had been to Wembley, but in football terms 33 years is an eternity and the Goodison club had not graced a Cup final since the Dixie Dean era of 1933. Harvey had been weaned on stories about that great side, and his and Goodison's yearning to emulate Dean's team had intensified through Liverpool's first-ever FA Cup triumph a year previously. Everton's conquest of Matt Busby's Cup favourites, who had thrashed Benfica in their own Stadium of Light in the European Cup just a month earlier, set pulses racing on Merseyside, whose red section was infused with Liverpool's charge to the League title. Championship and FA Cup final glory would illuminate Harvey's burgeoning playing career, and he was destined to take a team to Wembley as a manager and taste triumph at home and abroad as a coach. Yet that day at Bolton, when his strike decided the clash of the great north-west rivals, remains his shining memory:

"Manchester United, surprisingly, had gone out of Europe three days before the FA Cup semi. Although they beat Partizan Belgrade 1-0 at Old

Trafford, they lost 2-1 on aggregate. George Best had missed the European game through injury and he was still missing when they met us. They had a Liverpool lad called Willie John Anderson playing in his place - funnily enough, he looked a bit like George - and they had their big guns such as Denis Law, Bobby Charlton and David Herd in the team. Everyone outside Merseyside expected United to win. They were above us in the First Division and not long before produced that fantastic performance in Lisbon when they beat Benfica - including Eusebio, Torres and Coluna - 5-1 in their own Stadium of Light, when Best gave a dazzling two-goal display.

But the game at Bolton was very even. It wasn't a classic, which is so often the case in semi-finals, and neither side played well. Then, a clearance from Ray Wilson was headed by Alex Young into the path of Derek Temple, who made a break down the left wing. I got up as close to him as possible. Derek pulled the ball back to me and from just inside the box I hit it first time as hard as I could. There'd been heavy rain and the pitch was like a bog. The ball kept low and bounced just in front of Harry Gregg and I think that might have been the deciding factor. It must have put him off a bit. It wasn't a blinding shot but it was one of those awkward ones for a goalkeeper. Sometimes that bounce just gets them. Anyway, the ball went just inside the post...it might have just clipped the post. But it went in - and the feeling was fantastic. It was sheer elation. Right through my career I didn't get many goals and this one was with my left foot, too! My right was my strong one, although I could use my left and I practised to strengthen it.

The goal at Bolton was one of only two I got that season and when I realised I'd scored I just jumped for joy. The pictures show me leaping with both feet off the ground and our goalkeeper Gordon West came running all the way up the pitch to join the rest of the lads who were congratulating me. Late in the game Alex Young hit the post and I confess to being glad it hadn't gone in! Alex, quite rightly, was a superstar, loved by the fans and the press. But if Alex's effort had gone in it wouldn't have just taken the edge of my goal - I would hardly have got a mention in the papers!

When the final whistle went our fans invaded the pitch and it was mayhem for a while. As I finally walked off Harry Catterick, never one to be over-demonstrative, came and shook hands with me. For Harry that was almost the height of emotion! Others, too, came up and congratulated me and I felt quite literally as if I was walking on air. I'd grown up hearing stories from my dad and other older supporters about the previous time Everton had reached the

Cup final, which was long before I was born. They beat Manchester City 3-0 in 1933 through goals from Dixie Dean, Jimmy Dunn and Jimmy Stein...the names swirled round my brain. Now my goal had taken Everton back to Wembley and my dad, grandad and my uncles were there to see it. We'd also reached Wembley without conceding a goal, the first team to do so for 63 years since Bury did it in 1903, which was a pat on the back for our defence.

When we left Burnden Park after the match there was a blue van outside with 'Harvey Scored The Goal' painted right across the side of it. They hadn't wasted any time! Back in Liverpool I had a couple of drinks in the pub with family and friends and then my brother Brian and I went to the Beachcomber, a city-centre club. To be honest I didn't need a drink. I was drunk on the experience. I ended up at a party at one of my friends, with the old Dansette record player belting out the 1960s hits. I've no idea what time I got home.

Next day we had a team meeting at Goodison to organise the players' Cup final pool. In those days, long before mega money arrived and the average First Division wage was around 40-odd quid a week, if you got to a final you could make a few extra bob from players' pools. Perhaps my celebrations on the pitch at Bolton were a little over-enthusiastic, because we had to play United again in a League game on the Monday and I had to sit it out with a calf strain. It was a goalless draw but my thoughts were still dominated by action replays of that wonderful moment at Burnden Park."

The Second World War was dragging into its last winter and Franklin Delano Roosevelt had just won an unprecedented fourth term as President of the United States, when James Colin Harvey entered the world. On the day he was born, in the Fazakerley district of Liverpool on 11 November 1944, a desperate Adolf Hitler handed his henchman Heinrich Himmler control of the German Army, which was incorporated into the Nazi Party. That same day too, the flow of the conflict powerfully in favour of the Allies allowed the Home Guard to be stood down and 24 hours later the German warship Tirpitz was left crippled by an attack of Lancaster bombers.

The war at sea had been at the forefront of the Harvey family's thoughts, especially new mother Jessie, who originally hailed from Liverpool's famous Scotland Road area. Her husband Jim, from Bootle, was a serving seaman on HMS Implacable and was destined not to see his first child until after the youngster's first birthday. Colin recalled:

"We lived in my grandparents' house in Gribble Road, Fazakerley and that's where I was born. It was a two-up two-down and as well as my grandparents, my mum and me, her sisters Joyce and Peggy lived there as did my uncle Billy Mallon, a shore-based Royal Navy engineer, when he was home from duty in Scotland. So it was pretty crowded!

My mum managed to get news of my arrival to my dad, whose ship was on Russian convoy duty protecting merchant vessels in the Arctic sailing to the Soviet ports of Murmansk and Archangel. The Implacable was also involved in the development of anti-submarine sonar detection equipment. He was at sea when he learned I'd been born but it was more than 12 months before he saw me. I was christened James Colin. My dad wanted to call me James but my mother wanted me to have the name Colin. As my mother was at home she called me Colin from day one. That's how it stayed and through my life I've had a few funny moments and a few questions about my name. Once or twice I've had queries from banks and such like, checking on my initials for official forms. Then I've had friends, when they've discovered my registered names, joke: 'We'll call you Jimmy from now on.'

At the end of the war my dad had the idea of being demobbed by the Navy in Australia and staying there to live. He started making arrangements but my mum would have none of it. If we had gone to live there I almost certainly would never have played for Everton, possibly never been a footballer. As it was, I wasn't very old when we went to live with my Auntie Rose and Uncle George in Leta Street. It's one back from Gwladys Street, and although it's been partly rebuilt that street is still there today.

Although my dad's Australian plan had been scuppered, for a life-long Evertonian like him - just like his father and all my mother's family - it was heaven to live there when he came back from the war because from that house it was only 50 yards walk to his beloved Goodison. With that background there was never any doubt about my football allegiance!

Even though we weren't flush with cash my dad made sure we had the latest football books, particularly about Everton. We lived at my auntie's for about two years before my mum and dad managed to get a prefab in the Old Swan area. While there I started school at St Paul's but after three years, when I was seven, we moved back to Fazakerley to live in Grieve Road, which was the first house my mum and dad had. We later moved to another house close by in Manica Crescent. By then I was at Holy Name School in Moss Pitts Lane and I'd play football for them every Saturday morning. My dad, who came back from war to work as a labourer for English Electric and later Massey Ferguson, always came to watch me. It didn't matter where we were playing he'd be there - and on some occasions he even gave the team talk. Then in the afternoon, if Everton were at home, he'd take my brother Brian and I. We'd go in the boys' pen and he'd stand on the Gwladys Street terraces. After the match we'd meet up outside a pawnbrokers on the corner of City Road and we'd get the bus back home to Fazakerley.

We were not one of those families who would go to watch Everton one week and Liverpool the next. We were just Everton through and through, although I played at Anfield before I ever set foot on Goodison Park. The Holy Name School team got through to the final of the Collier Cup against St Matthew of Queens Drive in 1956-57 and the game was played at Anfield. I was only 12 and the rest of the side were 15 and due to leave school that year. Both sides changed in the same Anfield dressing room. Our team were big and many of the St Matthew's players were even bigger. They towered over me because I was very small at that stage. But I played quite well and we won 2-1. It was the only thing Holy Name ever won. I played inside right that day because teams still lined up in the old-fashioned 2-3-5 formation.

I'd always played either as an attacking wing-half or a deep inside forward, the two positions that were later amalgamated into the modern midfield role which worked out so well for me. I was basically right-footed although I could use my left and I worked a lot on building strength in my left foot. In fact, right through my football life from schooldays to my career with Everton, I always used to go through a series of personal routines to develop skills. As a boy I'd attempt to kick a tennis ball 100 times to keep it in the air and I wouldn't move on until I'd achieved it. When I'd done it I'd go into the garage, close the door behind me and fire the ball at high tempo at varying angles against the wall and try to control it as it rebounded.

On a Sunday we'd go to see my granddad, who would regale us with stories of the great Dixie Dean. He was also an avid reader of the Daily Express, especially articles by Henry Rose, who was to die in the Munich air disaster of February 1958 when he was travelling with Manchester United. 'The Express has always had the best football pictures, right back to Dixie's day,' my grandad would tell us. At that time, in the 1950s, Everton were a mediocre side. They'd been relegated from the old First Division in 1951 and I saw them play during the three seasons they spent in the Second Division. They had to win their last match of the 1953-54 season - away to Oldham on April 29 - to come back up and if they won by six clear goals they'd do it as champions. It was a Thursday night match and as I was only nine and Brian even younger we couldn't go. My dad went by coach straight from work but there was such traffic congestion that it was half-time before he got in. The outside walls of one part of the ground were painted with slow-drying tar in an attempt to prevent fans climbing over. But the fans just piled newspapers on top of the tar and got in anyway! Everton coasted to a 4-0 win through two goals from John Willie Parker - taking his season's total to 33 - with Dave Hickson and Tommy E. Jones adding the others.

Although Everton just missed out on the Second Division title - finishing level on 56 points with Leicester, who had a superior goal average - the only thing that mattered was that they were back in the top flight. To make it even sweeter for Evertonians, as we went up Liverpool went down. Liverpool were to spend eight seasons in the old Second Division and didn't come back up until 1962. Everton's promotion kept alive the city of Liverpool's unique distinction of staging top-flight soccer every season since the Football League's formation in 1888. I remember my dad coming home from Oldham absolutely overjoyed and with a souvenir of the occasion - a sliver of the Boundary Park pitch in an envelope!

As well as Hickson and Parker other players I enjoyed watching included wing-half Johnny King, later to become a successful manager with Tranmere, inside forward Wally Fielding and the Irish contingent of Peter Farrell, Tommy Eglington and Don Donovan. Cliff Britton was Everton manager from 1948 to 1956 before Ian Buchan took charge for two years prior to Johnny Carey's appointment in October 1958. It was only then, with players like Bobby Collins arriving and the later signings of Roy Vernon, Jimmy Gabriel, Billy Bingham and the 'Golden Vision' himself, Alex Young, that you began to sense that here was a club that could make an impact on the First Division.

When I was 13 I passed the exam to go to Cardinal Allen Grammar School - now called Cardinal Heenan - in the year it opened. It was a rugby union-playing school but they made a concession for our year to allow us to play soccer and we had games against other Catholic grammar schools in the city, such as De La Salle and St Francis Xavier. I was lucky in that respect. I don't know what I'd have done if I hadn't been able to play football at school, although later the school changed its policy and has since produced quite a few good footballers, notably Steven Gerrard.

The chance to play for the Liverpool city schoolboy team never presented itself to me because in those days lads from grammar schools were not selected, although at the time the two inside forwards in the Liverpool schools team were Tommy Wright and Tommy Smith, both future England internationals and stars of Merseyside football. So even if I could have been available for selection I would have had to dislodge one of that pair to get a game! To be honest, it's not something I regret because at that age my physique was very slight especially compared to Tommy Smith who, as Bill Shankly so memorably said, was born a man! In later years the city boys team, which has been superbly successful over a long period, was drawn from players at all state schools in Liverpool following the introduction of comprehensive education. However, new problems now exist. Clubs who have set up youth academies and centres of excellence over the past decade or so have stopped their youngsters playing for the city schoolboys' team. They feel that they are investing in the youngster and that they should call the shots. But I think that's a negative attitude and quite wrong. It robs the boy of the thrill of playing for his city, which may prove to be the only representative opportunity that comes his way.

I played a bit of rugby at school and really enjoyed it. To this day I like both rugby union and league and I go to watch games if the opportunity arises. Rugby players are not angelic, but I do admire the respect they show to the officials, the absolute recognition of the referee's authority. You will see a small official scolding a giant player who totally accepts it and walks away like a reprimanded schoolboy. Soccer can learn a lesson from that. When I was an Everton player the club physio at the time, Norman Borrowdale, who was from St Helens, used to invite some of the Saints players, including the great South African Tom Vanvollenhoven for treatment. Even then, I'd go to watch Saints when I could.

But I was playing soccer as soon as I was able to kick a ball. David Moyes, the Everton manager, made an observation that Wayne Rooney was one of the last of the street footballers. I know what he meant by that. Wayne grew up playing football in the street with his mates, just as I did. But it's something you hardly see any more. Society has changed enormously and traffic on the roads is now heavier than anything we saw when I was a boy. This lack of street games has certainly contributed to the dearth of British football talent because, for various reasons, you rarely see kids kicking a ball in the road. It used to be the raw, grass roots of the game and if it does not grow from that base it's little wonder we are finding home-grown talent in such alarmingly short supply. When Kevin Keegan was England manager he predicted, given the lack of native talent and the increase of foreign players in the Premiership, that one of his successors in the job would have to face up to picking players for the international team from the Nationwide First Division (now the Coca-Cola Championship).

My mates and I, lads I still see such as Jimmy, Paul and Henry Brown and John Stafford, played football morning, noon and night when we could. We'd play on Hawksmoor Park with lads joining in all the time so you'd often have 15 or 16-a-side! Then when it went dark we'd play in the road, using street lamps for light. We'd use the white Frido balls, made of a plastic-type substance. If they got a hole in them you could repair them with a hot poker. But your touch had to be right to seal the hole; otherwise you'd put the poker right through the ball. My brother Brian, two years younger than me, would also play and he's now head soccer coach at Oklahoma City University. He first went to the States in 1967 when the soccer leagues started there. He played for Dallas Tornado for a while, then spent a few years with clubs in Australia and Hong Kong. Then he got a call in 1978 from a friend who had gone out to America with him in the 1960s, who was opening a soccer school in the States. So Brian went back and he's been there ever since. He married to an American girl, Judy, and they now have a lovely daughter Nicole.

I was doing quite well in my school soccer team - even though we always seemed to lose - when a chance came up from a surprise quarter. An uncle of mine, Pat Bowe, who was married to one of my dad's sisters, knew a Liverpool FC director and he fixed me up with a trial in a match at their Melwood training ground on a Tuesday night. Ian Callaghan, who was a bit older than me, played in the same game. Little did we know that day early in 1961 that we'd soon be facing each other for Everton and Liverpool in front of massive crowds. I must have done reasonably well in that practice match because Liverpool asked me to go back the following week. But my uncle Pat struck again. He'd been in the pub business and had obviously built up quite a few contacts because after arranging for me to go for a trial at Liverpool he'd also been in touch with someone from Everton.

He arranged for me to go to Everton a week later, instead of going back to Liverpool, and I duly turned up at the floodlit training pitch on what is now the car park at Goodison. I met up with Les Shannon, who was Everton's youth coach. He invited me back and I started going there for a few weeks. Then Les asked me if I fancied playing against Blackpool in a 'C' team game at Everton's Bellefield training ground one Saturday afternoon in February 1961. I was already down to play for the Cardinal Allen team on the Saturday morning. But I didn't let Everton know that! So I played for the school and then went and played for Everton in the afternoon. We won 4-3 and I got invited to come back and play more games, which I did between then and the end of that season. I was still at school, had taken my GCEs and it was dependent on my results whether I stayed on or not.

During this time Les Shannon had invited me to join in Everton's pre-season training, which I did for six weeks that summer. Then I learned that I'd passed the GCE in English, Maths and History and it was decided that I'd leave school and look for a job. I managed to get fixed up as a National Health Service clerk based in Liverpool's Upper Parliament Street area, which meant I needed to catch three buses to get there from home in Fazakerley. I was due to start on the Monday but on the Saturday I played in an 'A' team game at Burnley watched by Everton's chief scout Harry Cooke, who came up to me after and said: "We're thinking of making you an offer. I'll call to see your mum and dad on Monday night." It was a bit of a shock for me and I said to Harry: "The only problem is that I start work at the NHS on Monday." But he came round as promised to speak to the family. He offered me an apprenticeship and my dad said to me: "Well, what do you want to do?" I said: "I want to play football." So, with great understanding, he replied: "In that case you'll have to go in tomorrow and hand in your notice to the NHS." Next morning, after just one day's work, I said to the departmental manager: "I've got to hand in my notice because I've accepted an Everton apprenticeship." He said to me: "If we were sacking you we'd give you two weeks notice. I expect the same from you." So I had to work another fortnight before starting at Everton, although I trained Tuesday and Thursday nights with the amateurs in those two weeks.

By that time the club was getting used to a new manager. Johnny Carey, who I had not met at that stage, had been sacked by John Moores in a London taxi in April 1961 when they were both attending a Football League meeting. Carey was dismissed despite taking Everton to fifth place - their highest post-war position in the old First Division up to that point - and making signings such as Roy Vernon, Jimmy Gabriel, Billy Bingham and Alex Young. Blonde-haired Alex, signed from Hearts, was a graceful player of class and charisma, idolised by Evertonians. He was so revered by the fans that it inspired a television play entitled 'The Golden Vision'. Moores, who had launched the Everton revolution by giving the club an interest-free loan of £56,000 in 1960, appointed Harry Catterick as Carey's successor.

Catterick arrived from Sheffield Wednesday with his assistant, Tommy

Eggleston, and the pair came fresh from guiding Wednesday to runners-up spot in the championship. It meant that Gordon Watson stepped down from first-team trainer to take over the reserves in place of another former Everton player, Stan Bentham. The staff changes meant you could feel Harry's presence immediately. As soon as he'd arrived there was a different atmosphere at the club. We heard the stories from Sheffield about him being a strict disciplinarian and we were all quaking in our boots.

In his first season at the helm the club finished fourth and in his second season in charge his team, with players from the Carey era supplemented by the likes of Gordon West, Dennis Stevens, Johnny Morrissey, Alex Scott and Tony Kay, stormed to Everton's first post-war championship. To do it they marched through a demanding backlog of fixtures after a fierce winter, leaving Everton inactive in the League for seven-and-a-half weeks. The first team went from December 22 to February 12 without playing a single League game yet went on to win the title with a club record 61 points - six ahead of runners-up Tottenham - remained unbeaten at home for the only time in the club's history and attracted a club record average crowd of 51,460, with their total attendances sweeping well past the million mark.

Alex Young and Stevens were the only two ever-presents in the team who clinched the title in the final game of the season on May 11, 1963 - a 4-1 home win over Fulham who included one of my favourite players in England star Johnny Haynes, who had become the country's first £100 a week player two years earlier. Everton's captain, Roy Vernon, a great Wales international, a superb penalty taker and cigarette smoker, scored a hat-trick and finished as top scorer with 24 goals. Alex Scott got the other and I was delighted to get to Goodison for the last 20 minutes of the match to see Roy complete his hat-trick. I was a regular in the 'A' team then but because the 'B' team had a chance of winning their championship I was switched to play for them against Burnley at Bellefield. Our game kicked off at two o'clock. We won, thereby clinching the title, and we got down to Goodison as quick as we could and got into Bullens Road. We saw only the latter stages but the atmosphere was incredible. Some older fans even likened it to the day in 1928 when Dixie Dean scored his record-breaking 60th League goal of the season. The team that day was, in the old 2-3-5 formation:

Albert Dunlop (deputising for the injured Gordon West); Alex Parker, Mick Meagan; Jimmy Gabriel, Brian Labone, Tony Kay; Alex Scott, Dennis Stevens, Alex Young, Roy Vernon, Derek Temple.

To see Roy go up to the directors box and be presented with the championship trophy sent a real tingle through me, both as an aspiring player and a fan. I was coming up against these great players on the training ground and as an Everton supporter since I was a toddler, it was the first thing I'd seen them win. In fact, it was Everton's first trophy since their last championship success in 1939.

This latest triumph came as Britain was being engulfed by the Mersey Sound. The Beatles had taken their first single 'Love Me Do' into the charts the previous autumn, Gerry And The Pacemakers had followed suit with a string of hits and a batch of other Liverpool groups were busy too. From the south The Rolling Stones, too, were on the rise. The club scene in Liverpool was also booming with the 'Swinging Sixties' in full flow. The Cavern was the most famous club but I went there on only a couple of occasions. I didn't go out socialising very often at that stage of my life. To be honest I was more scared of my mother than I was of Harry Catterick, because she was even more of a disciplinarian than he was! When I was a little older I did go out and probably went most to The Beachcomber in Seel Street, a club that was run by well-known Evertonian Jim Ireland. I'd also pop into The Mardi Gras and The Kardomah, a city-centre coffee bar.

We had a record player at home and on Thursdays, after we'd collected our wage packets, myself, Tommy Wright and a lad called Stuart Shaw - who later played against us for Southport in the FA Cup - used to go to Crease's, a local music store, to buy records. I used to like The Beatles stuff but most of my spare time was spent playing football with my brother Brian in the garden. Football dominated my thoughts and ambitions and I didn't really have time for anything else, apart from watching a bit of television. But as I stood on the terraces with the other Everton juniors, watching the League championship arrive that May day in 1963, little did I know that four months later I'd be lining up with the stars in the European Cup. It was a golden vision I could never have dreamed of."

EVERTON FOOTBALL CLUB, 1963-64

A. Rankin, K. Mulhearn, B. Harris, B. Labone, G. Heslop, D. McKenzie, J. Morrissey, R. Veall

R. Lewin (*Coach*), B. Rees, S. Shaw, T. Wright, C. Harvey, G. Thomson, J. Phillips, R. Parnell,
R. Vernon, G. West, J. Hill, G. Sharples, M. Meagan, A. Young, G. Watson (*Trainer*)

A. Parker, A. Scott, D. Stevens, J. Gabriel, H. Catterick (*Manager*), D. Temple, T. Kay, T. Eggleston (*Trainer/Coach*)

The official team photograph ahead of the 1963-64 season (I am pictured in the middle row fifth from left), my first as a member of the first-team squad and a proud moment. Although I did not help win the main trophies in the picture, I did help the 'B' team win the League, with the trophy also being pictured.

Chapter Two

Learning With The Blues

In the late summer of 1963 Goodison Park basked in the warm glow of Everton's first post-war League title, an achievement that enthralled teenage Colin Harvey. The team of Alex Young, Roy Vernon, Gordon West and Brian Labone bridged a gap of almost a quarter of a century since the side of Tommy Lawton, Joe Mercer, Tommy (T.G.) Jones and Ted Sagar lifted Everton to the championship summit in 1939. That triumph came only four months before the world was plunged into the darkness of the Second World War and when peace arrived and full scale League football re-emerged, Liverpool wrested the mantle of champions from their city neighbours.

History was destined to repeat itself in a traumatic season for Everton, which began with a four-goal Charity Shield trouncing of FA Cup winners Manchester United. Only nine days before the curtain-raiser against United, the nation had been stunned by the Great Train Robbery, when an armed gang ambushed the Glasgow to London mail train in Buckinghamshire and stole £1 million, a sum beyond imagination at that time. Just a week after the Charity Shield, pop music's new sensation The Beatles, soon to conquer America, joined Gerry and the Pacemakers and The Fourmost in a twice-nightly, week-long, sell-out stint at Southport's Odeon Theatre in an extravagant showcase of Merseyside's musical talent.

Like The Beatles, Everton were also about to spread their wings, entering big-time Continental competition for the first time in a Europe starkly divided politically between East and West following the dramatic erection of the Berlin Wall two years earlier. Yet 1963-64 was to be a campaign in which Everton would not only relinquish their championship crown, but also lose the impetus and driving force of the brilliant Tony Kay, on whom Harry Catterick had spent £55,000, then a British record for a wing-half, from his former club Sheffield Wednesday in December 1962. Catterick made him captain and red-head Kay's tigerish, inspirational qualities at left-half over the second half of that season fuelled Everton's drive to the title and earned him England recognition, which he celebrated with a goal in an 8-1 hammering of Switzerland in June 1963. Sadly, for Kay, for Everton, for England and for football in general, it was to be his only cap and the long-term greatness that surely beckoned him would be denied by one of English football's most unsavoury chapters. Newspaper revelations the following April launched a chain of events leading to criminal prosecutions for match betting during his time at Sheffield Wednesday. Kay - one of 10 players convicted in the scandal - received a four-month jail sentence and a life ban from football. Harvey, for whom Kay had been an exciting, exemplary player, particularly felt the sense of stunned shock. Harvey's memory of the night he first played alongside him, is burned deep into his memory.

"I trained hard on my own through the summer of 1963 and by the time I'd done the pre-season work I was in good nick and wondering what the new season would bring. I began it in the reserves but the first team returned to action with a great display in the Charity Shield to beat Manchester United 4-0 at Goodison, the goals coming from Jimmy Gabriel, Derek Temple, Roy Vernon and Dennis Stevens, who was a cousin, incidentally, of the late Duncan Edwards. That result certainly set pulses racing for the club's defence of the title and their looming collision with Inter Milan - or Internazionale to give them their correct name - in the European Cup.

It was a mouth-watering prospect. There could hardly have been tougher opposition for the club's first taste of Europe's top club competition. In stark contrast to today, when fourth place in the Premiership controversially guarantees a qualifying round slot in the Champions League, the European Champions Cup was then exactly what the label said - a tournament open only to national champions. Everton had played in European competition for the first time the previous season - and what an undistinguished baptism it was, losing 2-1 on aggregate to Dunfermline Athletic in the first hurdle of the Inter-Cities Fairs Cup. Inter were from a different football galaxy! However, in a mixed start to our League programme United got their revenge for their Charity Shield defeat when they beat us 5-1 at Old Trafford just a fortnight later, in our first away game. In the first six matches of the League programme we won three, lost two and drew one. Next up were Inter, who came to Goodison on Wednesday, September 18, 1963.

Then, as now, I was an avid reader of World Soccer magazine and I knew a bit about Inter...that Helenio Herrera, the Argentinian-born godfather of the defensive 'catenaccio' system was manager, and that they had great players. They included the legendary Spanish inside-forward Luis Suarez, the Italy forward Alessandro Mazzola, and Italian international full-backs Tarcisio Burgnich and Giacinto Facchetti, who would later captain his country. They were a glamour team of exotic superstars. I was among the 62,408 Goodison spectators for the first leg when the teams lined up like this:

Everton: West; Parker, Harris B.; Gabriel, Labone, Kay; Scott, Stevens, Young, Vernon, Temple.

Inter: Sarti; Burgnich, Facchetti; Tagnin, Guarneri, Picchi; Jair, Mazzola, Di Giacomo, Suarez, Szymaniak.

It was, as expected given Inter's reputation, a tight game. Their centre-half Guarneri made life difficult for Alex Young and West German midfielder Horst Szymaniak, who had been bought by Herrera specifically for away games in the European Cup, must have covered every blade of grass. Suarez was pure class, constantly feeding passes to Brazilian winger Jair who unleashed several shots at Gordon West's goal. For us, Tony Kay showed that he was a match for the Inter stars with his characteristic tackling and ball-winning qualities and Dennis Stevens gave a typically tireless display.

Our best chance came in the second half when Jimmy Gabriel headed on a Brian Harris cross and Alex Young's header brought a good save from Sarti. We were unlucky though, because Roy Vernon, who was shadowed all night by Tagnin, put the ball in the Inter net after Dennis Stevens had headed on Alex Parker's cross, only for the Hungarian referee G. Gere to disallow it for offside. BBC film showed that Alex Young was probably beyond the last defender as the ball is headed forward. Even in those days it was a debatable decision, but given today's interpretation of the offside law I'm sure a goal would have been given and we would have had a priceless lead going into the return. Nevertheless, the teams walked off to a standing ovation from the crowd who, despite the 0-0 scoreline, appreciated an absorbing evening. As I watched the players take the crowd's salute that night little did I know that I would be in the team facing Inter in the San Siro Stadium a week later.

On the weekend before the second leg, when the first team beat Sheffield Wednesday 3-2 at Goodison, I played in the reserves at Sheffield United. The motorway network was not very extensive in those days and we used to travel on the A road over the Pennines. Coming back from Bramall Lane that Saturday we stopped at Manchester's Belle Vue complex for a meal. While we were there, Gordon Watson, who was in charge of the reserves, rang Harry Catterick. The first-team squad were leaving for Italy early on the Monday morning and it had been arranged that Gordon would telephone Harry in case any of the reserves were needed to be called up for the trip. Gordon came back and said that Barry Rees - a wing-half or forward from Rhyl who was sadly to die in a car crash not long afterwards - full-back Roy 'Pancho' Parnell and myself were to report to Goodison on the Monday. Barry travelled up from Rhyl on the Sunday and stayed at our house overnight before we reported at Goodison, as ordered, early the next morning. We left as planned - but without the injured Jimmy Gabriel - only to spend all day stuck at Manchester Airport because of bad weather.

It was night-time before we flew out and on arrival in Milan we then had to travel to our hotel base in the famous motor-racing venue of Monza. Everyone was weary after the long delay and when we finally checked in it was straight to bed. We had a lie-in next morning and, feeling refreshed, we had a training session on a local pitch at Monza, although as far as Barry and I were concerned we were just there to carry the skips and to make up the numbers. Roy Parnell, though, was convinced he was going to play. Roy told Barry and I that he was sure Harry Catterick was going to switch Alex Parker into midfield and play him at right-back. I don't know whether he'd heard anything or it was just wishful thinking on Roy's part!

Just before we went for an afternoon sleep, a few hours before kick-off, we had a team meeting and Harry said: "As Gabby's injured and not with us, I want Dennis (Stevens) to drop back to No 4 and you, Colin, to come in at No 8." I was stunned. Even though Jimmy was out I'd never thought that I would get the nod. Being the old-style wing-half he was a different type of player from me so I felt it wouldn't be me who'd replace him. Now I'd just been told I was to make my debut as an 18-year-old at the San Siro Stadium in front of some of the most passionate, volatile fans in the world!

I went for my afternoon nap with my head full of images of being on the same field as Suarez and Inter's other stars, and lining up with the Everton players who I'd cheered on to clinch the championship a few months earlier. But the fact that I'd hardly got time to think about it, thanks to Harry's typical, low-key approach, showed great psychology and brilliant management on his part. I didn't even have the opportunity of letting my mum and dad know I was playing. They found out from the BBC Light Programme radio commentary.

Even though I'd been told I was playing it was still my job, along with Barry and Roy, to load the skips onto the team bus as we set off for the San Siro. As it was, we left the hotel too early and 'The Cat', as we called Harry, told the coach driver to drive around the city for 20 minutes or so because he didn't want us sitting in the dressing room for longer than was necessary. When, finally, we did approach the stadium it was a spectacular sight - a great, big illuminated bowl. That set the hairs on the back of my neck tingling. 'Here we go', I thought to myself. Yet, perhaps surprisingly, I wasn't too nervous. I reckoned that nobody would expect a great deal of me. I was just excited.

For the second leg Herrera brought in the Italy midfielder Mario Corso to replace Szymaniak, and his left-foot skills increased Inter's attacking qualities. But we gave a good account of ourselves in front of a 70,000 crowd containing 130 devoted, pioneering Everton fans who were tasting European away match travel for the first time on a charter trip that cost them £26. After making a couple of dodgy back passes to Gordon West early on, I settled down and even managed to get in two overhead kicks on goal. I was very physically fit and quickly adjusted to the leap from reserve football to European Cup action. Overall, I thought I did well, which was quite pleasing considering that my job was to try to quell the menace of Senor Suarez!

The only goal of the game - and of the tie - came immediately after the interval. Corso broke down their left flank, crossed and Suarez found Jair for the Brazilian to score. The match was quite heated and, at times, bad tempered, with lots of niggly fouls and body checking by Inter, gamesmanship which was par for the course in Italian football and very different from a typical English game. The Hungarian referee Horvath let them off with much of it but he did book four players - Brian Harris and Dennis Stevens on our side and Inter's Suarez and Jair. Probably our best moment came when Alex Scott went on a long, weaving run, only to shoot wide from 12 yards. We just couldn't find a way through and we lost 1-0.

There was no shirt-swapping in those days so as we walked off at the end I simply shook hands with Suarez. Obviously, it was disappointing to go out of the European Cup after our first taste of the competition but it was no disgrace to lose to a team who went on to become European and world champions for the next two years, which included a controversial defeat of Liverpool in the 1965 European Cup semi-final. As Harry Catterick said: "To play for three hours against one of the world's great sides and lose by only one goal is an achievement to remember. To do this with a makeshift, re-shuffled team made it a performance in the super class."

I was quite pleased, too, with the reaction when we got back to Liverpool. I got the bus from Goodison to the shops near our house, picked up the morning and evening papers and walked home reading them. Frank McGhee in the Daily Mirror wrote: 'At inside right Harvey had the toughest job of the lot - marking Suarez - and he made a courageous job of it. Thanks to Harvey, Jair got nothing like the service he had at Goodison from Suarez. It was 26 minutes before the great man got a ball through to his winger.' Another football reporter, Don Hardisty, wrote in the Daily Mail: 'Jair worked himself into such a frenzy when Harvey tackled him that he jumped up and started throwing punches at Harris, with whom he had already clashed several times.'

The fact that I'd played in Milan, done reasonably well and enjoyed the experience built my hopes about being involved in Everton's next match - the little matter of a trip to Anfield to confront Liverpool in the Mersey derby three days later. But, typical of 'The Cat', I found out on the Friday when the team sheets went up that I was playing against Liverpool - but against their reserves for our reserves in the mini-derby at Goodison. The manager hadn't said a word to me! That was my welcome to the world of Harry Catterick. I scored in the reserve match and we won 3-1 while the first team were losing 2-1 across Stanley Park.

A couple of weeks later, the day after I'd been in the reserve team beaten 2-1 by Burnley, Harry sent for me. As I walked up the old metal spiral staircase to his Goodison office, I was very apprehensive. When I got there he asked me: 'How did you go last night?' I said: 'Not so good, boss, and we got beat.' 'Well, I had a report that you played alright', Harry replied. 'Anyway, when we were in Milan the Inter club gave us a couple of presents and one of them was a gramophone. You may as well have it. It will be a souvenir of the game and bring back memories for you.' It was a suitcase-size record player and the fact that Harry had given it to me was his way of saying 'well done' without saying it in so many words.

But from walking off the San Siro pitch on that unforgettable night in Milan in September 1963, I had only one further taste of first-team action in the next six months. That came in November of that year in the second of two amazing matches we played against Rangers, in what was billed as the British Championship. Like Everton in England, Rangers had won the Scottish championship the previous season with an unbeaten home record and Ibrox Park, long before it had been re-built to its current splendour, was a hostile venue for visiting teams.

The first leg was played in Glasgow just five days after President Kennedy's assassination in Dallas, Texas. The world was reeling from Kennedy's killing but life - and sport - went on and we achieved a remarkable result at Ibrox. Andy Rankin, who'd been on the verge of quitting football for the police force until Harry Catterick became manager and persuaded him to stay, was in goal - having just displaced Gordon West - and saved a penalty from Scotland centre-forward Ralph Brand. George Heslop was at centre-back for the injured Brian Labone and goals from Alex Scott, Derek Temple and Alex Young gave us a superb 3-1 win, John Greig scoring for Rangers. Substitutes had not yet arrived in British football but they were allowed as a special dispensation in both legs and I was on the bench in Glasgow, although I didn't get on. Ibrox was packed to the rafters with a 70,000 crowd and the atmosphere was incredible. In fact, I found it more intimidating sitting on the bench there than playing in the San Siro.

On the morning of the second leg, a week later, we went into Goodison for some light training and when we left the ground at around 11.30am the roads were full of drunken Scots fans. Some locals reported seeing them drinking whisky from goldfish bowls! Everything was good-natured. There was no trouble. They were not belligerent. But I've seen nothing like it from that day to this and I thought: 'It's going to be a lively match tonight!'

My feeling was spot on. The game drew a crowd of more than 42,000 and the atmosphere was passionate and intense. I was again on the bench and near the end of the first half Jimmy Gabriel came off injured and I went on, so becoming the first Everton substitute used in a senior match. Again, I thought I did alright and we drew 1-1. Sandy Brown conceded an own goal but Alex Young, who'd scored in Glasgow, got another for us and we earned the title of British champions on a 4-2 aggregate. After that, though, it was back to reserve-team football for me right through to March, by which time the Beatles had taken America by storm and Cassius Clay, later Muhammad Ali, knocked out Sonny Liston in Miami to become world heavyweight champion for the first time.

Everton still had high aspirations of successfully defending the League title and the team's 4-2 win at leaders Tottenham on March 7 put us within two points of the top. Before the next game Catterick went out and bought a new centre forward, splashing £85,000 on Fred Pickering from Blackburn. He made an instant impact. Early in the season 'The Cat' had left the club's championship banquet and, still in his dinner suit, drove to Scotland to pay

Partick Thistle £38,000 for full-back Alex 'Sandy' Brown, who eventually took over on the right from his fellow Scot, Alex Parker. The manager also signed Northern Ireland inside forward Jimmy Hill from Norwich City, although Jimmy's seven appearances and one goal that season was the extent of his Everton first-team career. Pickering's arrival, though, was explosive. He had been moved up front from full-back at Blackburn and four days after he joined us he scored a hat-trick on his debut in a 6-1 home win over Nottingham Forest. It was Everton's biggest win of the season and the only first-team hat-trick, a feat Fred was to repeat on his England debut a few months later in a 10-0 trouncing of the United States in New York. At the end of the Forest game the rest of the Everton players stood back and joined the fans in giving Fred a standing ovation as he left the pitch.

A week later I found myself thrust into my League debut against Fred's former club Blackburn at Ewood Park. I found out I was playing when the team sheet went up the day before the game. Again, not a word from Harry. Blackburn, who had fine players like Bryan Douglas and Ronnie Clayton, were up there with us going for the championship but we did well. We won 2-1 and I made one of our goals for Derek Temple. During the game, nowhere near the ball and right out of the blue, I got an elbow in the face. Next minute Jimmy Gabriel was over. 'Who did that?' he asked. 'I don't really know but it must have been the left-back because he's the only one in that area', I replied. Five minutes later I saw the player laid out on the ground. That was justice, Gabby-style, and it gave me a dramatic welcome to life in the First Division, as the top flight was then called.

I played well at Blackburn in place of the injured Roy Vernon and, even though he was fit, I stayed in the team - again wearing No 10 - for the next game, at home to West Brom on Good Friday. The game drew an attendance of more than 61,000 but on the day I just wished the ground would swallow me up. We drew 1-1 and I had a nightmare. Before the end of the match the crowd, many of whom went to the game probably wanting to have a look at this promising 19-year-old who was keeping out Roy Vernon, were giving me dreadful stick. Nothing went right for me. I was falling over the ball, misplacing passes; everything that could go wrong did go wrong. To be honest, I couldn't get off the pitch quickly enough at the final whistle.

The next day the first team had a home game against Blackpool while the reserves were at Manchester City. Not only was I dropped from the senior side - I didn't even make the reserve team. I was named as 12th man for the reserves at Manchester City! The news was broken to me by the reserve-team trainer Gordon Watson, who came up to me and said: 'I'm sorry to tell you this, Col, you're travelling with us. But you're not playing - you're 12th man.' I think Catterick's feeling must have been that it was better to get me right away from the big stage. I suspect it was psychology on his part. But I was absolutely devastated. It left me almost in tears.

We had to leave on the coach for Maine Road almost right away. As I sat on that bus travelling down the East Lancashire Road to Manchester, I thought it was the end of my world. I feared I'd never play football again. I knew I'd played badly against West Brom, to put it mildly. I said to myself: 'That's me finished. Obviously I can't handle first-team football. I'm not going to be good enough.' I chatted on the coach to my best mate Tommy Wright and goalkeeper Ken Mulhearn, who later moved to Maine Road and became City's first-team keeper. But neither of them mentioned my demotion because they knew how upset I was.

I sat through the reserve game and came home on the team bus still feeling utterly depressed. I hadn't had the time or the opportunity to let my mum and dad know what was happening. To be honest, I wasn't in the right frame of mind anyway. My dad had gone along to Goodison for the League match against Blackpool hoping to see me in the team. He was a bit puzzled as to what had happened. When I got back home that night and told him the story he said to me: 'Son, you've just got to get on with it. These things happen and you've got to get over them.' He was right, of course. But I still felt devastated. Little did I know then how massively things were to change, both for me and for the club, and that my appearance at Blackburn a week earlier was to prove my second and last outing with Tony Kay. "

Arthur Proudler, Everton's reserve-team coach taking training at the back of Bellefield in the winter of 1967. Also pictured behind me are (left to right) Gerry Humphreys and Tommy Jackson.

Chapter Three

The Rise And Fall Of Tony Kay

Tony Kay played football with a swagger. He had style. He had panache and when Harry Catterick signed him from former club Sheffield Wednesday in the 1962-63 season, he provided an extra ingredient in the Everton team that lifted the title so gloriously the following May. In that era Kay was classed as a wing-half while today he would be catergorised as a midfielder. The photograph of Kay celebrating the success with a cigar in one hand and glass of champagne in the other is incongruous in football's current lifestyle-and-diet sensitive era. Yet it captures the personality of the player whose skills were feasted on by the fans and which illuminated his brief Everton career. That picture was worth a thousand words and if fate had held a different destiny for Kay another immortal photograph, of Nobby Stiles smiling up in jubilation at England captain Bobby Moore after the 1966 World Cup final defeat of West Germany, might never have been taken because it may well have been Kay, not Stiles, who played on that epic Wembley afternoon. Kenneth Wolstenholme, BBC TV's voice of football and immortalised for his 'they think it's all over - it is now' phrase at the climax of England's World Cup triumph, had no doubts.

"I could not conceive of a 1966 England squad that isn't built on Kay's great talents," said the iconic broadcaster. Sadly, it was not to be. "Sometimes I still feel sick", Kay admitted. "It was terrible having to watch the World Cup as a spectator and, of course, before that when my two clubs, Everton and Sheffield Wednesday, played in the FA Cup final. Football was my life, my everything. At 26, having won a championship, an England cap and with the World Cup coming up and then not being able to play - it hurt."

Corruption has reared its head in English football almost from the time the game became organised at national level in the late 19th century. One of its forms, bribery and betting, had been manifest from its earliest days when payments to players had strict ceilings in a game unrecognisable from today's television-driven Premiership bonanza. Nevertheless, Kay and his fellow miscreants placed their bets in the era when earnings had risen after the lifting of the maximum wage in 1961.

In 1900, Burnley goalkeeper Jack Hillman was banned for a year for trying to bribe Nottingham Forest to lose. Forest won 4-0 and Burnley were relegated to the Second Division. Five years later Manchester City captain Billy Meredith was banned for a season after attempting a £10 bribe on Aston Villa captain Alec Leake when the Maine Road club were challenging for the 1904-05 championship, eventually won by Newcastle United with City third, behind Everton. Meredith's response was to reveal widespread corruption at City. It led a year later to 17 current or former players being fined a total of £900, suspended and banned from playing for City again. The players were later auctioned by the Football League for £2,600.

City's chairman W. Forrest and secretary manager Tom Maley were banned 'sine die' and two other board members were suspended for seven months, just some of a batch of clubs, directors, managers and officials punished with varying severity over the years for illegal payments, deception and other financial irregularities. Yet such cases were sufficiently infrequent as to make headlines when they occurred and the word sleaze had yet to enter the game's lexicon when the Kay case stunned the nation. Indeed, Merseyside - at the forefront of football achievement through Everton and Liverpool - had remained largely untouched by unsavoury allegations since a remarkable case during the First World War.

The 'Dog and Partridge Affair' centred on a game on Good Friday, April 2, 1915 when Liverpool travelled to Old Trafford to meet relegation-threatened Manchester United. United duly won 2-0, and one match report observed: 'United scored an early goal through George Anderson but the quality of the match deteriorated. Liverpool appeared disinterested and in the latter stages the spectators were given to launch catcalls and jeers.' Liverpool's Jackie Sheldon, a former United player, missed a penalty, as did United's Patrick O'Connell, and rumours swiftly grew that the match had been fixed by a betting ring. Then it was revealed that bookmakers throughout the country had paid out considerable sums to people who had correctly forecast the result. Billy Meredith, who had left Manchester City and moved across town to United, played in the controversial match but subsequent League and FA Commissions accepted his protests of innocence.

Eight other players, though, were banned for life for betting large sums on the score at odds of 7-1. The United players banned were Alex 'Sandy' Turnbull (previously suspended in the Manchester City scandal), Arthur Whalley and Enoch West, the only one of them to have played in the match. The suspended Liverpool players were Tommy Fairfoul, Tommy Miller, Bob Purcell and Sheldon - all of whom played in the game. Also banned was Laurence Cook of Chester, for his part in the ring. United - who just beat relegation - and Liverpool were exonerated of any involvement, and the two clubs were praised by the authorities for their assistance. But United inside-left West protested his innocence and took the FA to court. The hearing seemed to be going in his favour until Sheldon, once Meredith's right-wing deputy at United, stepped into the witness box and declared:

"We went to Manchester and had a meeting in the 'Dog and Partridge' pub about laying the bets and Enoch was with us." If that was not enough to sink West, his team-mate George Anderson supplied the clinching evidence. The United forward, who scored both goals in the ill-fated match, told the court that West had earned more than £70 from illegal betting, a huge sum at that time. The judge, unsurprisingly, ruled that West's life ban should stand. When the suspensions on the other seven were lifted after the First World War, in recognition of their wartime service, West's remained in force and he never played again. His suspension was eventually lifted in November 1945 after 30 years - the longest ban in Football League history - and West died an embittered man in September 1965, still protesting his innocence.

Some 17 months earlier, on the morning of Sunday, April 12, 1964, the day before Sidney Poitier became the first black actor to win an Oscar for his performance in Lilies of the Field, and the independently minded Ian Smith was elected Prime Minister of Southern Rhodesia, Britain woke up to a football sensation. The People newspaper splashed a story that Tony Kay and his team-mates at Sheffield Wednesday, Peter Swan and David 'Bronco' Layne, had been involved in a match-fixing ring by placing bets. For all three it was a death sentence on their top-flight football careers. Seven other lower division players were named in subsequent revelations.

Kay, 26, who had captained Everton the previous day in their 3-3 draw at home to Wolves, never kicked a ball again in Goodison's royal blue. It was effectively the end, too, for his 27-year-old fellow England international Swan, an imposing centre-half, and Layne, 24, a potent centre-forward who had struck 52 goals in 74 League outings for Wednesday. Following the newspaper disclosures all three players were suspended on full pay by their clubs pending investigations into the accusations that they had placed a £50 bet on their side, Wednesday, to lose at League champions Ipswich Town on December 1, 1962, just weeks before Kay's £55,000 move to Everton set a new British record for a wing-half. Wednesday duly lost 2-0 and the three players won £100 each plus the return of their £50 wager. Yet the supreme irony was that The People newspaper, who broke the story of the match-fixing scandal, named Kay as its man-of-the-match in the very game at Portman Road on which he had bet and on which his career was to founder.

Everton manager Catterick also watched the Ipswich match and concurred with the match reporter's rating. "Kay was the best player on the pitch," said the man whose judgement and final decision to splash out on the tigerish red-head were confirmed by his performance that day. Another massive irony was the fact that 26 days after the fateful game Kay moved to Everton for which he would receive a signing-on fee estimated at around £3,000.

The series of newspaper stories was written by reporters Mike Gabbert and Peter Campling on paid evidence, much of it from secretly tape-recorded conversations, provided by syndicate leader Jimmy Gauld. An Aberdeen-born forward, Gauld's seven-club playing career in Ireland, England and Scotland included a spell at Everton between October 1956 and 1957 in which he made 26 senior appearances, scoring eight goals. His revelations to The People sparked police investigations that involved 100 players at 16 clubs and, in all, 33 individuals appeared in court charged with 'conspiracy to defraud.'

Ten of the players - including Kay, Swan and Layne - appeared at Nottingham Assizes before Mr Justice Lawton in January 1965 and were sent to prison, each of the famous trio receiving a four-month sentence which was followed, on their release, by life bans from football. Other, lesser-known players from various clubs were also jailed. Sammy Chapman, Ron Howells and Ken Thomson were given six-month terms and Dick Beattie nine months. Brian Phillips and Jack Fountain received 15-month sentences while ringleader and informant Gauld, who received £7,000 from The People, was sent down for four years and ordered to pay £5,000 costs. The football ban left Kay even more distraught than his jail sentence. "It destroyed me. I never cried so much in my life," said Kay, whose protest to the Press Council about methods used by The People was rejected and whose championship medal was stolen in a burglary.

As they were serving their jail terms, all those convicted no doubt reflected on the contrasting fate of Bristol Rovers goalkeeper Esmond Million and forward Keith Williams, some 18 months earlier. They, along with Brian Phillips of Mansfield, were found guilty of being party to an attempt to fix a Rovers v Doncaster match but escaped jail. Each was fined the maximum £50 with costs, while also receiving life bans from football.

Swan, for a short period with Wednesday and then with Bury, and Layne, in just four outings with Hereford, did taste League football again after their bans were lifted on appeal in 1972. Kay, who made 55 senior appearances for Everton, scoring four goals, was a bookmaker in Liverpool for a while, kept himself fit during the ban and surreptitiously played occasional games, always keeping a sharp eye for any photographers. For a period he lived in Benidorm and after his ban was lifted in 1974 he returned from Spain and briefly played non-league with Skelmersdale United. Later he became a London publican, playing Sunday League football for a team in Blackheath.

But the nagging, haunting reflections will not go away. "If only I'd turned down the bet," muses Kay, who insists that it was the only one he has ever had on a football match. "I've asked myself a thousand times and I haven't yet come up with an answer. I just thought we'd get beat. I think the FA used me as a scapegoat. They were appalled at the idea of football being corrupt and chopped off the limb of the game they believed to be cancerous. But I suffered more than anyone, as the player with the highest profile." Even Harry Catterick, a disciplinarian to his fingertips, declared that the prison sentence and life ban were "far too severe for the offence."

The case was dramatised on BBC television in a film entitled 'The Fix', screened in October 1997, which left Kay "deeply moved". He admitted to similar emotions when he returned to Goodison for the first time in almost 40 years to join a parade of great former Everton players before the opening match of the 2002-2003 season, Everton's record 100th campaign in the top flight. "I hadn't really known what to expect. But when they called my name and I heard the crowd cheer as I stepped onto the pitch it was quite overwhelming. I had the lovely warm feeling of 'going home'."

Colin Harvey, who drooled over Kay's talents both as a young, aspiring team-mate and also as a lifelong Evertonian, still wishes that Kay had stepped onto the Goodison stage a few hundred times more than he did. Instead, Harvey is left with the memory of a talent that fizzed across the Everton firmament like a shooting star and was gone all too briefly:

"I remember Tony joining the club and he didn't half make an impression!

He came in December 1962 and the day he arrived was a running day in training at Bellefield. I was with the reserves but as the first-teamers were running in a group he took off. He was running yards ahead of them. I thought: 'Hello, this feller looks a bit different'. Normally when a player arrives he eases himself in, sitting back in the pack and getting to know what's what. But not Tony. It was as if he was saying: 'Here I am - I've arrived'. And make no mistake - he could run alright. In one morning he showed us what he had and with his red hair and fiery temperament he was outstanding in every sense. He was coming from a slightly lesser club and he was out to prove that nobody was going to push him around. He wanted everyone to know what he had to offer. He was top dog.

He had a personality to match. I remember when we were playing one of the many first team v reserves matches we used to have and I was giving Tony a hard time because I could get up and down the pitch, too. On this occasion just as I turned round I got a set of studs from my chest down to my nether regions. It was him just letting me know: 'Don't mess about with me'. Tommy Eggleston, who was in charge of the session, spotted it. Everyone did. But it didn't make any difference to Tony. He just wanted to get his message across! As it happened, I wasn't the first member of our family to meet up with Tony. My younger brother Brian was an apprentice at Sheffield Wednesday for a season when Tony was there, before Brian left for Chester prior to moving to America. He told me about Tony. 'He's good company but he's as hard as nails', said Brian. 'Don't mess about with him.' I discovered the wisdom of Brian's advice very quickly.

Harry Catterick, of course, knew what he was getting in Tony. He wanted to toughen up the whole team. We had Dennis Stevens in midfield and he got through a tremendous amount of work. It was a good footballing side but it still lacked an edge. Harry had spotted that as soon as he had taken over as manager and knowing Tony very well he felt he would be the ideal player to supply that extra edge. The team had a good home record but a poor one away from home, which is why Harry went for Tony. Five months later we won the championship so Harry was proved absolutely right.

Tony was a great reader of the game and a tremendous tackler. He had a great engine and had a mean, arrogant streak in him. He knew he was a good player. He knew what qualities he had on the field and at the time he was probably the best defensive wing-half in the country. Off the field he appeared a stand-offish sort of person but once you got to know him he was alright. I roomed with Tony for our FA Cup fifth-round tie at Sunderland in February 1964, which we lost 3-1 on an icy day after they'd cleared bales and bales of hay off the pitch to make it playable. I was 12th man and I suppose I was told to share with Tony because all the other players had established room-mates and I was the new kid on the block. I have to say I got on reasonably well with him. He told me he liked the fact that I was competitive, loved my football and worked hard in training. Perhaps he saw some things in my game that he had in his, although certainly not his natural arrogance. We'll never know but in my opinion he would have gone on to play many more times for England than his one scoring appearance.

What he did in his short period at Everton was fantastic and he had the talent to become one of the all-time great midfielders. He could well have been a World Cup winner. To my mind he was better than Nobby Stiles and if that position had been up for grabs in Alf Ramsey's England team Tony would have taken it. Alf, like Harry Catterick, was strict. But I think Tony could have played for Alf. Sure, Tony liked a drink but he was a good trainer and a hard worker. He had an opinion - there's no two-ways about that. But others in Alf's squad thought for themselves, too. So I don't think that would have been an insurmountable hurdle. I'm sure that they would have set the parameters to enable them to get on together. Also, Alf knew you needed people like Tony.

So that famous Wembley picture of a jubilant Nobby Stiles after the 1966 World Cup win might never have happened if Tony hadn't been foolish enough to bet £50 on his Sheffield Wednesday side to lose at Ipswich. It was a tragedy for him, for football and for Everton who had paid what was then a fortune to sign him. They ended up losing his great captain's talents and, even allowing for the championship win, much of the £55,000 transfer fee went down the drain, too.

Even after the lifting of the maximum wage, which took players well above the average working man's pay packet, they earned nothing like the vast sums top-flight professionals are paid today. So Tony and his team-mates at Wednesday probably thought it was a chance to make a few bob. It was a bit of greed and very silly. Yet even having done it, Tony's competitive edge came to the fore in the very game he had bet his team to lose and he was picked as man-of-the-match by The People. He was the man of many matches he played because he was outstanding. Perhaps one positive by-product of the king's ransoms Premiership players are now paid is that the temptation to which Tony succumbed, to bet against your own side, is not there any more. Sure, many players like to gamble, some to the point of addiction - but not in the way Tony Kay and his team-mates did.

There's a famous championship celebration photograph of Tony smoking a cigar, which seems starkly out of kilter with today's health-dominated training and diet regimes. But at that time the majority of footballers did smoke. I remember being moved up into the first-team room and I was amazed at how many of them were dragging on cigarettes. In fact, there were only two or three of us who didn't smoke, myself and Johnny Morrissey included. Tony Kay didn't smoke cigarettes. He stuck to cigars and that fitted his flamboyance. He was a showman, a little larger than life.

When the betting story broke it was hard to take in. I just couldn't believe that footballers would get involved in anything of that sort. The enormity of it was devastating. Everton was a club in shock and, with the involvement of the Moores family, a decision was taken to make no public comment on the accusations. It was, after all, something that was alleged to have happened when Tony Kay was at Sheffield Wednesday. But the implications, including the loss of the captain and most inspirational player, were massive. Tony never played for the club again, which was a tragedy and raises more questions than it answers. For example, what would the future have brought for Everton if he had refused the bet and played on for many more seasons?

It might well have had an affect on many careers, including mine. I feel I would have broken through, anyway, but would Harry Catterick have still have gone out and bought some of the players he did if Tony Kay was still starring for him? Would I ever have linked up in midfield with those great players Alan Ball and Howard Kendall? Perhaps Harry would have felt he didn't need one or both of them if Tony Kay was still doing the business.

I feel sure that when the story hit the streets Tony's first reaction would have been: 'It'll all blow over and I'll be playing again next season'. He was that sort of guy - so positive. He would never have thought he'd be banned for life and go to jail. I certainly didn't - I don't think any of us did. But, with hindsight, the punishments were absolutely spot-on. It sent out a wake-up call and a warning to everybody in football."

However, within six months of the betting story sensation, Everton were to figure directly in further Sunday People allegations built on claims by a former Goodison goalkeeper.

Johnny Morrissey arguing on my behalf...I'd sooner have him on my side than against me!

The start of a long afternoon of wine tasting, on tour with Everton in Australia, 1964. Incidentally, the man with me who worked for the company was originally from Fazakerley.

Chapter Four

Down Under To The Top

If the mood at Goodison in the spring of 1964 was one of gloom, after seeing Everton's championship crown seized by Liverpool, Colin Harvey was in a personal trough of despondency. He was at his lowest ebb since embarking on his football career, trying to come to terms with the switchback ride of form and fortune, the roar of the crowd at his back one day, the boo-boys at his throat the next. An eye-catching display in Everton's win at Blackburn in March was followed by a nightmare experience six days later in a 1-1 Good Friday draw with West Brom. "I don't think I'd have won a toss-up that day," admits Harvey, whose outing earned him the ignimony of being made 12th man for the reserves by manager Harry Catterick. "He just wanted me off the scene, out of the way, whatever you like to call it. The crowd had really had a go at me and Harry must have thought: 'Right - let's get him completely out of the spotlight'." Harvey added:

"I was shattered because as far as first-team football was concerned, my season had ended prematurely. There were six games left after the West Brom match, which we had gone into with a good chance of retaining the title. Although the team won 3-1 at home to Blackpool the following day, defeats in the next two games - at West Brom and Stoke saw our hopes crumble. Another point went out of the window in a 3-3 home draw with Wolves, less than 24 hours before the Tony Kay revelations broke in the Sunday People, which were to bring an instant end to Tony's football career.

The team lost our final away game at Chelsea when the game's only goal came from a disputed Bert Murray penalty awarded by referee Jack Taylor. He judged that Andy Rankin had brought down Frank Blunstone, the England winger who had been sold by Harry Catterick 10 years earlier, when he was manager of Crewe Alexandra, and who had received a £5,000 testimonial cheque before kick-off. Fred Pickering, one of Harry's many shrewd signings for Everton, scored twice in our last match to give the team a 2-0 win over West Ham, taking Fred's tally to nine goals in nine games since his arrival from Blackburn. Fred's figures, however, were not enough to rescue our title ambitions and we finished third on 52 points, one behind Manchester United and five behind Liverpool. The disappointment had clearly been shared by the supporters. From a crowd of more than 61,000 against West Brom, only 33,000 turned out for the West Ham match.

When the season ended, in late April, I was devastated after my experience of being demoted from the first team. Fortunately, though, I didn't have time to dwell on it because suddenly I got a call-up for a close-season tour of Australia. We left the day after the season ended and we were away for almost six weeks, spanning the whole of May and into June, playing eight games. It seemed like it took three days to get there then! We flew from Manchester, touched down in Rome, landed again in India, had another stop in Singapore and arrived in northern Australia before flying down to Sydney. The whole thing was a great experience and it totally changed my horizons. I suppose for me it was like a football equivalent of doing national service. I'd never been away for anything like that amount of time. I got things into perspective and came home feeling more optimistic. You could say that going Down Under put me on the up again.

The first weekend we were in Australia we were invited to someone's house for a party. There were loads of British people present and the FA Cup final, between Preston and West Ham, was screened on television. I saw Howard Kendall become the youngest player to appear in an FA Cup final at Wembley aged 17, a record now passed down to Millwall's Curtis Weston, who was 17 years, 119 days when he went on as a substitute against Manchester United in 2004. I'd played against Howard in junior games but I didn't know him. I was just aware that he was a good wing-half who could tackle and kick you! It was strange being in Australia watching a lad younger than me play in such a big game on a stage like Wembley. Even though Preston lost 3-2, and Howard was still a few weeks short of his 18th birthday, he performed very well and he was an inspiration to me. You knew you were looking at a smashing player but, of course, I had no idea just how closely intertwined our lives and careers were to become in the years ahead. When we did finally meet I told him: 'I watched you in the Cup final when I was in Australia.'

Harry Catterick didn't go on the trip and Tommy Eggleston and Gordon Watson were in charge. We had two games against the Australian national side, which included former Everton and Blackburn centre-half Matt Woods, who'd moved there after a free transfer from Ewood Park. I played in central midfield in six of the matches and I regained my confidence and enjoyment of the game. Being away for so long, I got to know the first-team players quite well because we were living in each other's pockets. Before the tour I'd put players like Roy Vernon, Alex Young and Jimmy Gabriel on a pedestal but suddenly I felt part of them. The tour was an invaluable maturing period for me. When I came back I'd put on half-a-stone in muscle, which for my 5ft 8ins physique was a good thing, and it got me up to my playing weight of around 11 stone for the rest of my career.

Andy Rankin and John Hurst were in the squad but my best pal, Tommy Wright, didn't go and it was a great boost to me to be included. We played in several cities across Australia including Melbourne, Perth and Sydney, where we were based. At one of the games, against New South Wales in front of a 52,000 crowd at Sydney Cricket Ground, there was a pre-match commotion in the stadium just before we went out. A team of students, wearing blue strips, entered the stadium posing as Everton. The crowd, taken in by it, applauded until we began to take the field and the realisation set in that they'd been duped! The interlopers were led away by police.

I came home from that tour with my batteries re-charged and licking my lips at the prospect of the new 1964-65 season. During the summer Harry Catterick had paid Huddersfield Town £40,000 to sign Ray Wilson, one of the greatest left-backs football has ever seen, and destined to star for England in the 1966 World Cup. Catterick's plan was to pair Ray with Alex Parker on the right flank to form a dream Anglo-Scottish full-back partnership. However, his hopes were smashed by injuries and they were to play together only twice. Ray was hurt in only his second game for Everton and missed half the season. By the time he returned to action in December, Alex's career was effectively over because of hamstring damage. However, in football as in life generally, one man's misfortune can be somebody else's opportunity. In this case that applied to Tommy Wright. It meant that we were soon playing together in the team and we roomed together for the rest of our Everton careers. I returned in the eighth game of the season, taking over injured Roy Vernon's No 10 shirt in a 2-1 defeat at Manchester United. I must have done alright because I missed only another three matches that season, when I mainly wore No 8, but also appeared in the No 6 jersey.

Tommy Wright's career as an inside-forward, after his appearances for

England Schoolboys as a wing-half, seemed to be drifting nowhere by the summer of 1964. In fact, he was relieved he was given a further year's contract, which he didn't think he'd get. But in a pre-season practice match they were short of a right-back. Gordon Watson stuck Tommy there - and he went to make the position his own and play 11 times for England. He had all the necessary attributes. He was quick, a great crosser of a ball, good in the air and coming on to the game and overlapping as a defender, rather than having the action at his back, was tailor-made for him. The transformation was remarkable. It's amazing how these twists of fate happen and that one was certainly the making of Tommy. They played him right-back in the reserves and Alex Parker's injury gave Tommy his big chance. He was called up for his senior debut at Blackpool in mid-October and after a short spell of being in and out of the team he became a regular, going on to make 28 first-team appearances that season in domestic and European competition.

Our Continental campaign was in the Inter-Cities Fairs Cup - a forerunner of the UEFA Cup - although again we were pitted against British opposition after a 9-4 aggregate first-round win over Valerengen. My first European goal came against the Norwegians in the first leg at Goodison, which we won 5-2. We then faced Kilmarnock, beating the Scottish side 6-1 on aggregate. Once again I got on the scoresheet with one of the goals in our 4-1 second-leg win at Goodison. That took us through to a third-round date with Manchester United. Even though we drew 1-1 in the first game at Old Trafford, United came out on top 2-1 at Goodison to go through .

Three days before my long-awaited first-team recall, in the midweek League game at United on September 16, The People newspaper splashed dramatic new accusations that Everton players had taken drugs and had a bribes kitty to help them win the 1962-63 championship. The story, like the Kay exposure, was written by Mike Gabbert and based on information supplied by former Everton goalkeeper Albert Dunlop, who made 231 senior appearances before joining Wrexham in November 1963. Albert went to Norman Wynne, The People's Merseyside football writer, alleging that unknown to the directors he and four other Everton players, including Roy Vernon and Alex Young, were given an amphetamine, Benzedrine, by two Everton trainers. Benzedrine, a powerful stimulant with potentially serious side effects including depression and interference with vision, was banned from open sale in 1956 and available only on prescription.

Albert also alleged that players had taken another amphetamine Drinamyl, in tablet form, known as Purple Hearts. I never knew anything about drugs or pep pills until I read the allegations. Gabbert reported in The People that Albert had made 'a detailed written statement running to 39 foolscap pages, later sworn by Dunlop as affidavits before a Commissioner of Oaths.' Albert was quoted as stating: 'Many of the players started taking Benzedrine tablets regularly early in 1961. We didn't have to but most did. The tablets were mostly white but once or twice they were yellow. They were used in the 1961-62 season and the championship season that followed it.

On match days they were handed out to most of the players as a matter of course. Some of the players could not do without the drugs. It became a sort of ritual for them to be handed out by our head trainer Tommy Eggleston. We used to swallow them down with water. During training we could have the tablets on request from Eggleston or from our other trainer, Gordon Watson. The drugs were always kept under lock and key in the trainer's room or the trainer's portable medical boxes.' Gabbert also wrote that a State Registered Nurse, who helped care for Dunlop at Sefton General Hospital when he fell ill in 1962, said she had found a bottle three-quarters full of Benzedrine tablets in his possession which he said he had stolen from the club, a statement later sworn by her in an affidavit.

The article continued: 'The doctor who arranged for Dunlop's admission to hospital said that he had gone there because he was in a low-state mentally and physically, largely as a result of taking Benzedrine and other drugs. Dunlop had told him he was getting the Benzedrine tablets from officials at the club. The doctor was of the view that Dunlop was a truthful person and, despite his illness, there had never been any question of Dunlop's mind being impaired. A psychiatrist who treated Dunlop expressed the same view. We were also seeking independent corroboration of Dunlop's claim that other Everton players had taken the tablets at the club. We got the proof we needed. A player who was on Everton's books during the 1961-62 and 1962-63 seasons admitted to us in an interview that he and other Everton players took drugs during these seasons. He confirmed that Eggleston and Watson had handed out Benzedrine tablets in the way Dunlop had described. And he told us that Eggleston had warned players if they were ever asked about the tablets to say that they were only salt tablets.'

Gabbert, who stated that he had possession of this player's affidavit, also reported that the company secretary of a local chemist who supplied Everton said when shown a photograph of the bottle marked 'Benzedrine. EFC: 'I can definitely say that is one of our bottles. We are the official club chemists and Benzedrine has been supplied to the club on prescription. They do have it from us. We never let a bottle go out of here without writing on the label what the contents are. That is one of our bottles and one of our labels.'

Gabbert revealed that The People interviewed and had a signed statement from a woman who had worked as a doctor's receptionist. 'She admitted', he wrote, 'that she had got hold of blank National Health Service prescription forms, signed in advance by the doctor who employed her in readiness for patients requiring drugs and medicines. She had filled in the blank spaces left by the overworked doctor with prescriptions for Drinamyl tablets. Then she had obtained the drugs from chemists in the area and passed them on to a number of Everton players.'

The Everton allegations were aired again on BBC Radio 4's investigation into performance-enhancing substances in football in March 2004, the year Manchester United and England defender Rio Ferdinand was banned for eight months and fined £50,000 for failing to take a random drugs test at the club's training ground. The programme, presented by Alan Green, produced by Jack Enright and entitled 'Monkey Glands And Purple Hearts', traced substance-taking in the game from the Victorian era when miners and industrial workers took tonics and stimulants and the habit carried over into sport, including football.

It embraced the controversial use in the 1930s of monkey-gland injections - extracts from monkey testicles - by Wolves under the management of the redoubtable Major Frank Buckley. The practice was raised in parliament but the only outcome was a poster sent to every club stating that injections were optional. It was never displayed at Molineux. Players including Stanley Matthews and Manchester United's Harry Gregg and Albert Scanlon told of being given pep pills by club officials they trusted. It was an era, including the time of The People allegations, when there were no rules against doping, no list of banned substances. The 1966 World Cup was the first major international competition to hold compulsory, independent drugs tests.

Everton responded to The People dossier with an internal investigation supervised by club solicitor and director E. Holland Hughes, the outcome of which was reported in The Times. It read: 'Mr E. Holland Hughes, solicitor to the Everton Football Club, said last night that the homes of four Everton players had been wired for the use of tape recorders. The footballers were Jimmy Gabriel, Alex Parker, Roy Vernon and Alex Young. He said that the wiring had been done with the consent and knowledge of the players and their wives ('The wives were instructed to do what was necessary when the investigator arrived', he said). We knew that in investigations that had been, or were being carried out by The People newspaper, tape recorders were being made use of. We felt that we, in those circumstances, would employ the same methods so that whatever we were able to state could be substantiated by tape recordings in our possession in the same way as they would use their tape recorders. We did not want to be confronted by allegations made on tape recorders which could not be countered by statements that we were able to prove. We were also concerned to prove the methods by which statements were being obtained.

Regarding the pill business, through our investigations the Everton club has been unable to find any evidence whatever that there was any general use of a pill, as has been alleged. The pill, only a mild stimulant, was available for any player who wanted it before a match. Suggestions that it was in general use are false. The Everton club made sure that the particular pill was only a mild stimulant and did not have the serious effect which has been alleged.' Hughes also denied allegations in The People regarding the 1962-63 title campaign that 'if the bribery did not succeed, undoubtedly a plot was hatched by certain players to 'fix'one of the key matches of the season, that against West Bromwich Albion.'

The Daily Telegraph reported: 'Everton Football Club board of directors believes there was no bribery of opponents by their players in the season when they won the First Division championship two years ago. Mr E. Holland Hughes, a director and the club's solicitor, said: 'The allegations of actual bribery are not maintained. The suggestion is now reduced to one of 'a bribery plot' and of a collection of money in a coach. It is based, according to the article, mainly on hearsay, indirect evidence and the newspaper's interpretation of statements said to have been recorded.' Mr Hughes saw each of the players who had been in the coach, with the exception of Albert Dunlop, the goalkeeper. There was, he went on, a denial of any suggestion of bribery, attempted bribery or any collection for bribery.

Mr Fred Micklesfield - an Everton director who travelled in the coach - other officials, the coach driver and a sports journalist, had stated they they neither saw nor heard anything of the nature suggested. Mr Hughes added: 'I have seen, with West Bromwich Albion's permission, their player who was named by the newspaper in interviews with Everton players. He has denied there was any truth in the suggestions made about him'.'

More than 40 years on, it all seems so dated and incongruous. At the time on which all the allegations are centred I was a youngster who had little contact with first-team players. We changed in different dressing rooms so neither was I privy to any gossip and I have never been offered stimulants in my life. I do know that the players named, and others of that era, have flatly denied drug taking. I don't know anyone who did. So much hinged on the reliability of Albert Dunlop's evidence. Whether it was a figment of Albert's imagination or not, I honestly don't know. He said that he had become an addict and had been so high in one game that even after the final whistle he had stayed on the field and dived at the feet of a St John Ambulance man! He also claimed that he had tried to kill himself after losing his place in the team to Gordon West. Albert was a strange man with a personal life full of turmoil. Was it a case that he woke up one morning and had a flight of fancy, or wanted or needed cash? Who knows? I don't and, since Albert is dead, nobody ever will. Harry Catterick, Tommy Eggleston and Gordon Watson are also dead so it is impossible, too, to hear their side of the story and mature reflections on the allegations which, as far as I am aware, they never gave or never had the opportunity to give. Everton sent all their relevant material, transcripts of tapes and other documents, to the FA and Football League, but after deliberation the authorities took no action.

The drug story hit the streets just a week before my first senior derby game, which was at Anfield. Of course, the football world was agog with the allegations. The Liverpool fans verbally slaughtered us when we ran out onto the Anfield pitch for the match, and there were all kinds of banners relating to drug taking. Mind you, it did have its funny side because the Kop slightly changed the title of The Searchers' big hit and started to sing 'Needles And Pills!' And when Brian Harris needed treatment, they sang: 'Ee Aye Addio Harris Is On The Pills.' We had the last laugh, though, because we went there as underdogs with a weakened team, amidst boasts of what Liverpool were going to do to us, and we hammered them 4-0. What made it sweeter was that I scored one of the goals. The ball came out to me from the Liverpool defence. I chested it down and, before it hit the ground, lobbed it into the top corner of Tommy Lawrence's net. A wonderful feeling!"

As if the drugs and bribe allegations were not enough to contend with, Everton were on the receiving end of more negative headlines that same season when Catterick's team and Leeds were involved in the 'Battle of

Goodison' on November 7, 1964. It was one of the most remarkable afternoons in the history of the grand old stadium, when an air of menace pervaded the ground almost from the moment referee Ken Stokes of Newark blew for the kick-off. Leeds had returned to the top flight as champions of the old Second Division the previous season, and under Don Revie were beginning their journey to the forefront of English football with a team containing names that threaten, even in retrospect, to leap off the page and kick you. Their all-white kit painted a picture of wolves in sheep's clothing.

Their captain was Bobby Collins, the 5ft 4ins Scot who had left Everton, much to the chagrin of many supporters, in a £30,000 move to Elland Road in March 1962. What Collins lacked in stature he compensated for in heart, commitment, grit and massive skill allied to an often brittle temperament that took him where angels fear to tread. He could, as one pundit observed, spark a riot in a cemetery. We didn't witness a riot at Goodison that day but the frenzied, provocative events on the field whipped the crowd to such a fever pitch of hatred and fury it was amazing there was no mass pitch invasion. As it was, the temperature was too much for some and one supporter climbed onto the field intent on confronting Billy Bremner and Norman Hunter. Fortunately, Johnny Morrissey got there first, restraining the irate fan and preventing a tinderbox situation exploding.

Jack Charlton, who was to establish himself as England's World Cup-winning centre-half, reflected on the game thus: "The impression I had was that we'd been playing five minutes and the ball was still on the centre spot. You knew what sort of game it was going to be when Alex Young, of all people, immediately put the boot in." Everton left-back Sandy Brown did not even last five minutes. After the ball had been cleared he and Johnny Giles clashed and started wrestling on the ground - with only four minutes on the clock. Brown was sent off and, later, both teams were also ordered to the dressing room in an unprecedented event in top-class English football.

Willie Bell was fortunate not to suffer the same fate as Brown. His challenge flattened Derek Temple, who at first was feared to be seriously hurt. As a prone Temple was stretchered off, Leeds trainer Les Cocker told Bell to stay on the ground and also called for a stretcher. The ambulance man's terse, angry reply, to the effect that Cocker could fetch his own so and so stretcher, indicated the cauldron of emotion that Goodison had become. Bell escaped punishment and, compounding the injustice, was to score the only goal of the game. But in the 38th minute, as missiles began to be hurled from the

43,000-plus crowd, referee Stokes ordered off all the players "to allow them and the supporters to cool down."

The teams (in the old 2-3-5 formation) were:

Everton: Andy Rankin; Barry Rees, Sandy Brown; Jimmy Gabriel, Brian Labone, Dennis Stevens; Derek Temple, Alex Young, Fred Pickering, Roy Vernon, Johnny Morrissey.

Leeds United: Gary Sprake; Paul Reaney, Willie Bell; Billy Bremner, Jack Charlton, Norman Hunter; Johnny Giles, Jim Storrie, Rod Belfitt, Bobby Collins, Albert Johanneson.

Nobody had a clearer view of the bone-crunching mayhem that unfolded than Colin Harvey who, still in the pre-substitute era, was 12th man sitting on the Everton bench wincing at almost every challenge.

"The game had hardly started when Sandy went in with a late tackle on Bell. Sandy was a strong player and although he did go in I'm certain there was nothing malicious about it. But that was the spark that lit a forest fire of retribution. It became a case of forget the ball let's get on with the game! The worst incident was Bell's foul on Derek Temple. He laid him out and then did a bit of play-acting. For a few minutes it looked bad for Derek and he was carried off. Eventually, the ref felt he just had to take stern action. It had become a feud which, in today's strict, disciplinary climate would have meant the game being abandoned or, at the very least, the teams being severely depleted by a flurry of red cards. As it was, even though half-time was only seven minutes away, referee Stokes ordered off both sets of players with the crowd being told over the tannoy that it was a cooling-off period.

I learned much later from Daily Mirror sportswriter Dave Horridge, who was covering the match, that after ordering off both teams the referee said the game was abandoned but changed his mind when he got back to the dressing room. Dave also reported that Derek Temple had told him that Bobby Collins had gone over the top on him straight from the kick-off.

In the dressing room Harry Catterick told our players to clear their heads, regain their composure and try to concentrate on playing football. By the time the referee restarted the game 11 minutes later Derek Temple was ready to resume, too. Fortunately he had not suffered any breaks, just a heavy knock. Ironically, Willie Bell became very religious in later life after he'd gone to work in football in America in the late 1970s. He joined a sect called Campus Crusade For Christ and coached Liberty Baptist College. He was a villain at Goodison that day but apparently found God. I've often pondered on the fact that some players who are so quiet, polite and self-effacing off the field, acquire another streak to their character when they step onto the pitch. It's as if a kind of malevolence overtakes them as they walk out of the dressing-room door. Mark Hughes and Norman Hunter are just two whose on and off-field personalities starkly contrasted.

Bobby Collins, who was in the 1964 Leeds team, was a player well suited to their blend of skill and cynicism and I still have painful memories of the first time our paths crossed. He was a pugnacious little midfielder who could look after himself. He was one of my idols when I was a youngster supporting Everton because he was a great Scotland international player. He'd originally joined Everton as a junior straight from his native Glasgow, but homesickness drove him back to join Celtic, from where he returned to Goodison for £39,000 in September 1958. Shortly after I'd joined Everton as a teenager we were training one day on a pitch that was on the site of what is now the car park behind Goodison's Stanley Park Stand. Despite the fact that the first team had a First Division game that night, Bobby turned up and asked the youth coach Les Shannon if he could join in.

That was Bobby. He was a fitness fanatic and he no doubt felt he'd rather have a kick-about with the kids than stay at home waiting for the match in the evening. Les should have said no to Bobby, in case he got injured, but he let him join in and I was quickly aware of his presence. There was a 50-50 ball which I just nicked away from Bobby. The next moment I looked down at my shin and saw stud marks all the way down the front. It was the first time anyone had gone over the top on me. It was a welcome to the big, bad world of football. But despite that painful introduction I always got on well with him. Some time later, a writer doing a project on Bobby contacted me and I related the training pitch story. Years after that I attended a dinner at Liverpool's Adelphi Hotel and Bobby came up to me. 'I've got a bone to pick with you', he said bluntly. I asked him why. 'I never went over the top to you,' he replied. I said to him: 'Forget it, Bob. But you did. I can still feel it!' We shook hands and that was that. Clearly, he hadn't remembered.

He had taken that passion with him to Elland Road, where it flourished under Revie. Bobby would have been really pumped up that day at Goodison in November 1964, coming back with promoted Leeds to face the club who'd sold him. He was captain and desperate to do well. That feeling would have been transmitted round the Leeds dressing room, one of the reasons perhaps that things kicked off as much as they did. Apart from being a tough side, they were a very fine footballing team. But they had taken the physical aspect of the game to another level, beyond the likes of the Bolton team of whom it was said they would kick their grandmothers! Leeds were cunning, cynical and oozed gamesmanship. They were very difficult to play against, not only because of their skill but because you had no idea where the next challenge was coming from.

On that afternoon at Goodison I was disappointed not to be playing. I'd been in the team up to a fortnight earlier, got back in the week after the Leeds game and ended up appearing in 32 of our 42 League games that season. But watching the match hammered home to me how football had changed from when I was a schoolboy watching Everton, to what it had become in the 1960s. I realised, for example, that you had to learn the difference between the tackles you should try to make and those you shouldn't. If you went for the wrong one you'd end up with someone going over the top to you. I accepted that was what you had to come to terms with to become a top player. It wasn't just down to ability. You had to be able to look after yourself to a level that players of the 1940s and 1950s did not.

That Leeds team went to within a whisker of the championship the following spring, finishing runners-up with the same 61 points total as winners Manchester United and being denied the title only on goal average. They certainly rubbed salt in our wounds by beating us three times during that 1964-65 season. They followed up their win in November's frenzied encounter by returning to Goodison in February and knocking us out of the FA Cup in a fourth-round replay.

Prior to that I'd scored my first FA Cup goal in our 3-0 win over Sheffield Wednesday after we'd drawn 2-2 at home. Fred Pickering, who'd scored in the Goodison game, was on the scoresheet again in the replay along with myself and Derek Temple. Fred was on a roll because he got our goal in a 1-1 draw with Leeds, and scored again in the replay. But despite our home advantage it wasn't enough. Leeds beat us 2-1 and reached the final, where they lost to Liverpool. Even though we finished fourth in the League, three places above Liverpool, it was a period when Harry Catterick was beginning to lay the foundations of a new team. Roy Vernon left in a £40,000 move to Stoke in March 1965, Alex Parker joined Southport six months later and Dennis Stevens joined Oldham in December 1965 for £20,000.

I was just seeking the consistency in my game to establish me in the first team, some were nearing the end of their careers while Johnny Morrissey was re-establishing himself after making only seven League appearances the previous season. It wasn't until I'd started playing with Johnny in the reserves that I realised how good he was. John was very underrated. He had two good feet, he was a great crosser of a ball and he could tackle and look after himself. Although he wasn't the quickest of wingers, he had a great awareness and tactical brain and he could make space for himself with his movement. On top of that many opponents were frightened to go near him. Nobody took liberties with John. Whoever was captain in our five-a-sides in training would always choose John as his first pick.

An indication of Everton's bright future through the 1960s and into the early 1970s was provided when the club lifted the FA Youth Cup for the first time in its history, beating Arsenal 3-2 on aggregate in the final. It was a competition I was destined to become closely involved with many years later, and the team that won it in April 1965 included John Hurst and Jimmy Husband, both of whom went on to win League championship medals. Jimmy made his first-team debut nine days before the Youth Cup final while John made his breakthrough as Everton's first-ever substitute in the League game at Stoke the following August. The Youth Cup-winning goalkeeper was Geoff Barnett, an England Youth and Schoolboy international, whose first-team path at Goodison was blocked by Gordon West and Andy Rankin. It restricted him to just 10 appearances and he joined Arsenal in October 1969. At Highbury he had little scope because of Bob Wilson's hold on the first-team job but Geoff did play in the 1972 FA Cup final against Leeds.

I made my first trip to the venerable old stadium in May 1965 - to see Liverpool of all teams! They went in as the underdogs against Leeds but won 2-1 in extra time to win the trophy for the first time in Anfield history, ending 73 years of red yearning. As an Everton player I got a Cup final ground ticket from the club. One of my mates was a Liverpool fan, who'd managed to get a ticket and Tommy Wright gave me his ticket, which I gave to an Evertonian pal of mine and the three of us went to the game. The whole occasion and atmosphere made a tremendous impact on me. It was a dour, tight match but a fantastic experience and I dreamed of playing in a final. Little did I know that only a year later I would be back to sample the magic of a dramatic blue-and-white Wembley."

Wembley 1966, engaging in our lap of honour following the 3-2 victory over Sheffield Wednesday. Mike Trebilcock and Alec Young hold aloft the trophy, with manager Harry Catterick (far right) also pictured.

Chapter Five

Journey To The Temple Of Joy

Whenever the subjects of football and England are on people's lips the year 1966 is mentioned as naturally as taking the next breath. It was the crowning moment for the national game, with captain Bobby Moore joining the immortals as he raised the World Cup to the Wembley skies. It was a threshold England have never crossed again, that glittering moment assuming even greater iconic status with every subsequent failure by the international team to win another tournament at world or European level.

Merseyside had even greater reasons to celebrate 1966. Not only were Everton's Ray Wilson and Liverpool's Roger Hunt members of the triumphant England side, but their clubs landed the two big domestic trophies. The respective captains Brian Labone and Ron Yeats displayed Merseyside's football strength by parading the FA Cup and League championship trophy around Goodison Park, with Wilson and Hunt carrying the World Cup, on a unique August afternoon prior to the Charity Shield. The enduring magic of the occasion cannot be dimmed even by the subsequent revelation that the trophy held aloft that day by Wilson and Hunt was a fake, specially commissioned by the FA. The governing body undertook the deception because they feared that the eight-inch high, solid gold bauble would be stolen again after its theft in London the previous March, prior to the relief of its discovery by a dog called Pickles.

There was nothing artificial, though, about Everton's FA Cup joy. At a time when Britain's average wage was £20 6s 1d, and footballers in general earned little more than three times that amount, the Everton players thrilled the nation by staging what was probably Wembley's greatest comeback to topple Sheffield Wednesday. Thousands of exuberant Evertonians headed for the pub, where a pint of beer cost around two shillings, to celebrate the club's first FA

Cup win since the golden pre-war era of Dixie Dean in 1933.

Everton began the 1965-66 season in style, hammering newly-promoted Northampton Town 5-2 at Goodison in their opening fixture and going nap again in their second home game, a 5-1 hammering of Sheffield Wednesday. It swiftly avenged Everton's 3-1 defeat at Hillsborough the previous midweek and featured an Alex Young hat-trick that was one of the greatest seen at Goodison, to crown perhaps his finest display in a royal blue jersey. Two sizzling shots and a superb header gave Young his first treble in English football. Under the headline 'When Young Is In Mood There's No Finer Player In All Of Britain', match reporter Horace Yates wrote in the Liverpool Daily Post: 'If manager Harry Catterick had chosen to give 18-year-old John Hurst his first League start by leaving out Young instead of Dennis Stevens, no-one could have criticised him. Young last night and Young in the draw last Saturday at Stoke were alike in name only.

Wednesday hardly knew what day it was as this diminutive, darting devil of a problem ran them further and further into trouble every time he touched the ball. It is no disrespect to his opponent Gerry Young to say he had not a clue how to approach the shadow that was his namesake.' The Wednesday defender was to suffer even more fatefully against Everton nine months later, but Young's mercurial skills were symbolic of his team's inconsistency during a season which saw English football's first substitutes. John Hurst's name was etched into Everton's record books when he was the first used by the club, replacing Fred Pickering in the League game at Stoke on August 28, 1965, three days before his full debut against Sheffield Wednesday.

The promise of those displays was unfulfilled for Everton and their followers, who were anguished at their team's 5-0 humiliation in the derby at Anfield, and a run from the end of October to the start of December without a win - three defeats and a draw making it a dismal November. Their stuttering form continued into the New Year and prospects of silverware seemed bleak. Colin Harvey, who figured in 40 of the 42 League games that season - in which Everton finished 11th, some 20 points adrift of champions Liverpool - wore the No 10 jersey in all eight FA Cup games. He recalls:

"By the time we got to the Cup we were not playing particularly well and Harry Catterick had a few problems on his plate. A week before our third-round home tie with Sunderland, we lost 2-0 to Blackpool and I scored an own goal. The pitch was frozen hard and the game wouldn't have been played today. I attempted a back pass to Geoff Barnett, deputising in goal for injured Gordon West, unable to face his former club. The ball bounced a bit awkwardly but one you'd still expect a keeper to collect. As I half turned to go up the field I glanced back and saw the ball bobble through Geoff's legs and into the net. I don't know who was more mortified - him or me. That gave Blackpool their second goal and clinched it for them. Thankfully, it was the only own goal I conceded in my entire career. But overshadowing my misery and the defeat was what happened in the aftermath outside Bloomfield Road.

Catterick had dropped public hero Alex Young and caused a shock by plunging Joe Royle into his debut at the tender age of 16 years, 282 days to become the youngest player ever to appear in a senior match for Everton. That statistic disregards Andy Penman, who was only 15 when he played against Liverpool in a Floodlit Cup match but which, like wartime games, was not recognised as a first-class fixture. There are many versions of what happened outside the Blackpool ground that winter's afternoon but I was an eyewitness. There is no doubt there was a lot of discontent among the supporters, many of them angry that their idol Young had been dropped. The result, against a team we were expected to beat, only deepened their fury.

I was sitting on the team bus overlooking the main entrance. Harry was late coming out and when he did he was jostled and bustled by a section of the supporters as he walked through a crowd to board the coach. Contrary to some reports, he was not attacked or kicked and no punches were thrown. But he did go down and it was a frightening, upsetting experience for him. He was white-faced and clearly badly shaken when he got on the bus. He just sat straight down in his usual seat at the front of the bus next to Tommy Egggleston. The incident was very regrettable and it was something that should not have happened, however highly charged and emotional the fans felt. It was very unpleasant. Even to witness it, as I did, left a nasty taste. All round, our day out at Blackpool was one to forget. Jimmy Gabriel wasn't in the team, one of a batch of games he missed in mid-season, and Gordon West was out after breaking his collar-bone in a European game the previous October. It ruled him out of 18 League games that season, with Barnett and Andy Rankin sharing the job of deputising in goal.

Harry Catterick, well aware of Gordon's goalkeeping talents, was relieved to have him back for the FA Cup. Gordon had a mammoth throw. He could reach beyond the halfway line! But he also had a short fuse. Gordon, by his own admission, was pretty highly strung at the best of times. He'd warn the opposing player standing in front of him: 'Move out of the way or I'm going to catch you with my hand.' A couple of seasons later, at Newcastle in October 1967, the inevitable happened. As the ball was crossed, with five minutes of the game left, Newcastle's Albert Bennett challenged Gordon who, in his own words, "forgot about the ball and took the man." The result was a Newcastle penalty and Gordon being sent off for the first time in his career. Sandy Brown, who had been sent on as sub for Johnny Morrissey, took over in goal, thus achieving the distinction of replacing two players in the same game. His first job was to face the penalty, from which Jim Iley scored to give Newcastle a 1-0 win. Everton did not have a goalkeeper sent off in top-flight football again for 18 years, when Neville Southall was dismissed in 1985. Even so, it set an unwanted record of being the first club since the war to have two keepers sent off in top division football.

During 1965-66 I had my own problems about getting marching orders from referees, being sent off for the first time in our 3-2 defeat at Fulham in October, when I became only the 10th Everton player since the war to be dismissed. The next time I was sent for an early bath was more than three years later, at Leicester in the last match of the 1968-69 season. At Fulham I tangled with John Dempsey and was angry at the way he brought me down. I reacted and we each threw a punch. Some wag said it would have made a good boxing bill: (Len) Harvey against (Jack) Dempsey! Actually, it was something and nothing but I got my marching orders for the first time in my life.

In those days, after a player was dismissed he had to appear before an FA Disciplinary Commission, and the one dealing with my Fulham dismissal was held in a Sheffield hotel. At the hearing the Fulham manager Vic Buckingham, an extravagant dresser, sprang flamboyantly to my defence. He spoke up for me and even went down onto the floor in front of the commission members to demonstrate how John Dempsey and I had been rolling around on the pitch. The outcome was that I did not get suspended, the commission ruling that my sending off had been sufficient punishment. I experienced a similar fate at Leicester when Dave Gibson made more than one late challenge on me. The referee had spotted what was happening yet did nothing. Gibson did it again - and this time I kicked him back. The referee followed the flight of the ball and I thought I'd got away with it. But the linesman had seen it. He kept his flag up until the referee went over to him and I was on my way off again.

This time I had to attend a commission in Birmingham and again I found, a very influential voice speaking up for me. It was the linesman who'd drawn the referee's attention to what I'd done. He told the commission the full story of what had happened and, again, I escaped a suspension. It must be the first time a player has been sent off twice and not had to serve a suspension. I was never dismissed again in my career but, contrary to some reports, my dismissals were not in the same season. Since then several Everton players have suffered that misfortune including Neville Southall, Duncan Ferguson and Slaven Bilic, who was sent off three times in the League in 1997-98.

Back in 1966 the January game at Blackpool, which held such painful memories for Harry Catterick, also proved to be a watershed for him and the club's fortunes, which were very patchy in the League and disappointing in Europe. Our Continental campaign started positively when we knocked out West German club Nuremberg on a 2-1 aggregate in the first round of the Fairs Cup. Despite being without the injured Brian Labone and with Sandy Brown deputising at centre-half, we went to Germany and drew 1-1 in a bruising first leg that was dubbed 'The Battle of Nuremberg'. The Czech referee missed, or chose to overlook, some blatant fouls with Sandy Brown and Fred Pickering needing treatment.

The Germans took the lead midway through the first half, but we showed great character and determination to equalise early in the second half. From a right-wing corner Derek Temple gave the ball back to Tommy Wright, whose cross was met brilliantly by Brian Harris who headed us level. Gordon West kept it that way with a string of saves. There were 36 free-kicks in the game and five bookings. But only three of our players emerged unscathed, without some kind of injury. Harry Catterick pulled no punches. "I'm no softie", he said, "but Nuremberg are the dirtiest side I have ever seen. So far as they are concerned the war is still on. We shall be making a report on the referee, who was the poorest I have ever seen."

In the return match Nuremberg reacted to the first-leg criticism by showing a less aggressive attitude, but packed their defence with goalkeeper Wabra in defiant form. We suffered a blow when Gordon West broke his right collar-bone after half-an-hour in a collision with visiting centre forward Bast. Andy Rankin came on as the first goalkeeping substitute in the club's history - it would be more than 27 years before Everton would use another goalkeeping replacement - but Rankin was mainly a spectator. It wasn't until the 63rd minute that we beat the German keeper. Tommy Wright's cross was headed onto a post by Brian Harris - and Jimmy Gabriel, who'd earlier hit the bar, scored from the rebound to give us a 1-0 win on the night and a 2-1 aggregate victory.

Having seen off Nuremberg, we were deeply disappointed to fall at the next hurdle to the crack Hungarians of Ujpest Dozsa, losing the first leg 3-0 in Budapest. Ujpest paraded several players who travelled to England in the Hungary squad for the World Cup the following summer, notably centre forward Ferenc Bene, defender Kaposzta and goalkeeper Szentmihalyi. The keeper's form caused us problems on the pitch and his name provided headaches for the visiting press corps battling to dictate their match reports back to Britain from behind the Iron Curtain over faint and crackling East European telephone lines. When Colin Wood of the Daily Mail referred to Szentmihalyi in his report, the copytaker on the other end of the line in Manchester said tartly: "I presume that will be the usual spelling."

We had Dennis Stevens in for the injured Jimmy Gabriel and it was a bad day all round. There was an eerie atmosphere with only 5,000 spectators in the 100,000 capacity stadium and we were up against it with the game less than 10 minutes old when Egor Solymosi struck a 25-yard curler that flew past Andy Rankin. Ujpest were soon two-up after I'd fouled Bene. The free-kick, taken by Solymosi, swerved past Rankin, hit Tommy Wright on the goal line and rebounded for Bene to score. Harry Catterick sent Brian Harris further forward but it took us all our time on a hard pitch to contain the lively Ujpest players. It was no real surprise when they added a third goal in the second half through Kuharsky. It needed Rankin to produce the save of the match from a fierce Bene shot to prevent us conceding a fourth on a dismal trip that is also recalled by the press corps for a fight in a Budapest nightclub. It has to be admitted that one or two players accompanied the sportswriters sheltering under tables as bottles flew through the air.

Unfortunately we were unable to turn the tables on the pitch in the Goodison return. Although we won 2-1, through Brian Harris and an own goal, we went out on a 4-2 aggregate on an arctic, wind-tossed night, memorable only for Jimmy Husband being called into the side to become Everton's youngest player in Europe. Jimmy was aged 18 years, 32 days, lowering my record of 18 years, 313 days set when I played against Inter. There was no doubt that Ujpest looked a classy outfit, but their hopes of repeating the feat of their compatriots Ferencvaros, who won the Fairs Cup the previous season, ended in a 5-2 quarter-final defeat by Leeds. So after our early exit from Europe and a mediocre showing in the League, we needed something to brighten our season. A week later we started on the road that would do just that - the FA Cup.

We were drawn at home to Sunderland in the third round and many fans were still irate at Catterick dropping Alex Young the previous week. One fan ran onto the pitch before kick-off carrying a placard with a message that, ironically, wrongly spelt the manager's name. 'Sack Cattrick Keep Young', it read. The pitch invader was led away by a policeman and his demand was overshadowed by events. Harry immediately recalled Alex in place of Joe Royle, who figured only once more in the first team that season. Also back were Gordon West, Jimmy Gabriel and fit-again Ray Wilson, for whom Sandy Brown had deputised at Blackpool. The team lined up like this:

West; Wright, Wilson; Gabriel, Labone, Harris; Scott, Young, Pickering, Harvey, Temple.

Whatever Harry's reasons for the shock change at Blackpool, his response to what happened was inspired. The team he picked the following week was to be, with one dramatic exception, the side that would share in an unforgettable experience four months later. We beat Sunderland 3-0, with Alex Young celebrating his swift return to action with a goal and an impressive all-round performance. Fred Pickering and Derek Temple scored the others on a day which ended with Evertonians suddenly feeling happier.

While we were on the way to victory watched by a crowd of 54,097 at Goodison, there were another 47,430 at Anfield witnessing holders Liverpool losing 2-1 to Chelsea. Pickering and Temple were on target again to ease us through our next Cup mission at non-League Bedford. Derek scored twice and Fred got the other goal as we ran out 3-0 winners. We were paired with Coventry at home in round five and for the third successive cup game Pickering and Temple scored, with Young getting the other in our 3-0 win.

For the sixth round we were pitted against Manchester City at Maine Road. Although they were then in the old Second Division, it was no easy task because City had been revived under former Everton star Joe Mercer, and went on to win promotion a couple of months later. In Mike Summerbee, Colin Bell, Alan Oakes, Mike Doyle, Glyn Pardoe and Neil Young, they already had a batch of the players who would go on to help City win the League title, the FA Cup, the League Cup and the European Cup Winners' Cup later that decade. Also in the City line-up was my former team-mate George Heslop, a Geordie centre-half who had made 11 first-team appearances for Everton in over three years at Goodison before moving to City the previous September. He was very impressive against us in a very tight game at Maine Road, which finished goalless. George played well, too, in the Goodison replay which also finished with a blank scoresheet.

Jimmy Gabriel missed the first two games through injury but was back for the third meeting at Molineux, the venue switched from Blackburn to beat the weather. This time we won 2-0, with Temple and Pickering extending their run of scoring in every round. 'Everton showed the quality of Cup fighters,' observed Liverpool Echo reporter Leslie Edwards. He was right. We'd got to the semi-final without conceding a goal. A later Everton manager, Gordon Lee, used the colourful phrase "sniff of the hot dog" if the possibility of a trophy shimmered into view. I know exactly what he meant because, for me, reaching the semi-final represented my first chance of winning something.

First, we had to take on and overcome Manchester United, then the reigning champions. Even without the injured George Best they were still formidable with Footballer of the Year Bobby Charlton, Denis Law and Nobby Stiles in their ranks. A week before the semi, Catterick fielded a reserve side at Leeds. All the recognised first-team players, including me, were rested and the team included Frank Darcy, Gerry Glover, Gerry Humphreys, Derek Smith and Joe Royle. With an average age of 20 years 11 months it is thought to be the youngest-ever Everton side. Not surprisingly, they lost 4-1, with Mike Trebilcock scoring our goal, and the Football League, for failing to field a full-strength team, fined the club £2,000.

For the semi-final we were without the injured Tommy Wright and Fred Pickering, unfortunately ending Fred's run of scoring in every round until then, which meant call-ups for Sandy Brown and Trebilcock. The game was staged at Bolton's Burnden Park, the first semi-final on the ground since March 1907 when Everton beat Second Division West Bromwich Albion 2-1, only to lose 2-1 in the final at Crystal Palace to...Sheffield Wednesday.

This is how the semi-final teams lined up (in the old 2-3-5 formation) in front of a 60,000 crowd on April 23, 1966:

Everton - Gordon West; Sandy Brown, Ray Wilson; Jimmy Gabriel, Brian Labone, Brian Harris; Alex Scott, Mike Trebilcock, Alex Young, Colin Harvey, Derek Temple.

Manchester United - Harry Gregg; Shay Brennan, Tony Dunne; Pat Crerand, Billy Foulkes, Nobby Stiles; Willie John Anderson, Denis Law, Bobby Charlton, David Herd, John Connelly.

As I recounted in the opening chapter, the match produced my most cherished football memory, that moment late in the game when my shot bounced on the muddy pitch, beat Harry Gregg and nestled in the United net.

We had toppled United, upset the odds and booked Everton's first visit to Wembley for 33 years. Sportswriter Dave Horridge, who reported the semi-final for the Daily Mirror, recalled an interesting aside as I was talking to him and other newspapermen after the match. "I asked Colin whether he was inside or outside the box when he shot - and received a reply from an unexpected quarter", Dave recounted. "Nobby Stiles happened to be walking past, heard my question to Colin and said: 'He was definitely inside the box. If he'd been outside I'd have made sure he never had the chance to shoot,' indicating he would have had no compunction about chopping Colin." In that case I'm glad I made the extra yard or so into the box!

Our League form and results, in contrast, ended on a downward spiral. We won only one of our last eight First Division games and finished our programme with successive away defeats at Sunderland and Leicester. We lost 3-0 at Filbert Street in our last League game and a young man called Peter Shilton made his League debut in Leicester's goal at the age of 16 years, 228 days. With the Cup final looming Harry Catterick rested Gordon West, Ray Wilson, Derek Temple and Alex Young and brought in Andy Rankin, Sandy Brown, John Hurst and Gerry Humphreys, a 20-year-old Welsh forward who had made the first of 14 League appearances for the club in the weakened team at Leeds prior to the semi-final. But all our minds were elsewhere. The FA Cup dominated our thoughts and because the Wembley countdown had begun, Shilton's debut went largely unheralded.

It left us with 10 days to prepare for the big game against Sheffield Wednesday, who had beaten Chelsea 2-0 in their semi-final at Villa Park after winning at Blackburn, Huddersfield, Newcastle and Reading in previous rounds. They'd reached Wembley without once playing in front of their own fans at Hillsborough, only the second team in the 20th century to achieve that feat, to underline the threat they posed.

There had been some discord in the Wednesday camp between manager Alan Brown and his players. Brown was a man with strong views so when it came to the topic of Cup final tickets and links to the black market, he laid it on the line. He told his players that the club would be sticking to the official allocation of 25 tickets each. He was confronted by a discontented dressing room delegation but Brown told them flatly: "That's all the tickets you're getting. If you don't think it's enough then don't bother to turn out at Wembley. I'm prepared to use the reserves but you can be sure that the world will know why." It was drastic stuff from a manager in the build-up to a Cup final but you have to admire his principles and from the evidence of his side's display, his stand certainly didn't have a negative effect on the players.

I don't recall any ticket problems in our camp, apart from the public scramble to get their hands on them. The club could have sold their 15,000 allocation at least four times over. Our squad travelled south a few days before the May 14 final to stay at Selsdon Park near Croydon. I roomed, as usual, with Tommy Wright and I remember on the morning of the game we were tuning in to the room radio and managed to get the pirate station Radio Caroline. That had just gone on the air and it was all new to us. We'd never got beyond Radio Luxembourg. The first record we heard that morning was Frank Sinatra's 'Strangers In The Night' and even though we'd been trying to tune into some pop music, I thought that was a good omen because my dad was mad about Sinatra.

As we approached Wembley on the team bus everywhere was just a sea of blue and white, the colours of both clubs, although while we wore our familiar strip in the final, Wednesday wore all white. Travelling down Wembley Way amidst the pre-match buzz remains one of the great, unforgettable experiences of my life. The occasion was something to cherish for the fans, too, because only the older supporters had memories of the last time Everton had been in the final, when Dixie's side beat Manchester City 3-0 in 1933. Fans began arriving in London from the early hours. Some of them went to Downing Street and were given an impromptu personal greeting by the Prime Minister, Harold Wilson. Another group of supporters got a sporting bonus. As they wandered through Hyde Park they came upon a hooded, track-suited figure shadow boxing under the trees. It was Muhammad Ali in training for his world-title fight with Henry Cooper. Like the showman he was, Ali stepped up the tempo to give his admiring gallery a special exhibition of his agility, unique in heavyweight boxing. Sadly for Cooper, a cut eye forced him to retire in the sixth round when the pair met at Highbury a week later.

Harry Catterick sprang a pre-match shock when he announced the team without Fred Pickering at centre-forward. Fred had scored four goals in his five Cup appearances, although he'd missed the semi-final because of knee trouble. That had given Mike Trebilcock his chance and to many people's amazement, including his own, the 21-year-old Cornishman, who'd been signed in a £20,000 move from Plymouth the previous New Year's Eve, found himself playing in the final. Harry had told the two players of his decision the day before the game. Fred was devastated. He'd expected to play after appearing in our last three League games and when he learned he wasn't, he told us he was never going to play for the club again. Although he never carried out that threat, Fred made only eight more appearances before Catterick sold him to Birmingham City for £50,000 the following summer.

Mike, in contrast, was stunned at his selection and admitted: "I had been looking forward to going to Wembley because I'd never been before and I was excited at the thought of sitting and watching the game in a new suit. Then, after lunch the day before the game, the manager called me. I expected to have to help to put out all the Wembley gear. Instead, he told me I'd be playing in place of Fred. If ever I've fallen off the back of my seat that was it. My name wasn't even mentioned in the Cup final programme!" In fact, he never made another FA Cup appearance for Everton after Wembley and after a total of only 14 senior outings, in which he scored five goals, moved to Portsmouth 18 months later. Mike married a girl from Bootle and after ending his career with Torquay, he emigrated to Australia but his name endures in the annals of Everton achievement.

Catterick's gamble in picking him proved the hand of destiny for Mike and us. "Fred was popular and could score but he'd been injured and had gone off the boil a bit", Harry explained later. "Trebilcock was a first-rate goal poacher. I always felt his sharpness would show." These were the line-ups:

Everton: Gordon West; Tommy Wright, Ray Wilson; Jimmy Gabriel, Brian Labone (captain), Brian Harris; Alex Scott, Mike Trebilcock, Alex Young, Colin Harvey, Derek Temple.

Sheffield Wednesday: Ron Springett; Wilf Smith, Don Megson (captain); Peter Eustace, Sam Ellis, Gerry Young; Graham Pugh, John Fantham, Jim McCalliog, David Ford, John Quinn.

Referee: Mr J.W. (Jack) Taylor (Wolverhampton). Attendance: 100,000

For the whole of the first half and into the second Wednesday boss Brown won the tactical battle by playing four men in midfield. We had two wingers in Alex Scott and Derek Temple out wide. With just me and Jimmy Gabriel in the middle, Wednesday ran us ragged. We just couldn't get the ball. They had some good footballers, notably the elegant Peter Eustace and the crafty Jim McCalliog, who'd drop a bit deep. Gabby was looking at me and I was looking at him and we were desperately wondering: 'How are we going to get hold of this ball?' Only four minutes had gone when we went behind, fortune favouring Wednesday when a McCalliog shot deflected off Ray Wilson's heel past Gordon West.

A linesman's offside flag also went their way 10 minutes later after Alex Young had netted and nine minutes after that Alex rounded goalkeeper Ron Springett and was bundled over. But Jack Taylor, who was a good 20 yards away, gave nothing. I've watched the game on film and video several times since and I have to say that it was only for brilliant defensive performances from Brian Harris and Brian Labone that kept us in the game. In the dressing room at half-time Harry Catterick tried to pick us up. He told us that we had the ability but had to find the determination to go with it. He reminded us that we couldn't bank on coming back for another Cup final.

But things got even bleaker for us in the 57th minute when Gordon West could only parry John Fantham's shot and David Ford swept the ball in to put us 2-0 down. Everything now was stacked against us. Then, suddenly, two minutes later the tide changed. We scored and the game began to turn. I managed to play the ball forward to Derek Temple. He flicked it down with his head into the path of Trebilcock, who struck it first time - and the ball flew into the bottom corner of the net beyond Springett's groping left hand. "All I wanted to do was keep my shot low," said Mike, who became the first black player to score in an FA Cup final. He added: "It's so easy to get under the ball but I knew if I did keep it low it must have a chance of going in."

Trebilcock's goal transformed us. We'd been feeling drained due to the nervousness of the occasion, the warmth of the day and the lushness of the pitch. That was something players then were not used to, and probably gave rise to the injury jinx that clouded so many finals. In those days from Christmas onwards you were just playing on mud on First Division grounds. The surfaces were dreadful. Then you suddenly stepped out onto the rich, green sward of Wembley and, in our case, were getting chased all over the place. We were dead on our feet and I felt there was no way back. I wasn't alone. When Wednesday's second goal went in my grandad, Billy. Mallon, left the ground. He couldn't stand watching any more. But when he heard the roar for our first goal he got back in again.

It was as if someone had flicked a switch. It gave us an adrenalin rush. We had energy again. It must have been a downer for Wednesday, who were flattened five minutes later when we equalised. Alex Scott's free-kick dropped for Trebilcock to hammer home on the half volley from 15 yards. It was the signal for one of the moments committed to Everton folklore, an incident not to be encouraged but one that briefly relieved the tension and brought smiles to thousands in the stadium and millions watching on television.

Former Everton youth-team players Eddie and Jimmy Kavanagh, both of whom I knew, were standing together on the terraces when Eddie said he was going to the toilet. Instead, elated Eddie ran onto the pitch and his ecstatic dash across the Wembley stage, captured for posterity by the cameras, was stopped only by a policeman's flying rugby tackle. Brian Harris gave the crowd further delight by donning the officer's fallen helmet. "He just ran and nobody seemed able to catch him," recalled Micky Cullinan, one of Eddie's fellow supporters that day. "He even got his coat off just as one bobby was about to grab him. I'll never forget seeing his braces as he slipped away from his pursuers. Everyone just cheered and when they finally got him everyone booed. You could even see the players pleading with the coppers not to chuck him out." Eddie did get ejected from the stadium but he got back in again. I know that because when we were doing our after-match lap of honour he popped up right beside us! He was a great character. Sadly, Eddie died in 1999 but his excursion onto the Wembley pitch is preserved to this day on Everton's official history tour tape.

The flow and momentum of the game was now powerfully with us and the Cup was won appropriately by a majestic strike from Derek Temple, the type of goal that was his speciality. Little more than 10 minutes remained when I lobbed the ball forward. It looked as if Gerry Young would deal with it easily but the ball slipped under his foot and into the path of the lurking Derek. Springett began to advance and most players in Derek's situation would have opted to take the ball on and try to make sure. But not him. He just launched his shot and it sped into the net. We felt sheer, unbounded joy. Derek was a sweet striker of the ball, with magnificent timing, but none was as sweet as his shot at Wembley. As Mike Trebilcock, himself a hero on the day put it: "Every schoolboy dreams of playing at Wembley and scoring the winner in a cup final. But I didn't score the winner. Derek did that - and what a magnificent goal it was."

Derek, with typical modesty, talked us through his wonder-strike like this: "I didn't have time to feel sorry for Gerry Young. When I saw Springett coming out I was going to try to chip the ball over him but he stopped on the six-yard line. Then I was torn between taking the ball up to him and either hitting it or trying to dribble past him. I decided to hit it and it paid off. I knew the instant I hit it that it was going in. But I wouldn't like to be in that position again at Wembley...unless there was the same outcome."

Only two months later, Alf Ramsey would signal the death of wingers when he dispensed with them and won the World Cup for England. But when you had versatile flank-men like Derek, who hit 15 goals that season including a top-scoring six in the FA Cup, they were invaluable. He scored 82 goals in 273 senior Everton appearances and although he won only one England cap, against West Germany in 1965, his place in Goodison's hall of fame is assured. He did it, too, after an awkward period when he was the butt of crowd jibes, something Derek put down to the fact that he was a local boy. But in the end he deservedly won their applause. Almost four decades after that magical afternoon at Wembley I was at Liverpool's Royal Court Theatre for an Everton pantomime, and when Derek walked on stage for a guest appearance his entry brought the house down. In that moment it was evident that he was a hero for all seasons, his status handed down the generations. After his Wembley goal we knew we were going to win the Cup although Wednesday, to their credit, kept battling to the end. In the dying minutes Gabby took the ball up to the right-hand corner flag and kept it there. To be honest, I think he did that because he was knackered.

Jack Taylor's final whistle lit the blue-touch paper for wild celebrations by us and desolation for Wednesday in general and in particular for Gerry Young, whose mistake had proved crucial. "I am inconsolable", he lamented. "Ninety-nine times out of a hundred I'd have dealt with that ball - the hundredth had to be in the final." His manager Alan Brown said generously: "After being two goals down, Everton deserved their success." Jack Rowe, in his Liverpool Daily Post match report, wrote: 'Don't let anyone try to kid you that this was the finest Cup final fightback since Stanley Matthews hauled Blackpool to victory over Bolton in 1953. Nobody is going to kid me because I put Everton's triumph above that - for two reasons. In 1953 Bolton were handicapped by an injury to a defender and even when you're leading by two goals, with a man like Matthews on the opposing side anything can happen.

But this time it was all so different. Wednesday had grabbed their two goals, they were riding as high as any team could and Everton, with 29 minutes to play, looked down and out. What then enables Everton literally to drag themselves up off the deck and in 14 of the most dramatic, exciting and stupendous minutes, deliver the most historic knock-out blow ever seen at Wembley? The captain Brian Labone gave me the answer when he said it was team spirit. Every player lifted himself up when the chips were down.'

Me? I was living the football cliche. I was absolutely over the moon as I followed our skipper Labby up the 39 steps to the royal box to receive my winners medal from Princess Margaret. How fortune had changed for Harry Catterick, jostled by fans in January and now lauded by them in May. We chaired Harry off the pitch, apparently the first time a team had done that in a Cup final - but he deserved it. His team selection against his former club had been gloriously vindicated and he said later: "I wasn't panicking when we were two down but nobody feels on top of the world when they're trailing against a fast, competent team in the Cup final. But the lads clicked and I was delighted with all 11 of them."

In the after-match banquet, at London's Grosvenor House Hotel - attended by the 1933 Cup-winning side apart from Warney Cresswell, who was ill - Harry was presented with the gift of a silver tea service from director and former chairman John Moores, the power behind the club who had a second spell in the chair during the 1970s. I and the team, as well as Fred Pickering, Sandy Brown and Johnny Morrissey, received gold watches. The fact is, though, that whenever I wish I can rewind my memory clock, it is to the day I was part of something magical at Wembley on a May day in 1966."

One of my proudest pictures, with Harry Catterick at Bellefield.

Chapter Six

The Enigma Called Catterick

Ariddle wrapped in a mystery inside an enigma: Churchill's famous description of Russia applies perfectly to Harry Catterick, the Everton manager whose brilliantly-consistent record during the 1960s has been woefully unheralded in the annals of English football. The reasons are many but his personality was a huge obstruction to Catterick being granted the public recognition his achievements deserve. Those, including me, who knew him - in so far as anyone outside his family could claim to know him - will talk of a man who could be likened to an iceberg. Two thirds were always looming unseen below the surface. They will talk, too, of his charm on the one hand contrasting with his coldness and remoteness on the other.

Given the context of his management years at Everton, Catterick was an alter-ego to his era of the Swinging Sixties. He was as introverted as his great Liverpool rival Bill Shankly was extrovert. He shunned publicity with as much Machiavellian determination as his Scottish counterpart grasped and courted it. His psyche ensured that he could never become a cult figure beloved by Gwladys Street as Shankly was by the Kop. Yet, as this book exclusively reveals, Catterick's remarkable, surreptitious operations in the transfer market led to a shocked Shankly resigning in the 1960s, a situation that required desperate pleading by the Anfield hierarchy to persuade the iconic Scot to resume his reign. A few minutes in the company of those who played and worked for Catterick reveal a deep respect for the man, even if his methods often left them puzzled and sometimes fearful.

It is accepted, if entirely unconfirmed, that sometime between his birth in Darlington on November 26, 1919 - the son of Stockport player Henry also known as Harry - and his entry into management in the 1950s, Catterick underwent an Alf Ramsey-style voice makeover. An immaculate dresser, in finely cut suits often with waistcoat, he took great care and pride in his appearance. That is why his characterisation by actor Colin Welland as a bluff, gruff 'where there's muck there's brass' Yorkshireman in the 1997 BBC TV drama 'The Fix', about Tony Kay and football's 1960s betting scandal, attracted such derision. 'It was one of the worst theatrical take-offs since Dick Van Dyke essayed his gor-blimey Cockney in Mary Poppins', was the acerbic view of Len Capeling in the Liverpool Daily Post. It was echoed by Catterick's grandson Tony Smith after he had seen the programme, which also purported to show his grandfather handing his new capture Kay a then illicit signing-on fee in the Sheffield Wednesday boardroom following the player's transfer. 'It made my grandad look like Mr Blobby but he was not like that - it almost made me want to cry', said Tony. 'But I was pleased that they didn't portray him taking any bungs himself.'

Catterick was an apprentice marine engineer playing centre-forward as an amateur for Stockport - where his father was coach - and Cheadle Heath Nomads when Everton signed him as a part-time professional in March 1937. Standing a shade over 5ft 9ins with a playing weight of 10 stone 10 lbs and described as 'hard, rugged and uncompromising', Goodison's new recruit made a handful of reserve appearances alongside Dixie Dean during the iconic star's latter days at Everton. Catterick made his first-team debut in the War Regional League in March 1940, becoming understudy to the great Tommy Lawton and, later, finding Jock Dodds and Jimmy McIntosh ahead of him in the pecking order. Yet Catterick's scoring ratio in wartime football was an impressive 55 goals in 71 appearances. His haul included four hat-tricks, one of them notably in a 3-1 win at Liverpool in February 1941.

He made his League debut on the resumption of national organised football in August 1946, having had his FA Cup baptism in a two-leg defeat by Preston the previous January. Fortune, though, failed to smile on Catterick who suffered from a series of injuries and, when peace resumed, he sustained two broken arms. But he did have his memorable moments, none more so than his hat-trick at Craven Cottage in a 5-1 win over Fulham in October 1950. As Dave Hickson emerged Catterick, having scored 24 goals in 71 League and FA Cup outings, left in December 1951 to become player-boss of Crewe, hanging up his boots the following year to concentrate on management.

At Gresty Road he discovered and developed local-boy Frank Blunstone, who was sold to Chelsea for the-then impressive sum of £10,000, his left-wing talents gaining England recognition. Catterick moved on to take charge of Rochdale in June 1953 where his managerial skills became evident, assembling a side of free-transfer signings and steering them into the newly-formed Third Division before he managed Sheffield Wednesday. It was there that he first linked up with Tommy Eggleston, a partnership that would later lead Everton to glory. Catterick appointed Mitcham-born Eggleston as his coach on the recommendation of Bill Dodgin Senior, who had been his manager when Egggleston was trainer at Brentford.

Catterick's achievement at Hillsborough was to stabilise the 'yo-yo club', which had been promoted twice and relegated twice during eight seasons in the immediate post-war period. He led them to the championship of the old Second Division in 1959 and in successive seasons Wednesday finished fifth in the top flight and reached the FA Cup semi-final, and then took the runners-up spot behind Double-winners Tottenham. That impressive record alerted Everton supremo John Moores and in April 1961 he famously sacked the popular Johnny Carey, as the pair travelled in a London taxi after attending a Football League meeting.

Moores allowed the affable Irishman one more game in charge, the penultimate home match of the season against Cardiff. It was perhaps a masochistic decision by Moores. He was jeered and booed by the fans, who were as angry as the players at Carey's dismissal. Under Carey's stewardship Everton were heading for fifth place - their highest-finishing position since the 1939 championship win - a distinct change of fortune after a post-war period in which, having suffered relegation in 1951, they scrambled just five points clear of relegation to Division Three North two seasons later. But rumours that Moores wanted more iron fist than velvet glove in his manager, and of a personality clash, were confirmed by his sacking of the former Blackburn manager and outstanding captain of Manchester United and Ireland. Catterick's hard-headed management approach appealed to Moores who saw in him the qualities to deal with star players. Skipper Bobby Collins, who saluted Carey on behalf of the team in a dressing room farewell speech before kick-off against Cardiff, put his words into action with a hat-trick in a 5-1 win, Alex Young scoring the other two goals.

At that stage Catterick had been out of work for 10 days, having resigned from Wednesday after resenting interference by the board. Moores gave him the task of bringing success and silverware to Goodison when, 48 hours after the Cardiff game, he appointed Catterick as manager. The job came with a terse challenge. "Our fans demand success - and that is what they will get", pledged Moores. "I will give Mr Catterick all the support I can. The rest is up to him." Perhaps it was that Moores mantra and the pressure emanating from it that determined Catterick's management style, maybe his very persona. "Harry could be a real tough man who demanded 100 per cent from his staff," said Eggleston, who followed Catterick to Goodison to resume a partnership many likened to the 'bad guy, nice guy' duo so hackneyed in police dramas. "I was a little bit more placid than Harry and could calm things down a bit", Eggleston added. "Harry was a very good manager when it came to buying and selling players. He knew the game and he got the best out of his players. He wasn't in the Shankly class for public relations. He was a bit reserved and kept to himself. But that was natural. He was true to himself and I think he believed there's no value in false habits."

Catterick enthused over his return to manage his former club. "It has been one of my ambitions to come back. Everton is a club of wonderful traditions. I only hope I can fulfil expectations and put them back amongst the game's major honours." However, he soon felt the need to stamp his presence. "There was an air of complacency about the place", he declared. "Everyone seemed too easy going. Some of the staff seemed afraid to make minor decisions affecting training and coaching. I had to make changes and I didn't like what I had to do because I'd known some as players."

To the outside world, though, Catterick was a perplexing figure, authoritarian in his management style, distant to the fans and frustratingly uncooperative to the media. He was instrumental in Everton's stance on the newly-arrived creature called televised football, of which he was highly suspicious. The BBC's now celebrated 'Match of the Day' began in August 1964, Kenneth Wolstenholme introducing it from Anfield for Liverpool's 3-2 win over Arsenal. At the outset of a programme that was to become a national institution, the BBC were restricted to 45 minutes edited highlights of just one League game and was not permitted to reveal its selected match in advance. The FA also dictated that analysing controversial incidents and referees' decisions were not allowed. Catterick went further. He saw television as a threat but unlike others of his contemporaries who were apprehensive about television's affect on attendances, he feared it for a different reason. The cameras, he believed, would reveal far too much to opponents about his players and his tactics.

His fears of the cameras led to a remarkable Everton request to their neighbours Liverpool, revealed for the first time in this book. They wanted Merseyside's big two clubs to form an anti-TV alliance, an idea that seems utterly bizarre in this television-driven football age when, for good or ill, small screen coverage of our national sport fuels the game's finances.

Peter Robinson, who was then Liverpool FC secretary, disclosed: "We received an invitation from Everton to discuss the new development of televised football. I went to Goodison with one of our directors, Eric Sawyer, who was our finance committee chairman. We met the then Everton chairman, E. Holland Hughes who was accompanied, if memory serves me right, by another Everton director, George Watts.

Holland Hughes was a powerful debater and he put forward the view that televised football was bad for the game and that their manager, Harry Catterick, was strongly opposed to it. He felt that the more his team were seen the more advantage it gave to forthcoming opponents. They said that Everton wanted us to join with them in resisting television, not only with regard to the number of occasions on which a team should be televised but also the length of the transmission.

Everton's request put us in a difficult position on three counts. First was the fact that John Moores, as well as being a powerful and influential Everton figure, was also a substantial shareholder in Liverpool. Second, we held the view that television was to be encouraged, one of the reasons being that we were in the process of building Liverpool's image and identity because it was only a few years previously that we'd won promotion. Indeed, we were proud that Liverpool featured in the first black and white and colour editions of Match of the Day.

And, third was the fact that our manager Bill Shankly held a diametrically opposed view to Harry Catterick. Bill was all for his team being screened. He believed that when other clubs and managers saw Liverpool play it would frighten them! We expressed our views and said we would go away and reflect on what Everton had said. But events took over. Televised football was a tide that could not be turned. Football League secretary Alan Hardaker got involved and said that clubs should welcome and co-operate with television.

At that time I understand the production team used to edit the film with scissors and when Match of the Day came to Anfield they used my office as a studio. It's astonishing to reflect on the march of televised football in the ensuing 40 years." Catterick, though, was unmoved and did all he could to throw obstacles in the way of this new phenomenon which he saw as a grossly unwelcome intrusion. The upshot was that Everton requested not to be featured in televised games and followed up with a proposal that action replays of controversial incidents should be banned.

Although Everton's home FA Cup clash with Sheffield Wednesday in January 1965 was screened on Match of the Day, they did not feature in a televised League game at Goodison during the first three seasons of the programme. That was delayed until August 1967, when the nation's viewers saw two Alan Ball goals and another from Alex Young give them a 3-1 win over Manchester United. By then, even Catterick had realised that trying to stem the flow of televised soccer was a football equivalent of Canute ordering back the tide - but his secretive traits persisted. His policy of announcing his match squad in alphabetical order the day before the game belied his reluctance to be informative, as much as his desire to keep the opposition in the dark. The late Chris James, in his first week as a Liverpool Echo sportswriter in 1967, decided he would interpolate Catterick's announced squad and reported what he believed would be the likely line-up. No sooner had the paper hit the streets than James received a telephone call: "This is Harry Catterick. If you've started the way you intend to continue you'll get no cooperation from me." Then Catterick curtly ended the call. James, always a man to confront problems head on, went straight to the club's Bellefield training ground to see the Everton manager, telling him in no uncertain terms that while it may be Catterick's desire to keep people guessing, his job was to inform the public and it would continue to be so.

Thus was born one of many uneasy relationships between Catterick and media men which also manifested itself after James had unavoidably missed Everton's team coach following a midweek match at Southampton. The volume of his newspaper commitments meant that James had not completed his work before the team bus departed, but Catterick officially reported him to the Echo, warning that a repeat would jeopardise the privilege of local pressmen travelling with the team. Later, James was succeeded as the paper's Everton reporter by the late Michael Charters, who recalled: "I got to know Harry as well as any journalist, but he always maintained a professional barrier. He admitted to me frankly that he was an introvert and found it difficult to let down that barrier with the media, even though he and I became good friends. I believe that he had a fear, a complex, about Littlewoods, who wielded such influence at Everton and whose founder and owner John Moores appointed him as manager. Harry always seemed to be looking over his shoulder. I think he was frightened of the power of Littlewoods. But I admired him for his dedication to the cause of Everton. He set a high target for his players and punished himself to maintain that."

Dave Horridge, who covered the Mersey football beat during the 1960s and early 1970s for the Daily Mirror, was also the subject of a complaint from Catterick, involving Fred Pickering. "One day I bumped into Fred outside Goodison and we started chatting", recalled Horridge. "Then, from an upstairs window, Harry's assistant Tommy Eggleston shouted that Fred was wanted. A couple of days later, the Mirror sports editor Peter Thomas received a letter from Catterick complaining that I had been seen talking to Pickering and pointing out that it was against League and club rules for a player to talk to the press without permission. Peter replied by pointing out that he had no control over whether reporters spoke to players and that it was part of their job. If journalists didn't talk to people, he told Catterick, newspapers would go out of business. Harry, like many others in football, made the mistake of thinking that while they may try to stop players talking to the press, they couldn't prevent the press trying to talk to players."

Another sportswriter Mike Ellis, who has covered Merseyside football for 40 years for the defunct Daily Herald and The Sun, has some vividly revealing recollections of Catterick, the man and the manager. "My boats were burned with Harry the first time I met him", he admits. "In 1963 I was living in Rhyl and I'd just come down from working on a paper in Hartlepool, and joined the Herald. One of their sportswriters, Alf Ballard, was ill so I was told I'd be standing in for him on Merseyside. As it turned out, Alf didn't come back and it became my patch permanently.

The sports editor Jimmy Stevenson and I made an appointment to meet Harry at Goodison. We duly reported to reception and were told to take the lift. A lift! That impressed me! Harry met us and invited us into the boardroom for a drink. 'This is the life', I thought. Then Harry said in that far-back voice of his: 'Come and meet some of the players.' He took us to the snooker room and the first player I spotted was Jimmy Gabriel, who was playing a shot on the table. 'This is Mike Ellis, he's going to be working for the Daily Herald,' said Harry. Suddenly, a guy leaning over the top of the table with a fag in his mouth, exclaimed: 'Bloody hell, Mike, what are you doing here?' It was Roy Vernon, who I'd grown up with and gone to school with in North Wales. Harry's face was an absolute picture as he realised that I had a contact in the dressing room amongst his players and he didn't like it. I think from that moment my relationship with Harry Catterick was always going to be difficult - and so it proved.

In 1966 Everton's star centre-forward Fred Pickering, who'd cost the massive sum in those days of £85,000, was carried off in a match and the club wouldn't say what was wrong with him. My sports editor told me to see if I could find out by going to see Fred. He was in Liverpool's Broadgreen Hospital and I reported to reception, told them who I was and what I was there for. The receptionist went away to check with those in charge and she came back to say permission had been given. They'd spoken to Fred, who I knew, and he said he'd be delighted to see me in his private room. 'Great to see you, Mike, because nobody from the club's been in', said Fred. Fred told me what his injury was, a cartilage in his knee, and we had a chat. I wrote the story in next morning's paper and Catterick was straight on the phone to the sports editor. He claimed I had trespassed on hospital property and spoken to Fred without permission and said he was going to make a complaint to the Press Council against me and the paper. The editor told Catterick: 'If that's what you're threatening to do, do it.' But Harry didn't. His bluff had been called.

The following March I got a shock when Harry told me he had an exclusive for me. He told me he'd lost out in the battle for Howard Kendall and that Liverpool were signing him from Preston the following day. I knew how highly Bill Shankly rated Howard so I wrote the story which appeared next day as a back page lead under the headline: 'Shankly Swoops For Kendall.' As I was driving to Merseyside from Rhyl I switched on the radio to hear William Hardcastle, presenter of the BBC radio programme 'The World At One', announce: 'In sport, Everton today signed Howard Kendall from Preston.' I was stunned. I couldn't believe it. I drove straight to Bellefield to confront Harry. 'You've turned me over,' I told him. Harry just grinned and said: 'That's football.' Then he got the bottle out. He'd used me to make Bill Shankly look small and embarrass Liverpool. It was Harry's way of scoring points off Bill." What Catterick did not know, and something that this book can now reveal, is that his capture of Kendall devastated Shankly and prompted his written resignation as Liverpool manager.

Shankly was a huge admirer of Kendall and had been keen to take him to Anfield as his fourth capture from his former club Preston, following his earlier signings of Gordon Milne, Dave Wilson and Peter Thompson. Kendall had built on his assured performance at Wembley three years earlier, when he had become the 20th century's youngest FA Cup finalist at the age of 17 years, 345 days - a record lowered by West Ham's Paul Allen in 1980, with Millwall's Curtis Weston becoming the youngest FA Cup finalist in history as a substitute in 2004, aged 17 years, 119 days.

Shankly and Catterick were in the vanguard of top-flight managers coveting Kendall's rising talents but Shankly's initial overtures were rebuffed by the Deepdale club. When Shankly arrived for work at Liverpool's Melwood training ground on Friday, March 10, 1967, the day before a Saturday evening FA Cup fifth-round collision with Everton, he was puzzled to read the Sun story of his imminent swoop for Kendall. His mood changed to abject disappointment a few hours later when news broke of Kendall's £80,000 move to Everton after the player had rejected an offer from Stoke. Liverpool contacted Preston desperately hoping the deal with Everton had not been signed and sealed but discovered that negotiations had been completed. Shankly was obsessively driven in his rivalry with Catterick. If Arsenal or Manchester United had signed Kendall, it would have been a jolt to him. But for his great Goodison antagonist, a man he labelled on radio as "devious", to have staged such an audacious coup was a savage blow to the Scot, whose outward bravado often masked deep anxieties.

Compounding Shankly's woes was his side's fate at Goodison next evening - a 1-0 Cup defeat by Catterick's team. Kendall was among the spectators in a combined crowd surpassing 105,000 - an FA Cup record - with the tie beamed back to Anfield on closed-circuit television screens. The deciding goal had come from Alan Ball, the flame-haired World Cup hero whose £110,000 signing from Blackpool had come within hours of Everton's 1-0 Charity Shield defeat by Liverpool the previous August. Kendall's arrival meant that, with Ball and Colin Harvey, Catterick now had the three players who were to form a majestic midfield trio that would carry Everton to glory. But Shankly's anguish at losing out to Catterick for Kendall intensified to the extent that he sat down and wrote his resignation letter on the typewriter that now has pride of place in the Liverpool FC Museum.

Shankly threatening to quit was not new. Almost every summer he would tell his right-hand man Bob Paisley and club secretary and later chief executive Peter Robinson that he was finishing. People at the club even called it affectionately 'Bill's summer madness', probably born of stressful, new-season trepidation. This, though, was something different - a calculated, written resignation during the season. Shankly handed the letter to Robinson and departed Anfield, taking his typewriter and other personal belongings with him. Robinson passed on the letter to club chairman Sid Reakes, to whom it was addressed, and the Anfield hierarchy were plunged into crisis. Somehow they kept the situation under wraps and told Paisley and the players that Shankly's absence was due to a heavy cold.

Meanwhile, frantic efforts were made to bring him back. Reakes, Robinson, former chairman Tom Williams and finance committee chairman Eric Sawyer all spoke to Shankly at home by telephone, pleading with him to reconsider. Suddenly, two days later, Shankly re-appeared and resumed managerial duties as if nothing had happened. It would be more than seven years before he would irrevocably leave Liverpool but strangely, even in 1974, his resignation was verbal. There was no letter as there had been in 1967, a letter that was never rescinded and which remained in a filing cabinet at Anfield until it was lost during office renovations in the 1980s.

An example of Catterick's complex personality manifested itself on the club's European Cup Winners' Cup first round, first-leg trip to Aalborg, Denmark in September 1966. Members of the press travelled on the club's charter flight and as the aircraft began its descent, a sportswriter who had been having a stony, unproductive relationship with Catterick got a shock. "Harry, who I didn't get on with very well, suddenly slid into the empty seat beside me and asked me if I'd been to Aalborg before. I told him I hadn't and he replied: 'I was here last week, taking a look at the opposition, and it's a great place. If you're going out tonight knock on my room door and I'll come with you.' I was totally gobsmacked.

Sure enough, when we checked into the hotel he gave me his room number. That evening I knocked on Harry's door as he'd suggested and out we went on the town. He couldn't have been better company. He introduced me to a beautiful blonde girl and ensured I had a fantastic night. On the flight home I went up the plane to where Catterick was sitting and asked him about the match, which was a goalless draw, to write a follow-up. But the shutters had come down again. The man who I'd been on the town with 24 hours earlier didn't want to know and by the time the plane's wheels touched down at Speke Airport normal, chilly, relations had resumed." His split personality was evident, too, on another European trip when a member of the British press party chatted up one of the local girls much to the chagrin of her boyfriend, who stormed into the foyer of the team's hotel and confronted the sportswriter. Flying fists were a split second away when Catterick stepped in to protect the threatened journalist and pacify the situation. "I was amazed because Harry would hardly speak to me at home," said the relieved but puzzled member of the press corps.

Catterick was famed for his transfer market modus operandi, which invariably earned the cliche media label of 'cloak and dagger'. When questioned about it, though, Catterick was dismissive, as Bob Azurdia of BBC Radio Merseyside discovered when he interviewed him in the late 1960s. "You have a reputation for being very secretive about your transfer actions then suddenly swooping," said Azurdia. Catterick responded: "This question of swooping isn't really on because I never move quickly. The point is that I negotiate for quite some time. But I always feel that transfer business is essentially between the two clubs until it becomes an established fact and then it's time to release it to the public."

In the 1960s his secretive transfer raids were legendary. Tottenham boss Bill Nicholson, for example, was about to light a cigar to celebrate winning the battle to sign Alex Scott from Rangers in February 1963. A London evening paper actually ran a story proclaiming Scott was a Spurs player. They reckoned, though, without Catterick who stole in to land the Scotland winger for £40,000, and leave White Hart Lane and the football press stunned. Seven months later Catterick and his assistant Tommy Eggleston, in evening dress and bow ties, were dining at Everton's championship banquet at Liverpool's Adelphi Hotel when the Goodison boss told his right-hand man they were leaving. The pair slipped away and drove straight to Scotland to sign utility man Alex 'Sandy' Brown from Partick for £38,000.

Taciturn though he was with the media, Catterick was not afraid to air his views when the mood took him, as long-serving, highly respected football writer Colin Wood can testify. "I'd written an article in the Daily Mail about the Scotland international squad", Wood recalled. "The selectors had included Liverpool's Ian St John and in my piece I questioned why Alex Young of Everton had not been named. The day the article appeared I was at Everton, making a customary news call, when Harry rounded on me. He was very upset at what I'd written and said: 'You've insulted the fellow across the park, who's one of the best around.' I think his outburst showed the extent of his feelings about Young, which we were well aware of anyway."

Yet if it was difficult to warm to disciplinarian Catterick, who registered minus on the communication chart, his judgment of football flesh and his ability to build winning teams, the two greatest yardsticks of a football manager, soared almost off the scale. Gifted, charismatic managers adorned the 1960s. Shankly, Matt Busby, Don Revie, Bill Nicholson and Joe Mercer amassed 33 major trophies between them. Yet Catterick had nine top-six

League finishes during that decade and his record included two championships, a runners-up spot and two third places.

During those 10 years Everton lost only 25 home games and scored an average of 46 goals per season at Goodison. In the Cup they lost only one of 25 home ties and only once in Europe. In addition, Catterick sides lost in two FA Cup semi-finals and in a final after extra time while the club's youngsters lifted the 1965 FA Youth Cup and players like John Hurst, Jimmy Husband, Joe Royle, Tommy Wright, Alan Whittle and Andy Rankin graduated through the ranks to become accomplished first-team performers. Colin Harvey was another who saw his career take off under Catterick. He was at Goodison throughout the Catterick era and his recollections offer a revealing and intriguing insight into football's most mysterious manager:

"I never had a single problem with Harry. In fact, I got on quite well with him. After all, he brought me through into the team and I think he got a kick out of that which, for a manager, is understandable. You get fulfilment from guiding youngsters up the ladder and seeing them make it to the top. He was receptive to people who worked hard for him because his management creed was based on the work ethic. I remember I had a bad match at Coventry in 1970. We'd played in Iceland against Keflavik in the European Cup in midweek and we lost 3-1 at Highfield Road. Harry had a go at us afterwards but he let me down lightly when he said to me: 'I know you gave 100 per cent but it wasn't good enough. It wasn't your usual 100 per cent!'

Others, though, had different experiences with him. His relationship with Alex Young could be quite fraught. For a start, Alex was a player he'd inherited after being signed by Johnny Carey and Harry was distrustful of so-called flair players. His signings underline that. People like Dennis Stevens, Tony Kay, Ray Wilson, Sandy Brown, Johnny Morrissey, Alan Ball and Howard Kendall were all tremendous players, but they were also diligent and hard-working.

Alex was also a great player but his contribution was skill-based, talent that thrilled the fans who lauded this blonde forward who scored spectacular goals. But he was a player Harry would never have gone out and signed and I can quite understand why Ian St John at Liverpool was far more Harry's type of player than Alex. He scored goals and worked 100 per cent, but lacked the artistry or touch that Alex had in abundance. With St John you knew what you were going to get. With Alex, in some games you'd just stand back and admire him and in others you were a man short.

There is a certain parallel with the later situation when Gordon Lee became manager and inherited Duncan McKenzie, just as Catterick had inherited Alex. Duncan was not Gordon's type of player. His eccentricities on the field offended Gordon's rigid work ethic and their professional relationship was, at best, uneasy. 'I consider Duncan what you might call a cream-on-the-cake player - but first of all you've got to make sure you've got a bloody cake!' was one of Gordon's observations about McKenzie.

Similarly, there was strain between Harry and Alex. Many years later Alex declared publicly on BBC Radio Merseyside that he would far rather have been managed by Shankly than Catterick, having experienced playing for his compatriot in the Scotland side drawn from Everton and Liverpool players that faced a locally-composed England side in Dixie Dean's 1964 testimonial match. Another factor was that Alex suffered, literally, from very tender feet which ruled him out of matches and which didn't endear him to Harry, for whom Alex was never The Golden Vision idolised by the supporters.

Harry was a strict disciplinarian and we had to 'clock on' for work each morning. We had to be in by 9.45am and there was a book we had to sign when we arrived for training at Bellefield. There was a pencil for us to use. If we were late the pencil had gone and Tommy Eggleston or Wilf Dixon, on Harry's instructions, would put a red pen in its place. At about 10 o'clock the book would go upstairs and Harry would inspect it. Anyone who signed in red was in for a fine. I remember I got caught by the book when I got married in January 1970.

My wife Maureen's background spans the entire British Isles. Her late father and mother met in Scotland but were Irish - Tommy Murray born in Belfast and Kathleen, a nurse, born in Cork. Maureen was born in North Wales as the second girl in a family of two daughters and two sons. Her eldest brother and sister were born in Scotland, where Tom had a job that serviced the building industry. His work then took him to North Wales where Maureen and her younger brother were born - and that's where I met her. My grandmother had a couple of caravans there and one night in June 1967 I went for a drink with friends in the old Lido in Prestatyn. Maureen, who was home for the weekend from Liverpool, where she worked as a clerical officer at Mill Road Hospital, was having a drink with her dad.

We got talking and I learned that she had to be back in Liverpool for Tuesday so we offered to give her a lift to the flat in Walton where she lived with her sister Kathy, a nurse at Aintree Hospital, and a couple of other girls. We

We dropped her off as I made my way home to Fazakerley. I didn't see her again until I was driving past a bus stop one night on my way into Liverpool and saw her standing there, as The Beatles song put it. I asked her if she'd like to go to the pictures, she said yes - and that's the start of how, two-and-a-half years later, Maureen became a footballer's wife. Later we celebrated the arrival of three daughters: Joanna, now a married teacher; Melanie, who is features editor on the Daily Record in Glasgow; and Emma, who's a podiatrist, which is a fully-qualified chiropodist. She took a course at Salford University, the same one Norman Whiteside took to qualify also as a podiatrist.

My wedding was in North Wales on a Wednesday, my day off, and Maureen and I stayed at a friend's bungalow in Rhyl overnight. The next day I'm driving into training and, when I reached the Mersey Tunnel toll-booths, I realise that in the rush I'd come out without any money. I went to the booth and fortunately the guy recognised me. He paid the two bob toll and I arranged to repay him the following day. But by the time I get to Bellefield I'm late. The book's gone, there's a tap on the window upstairs and it's The Cat looking down at me. He summoned me upstairs and I went up with some trepidation. 'Want a cup of tea?' he asked. I said: 'No thanks boss, I'm going out training in a minute.' 'Oh, you're alright, sit down', said Harry. 'How did it go yesterday?' 'Fine', I replied. 'Everything went well and I didn't have a late night.' 'Good. Off you go,' said Harry.

Next day I got to the Tunnel entrance and found there'd been an accident. So I'm delayed and I'm late arriving for training again. I went flying into Bellefield after parking the car, trying hard not to look up at the window. But Harry's there again and beckons me up. 'What's the problem?' he asked me. 'You won't believe it, boss, I set off even earlier and there'd been an accident,' I replied. 'Well, don't worry, don't panic, but we've got a game tomorrow - you're not going to be late for that, are you?' 'Rest assured, boss, I'm not going back to Wales tonight. I'll phone Maureen and tell her I'm staying at my mum's in Liverpool.' So I got away without a fine for being late on successive days. I don't know of anyone else who could say that and I think it illustrates how well I got on with Harry.

Tommy Wright said to me once: 'Have you noticed that when you've had a good game The Cat helps you take your shirt off.' That was a big thing by Harry, a man from whom 'well done' was fulsome praise. Perhaps that was psychologically good. If a manager overdoes praise you tend to let it wash over you. But with Harry you seized on every word and when he helped me off with my shirt, I knew I must have done well.

But Harry never got the recognition he deserved and that was almost certainly down to his natural stand-offish attitude not only towards the media, but also to people in general. That's the way he was. His record is up there with the great managers. For example, the only time we finished outside the top six under his management during the 1960s was in 1966 - and we made up for that by winning the FA Cup, which was then a cherished, prestigious trophy. Our finishing positions under Harry from 1961-62 to 1969-70 were: 4th, 1st, 3rd, 4th, 11th, 6th, 5th, 3rd and 1st. That's what you call consistency.

He came from the north-east but you'd never have guessed that from his accent. It was almost classless and it was generally accepted that he'd had some kind of elocution or a vocal makeover as it would be called today. Perhaps the reason for that stemmed from a sense of personal insecurity. He was always introverted and to the players he often seemed a distant figure. During the week we hardly saw him. Tommy Eggleston, who had two spells at Everton working with Harry, or Wilf Dixon took the training sessions. Harry wasn't a tracksuit manager but he made sure the training went exactly to his requirements. He was old school and had come up the hard way. The only time you'd see him in a tracksuit would be at the start of a season when we got new ones or when the cameras were at Bellefield. Joe Royle used to joke: 'The Cat's got a tracksuit on...the BBC or ITV must be here!'

The norm for Harry, though, was that he was immaculately dressed in suit, collar and tie. He was always smartly attired and delegated training responsibilities to the coaching staff. But he knew precisely what he wanted. Each morning the coaches had to go to see him, tell him exactly what they were going to do and how long it would take because everything was done by the stop-watch. Then the coaches would report back to Harry to tell him how training had gone. He was very astute on training and in match situations. At half-time he would pick on two or three pertinent things. He was sharp tactically and was quick to spot things that needed changing.

The day before a game we'd have a team meeting and discuss the opposition and the reports we'd had on them. Prior to the building at Bellefield being completed, we spent more time at Goodison where there was a table in what we called 'the bollocking room', for obvious reasons! He used a board with football pitch markings to give us his match instructions and when we moved to Bellefield permanently he had a similar table and also a magnetic wall-board with model plastic players. Harry was very thorough in how the opposition were going to play and how we would counter it.

His office, which had an outside metal staircase leading up to it, was situated on the corner of the building at Bellefield so he could see virtually everything from his windows. One part he couldn't see was an old bowling green where we'd play five-a-side. Harry would suddenly appear from nowhere and as soon as he was spotted the pace of the game would increase about 100 per cent and the ground staff, who'd been watching, would start working away! Howard Kendall used to say: 'When The Cat got the gym built I'm sure he got a set of tunnels built as well because he can appear anywhere, at any time, without any warning.'

If the first team was worked hard, it was even tougher for the younger players. They were back every afternoon to train - and not just ball work. It was hard running, too. The subject came up when I was sitting with Howard Kendall at a 'Goodison Greats' dinner. Frank Darcy and Harry Bennett, two reserves from the 1960s and early 1970s, were at a table opposite. They started going on to us about their training and said: 'Some of you lot in the first team should have had a word with Catterick because he didn't half drive us hard.' Howard, though, left them speechless when he said: 'I'll tell you something, lads. We used to meet in the pub, discuss the matter and we'd say to each other: 'He's a bastard that Catterick for the way he treats those lads'.' He made it up, of course, but Harry and Frank had no answer to it!

There were similarities in the management creeds of Harry Catterick and Sir Alf Ramsey. Both were strong disciplinarians and disciples of the work ethic. Yet I believe Harry was more adventurous. Alf dispensed with wingers and won the World Cup, whereas Harry went for wide men. He signed Johnny Morrissey from Liverpool and Alex Scott from Rangers and they were both hard-working wingers. Johnny was the first of a breed. He was the archetypal midfielder-cum-winger, who would have a tremendous impact in today's football. He could attack, he could defend and he could tackle and provided a great outlet for us. I used to love linking up with Johnny, while on the right flank we had the pace and shooting power of Alex Scott. We also had Derek Temple, who could play on the wing or inside. So Harry liked to attack but his philosophy was always 'get your defence right, first' and with that in mind went out and bought the world's best left-back, Ray Wilson, and a fine goalkeeper in Gordon West.

He was also the first manager at club level to use a double centre-half ploy. The seed was sown when Tony Kay came back from England duty and talked about Alf's twin centre-back experiment using Bobby Moore and Maurice Norman, with Jack Charlton coming in later. Harry picked up on it very quickly. I remember Tony having arguments with Jimmy Gabriel about the system. In fact, Tony played the role once or twice, I think to show everyone how it was done! Brian Harris also did it and then Jimmy started to play alongside Labby. Eventually, John Hurst, who had joined the club as a striker, succeeded Jimmy. He was an England Schoolboy centre-forward but moved his way back, via midfield, to play alongside Labby. Other teams followed suit, Liverpool moving Tommy Smith back alongside Ron Yeats and Leeds fielding Jack Charlton and Norman Hunter.

Harry was a superb judge of football flesh when he was in his prime until his health began to suffer in the 1970s. His signings bear testimony to that even if, like all managers, he saw one or two get away. For example, he dismissed a Scunthorpe youngster called Kevin Keegan as 'just another busy midfield player', although to be fair to Harry many managers were dubious about Kevin's qualities at that time. Even Shankly signed him for Liverpool as a midfielder, ostensibly to replace Ian Callaghan. The fact that he became a striker through a training-ground switch and that Callaghan played on for another seven years underlines how capricious football can be.

Harry's signing missions were legendary for their secrecy and stealth. He would say to chief scout Harry Cooke: 'We're going for a game of golf but bring some clothes - we might be away a couple of days.' They'd play golf and then Harry Cooke would be told to drive to a certain destination to meet a player and his club representatives to clinch a deal...and all hush-hush without the media knowing a thing. But he was still clever enough to use the media when he wanted to. Michael Charters of the Liverpool Echo travelled on our team bus to and from away matches. He had Harry's ear and vice versa. Harry would use him to get his feelings across in print. So if the Charters match report was highly critical we knew what Harry felt.

Generally, though, he was suspicious of the press. I remember Alan Ball had done an article in one of the papers during the build-up to our 1969 FA Cup semi-final against Manchester City. It was announced that Harry had fined him, although it turned out later that he hadn't, but had put out that he had to scare the rest of us. It was his way of ensuring nobody said a word. The club secretary Bill Dickinson was not given to feeding material to the media while Littlewoods employed publicity officers in the hope of managing the news.

Harry's method was control by fear and yes, it was a sign of insecurity on his part and perhaps he did live in fear of the power of John Moores and Littlewoods, which was the biggest private company in Europe. But we all had insecurities then because we didn't have the earning capacity or the lucrative contracts that have revolutionised top-flight football since the advent of the Premiership. In our day Harry earned a lot less than his players and we weren't paid fortunes. What other profession in the world would pay the man in charge less than his staff?

After leaving Everton, having suffered a heart attack in January 1972, being moved sideways into a vague consultancy role then spending two years as Preston manager, Catterick revealed his Goodison pressures: 'I found the demands from the directorate were rather more than I'd had anywhere else. They were very ambitious. There's nothing wrong with ambition but there was a great desire to win everything when, prior to my going there, they hadn't won anything for years.'

As far as the players were concerned, Harry was not well-liked but he was deeply respected. His personality was thrown into focus by Shankly being the exact opposite and because of that I think Harry would try to play mind games with Bill. He didn't want Shanks to know anything. In fact, the less anyone knew about his team the happier Harry was. It was right up his street one day at Leeds when Gordon West and Ray Wilson led Ken Wolstenholme and the BBC up the garden path. Ken was waiting outside when Gordon, having wrapped his arm in a bandage, walked out to the toilet. Then Ray pulled on a No 8 jersey and he, too, walked out to the toilet, leaving Wolstenholme baffled. Harry not only went along with it, he loved it because the media were being misled! When he did emerge before kick-off to give the BBC his team, he just kept deadpan when they asked him about Gordon's arm being bandaged. 'I don't know anything about it,' he said.

What Catterick did know about, though, was team building, finding that elusive balance between various strengths and weaknesses of players. Perhaps the greatest testimony to those Catterick qualities is provided by three words. In alphabetical order they are: Ball, Harvey, Kendall.

In the old first-team dressing room at Goodison, after clinching the 1970 championship. Harry Catterick holds the trophy with me on the back row next to Howard Kendall.

At least I'm keeping my eyes on the ball! With Howard in training at Bellefield - the start of a long relationship at Everton.

Chapter Seven

The Holy Trinity

The statement that 'football is like a religion on Merseyside' is one of the most hackneyed in the game's lexicon. Yet despite its place in the category of well-worn clichés, its accuracy is indisputable. The sheer passion and intensity of football followers on the banks of the Mersey has a religious fervour. Supporters are zealots in their loyalty to their team, perhaps indicative of the strong Celtic flavour in the blood of the city. So when three midfield players of wonderful skills and ability came together in Everton's royal blue during the 1960s, it is unsurprising that the fans acclaimed them in biblical terms. Irreverent it probably was but when Alan Ball, Colin Harvey and Howard Kendall were dubbed from the adoring terraces as 'The Holy Trinity', the supporters were bestowing upon them the mantle of greatness, a tribute to their enduring, legendary status in Everton history.

The trio was assembled in the early days of midfield as a recognised entity in a team. The old W formation, when half-backs and inside-forwards contested the middle of the park, had only just been consigned to history in a tactical revolution in the game. Sir Alf Ramsey dispensed with wingers and opted for players who could operate wide, but tackle back as part of a new work ethic which took England to World Cup glory. One of the national heroes on that July day at Wembley in 1966 was Blackpool's Alan Ball, a red-headed bundle of energy, skill and commitment.

Two weeks after the capture of the Jules Rimet trophy, Everton's defeat to Liverpool in the FA Charity Shield, when Roger Hunt's only goal of the game was scant reflection of the Anfield side's superiority, prompted urgent action by Harry Catterick. Within 48 hours the Everton boss had splashed a British record £110,000 to sign Ball. It was a move born of desperation by Catterick yet it proved to be one of his most inspired. Ball became, in the view of a host of pundits and punters, Everton's finest post-war player.

One of the first messages Ball received after signing was from Bill Shankly. "Congratulations, son, you'll be playing NEAR a great club," was the Liverpool manager's mischievous greeting. In reality, Shankly was a fervent admirer of the 21-year-old and, as he had previously, was to find to Liverpool's cost and his own chagrin just how devastating the England man's talents could be. Ball's arrival meant that two of the famed midfield trio were in place, his fellow 21-year-old Colin Harvey having made the graduation from boyhood fan of his local club to first-team star and FA Cup winner. A fortnight after the Charity Shield humiliation by Liverpool, the old enemy were back at Goodison for a League encounter but the difference was profound. Ball's influence was massive and he crowned a great personal display with two goals as Everton gained sweet revenge with a 3-1 win. Liverpool would also figure in the arrival of the third member of the midfield triumvirate, Howard Kendall. Saturday night, March 11, 1967 provided an historic landmark in Merseyside football history.

Everton and Liverpool collided in the fifth round of the FA Cup at Goodison and demand to see the game was such that it was switched to an evening kick-off with the game beamed back to Anfield on closed-circuit screens. A total attendance of 105,000 - 64,851 at Goodison and 40,149 at Anfield - was the biggest-ever for any FA Cup game outside a final. This huge gallery saw Ball again prove decisive, firing past Tommy Lawrence from an outrageous angle. Among the Goodison spectators that wind-tossed night was Kendall, signed by Catterick from Preston the previous day for £80,000, the Everton manager beating off competition for the 20-year-old Tynesider from Liverpool and Stoke, among others.

The first two games that Ball, Harvey and Kendall played together, in the numbers 8, 10 and 6 shirts respectively, were distinctly inauspicious: successive 1-0 home defeats by Southampton and Tottenham. Their first win in harness was a 2-0 victory at Sunderland, before injury ruled out Kendall for virtually all of the last two months of the season. Everton, having seen their defence of the FA Cup end at Nottingham Forest in round six following their early-season Cup Winners' Cup knockout on a 2-1 aggregate to Real Zaragoza, finished sixth in the League on 48 points, three behind fifth-placed Liverpool. Manchester United were champions with 60 points.

It was a period of change and challenge at Goodison. Jimmy Gabriel, only 28 but whose place was under threat from Kendall, left for Southampton, Fred Pickering joined Birmingham, Alex Scott moved to Hibernian, Derek Temple to Preston and Mike Trebilcock to Portsmouth. The idolised Alex Young also moved on, taking charge of Belfast club Glentoran in August 1968. Into Goodison came Ernie Hunt, an £80,000 Catterick buy from Wolves. His failure to settle and make an impact at Everton - he made 14 senior appearances, scoring three goals - saw him sold on six months later in March 1968 for £70,000 to Coventry.

Hunt's place in football history would come later with his famous 'donkey kick' goal against Everton in October 1970, volleying the ball beyond Andy Rankin after Willie Carr had flicked the ball into the air with both feet from a free-kick. The FA later banned the ploy although Rankin was not altogether distraught about being on the receiving end of the strike. "Film of the goal was used as part of the opening sequence on Match of the Day, so at least it meant I was on the telly every week," he mused. If Hunt - whose first name, ironically, was Roger - had a brief Goodison tenure, the new face of Everton was represented by Joe Royle, John Hurst, Jimmy Husband and, a little later, Alan Whittle, all of whom graduated through the Goodison ranks. They were supplemented by the signing of Tommy Jackson from Glentoran, to bed into a team orchestrated by its new midfield trio.

In their first full season together, 1967-68, Ball at No 8, Harvey at No 6 and Kendall in the No 4 jersey helped steer Everton to the FA Cup final. Alas, the favourites suffered a shock 1-0 defeat to West Bromwich Albion in extra time at Wembley, an outcome Goodison fans and players alike still find inexplicable. Jeff Astle scored the winner for opponents that Everton had beaten home and away in the League that season, their 6-2 win at Goodison seeing the rampant Ball score four. Everton finished fifth in the League on 52 points - three points and two places behind Liverpool – with Manchester City succeeding rivals United as champions on 58 points.

The following campaign, though, was to witness the talents of Ball, Harvey and Kendall blossom as Everton climbed to third in the League - behind champions Leeds and Liverpool - and reach the FA Cup semi-final. It was the prelude to one of the most glorious campaigns in Goodison history, the championship season of 1969-70 when the squad, bolstered by Catterick's £80,000 capture of England full-back Keith Newton from Blackburn, provided some of the finest football ever seen from an Everton side, rivalling the teams of the 1930s and the side Harvey had watched secure the title in 1963. Catterick had conjured a thrilling balance between defence and attack - and the fulcrum was the dazzling and consistent midfield. Of the 42 League games, Harvey played in 35, Ball in 37 and Kendall in 36. Between them they contributed 17 goals to Everton's total of 72. It was a goal from Harvey that clinched the title on April Fool's Day, April 1, 1970 and he provides a unique insight into the factors that propelled that midfield trio to iconic status:

"I had played against both Alan and Howard at junior level. I also faced Alan at reserve level and also in the first team when he was at Blackpool. So I knew something from personal experience about both of them, to a greater or lesser degree, before they joined Everton. Of course, just before Alan's signing he had become a national hero by helping England win the World Cup, and the contrast between his arrival and Howard's was stark. Howard took time to settle. He was jumping up a division and was then hampered by an injury soon after arriving. So he took a bit of time before showing what a great player he was. But Alan blazed into Goodison already a great player. He scored the only goal of the game on his debut at Fulham and never looked back. He was an instant hero.

There's no doubt that it was our performance against Liverpool in the Charity Shield that prompted Harry Catterick to sign Alan. It was a 1-0 massacre. It could have been five or six. That was on the Saturday and on the Monday The Cat struck by signing Alan, who had been in dispute with Blackpool over a new contract. Apparently, the Blackpool manager Ron Suart called Alan in and told him: 'We've received an offer for you from one club - and that's Everton. You've got to talk to them.' Alan knew for a fact that Leeds were in simply because - as he revealed in print years later - he'd had several clandestine meetings with their manager Don Revie, who was desperate to sign him but was waiting for Blackpool to put him up for sale. Bally's dad, Alan Senior, said to him: 'Everton are one of the best clubs you could join so go ahead and sign for them.' So Harry Catterick got his man and it was authoritatively reported that Revie was close to tears at missing out on a player he thought would combine devastatingly with Billy Bremner and Johnny Giles at Elland Road.

Be that as it may, what good advice Alan's father's turned out to be. Goodison was a stage just awaiting Alan. He was tailor-made for a club with the label of the School of Science. It wasn't just his talent. It was his personality as well. He was lively, enthusiastic and bright. He was cocky and brash - he had to be to wear those famous white boots - but without the arrogance of another red-head, Tony Kay. Like Tony, Alan was a fine player, full of energy and he had a hair-trigger temperament. But he was more of a team performer than Tony. He linked the back four with the front men and scored his fair share of goals. He played wide for England and in the middle for us. His Everton role was in between Howard and myself and as a support man for Joe Royle, because we didn't play with two recognised strikers. We had Jimmy Husband who broke in from the right to support Joe and Alan from the middle. I was, in the terms of the old system, a wing-half or inside-forward who could get forward while Howard had those old-fashioned half-back qualities of being a great tackler and passer who played a bit deeper.

He'd actually appeared at the back for Preston and Harry Catterick picked him in defence once for Everton, too. That was at Arsenal in October 1970 when Henry Newton, a £150,000 signing from Nottingham Forest, made his debut. In an attempt to accommodate people in the team Harry left out John Hurst and switched Howard to centre-back alongside Roger Kenyon. We endured a nightmare afternoon and lost 4-0. Needless to say the experiment with Howard was not repeated. I know Howard found it difficult there because playing in defence is a totally different game from midfield. I'd played against Howard in the 'A' and 'B' teams and I'd seen him play as a 17-year-old youngster in the 1964 FA Cup final. So I knew we were getting a good player.

To put Alan, Howard and me together in midfield was a great feather in The Cat's cap. One of Harry's greatest attributes was his judgement of players. He had a great eye for players who were also winners. He knew the types of player our crowd would accept - and some like Bally, they idolised. I think when Howard, Alan and I came together we discovered there was an instant chemistry between us. Neither Harry nor any of the coaches told us how we were going to play. We worked things out for ourselves, obviously with the help of others including Joe Royle, Johnny Morrissey and Jimmy Husband. Certain moves developed through good players playing together. Yet, ironically, on the thankfully few occasions when we weren't quite hitting it off, the coach Wilf Dixon tried to tell us that we weren't doing this or doing that when we'd been the ones who'd originated the moves anyway!

One of the moves would involve me picking the ball up on the left off Johnny Morrissey, Jimmy Husband would make a run across to Joe and Howard would appear on the right for me to play him in. We often found with a lot of London clubs at that time that they'd mark man-for-man. So when Jimmy made his run the opposing full-backs went with him and left a lot of space in the left-back position - and Howard would break in there. When we weren't playing well and the full-back was staying in position to deny us space, Wilf would have us in on the Monday working on a move that we'd invented ourselves!

I used to explain to Wilf: 'I couldn't knock the ball in there because the full-back stayed.' And Howard would tell him: 'I couldn't make the run in because there was no hole to run into.' Wilf would still respond by saying: 'Well, you've got to work at it.' It was bizarre considering we'd devised it ourselves. That used to get under our skins but overall Wilf was good to work with and always enthusiastic, bubbly and lively. He'd joined us from Blackpool, taking over coaching duties after Tommy Eggleston left to take over as Mansfield manager in August 1967. Tommy later managed Greek clubs Ethnikos and Panahaiki, before returning to Everton in 1972, first as youth-team coach and then, once again, as Harry's right-hand man. Prior to that, Wilf was in charge of the team for our 1971 FA Cup semi-final against Liverpool, which Harry missed through illness. Wilf took over again after Harry suffered a heart attack while driving home from watching a match in Sheffield on a snowy night in January 1972, which kept him off managerial duties for 10 weeks. By the time in April 1973 that Harry, then 53, was pushed upstairs into 'a senior executive capacity not responsible for team selection and management', Tommy Eggleston had returned to the club, first as youth-team coach and then once more as Harry's right-hand man.

John Moores, then in his second spell as Everton chairman, explained the decision to move Harry by saying: 'Harry's only trouble is that he works too hard. We asked him to choose an alternative position at the club because, after his illness, we felt the manager's job was too demanding. The championship side had fallen apart.' It meant Tommy Eggleston acting as caretaker from mid-April until the end of the 1972-73 season prior to Billy Bingham's arrival as manager, when Tommy left the club to study and practice physiotherapy. He worked in that capacity for Plymouth and then for Ipswich during the heady days at Portman Road under Bobby Robson. Fate, though, was to decree that Tommy would be back at Goodison with Ipswich on the day in March 1985 when Harry Catterick, his long-time friend and colleague, collapsed and died watching our FA Cup quarter-final. Football has conjured many poignant situations and that was certainly one, coming five years to the month after Dixie Dean's death in sadly identical circumstances at Goodison.

History will measure Harry as an astute, successful manager. Given his justifiable reputation as an authoritarian character, it might surprise many people to learn that after bringing together Alan, Howard and myself, he just let us get on with playing. He left the daily training routines to the coaches, anyway, but I can't recall a single occasion when he got the three of us together for a tactical talk. I think his attitude was: 'You're all top-class players. Just go out and do what you're good at and what I signed you for.' On the field he gave us our head. He knew that between the three of us – Bally, who would take the ball off anyone and go and attack; Howard, who was a great tackler and could shut up shop across the middle; and myself, who provided a mixture - he had the ideally balanced unit. Harry never told us whether that was by some grand design of his or that the chemistry between us just happened to be right. As it turned out, for several years it was magnificent to play with Alan and Howard.

To have Alan in the team, a World Cup winner and a future captain of both club and country, had a tremendous impact on us. *Ball of Fire*, the title of his first book, was perfectly appropriate. That's exactly what he was. His temperament led to him being sent off eight times during his playing career, but only once for Everton - against Newcastle in our 1-0 home win in March 1968. But if you'd taken that committed, winning attitude away from him, he would have been a much lesser player. When he arrived I said to myself: 'We've got a World Cup winner here now. I've got to drive myself harder. I've got to match him, even try to better him.' We had another of the World Cup team, of course, in that great left-back Ray Wilson but he was nearing the end of his career and left us in July 1969 to join Oldham.

But what endeared Alan to the Goodison fans, as well as his great ability, was the Indian sign he had on Liverpool. He was the scourge of Anfield, ever since the day as a 17-year-old in August 1962 when he made his League debut for Blackpool in front of the Kop and starred for the visitors in their 2-1 win. It was Liverpool's first game back in the top flight after promotion from the old Second Division - and Alan continued what he had started! In his five-and-a-half years at Everton he faced Liverpool in 13 League and Cup games and was on the losing side only four times. Even after his move to Arsenal, he continued to be a thorn in Liverpool's side, etching his own entry in the record books by being victorious in four League games at Anfield during the 1970s. Amazing, really, when you consider that Liverpool lost only 11 games at home in that entire decade! Three of Alan's wins there were with Arsenal and the other, memorably, was with Everton to put us on our way to the 1970 championship. 'I don't feel one ounce of fear when I enter Anfield', Alan would say. 'I believe in myself, and my ability. Those who are terrified should stay at home. The Kop will applaud all good players but they smell blood instantly if they see faint hearts.'

Even the training in those days was a fantastic experience. Alan, Howard and I were good trainers and everything was done at pace. We bubbled all the time and we got on well socially, too. Alan lived near Bolton, Howard in Southport and I lived in Fazakerley, Liverpool. Together with lads like John Hurst and Tommy Wright we had nights out together. For a spell Alan moved to Southport and as we had Wednesdays off, we'd meet up there on a Tuesday night and go to the Kingsway Casino where they staged different groups and acts. Ernie Hunt was staying in a small hotel on the promenade where they had a piano. He fancied himself as a bit of a Frank Sinatra and, to be fair, he was quite a good singer. Howard could play the organ and piano so after a night out at the Kingsway, we'd go back to Ernie's place and have a sing-song. It was all part of a great camaraderie we had. I'm sure Harry Catterick knew about our nights out and I don't think he approved. At the same time he probably mulled over the saying that the team that had a drink together played together and stuck together.

Such things are now gone in football. It is a different era. We were well paid then, don't get me wrong. But we weren't multi-millionaires like today and we could mix with the fans and have a drink with them. I thought it was great. We played our hearts out on a Saturday together and then we enjoyed ourselves on a night out together. The football culture has been revolutionised and a massive factor in that has been the influx of so many foreign players into our game. Premiership team buses don't stop now outside off-licences on their way home from games to get a crate of beer on board - and that's understandable. I can't criticise today's regime on diet and lifestyle. Players earn mega bucks and are expected to behave accordingly. Perceptions have changed radically. Modern football is more athletic but I'd still back the likes of Alan, Howard and myself to find ways of countering it. Good players always find an answer. Talent will out. And don't be under any illusions - we trained very hard then and we were supremely fit.

It wasn't long after the three of us came together that the press and the public latched onto us and the fans quickly nicknamed us as 'The Holy Trinity'. But despite the attention we got there were certainly no feelings of antipathy or jealousy from any of the other lads in the squad. We were all just glad to be part of a good side. In fact, to this day our captain Brian Labone still jokes whenever he meets up with Howard, Alan or me: 'Here he is - one of the only three-man team ever to win the championship!'

What a season 1969-70 proved to be. I'm sure all Evertonians will forever fondly remember it. Certainly I'll never forget it. Perhaps what happened in our opening game was a sign of the glory to come because we went to Arsenal without Bally, who was suspended, and won 1-0 through a John Hurst goal. In our next three outings we beat Manchester United home and away - 2-0 at Old Trafford and 3-0 at Goodison, where we hardly gave them a kick - and beat Crystal Palace 2-1 at home. It set us up for a great run in which we lost only one and won 15 of our first 18 League games. It included a home win over Leeds at the end of August.

Don Revie's formidable side arrived at Goodison as champions and unbeaten in 34 League games. But Billy Bremner, Johnny Giles and company were undone by a great performance, crowned by a magnificent display of wing play from Johnny Morrissey. Many people rate it as the best 90 minutes Johnny ever turned in for us. He tormented Paul Reaney, who was one of the best full-backs around. We took an early lead when Jimmy Husband scored and midway through the first half we went further ahead when Joe Royle, who gave big Jack Charlton a torturous afternoon, connected with a great Morrissey cross to head past Gary Sprake. Just after half-time it looked as if we'd reached the comfort zone when big Joe scored again, firing home our third goal from more than 20 yards after being set up by Hurst and Husband.

To their credit, though, Leeds refused to throw in the towel and, frankly, you wouldn't have expected them to because they were a terrific team. Bremner reduced our lead just past the hour mark and when Giles delivered an inswinging corner with a quarter of an hour remaining, Allan Clarke pounced to clip our advantage to a single goal. Leeds, sensing they might just salvage their remarkable unbeaten run, poured forward in the closing stages but we came through for a terrific 3-2 win.

'Everton could well be the team of the season', observed Horace Yates in the Liverpool Daily Post. 'Playing as they are not only are they a delight to watch, but their daintiness is merely an attractive cloak for the devastation they pack.' Perhaps such praise adversely affected us because a week later we suffered our first defeat of the season, losing 2-1 at Derby, managed by a certain Brian Clough and marshalled and organised brilliantly on the field by Dave Mackay. We responded by embarking on a 10-game sequence of nine wins and a draw to consolidate our position at the top before losing 2-0 at West Brom on November 8. Even so, in that era of two points for a win, we stayed top with

32 points from 19 games, six ahead of Leeds who had played one match fewer, and seven ahead of third-placed Liverpool.

That autumn, the British public were getting used to a strange new object with the 50 pence coin replacing the 10 shilling note and when it came to money, I'm sure the Goodison fans felt they were getting good value for their admission price of 8 shillings (40 pence) in the stand and 5 shillings (25 pence) on the terraces. But for me it became a time of high anxiety. I'd been an ever-present in our first 20 League games and I'd also played in three League Cup matches before I was ruled out with an eye problem. I just woke up one morning with blurred vision. I tried to wipe my eyes thinking my vision would become clearer. But when I opened some letters I couldn't focus to read them. I phoned Bellefield and spoke to our physio Norman Borrowdale. He told me to get down there right away and I was soon being examined by an optician. That afternoon I was in St Paul's Eye Hospital in Liverpool having treatment for what was diagnosed as inflammation of the optic nerve. I had a lumbar puncture done, I was treated with daily steroid injections and I was in the hospital for 10 days.

It was the prelude to dramatic newspaper headlines, one of them even stating there were fears for my sight. When the stories appeared I was out of hospital recovering and my dad was so incensed that he rang the Daily Express to complain. When I left hospital I still couldn't train because of the injections. For five or six weeks I used to go into Bellefield, walk a couple of laps and then get my injection off the club doctor. In all, despite being out from mid-November to mid-January, I missed only seven League games and our FA Cup tie at Sheffield United. It would have been more but for postponements due to bad weather and the abandonment of our game at Tottenham due to floodlight failure. Tommy Wright and Johnny Morrissey, as well as myself, were ruled out of that White Hart Lane game so fortune smiled on us when the lights went out because all three of us played in the re-arranged game in March, when an Alan Whittle goal gave us a crucial 1-0 win.

One of the games I missed was the derby at Goodison in December, when Sandy Brown had the agonising misfortune of heading a spectacular own goal. With Emlyn Hughes and Bobby Graham also getting on the scoresheet, the outcome was a chastening 3-0 defeat. It would prove to be our only home reverse of the season, but one we would sweetly avenge. After making my comeback in a reserve game - in which I played for an hour and felt drained because I'd missed so much training - Harry Catterick put me back in the first team a week later at relegation-threatened Southampton, when we lost 2-1. The game centred on Mick Channon, then 21. With 20 minutes left it was goalless but Channon headed Southampton in front, conceded an own goal when a Morrissey shot deflected off him and in the last minute he headed a second goal to give his side their first win in 21 League games. It was a defeat that cost us the First Division leadership. Leeds beat Coventry 3-1 the same day to leapfrog us with 44 points from 29 games. We were a point behind but had a game in hand and were seven points clear of third-placed Chelsea.

Tommy Jackson, who'd deputised for me in the No 6 shirt during my absence, replaced me as a substitute at Southampton and on the journey back I felt devoid of any energy, the result of all those missed weeks of training. It was hardly the best preparation for what was to happen the following Wednesday - my wedding to Maureen. We got married in Wales and I was back at Bellefield to train the next morning. Maureen learned instantly the realities of life for footballer's wives! Despite my battle for full fitness and struggling through games, I was delighted to stay in the team through to the end of the season, which was shortened to finish in April because of the World Cup finals in Mexico that summer. My Goodison return came in a goalless draw with Newcastle, the first of four consecutive home games. We beat Wolves then drew 2-2 with Arsenal, whose captain Frank McLintock came over to me before kick off and asked how I was after my eye trouble. I thought that was a kind gesture, especially for Frank to do it pre-match when the last thing most players have on their mind is the welfare of an opponent.

In the last of that quartet of Goodison home games we were held to a goalless draw by Coventry and we also drew our next match, at Nottingham Forest, 1-1 at the end of February when Jimmy Husband was injured and ruled out of all but one of our remaining games. However, it meant that opportunity knocked for Alan Whittle - and he grasped it with a great scoring run. The draw at Forest left us in second place on 49 points from 33 games with Leeds, who'd beaten Crystal Palace 2-0 the same day, two points ahead having played a game more. It was nip and tuck at the top - but that weekend was to prove a watershed in the championship. Leeds, who needed two replays to beat Manchester United in the FA Cup semi-final, were to win only two of their final eight League games.

As March came in, the month that The Beatles released their final single 'Let It Be', we also found perfect harmony and set off on a run of eight straight wins and a draw in our final nine games. I began to feel stronger and our winning sequence began against Burnley at Turf Moor where goals from Alan Ball and John Hurst gave us a 2-1 win. It was amazing the game was played at all. Heavy overnight snow had covered the pitch and our captain Brian Labone and goalkeeper Gordon West were so sure the game would be postponed that they ordered double breakfasts in the hotel. They were unaware that Burnley had organised a huge volunteer force to clear the pitch and terraces - and the referee declared the match on.

It just wasn't Labby's day. As he tussled for possession with Burnley's Steve Kindon, Westy ran off his line to try to clear the ball. Kindon took evasive action and Westy collided with Labby. Brian was clearly in pain and although he finished the match, he passed blood afterwards and hospital tests revealed he had suffered kidney damage, which ruled him out of our remaining eight games. That meant a call-up at centre-half for Roger Kenyon with Alan Ball taking over as skipper. Despite the blow of losing Brian's experienced leadership, our title hopes were given a massive twin boost when we beat Tottenham twice in three days. In the White Hart Lane game, re-arranged in midweek after floodlight failure earlier in the season, Alan Whittle scored the only goal. The goal came from a 20th minute free-kick by Keith Newton and it put us back on the top of the table for the first time since mid-December. But for Keith, making his 13th appearance since joining us from Blackburn before Christmas, it was an unlucky evening. He went off injured and played no further part in the title run-in.

Sandy Brown stepped into the left-back berth and we swiftly renewed battle with Tottenham at home on the Saturday. It was an eventful afternoon with Alan Whittle striking again on the half-hour mark to put us ahead, only for Alan Gilzean to equalise three minutes later with a thunderous shot. Five minutes before the interval Mike England fouled Joe Royle in the box and Alan Ball beat Pat Jennings from the spot. Another foul on Royle gave Bally the chance for a repeat - but this time Jennings produced a brilliant save from the penalty. The clock had ticked into the 73rd minute when referee David Lyden awarded penalty No 3 - this time to Tottenham. Dennis Bond stepped up and scored to level at 2-2. That scoreline, though, lasted only a couple of minutes before Joe Royle struck with a shot that Jennings managed to touch but failed to prevent crossing the line to give us victory.

For our next mission we made the shortest trip of all - a mile-and-a-half across Stanley Park to take on Liverpool. Quite apart from the fact that our lads had a score to settle with them after their Goodison win earlier in the season, we needed the points for out title battle with Leeds. The day went like a dream. It was one of the most memorable 90 minutes of my career and when the final whistle sounded I had a feeling it was the result that was going to propel us to the championship. This is how the teams lined up:

Liverpool: Ray Clemence; Chris Lawler, Geoff Strong, Tommy Smith, Ron Yeats, Emlyn Hughes, Peter Thompson (Alun Evans), Dougie Livermore, Ian St John, Ian Callaghan, Bobby Graham.

Everton: Gordon West, Tommy Wright, Sandy Brown, Howard Kendall, Roger Kenyon, myself, Alan Whittle, Alan Ball, Joe Royle, John Hurst, Johnny Morrissey.

We got off to a great start, taking the lead after only 10 minutes. Howard, Bally and I combined to send Johnny Morrissey in on the left and when he delivered a cross Joe Royle beat Ron Yeats and Clemence to send a header just under the bar. Liverpool failed to take a couple of chances to equalise and we went in at half-time in front. When we walked out for the second half our fans began to chant 'champions, champions' and they were soon in even better voice. Just three minutes after the re-start big Joe met a Sandy Brown free-kick and headed down. I managed to collect the ball on the edge of the box and shot through a packed goalmouth. The ball came back off the post and fell for Alan Whittle to loft it into the net to make it 2-0.

I don't think we were in any danger of losing afterwards and that's how the game finished to keep us firmly on course for the title. 'Everton's revenge for their defeat by Liverpool at Goodison was unequivocal, complete and timely in the championship race', wrote Max Marquis in The Sunday Times. 'Nearly all of Everton's players did well but Ball, Harvey and Kendall were quite devastating. This was the firm triangular base for victory. Liverpool, unhappily, were a group of journeymen against the Everton artists.' Walking off the Anfield pitch that day was a marvellous feeling, although none of us were to know that an Everton team would not taste victory there again for more than 14 years.

A week after our triumph at the Kop, we rattled in five against Chelsea in a seven-goal Goodison spectacular, big Joe's brace taking him to 23 in the League, and two days later on Easter Monday another Alan Whittle goal gave us a 1-0 win at Stoke. Destiny beckoned 48 hours later. Six straight wins had taken us to the title threshold. Victory over West Brom at Goodison on April Fool's Day, Wednesday, April 1, would secure the prize. By this stage I was flying. I had been getting fitter and fitter after my mid-season absence and here I was on the verge of a championship medal. Goodison was throbbing with 58,523 people packed in - which took Goodison attendances for the season past one million - and Harry Catterick used a cunning, psychological ploy before kick-off - he ordered pre-match bubbly to be sent to the West Brom dressing room! Tony 'Bomber' Brown, that fine West Brom forward, revealed: 'We were all in the dressing room psyching ourselves up, saying how we were going to do Everton and that they'd win the title over our dead bodies, when there was a knock on the dressing room door. There was a little old bloke waiting outside wearing a white chef's outfit and pushing a trolley loaded with champagne on ice. He explained that the drinks were for us to toast the new champions! We were so deflated. We'd virtually lost the game before we even got down the tunnel - and, sure enough, we were beaten 2-0. But it was an incredible atmosphere and Everton were worthy champions.'

Obviously we had to go out and do the business but I felt our name was on the trophy because of the fantastic run of form we'd shown. I knew we were the best team in the country. With 20 minutes gone my attempted shot fell to Alan Whittle who extended his remarkable goal spree with a deflected shot past John Osborne - his sixth goal in six games. Just three minutes later I experienced one of the greatest moments of my life - hitting a spectacular goal that clinched the championship. It was probably more by accident than design, but that doesn't detract from it one iota! I got the ball and set off running with it. A couple of half challenges came in but I went past them and found myself approaching the box. I thought: 'I'll just blast it.'

Well, the ball flew into the top corner and the place went mad! I intended to shoot - whether the top corner was in my mind is another matter. But we'd won the title and it was richly deserved. Into my mind flooded images of the day in 1963 when I'd got back to Goodison after a junior game in time to see that Everton side win the championship in front of our own fans - now we had done the same. I've still got my cherished 1970 medal and club plaque with the names of all the players, staff and directors involved. Alan, Howard and I had played our part in a great effort by a 16-man squad, from Gerry Humphreys, who made one appearance, to Joe Royle who was a 42-match ever-present and scored 23 goals. Gordon West, Tommy Wright and John Hurst were also ever-presents. Then there were lads like Alan Whittle, who'd come in at 19 and responded brilliantly with 11 goals in 15 appearances and Roger Kenyon, who at 21 had stepped into the heart of defence, replacing the injured Brian Labone, and performed manfully in the title run-in.

There were great scenes at the end of the West Brom game and The Cat was first on the pitch to congratulate each of us. Even his mask slipped that night. We got Labby out in his overcoat to join us in a lap of honour before Bally received the championship trophy. Unforgettable. I've got some great memories - and photographs - of Harry opening the champagne in the dressing room and congratulating everyone. I think he helped everyone to take their shirt off that night. He was beaming and justifiably proud of our achievement. The next day we all went to Aintree for the races.

We still had two games left and when we ran out at Sheffield Wednesday on the Saturday the message on their scoreboard read: 'Welcome to the Champions' and their players formed a guard of honour and clapped us onto the pitch. But we were so drained from the midweek emotion that we were awful. How we won 1-0 - through a Johnny Morrissey goal - I'll never know. Jack Whitham, who later joined Liverpool, should have scored four against us. Yet as we got off the team bus back in Liverpool The Cat came over to me and said: 'This season could go on for another six months for you, couldn't it? I've just seen you get fitter and fitter.' It was rare he would make observations like that to an individual player so it was praise indeed.

During the season we set a post-war club record - later equalled in 1985 - by beating every other team in the top flight at least once and a goalless draw in our final match at Sunderland gave us a points total of 66, nine more than runners-up Leeds and 11 in front of third-placed Chelsea. Under the modern three-points-for-a-win system our total would have converted to 95 points, the same as Chelsea's record Premiership total set in 2005 and five more than Everton's total in 1984-85. So statistically, the 1969-70 team proved the finest in Everton history. Its reign, though, was to be bafflingly brief. The crown would swiftly be snatched away and precede years of agonising limbo at Goodison as the 1970s took shape.''

Off on a pre-season tour to Sweden 1973 with Joe Royle (left) and Mick Bernard (right).

Chapter Eight

Broken Dreams And New Beginnings

In the summer of 1970, when England's ambitions of retaining the World Cup won on home soil four years earlier died with quarter-final defeat to West Germany in the baking heat of Mexico, Everton stood at the pinnacle of domestic football. Their championship triumph the previous season took them into the new decade ready to scorch through the Seventies. The side assembled by Harry Catterick was wonderfully balanced between defence and attack with the Alan Ball-Colin Harvey-Howard Kendall midfield as its heartbeat. Everton's quality was reflected in the fact that four of their players - Tommy Wright, Brian Labone, Keith Newton and Ball - were in Alf Ramsey's England squad. A fifth, goalkeeper Gordon West, would have been in the World Cup party too, but asked not to be considered for personal reasons. "This Everton team", Ball declared in the aftermath of the title triumph, "can dominate English football for the next five years. We have talented players who all work hard for each other. So how can we fail?" Ball's confidence merely echoed the views of many pundits and punters who identified in the Goodison squad the pre-requisites for long-term success.

It is one of the game's enduring mysteries that far from presaging a glorious 1970s for Everton, the championship preceded a barren decade when not a single major piece of silverware would adorn the club's trophy cabinet. The title-winning side was swiftly broken up and the approach of Christmas 1971 brought the stunning and sickening shock for Everton fans of Ball being sold to Arsenal on December 22. Catterick's decision caused outrage amongst the Blues faithful, who scorned the financially profitable aspect of the deal, which had seen Ball sold for twice the £110,000 he had cost five-and-a-half years earlier to set another British record. Their anger was compounded by the fact that earlier in the year Catterick had seemingly closed the door on such a prospect when he stressed: "I'd consider offers only in the region of £1 million

- and then say no." But, after selling Ball, Catterick said mysteriously: "Aspects of the deal will never be told."

Rumours of gambling debts and friction in the dressing room swept Merseyside. There was gossip that other players had begun to bristle at Ball's outspoken manner, which had once prompted the great Sir Stanley Matthews to tell Blackpool manager Ron Suart during a match: "Take Big Mouth off or I go off." The same Ball who used to whistle at opponents deputed to man-mark him, click his tongue at them and shout: "Come on boy!" Ball, however, insisted: "I was sold purely and simply for business reasons. Harry Catterick called me to his office and told me it would be a good move for me and that I'd make some money out of it. It was then that I realised what this game of football really is. It's a business. I was shocked. There was no way I wanted to leave Everton." Ball, who had made 250 senior appearances and scored 78 goals, was only 26 when he departed Everton. He was to play on for another 12 years, take his total of England caps to 72 and have the honour of captaining his country. "I think we all knew a great era was over the day Bally was sold to Arsenal", his colleague Joe Royle reflected. "Once he'd gone things began to crumble."

It was a period when Goodison itself was undergoing transformation with the main stand undergoing a £1 million makeover with seating for 10,000 and inside the stadium new-look dressing rooms, treatment room, gymnasium, laundry, offices, a restaurant and the 300 and 500 membership clubs. The floodlight pylons, which had stood since the 1950s, were replaced by a series of powerful bulbs on the stands. The changes Catterick made in the playing staff were equally dramatic, if not as illuminating. Amazingly, in a little more than two years since winning the title, seven members of that squad had gone. Adding to the departures were career-ending injuries to captain Brian Labone and Tommy Wright. Labone, whose service to the club embraced 533 senior appearances stretching across three decades from the 1950s to the 1970s, hung up his boots after sustaining Achilles damage. He recalled that Catterick, appearing unsympathetic if tongue-in-cheek, told him: "If you were a horse they'd shoot you."

The 1970s, which saw three Everton managers in office with Billy Bingham and Gordon Lee following Catterick, was not without promise for Goodison and transfer activity continued to be brisk, with big money splashed. England players Bob Latchford (who cost a British record £350,000 in a package deal), Martin Dobson, Dave Thomas and Colin Todd, Scotland internationals Bruce

Rioch and John Connolly and Northern Ireland midfielders Dave Clements and Bryan Hamilton were signed at various stages during the decade. Among other recruits were Henry Newton, Duncan McKenzie, Andy King, Mike Bernard, Joe Harper, John McLaughlin and goalkeepers Dai Davies and David Lawson, whose £80,000 fee from Huddersfield made him the country's most expensive last line of defence. Other new faces came from within with Mick Buckley, Mick Lyons, Gary Jones, Terry Darracott, Steve Seargeant, Archie Styles, Ronnie Goodlass and Ken McNaught following the emergence of John Hurst and Roger Kenyon.

But the sad fact for Everton was that the jigsaw never quite slotted into place and the club failed to replace Harvey, Ball and Kendall, all of whom had departed Goodison before the halfway point of the 1970s. And if some of the signings were dubious, others were highly suspect. Catterick's acquisition of forwards Bernie Wright, Rod Belfitt and Joe Harper fell distinctly into the latter category, especially as Belfitt's signing from Ipswich in November 1972 meant the departure of rising star David Johnson in the opposite direction, scant value for a financial makeweight of £50,000. Johnson would play for England and join Liverpool for £200,000 later in the decade. Belfitt made a mere 19 senior Everton appearances, scoring three goals, before being sold to Sunderland 11 months later.

Wright, a tall, burly, combative striker known as 'Bernie the Bolt', was signed from Walsall for £20,000 on the strength of a scoring FA Cup performance against Everton in February 1972. He had only 11 senior outings, scoring twice, before rejoining the Midlands club, bizarrely departing Merseyside by hitching a lift on a lorry and leaving behind stories of training ground bust-ups and wind-ups by other players, one of them going perilously close to the player confronting Catterick! Harper, another forward and at 5ft 6ins almost eight inches shorter than Wright, arrived from Aberdeen in December 1972 for a Scottish record fee of £180,000. He lasted 14 months, which brought him 14 goals in 51 senior appearances. Homesick, he returned to his native heath to join Hibernian for £120,000.

Not only was Everton a trophy-free zone during the 1970s, but also the agony for the supporters was compounded by the team's failure to beat arch-foes Liverpool at Anfield in League combat for another 14 years after their memorable victory there in March 1970. During the same period they managed only two derby wins at home. Indeed, the 1980s would be in full swing before Everton could assemble a midfield with the chemistry to transform promise into achievement and once more bring glitter to Goodison. Colin Harvey was to be hugely influential in that glorious renaissance but in a role he could not have contemplated at the start of a decade which was to prove a switchback ride for his life and career:

"We embarked on the 1970-71 season with great eagerness and optimism, especially after lifting the Charity Shield with a 2-1 win over FA Cup holders Chelsea at Stamford Bridge. But our title defence started poorly and we never recovered. We failed to win any of our opening six League games - losing three and drawing three. We were also back in the European Cup, a campaign we began with a 6-2 home win over Keflavik. The Icelandic side went ahead through a Gordon West own goal but Bally got a hat-trick that night - the club's first in European competition - Joe Royle scored a couple and Howard Kendall got the other. That remarkable statistician Gavin Buckland informs me that it was the game in which Everton collected the most corners in their history - a total of 27 - and only a superb display by visiting keeper Olafsson prevented us reaching double figures on the night.

Three days later we went to Bloomfield Road and beat Blackpool 2-0 with Jimmy Husband and Johnny Morrissey on target - but Harry Catterick was far from happy. He felt we were guilty of taking our feet off the gas and on the Monday we were called into the bollocking room at Bellefield. Harry really tore into us. 'You think you're entertainers, do you?' he barked. 'Well, you lot are in danger of becoming the West Ham of the north.' That episode graphically revealed the Catterick football creed. He was making the point that West Ham, despite having gifted players, by repute had a soft centre and he demanded that we showed northern grit. In Harry's eyes, that didn't include easing up in matches even though we were on top and winning. I wonder whether that gave him the first cursory ideas about rebuilding the team. If so some of the results we had after that would have strengthened such thoughts.

After beating Crystal Palace at home, when I scored in our 3-1 win, we completed a 9-2 aggregate win over Keflavik before a run of only two wins in our next 10 League games. By the turn of the year we'd won only seven of 23 First Division games. We had a decidedly unhappy Christmas. We lost 1-0 at home to Leeds, Jack Charlton heading an early goal which took them top of the League, later to be displaced by Double-winners Arsenal. Our last match of 1970 was a 2-0 Boxing Day defeat at Wolves when Derek Dougan, who got both goals, became the first player to score against Everton for four different clubs, having previously done so for Portsmouth (1957), Blackburn (1959) and Leicester (1966). During the second half of the season we collected only another five wins and slumped to finish a hugely disappointing 14th. We began our FA Cup campaign with a brace of goals from Jimmy Husband securing us a 2-0 win over Blackburn but that day, January 2, 1971, was overshadowed by the grim events at Ibrox Park, when 66 people were crushed to death at a Rangers v Celtic match. Little did we know then that football disasters would haunt Merseyside in coming years and that I would be a manager in the terrible aftermath of one such tragedy.

In the October of the 1970-71 season Catterick spent £150,000 to sign Henry Newton from Nottingham Forest, the third highest fee in English football after Martin Peters and Allan Clarke, adding more weight to Everton's media nickname of the 'Mersey Millionaires'. Henry made his debut at Arsenal when Catterick, to accommodate his new signing in midfield, switched Howard Kendall to centre-back and dropped John Hurst. It was a silly decision that rebounded on him. We lost 4-0 and Howard swiftly resumed his midfield role with Henry going on to fill a variety of berths, including left-back in a three-year spell at Goodison, before joining Derby. There was speculation that Henry had been bought to replace Howard. Whatever was in Catterick's mind, Howard's form made that impossible. Four days after the Highbury debacle we travelled to take on Borussia Moenchengladbach, the crack team of Gunter Netzer, Berti Vogts and Jupp Heynckes. Howard played a starring role and, with new signing Henry Newton ineligible for the European Cup, Catterick named this team:

Andy Rankin; Tommy Wright, Keith Newton; Howard Kendall, Roger Kenyon, Colin Harvey; Alan Whittle, Alan Ball, Joe Royle, John Hurst, John Morrissey.

We battled to keep out the Germans until 10 minutes before the break when Vogts smashed the ball through a forest of legs into our net. But early in the second half we were level thanks to Howard's quick thinking. Home keeper Wolfgang Kleff left his goalmouth to remove toilet rolls that had been thrown onto the pitch and, spotting his pre-occupation with the litter, Howard unleashed a superb shot from more than 20 yards which flew over the stranded Kleff into the net. Howard rated it one of the best of his 30 Everton career goals and the Germans reacted by blaming Everton fans for throwing the toilet rolls in the first place. Visiting supporters counter-claimed that they had been thrown at them by home fans. One wag observed: 'Someone's telling a tissue of lies!' Whatever the truth, after that equaliser the result could have gone either way. Joe Royle headed over an Alan Ball free-kick and, at the other end, Sielhoff shot wide from 12 yards with Andy Rankin off his line to ensure we got a great 1-1 draw.

The return leg was one of Goodison's great occasions, with nail-biting tension and drama witnessed by almost 43,000 spectators. It was also a night for the record books - the first time Everton had been in a penalty shoot-out, the first one involving an English club in Europe. It also meant that Everton were only the third English club to take part in this new-style decider following Manchester United's victory over Hull in the Watney Cup semi-final three months earlier, when George Best became the first Briton to score in a penalty shoot-out. After what happened in the first minute of the return game we just didn't contemplate such an outcome. Straight from the kick-off Johnny Morrissey flew down the wing and his shot slipped through Kleff's clutches into the net. The goal, to put us 2-1 ahead on aggregate, was clocked at something like 23 seconds, one of the fastest-ever at Goodison and one that made Johnny the only Everton player to score in three different European competitions, having done so previously in the old Fairs Cup and the now defunct Cup Winners' Cup.

Kleff, determined to atone for his calamitous start, proceeded to make a string of magnificent saves as we tried to finish off the Germans. Yet one brief respite in the bombardment let in Borussia. Andy Rankin, who had taken over from Gordon West a couple of months earlier, found himself facing a rare Borussia attack and could only parry a shot from Herbert Laumen 11 minutes before half-time. The German international got to his feet and steered the rebound into the net to stun the home fans.

Try as we could we failed to beat Kleff again during the 90 minutes and the tie went into extra time. Amazingly, we came within a coat of paint of going out when Horst Koppel's shot hit the woodwork. So we came to the adrenalin-pumping theatre of penalties, staged at the Gwladys Street end. Joe Royle stepped up for the first spot-kick, which Kleff saved. At that point one radio commentator, unaccustomed to this new method of deciding games, handed back to the studio with the words: 'That's it - Everton are out.' We weren't - but the advantage was certainly with the Germans. Sielhoff and Alan Ball both converted their penalties before Laumen shot wide. Now we had one failure each. Johnny Morrissey, Heynckes, Howard Kendall, Koppel and substitute Sandy Brown all scored to leave us 4-3 in front with Borussia's fifth penalty left. Ludwig Muller took it and hit the ball with power - but Andy

Rankin dived to his right to push the ball away and grasp our ticket into the quarter-finals. Needless to say, Andy was engulfed in our congratulations and celebrations, but admitted modestly: 'The German lad hit the ball well and, to be fair, I think I moved about half-an-hour before he took the kick! I managed to get two hands to it and push it away. Gordon West came onto the pitch and was the first to reach me, delightedly throwing me about like a rag doll.'

By the time we met Panathinaikos in the last eight, we had booked an FA Cup semi-final encounter with Liverpool, having enjoyed a home run to the last four without conceding a goal. So despite the fact that we had lost our championship crown we had a double vision of Wembley. As well as having our eyes on playing there in the FA Cup final, the European Cup final was also to be staged in front of the old Twin Towers. At that time the only European Cup triumphs by British clubs had been Celtic in 1967 and Manchester United a year later. We felt that with the final on English soil we had a great chance of emulating them. Alan Ball, who had succeeded Brian Labone as captain, got some publicity for saying so at a dinner - but he was only voicing what we all felt. After our 2-0 FA Cup third-round home win over Blackburn, we beat Middlesbrough 3-0 - when I got on the scoresheet - Derby 1-0 and Leeds' shock fifth-round conquerors Colchester 5-0. Three days after our big win over the Fourth Division side we faced Panathinaikos in the first leg of the European Cup quarter-final. What a frustrating experience it proved to be!

The Greeks, in total contrast to the compelling football symbolised by their Hungarian manager Ferenc Puskas, came to shut up shop and waste time. They carried out that policy with total, niggling commitment. In the end it was only a late strike from David Johnson, as a 19-year-old substitute, that rescued us from what would have been an unthinkable defeat. Our waves of attacks came to nothing as Chris James, reporting for the Liverpool Echo and later the Daily Mirror man on Merseyside, underlined in his match notes: 'Royle has header cleared off the line, has three headers over the bar and another wide, Wright's header hits the bar, Johnson has shot saved, Ball's header saved, Kendall shoots just wide, Johnson's shot hits the bar, Ball's free-kick hits the bar, Wright shoots over, Wright heads wide, Ball misses the easiest chance of the game, Wright heads wide.'

With eight minutes left Greek forward Antoniadis took a return pass from Grammos to put Panathinaikos in front. The game had ticked into the 90th minute when Joe Royle headed down our 17th corner of the night and David, who'd been an early replacement for the injured Jimmy Husband, blasted an equaliser to extend his remarkable sequence of scoring on his debuts in League, FA Cup and European Cup. Howard Kendall and some of the other lads told us in the dressing room afterwards that during the game some of the Greek players kept repeating 'Athens, Athens' in threatening tones - so I suppose we should have known what to expect in the second leg.

Successive away League defeats at Newcastle and Nottingham Forest preceded our trip to the Greek capital, which was a total nightmare. We stayed at a city-centre hotel and I roomed, as usual, with Tommy Wright. All night before the game Greek fans drove round and round the hotel on motorbikes and scooters making a terrific noise. It didn't affect Tommy, who was out like a light, but I couldn't sleep. I remember at one stage opening the room door and coming face-to-face with Michael Charters, the Liverpool Echo reporter, who had the next room. We asked each other what was going on. It was only then that I realised I was stark naked! It was almost four o'clock in the morning before I got to sleep and most of our party had a very disturbed night. I don't know whether the hotel had been recommended or it was just an unlucky choice. Experiences like ours led in due course to clubs trying to carefully vet team accommodation. The following morning our club secretary Bill Dickinson received a telephone call at the hotel and the caller said, as if in a scene from some bad 'B' movie: 'Everton, you die.'

When we arrived for the match some of our lads were stopped outside the players' entrance by people who opened their jackets to reveal guns! It was that frightening. The stadium was decrepit, the pitch was bare and bumpy and the hostile atmosphere made it more like a bear pit. Although the crowd were caged in behind fences they still felt right on top of us. Our lads were spat on when they went to take throw-ins and when John Hurst ran into the Greek penalty area one of their players, who were on £2,000 a man to reach the semi-finals, just stuck two fingers in his eye. I'll never forget Alan Whittle being brought down about five yards inside the box and the referee gave us a free-kick on the edge of the area! Had he succumbed to the hate-filled atmosphere or was there something even more sinister behind that and other decisions? The Panathinaikos skipper Mimis Domazos, a Greek international midfielder, received only mild rebukes for several fierce tackles while the official seemed to clamp down hard on anything we did. It was a terrible game and, armed as they were with their away goal, the Greeks knew a goalless draw would take them through and that's what they got.

There were few chances. Their best came when Domazos shot against the post. For us, Howard hit a volley which brought a fine save from their keeper with the almost unpronounceable name of Oeconomopoulos, while Joe Royle had a goal-bound shot cleared by Vlahos. Going out in those circumstances was a bitter pill to swallow. We knew we were a better team than Panathinaikos and that we'd missed our big opportunity in the first leg. What made our elimination even more galling was that the Greeks went on to beat Red Star Belgrade, also on away goals, to become the first team to win both a quarter-final and semi-final by that rule. Amazingly, after losing 4-1 in Belgrade, they won the return 3-0, a result that once again raised more questions than it answered. But the Greeks were outclassed by Ajax and Johan Cruyff in the final at Wembley, when the only puzzle was how Panathinaikos escaped with merely a 2-0 defeat.

Our fate in Athens on the Wednesday was hardly the best preparation for our Saturday collision with Liverpool in the FA Cup semi-final at Old Trafford. Liverpool, too, had been in European midweek action, their 1-1 draw at Bayern Munich taking them through to the Fairs Cup semi-final. However, as well as our deep disappointment, several of our party came back suffering from a chest virus. I was one of the victims and so was Harry Catterick. We flew back and went to stay on the Thursday night at the Lymm Hotel, resumed training at Bellefield the following morning and on Friday night stayed at the Dunkenhalgh Hotel, near Blackburn. I went to bed early because I wasn't feeling brilliant. I played but Harry didn't even make the game next day. He was confined to his Southport home and had to follow the semi-final on radio, later suffering the taunt from his counterpart Bill Shankly: 'I'd have climbed out of my coffin rather than miss a semi-final.'

First-team coach Wilf Dixon took charge of an unchanged side and we started well, watched by what was then a capacity Old Trafford crowd of more than 62,000. Alan Ball gave us the lead with a close-range 10th minute angled drive after a good combination between Joe Royle and Johnny Morissey, whose pass was flicked on to Bally by Alan Whittle. Although Liverpool had the ball in our net a minute later, it was disallowed for handling by Ian Callaghan and we might have gone two-up shortly after, when Whittle fired wide with Bally crying out for the ball on the far post.

We went in at half-time a goal to the good and quite pleased with the way things had gone. But the second half was only five minutes old when Brian Labone went off with a pulled hamstring. The loss of Labby's commanding figure was a mental blow to us and a boost to Liverpool. They equalised only nine minutes later through Alun Evans and in the 73rd minute they scored again when Andy, challenged by John Toshack, failed to hold a snap centre from Evans and when the ball dropped Brian Hall hooked it into the net. Our misery was complete. Our double hope of Wembley was shattered and our season was wrecked. Indeed, many maintain that those four days in March inflicted such crushing psychological damage that it ended an Everton era and needed years of recovery. I have since wondered whether what happened at Old Trafford was instrumental in Harry Catterick's proposal to the FA only weeks later that two substitutes should be permitted in domestic competitions, because another fresh pair of legs could have been invaluable to us. Certainly, I don't think Harry was ever the same again. Some of his transfer dealings, once such his strong suit, were strange to say the least. It seemed that the magic just evaporated in a man who is too often unforgivably forgotten in the litany of great managers.

After playing in the semi-final with my chest problem I was sick in the dressing-room toilets after the game. I had never felt as drained and low in my entire career. The previous month everything had seemed so promising and I'd also won an England cap. I'd already collected five Under 23 appearances, all during a three-month period in 1967, and appeared for the Football League. Alf Ramsey called me into the squad for the home internationals against Scotland and Wales in May 1969 because Nobby Stiles had a knee problem. Because of that, and Alan Mullery's struggle for form, I think I had a good chance of winning my first cap. Unfortunately, I had to withdraw with an ankle injury although I was fit enough to travel in the England squad the following month for the tour of Mexico and South America, which was a conditioning exercise for the following summer's World Cup finals. Ramsey named me in an 18-man tour squad that also included my Everton team-mates Gordon West, Tommy Wright, Brian Labone and Alan Ball as well as Blackburn's Keith Newton, who would later move to Goodison.

On June 3, 1969 I played against Mexico in an England side in Guadalajara, where Ramsey's squad was to be based in the following summer's World Cup. So it was an important conditioning match. Peter Shilton wore an England jersey for the first time in that game as deputy to Gordon Banks and we won 4-0. As far as I was concerned I'd made my England debut and it wasn't until some time later that we were told it wasn't classed as a full international, so I didn't get a cap. I hurt my big toe during the game but I didn't tell anyone in case it damaged my selection chances later in the tour. As it was, I wasn't selected. At the start of the following season an X-ray revealed that I'd actually broken my toe in Mexico. It showed that the bone had healed out of alignment and I still have an arthritic legacy of that injury. To deepen my disappointment I was omitted from Ramsey's World Cup 22 the following year.

I had to wait until February 1971 to collect a cherished first - and what turned out to be my only - cap. It was a Nations Cup tie in Malta and Joe Royle, Roy McFarland and Martin Chivers were also making their England debuts. On a baking-hot Mediterranean day we won 1-0 through a 35th-minute goal from Martin Peters and the team was:

Gordon Banks (Stoke), Paul Reaney (Leeds), Emlyn Hughes (Liverpool), Alan Mullery (Tottenham, captain), Roy McFarland (Derby), Norman Hunter (Leeds), Alan Ball (Everton), Martin Chivers (Tottenham), Joe Royle (Everton), Colin Harvey (Everton), Martin Peters (Tottenham).

I was destined never to play for England again which, of course, I'd have loved to have done. But at least I've had the honour of representing my country, which is something that eludes many, many players. Howard Kendall, for example, never won a cap which is inexplicable in my view. He must be the best uncapped player in the history of English football.

After our European exit in Athens and semi-final defeat by Liverpool, our squad was so flat that we won only one and lost five of our remaining eight League games. Then we had to play in the FA Cup third and fourth-place play-off match, a fixture which was thankfully short-lived. The games, between the losing semi-finalists, had begun in 1970 to replace the traditional eve-of-final match between England and Young England - but they lasted for only five years. We met Stoke at Selhurst Park on the Friday evening and the event was clearly as unpopular with fans as it was with players. A total of only 5,031 spectators turned out to see us lose 3-2. We were 2-1 up at half-time through Alan Whittle and Alan Ball but we also missed a penalty and Stoke hit back, John Ritchie scoring twice and Mike Bernard, who would sign for us a year later, getting the other. Naturally we'd rather have won but the importance of the game is summed up by the fact that many record books don't even list the match as having taken place.

During the summer of 1971 I was troubled with what I first thought to be a groin strain but turned out to be the problem with my left hip that would blight me over the next few years, and eventually finish my playing career. I felt it the day before we were due to fly out to play Shamrock in a friendly and I missed the first three League games of a season which saw the introduction of a new disciplinary code - that brought 329 bookings in the first two months - and a report on players wages which makes fascinating reading. English football's highest wage earners were paid between £13,000 and £16,000 a year. Only 27 players collected more than £10,000 and the biggest percentage of players - 709 out of a total of 1,800 - earned between £1,000 and £2,000 a year, or between £20 and £40 a week. My concern then was not money but fitness. Up to then my appearance record had been good but I started to suffer all sorts of niggles, including ankle and Achilles, probably caused by trying to compensate for my hip and the fact that I wasn't training properly.

In my first game that season I scored both goals in a 2-0 win over Chelsea. I went on to make 20 appearances and score four goals, but my longest run of consecutive games was four. I had a couple of cortisone injections and there were periods when the hip would be fine. But if it was a bad season for me it was a traumatic one for the club in general.

We could have used some help from the heavens as we won only four of our first 16 League games and were knocked out of the League Cup by Southampton. Hopes rose briefly during one week in November when we beat Liverpool 1-0 at Goodison - David Johnson extending his sequence of debut goals to incorporate the Mersey derby - and the following Saturday, a game I missed due to injury, we demolished Southampton 8-0. It was a day of scoring feats because on the same afternoon Ted McDougall hit nine goals for Bournemouth against Margate in the FA Cup first round. Our win was emphatic revenge for our earlier League Cup defeat at The Dell with Joe Royle scoring four, David Johnson three and Alan Ball getting the other goal to complete one of the biggest wins in Everton history and equalling the club's highest margin of victory in the 20th century. It was to prove the biggest top-flight win by any team during the 1970s and it's unprecedented in League history for any side to score such a large proportion of one season's goal total in one match. In all, we scored only 37 League goals and our next eight goals were spread over 14 games. The haul was only one goal less than the nine we scored in 21 away games that season!

The late John McGrath, one of Southampton's defenders that day, related a story that put the lid on their forgettable afternoon. "We were having a meal on the train journey from Lime Street back to Southampton", John recalled. "One of the lads asked the steward, a Scouser, if the fruit salad dessert was fresh. 'It should be', he replied 'we've only just opened the tin!'" The following March, Southampton suffered another humiliation when they were thrashed 7-0 by Leeds. However, our win was to prove a false dawn. It was the feast before the famine. The team failed to score in the next four games and by the time we did find the net again, with Johnson and home-developed defender Peter Scott scoring in a 2-2 Christmas draw with Huddersfield, the Everton supporters were in a state of outrage and bewilderment. Harry Catterick's £220,000 sale of the idolised Ball to Arsenal three days before Christmas left fans and players stunned. At the time Catterick probably felt it was good business to get twice what he'd paid for Alan. We weren't playing well and he obviously thought it made sense to double his money on Bally. In retrospect, though, it was an awful decision.

My good friend Howard Kendall has publicly cited a training-ground incident when an exasperated Bally turned to one of the coaches and said: 'How can I play with this lot?' Howard's view is that no player should be allowed to talk down his team-mates, and he said he could understand the manager selling Alan for the sake of the team. I go along with that to an extent but I think Harry deliberately sought to break up the championship side and build another one. That was his style and managers had the time to do those things. But if he felt things needed changing then I'm sure Bally could have changed with them. He was such a great player as he continued to demonstrate after leaving Everton with his performances for Arsenal, Southampton and England. Harry surely could not have envisaged that.

Alan's last Everton appearance, captaining the side at Derby in another game I missed through injury, was not a happy one. The team coach broke down en route, the players missed their pre-match hotel meal and had to make do with the pre-packed food intended for the return journey. They lost 2-0 to the team who would go on to win the championship and we slipped to fifth-from-bottom. The pressure of this fall from grace, the controversy over the sale of Ball and perhaps Catterick's failure to land any of the players on his wanted list, said to include Trevor Francis, Brian Kidd and Ian Storey-Moore, must have been contributory factors in his heart attack. It happened on January 5, 1972 only a fortnight after Ball's departure. Catterick was driving home from Sheffield after watching a League Cup semi-final replay at Hillsborough between Stoke and West Ham, who were Everton's next First Division opponents.

'It was an icy, snowy night and I opted to come back over Mam Tor which was the quieter route,' Catterick recounted in *Everton: The Official Centenary History* by John Roberts. 'Just before I reached Mam Tor the attack came. I pulled into the side of the road and walked across to where I could see two lights, hoping they would be cottages. They were and, fortunately, a district nurse lived at one of them. That probably saved my life. Subsequently, I was in intensive care for some time.'

During his absence coach Tommy Casey took charge of team affairs. Tommy, a former Northern Ireland international wing-half, played for a number of clubs and made more than 100 appearances each for Newcastle and Bristol City during the 1950s and early 1960s. Tommy had a completely different football ethic from Catterick and one that didn't fit easily into the Everton tradition. He was one of the original long-ball merchants but apart from his first two games in charge, in which we beat West Ham and West Brom both by 2-1 and both at home, it was a bleak period. We didn't win another League game under Tommy, our only other victories during his period in charge coming in an FA Cup third-round replay against Crystal Palace and a fourth-round win over Walsall, before going out 2-0 at home to Tottenham. In fact, from the win over West Brom on January 22, we won only one more League game in the remaining 16 to the end of the season, finishing 15th with 36 points from the 42 games.

Bernie Wright, who'd played against us for Walsall, was signed the following week. Clearly, he'd done enough to impress Tommy and after he'd consulted the convalescent Catterick the deal was done. Wright's arrival followed the £65,000 signing earlier in the season of Falkirk full-back John McLaughlin. Yet despite the breakthrough of youngsters like Mick Lyons, Terry Darracott, Steve Seargeant, Gary Jones and Manchester lad Mick Buckley, the squad had taken a distinct dip in strength from the heady era only two years previously. Ball's departure, which had a massively negative impact, followed the sale of Sandy Brown to Shrewsbury and injury to Brian Labone, which led to his retirement at the end of the 1971-72 season. Catterick left his sickbed to spend £75,000 in acquiring winger John Connolly from St Johnstone, but was back on duty in the middle of March. His return came 10 weeks after his heart attack and shortly after our 4-0 hiding by Liverpool at Anfield, when a young Kopite presented our goalkeeper Gordon West with a handbag. Our agony was compounded by own goals from Tommy Wright and John McLaughlin.

As the 'welcome back' messages from other managers poured in for Harry, there was one conspicuous by its absence - from his Liverpool rival Bill Shankly. Then, late one afternoon there was the sound of footsteps up the spiral staircase to Catterick's Bellefield office, a knock on the door and the arrival of Shankly with a cup of soup. 'Here you are Harry, hope you're better', he declared. 'Now how much do you want for Joe Royle and David Johnson?' Shankly was serious. Catterick laughed it off. Yet only eight months later he allowed Johnson to leave for Ipswich in the deal that brought Rod Belfitt to Goodison. Like Wright, Belfitt was not good enough for Everton and, to me, his signing revealed that Harry had lost his touch.

At the end of the 1971-72 season Johnny Morrissey joined Oldham and Keith Newton left for Burnley, but Harry opened the club's cheque book to sign Mike Bernard from Stoke for £140,000 and England Under 23 goalkeeper David Lawson from Huddersfield, who joined fellow keeper Dai Davies, a £20,000 acquisition from Swansea in December 1970. Andy Rankin had been sold to Watford for £20,000 the previous November and Lawson's arrival effectively ended Gordon West's long reign as first choice. Lawson took over and Gordon made only four more first-team outings the following season before retiring after 402 senior appearances for Everton, in which he proved one of the club's greatest goalkeepers.

Another great Evertonian Brian Labone, also retired. Labby decided to call it a day in June 1972 after succumbing to an Achilles injury. What a fantastic career he had, spanning the 1950s to the 1970s, captaining the club, collecting two League championships, FA Cup winners and runners-up medals and 26 England caps. He was one of the country's finest centre-halves and, as Catterick observed, played with a Corinthian attitude. Brian received only two cautions in 533 senior appearances, an all-time club record for an outfield player and surpassed only by goalkeeper Neville Southall. The fans paid tribute to Brian in March 1973 when more than 25,000 turned out for his testimonial match which raised around £15,000. I'm glad to say that Brian and another Everton luminary, Dave Hickson, still grace Goodison. They're both there on match days while Dave guides sightseers around Goodison on the club tours. I'm proud to say that I share one Everton record with Brian. We appeared in 19 European games, which is more than any other Everton player.

The 1972-73 season was Harry Catterick's last as manager and during the summer leading up to it I broke my own custom of training hard during the break. Given my hip problems, I gave it a miss. Instead, I underwent what was then a revolutionary regime of weight training. The outcome was that the rest from normal training did me a lot of good and I played in our first 19 games through to the end of November. The season started well and we were unbeaten in our opening eight matches, which saw us top the table for the first time since our championship win. Our run included wins over champions Derby and Manchester United and City and saw Joe Royle score in five consecutive games. But after seven goals in the first 14 matches Joe suffered a serious back injury, ruling him out for the rest of the campaign.

It proved a crucial turning point. We never recovered from the loss of England striker Joe, who'd been in top form. David Johnson took over Joe's No 9 jersey for one match before he was transferred to Ipswich in the deal that brought Rod Belfitt to Goodison. Belfitt made only 14 League appearances, scoring two goals, before being sold on to Sunderland within a year. Another forward, Joe Harper, who cost a Scottish record £180,000 from Aberdeen, lasted only slightly longer. He arrived in December 1972 - following Alan Whittle's £100,000 departure to Crystal Palace - and 14 months, 51 appearances and 14 goals later, Harper joined Hibernian for £120,000. Bernie Wright, his contract terminated by Catterick for disciplinary reasons, returned to Walsall halfway through the season after an 11 month-stopover at Goodison which brought him two goals in 11 senior appearances. One of his goals came from a header in a 2-1 defeat by West Ham in November, when Wright partnered Belfitt in attack. It was a memorable moment. The Liverpool Echo reported: 'Such was the physical condition of Bernie the Bolt that the powerful Brummie celebrated his strike by marching back to the halfway line, bending forward, placing his hands on his hips and promptly vomiting.'

After Joe Royle's injury our fortunes plunged. We suffered six straight League defeats in which we scored only three goals. During that sequence, which equalled the worst run in Everton history, I was dropped for the first time for our match at Coventry on December 2. In my place Harry called up Mick Buckley, who had just had his 20th birthday and had made his debut the previous season. I was named substitute. We lost 1-0, I was back in for the next match, on the bench again for the game after that and then recalled and substituted in the 1-1 pre-Christmas draw at Chelsea.

I missed the next four games which took us into the New Year, and I returned to the team in a goalless draw at Southampton in February, a week after we'd gone out of the FA Cup 2-0 at home to Millwall, a tie marred by the stabbing of a group of visiting supporters on the Gwladys Street terraces. Everton's poor display against what was a mediocre Second Division side was greeted with cushions hurled in disgust from the stand to compound our winter of discontent. The terrace anger and frustration and slumping attendances, which dropped to a low of less than 22,000 for the 2-2 draw with Norwich, prompted Catterick to say publicly - and probably foolishly - that he felt his players preferred to play in away games. 'They are frightened to try something different', he said, 'because they feel the crowd will be on their backs as soon as they make a mistake.' Chairman John Moores, or 'Mr John' as he was known around the club, was worried about the situation. Failure was not on his agenda. A self-made man, who had built Littlewoods into the biggest private company in Europe, held talks with Catterick after being alerted by the team's position and the public response.

After our precious point at The Dell I was in the side that lost 3-0 at Tottenham and my last appearance of the season came in a 2-1 defeat at Leeds in March. I was carried off after a late tackle by Trevor Cherry, which damaged the medial ligaments in my left knee. I'd just laid the ball off and got hit on my standing leg. It kept me out until the start of the following season, which opened a new chapter in Everton history. Unknown to me then, my departure on a stretcher was also my farewell to playing under Catterick who, in his pomp, was one of the greats and the circumstances of his final days in charge were sad. From Joe Royle's last appearance that season, a 1-0 win at Sheffield United on October 21, to the game at Leeds on March 10, we lost 10 and won only two of 17 League games.

April saw Value Added Tax introduced in Britain and we certainly got value that month from back-to-back wins over Sheffield United and Ipswich. Versatile Mick Lyons, handed the No 9 shirt for a spell late in the season, scored in the victory over Sheffield and we managed to escape the drop and finish 17th. Deepening our gloom was the stark contrast of Liverpool winning the championship. They won it with 60 points, three ahead of Arsenal, and the end of the season also marked the end of the careers of the Charlton brothers, Bobby and Jack. Bobby made the last of his 606 League appearances for Manchester United in a 1-0 defeat at Chelsea - United finishing one place below us on the same 37-point total - while Jack limped off in a 3-1 defeat for third-placed Leeds at Southampton. A week later Bobby became boss of Preston while Jack took charge of Middlesbrough.

A new era dawned, too, at Everton. Even before the season was over, the Catterick era was ended by Moores, whose anxiety over the club's steady decline resulted in Harry, at the age of 53, being relieved of his managerial duties on April 11. The club, facing a £50,000-plus pay-off to Harry - who had four years remaining of a 10-year contract - decided instead to move him into 'a senior executive capacity not responsible for team selection and management'. Harry responded with dignity, reflecting: 'This is a very sad moment and a blow for me. I was back in harness too soon after my heart attack and I couldn't pick up the pieces as quickly as I wanted to. Although I feel well enough, I think the club were concerned about my health. But I am an Evertonian and I'll always continue to be so. I'm not an extrovert but no matter how loudly anyone shouts they'll never feel more for Everton than I do. I'm grateful to and appreciative of the efforts the players have put in.' His great rival and contemporary Bill Shankly said: 'Harry's record speaks for itself. He has shown shrewd judgment when it comes to assessing players. The combination of Harry and John Moores has been formidable. But opposition can be a good thing. It made me fight even harder.'

Everton later announced that Harry would fill a consultancy role which was a grand title for scouting until he severed his Goodison ties and became manager of Preston in August 1975, spending two years at Deepdale before retiring from the game in 1977. Tommy Eggleston, who had returned to Goodison as youth-team coach in 1972 before becoming Harry's assistant, took charge of the first team for the last six games of the 1972-73 season as the directors launched their hunt for a new manager. Speculation raged about who the new man would be. Brian Clough, then managing Derby, and Bill McGarry of Wolves were among the names in the media frame. So, too, were Bobby Robson and Jimmy Armfield.

Robson, ensconced in his Suffolk citadel of Ipswich Town, was greatly admired by John Moores and was top of Everton's wanted list. Robson, though, spurned Everton's advances. So, too, did Jimmy Armfield, who had just led Bolton Wanderers to the Third Division championship as part of a Lancashire clean sweep of the four divisional titles, Southport winning the Fourth, Burnley the Second and Liverpool the First. 'I went to see John Moores at his house in Formby', recalled Armfield, the former Blackpool and England full-back. 'I rather liked him. He showed me his paintings and he was very interested in music. In fact, we spent more time talking about music than we did about Everton! But he offered me the manager's job and I promised to give him a decision within 48 hours. As it was, I rang him back the following day and declined. He couldn't believe it. But I didn't think I was ready. I knew Everton well and I didn't think it was right for me then.'

The shock decision by Armfield - who took charge at Leeds 16 months later - plunged Moores and the Everton board into turmoil. With none of their target list biting on the hook the Everton chairman called an emergency board meeting at which it was decided to approach Don Revie. After a long wait Revie, still smarting from the wounds of his Leeds side losing to Sunderland in the FA Cup final and to AC Milan in the Cup Winners' Cup final and a year before his appointment as England manager, informed Everton that he was staying at Leeds.

Everton had to cast their net wider - and it fell on the Greek capital of Athens and Billy Bingham, who I'd played alongside in the reserves during his Goodison playing career which ended just before I made my first-team debut in the 1963-64 season. Billy was a talented Belfast-born Northern Ireland international winger who won 56 caps. He'd joined us as a player from Luton in 1958 and made 23 appearances, scoring five goals, in our 1962-63 championship season. He moved to Port Vale that summer but hung up his boots two years later after breaking a leg and became Southport trainer-coach in July 1965, taking over as manager the following December. Billy was in charge when we played Southport in the FA Cup third round at Haig Avenue in January 1968. A crowd of 18,795 packed in while gate receipts of £6,175 set a Southport record. We won with the game's only goal, scored by Joe Royle 11 minutes from the end, and went all the way to Wembley and that bitterly disappointing defeat by West Brom.

Billy's journey took him to Plymouth as manager after resigning the Southport job a fortnight after the cup tie. He was also appointed part-time boss of Northern Ireland the same year. In June 1970 he became manager of Irish League club Linfield before being appointed national coach of Greece a year later during the tense era of the military junta, who had seized power and removed the king in the 1967 army coup. Billy not only saw out his two-year contract but was considering an offer to stay and return to club management with AEK Athens when a funny thing happened, almost literally on the way to the forum! A Daily Mirror story about Billy's new job prospects in Greece was brought to the attention of John Moores, who decided he would contact him and ask if he was interested in managing Everton. The outcome was that on May 28, 1973, at the age of 42, he was appointed as Everton's new boss and hailed by Moores as 'a true Evertonian'. Billy declared: 'I have blue blood in my veins and I'm dying to have a go. If I could have picked a club to manage it would have been Everton and I hope I can bring back the standards they enjoyed before.'

One of his first acts after being appointed was to call together the older players, including myself, for a talk. Although we knew each other as players he quickly told me: 'From now on it's not Billy, it's boss.' Right away I think he wanted to bring in his own players, to dispense with the old guard and play it his way. I have to admit that it wasn't an enjoyable time for me. I was beginning to get my nose pushed out and it was upsetting because I knew I'd be on my way sooner rather than later. I was wondering where I was going to go from a club which had been such a part of my life.

On reflection, though, Billy's desire for change was understandable. It's what new managers do and one of his first decisions was to bring former Halifax manager Ray Henderson onto the backroom staff in place of Tommy Eggleston. I'd had a good pre-season training although our tour of Sweden, the first games of Billy's management, was marked by a few players breaking curfew at Helsingborg and a couple falling off a drainpipe trying to get back into the team's hotel. The story broke in the papers the next day and led to a midnight confrontation with the travelling press by a deputation of the players, led by our captain Howard Kendall and including myself. It also brought fines by the new manager for the late arriving players. The row rumbled all the way to Copenhagen airport for the flight home and a heated exchange in the check-in area between Joe Harper and sportswriter Chris James, which briefly threatened to come to blows.

By the time the season began normal relations between the players and the press had been restored, but the experience had shown that Bingham was not a manager to be toyed with. I was in the team that began the Bingham era in the League opener at Leeds. The line-up was:

David Lawson; John McLaughlin, Mick Lyons, Roger Kenyon, Terry Darracott; Howard Kendall, myself, Mick Buckley, John Connolly; Joe Royle, Joe Harper.

We lost 3-1 and I stayed in the side for the next four games but went over severely on my ankle in our 2-1 defeat at Derby, a game in which Howard was also injured. Apart from two injury-hampered appearances on my part we were both ruled out for five months and made our comebacks together in the 1-1 draw at Sheffield United in February. By that time the team had gone out of the League Cup at home to Norwich and lost a fourth round FA Cup replay at West Brom, our goalless home draw against the Second Division club making history and - quaint as it seems now - stirring fierce controversy and debate by being played on a Sunday.

That winter's power cuts and three-day week during the miner's strike, in addition to a fixture clash with Liverpool who had a Saturday home tie against Carlisle, led to Everton's game being put back 24 hours to January 27, 1974. It was Merseyside's first FA Cup tie staged on a Sunday and a floodlight ban because of the power crisis meant it had a 2.15pm kick-off, a starting time which was a throwback to the cloth-cap era. Several other ties and League games had been staged at other clubs earlier in the month and although Sunday football is now commonplace, there were many then, church and religious interests among them, who condemned the experiment. But it was certainly box office because the 53,509 attendance for the West Brom game was our third highest of the season, surpassed only by the turnout for our League games against Liverpool and Leeds. It was also English football's first 50,000-plus attendance for a Sunday match.

However, when the power emergency was over so was Sunday football and it did not return for another seven years until February 1981, when the League gave the go-ahead for games on the sabbath. As well as the club's early exits from the League and FA Cups we lost on aggregate to Hearts in our first - and last - engagement in the Texaco Cup, going down 1-0 at home and playing a goalless draw in the Edinburgh return. The first game was the 19th and last of Rod Belfitt's Everton appearances before Bingham sold him to Sunderland for £65,000 in October 1974.

Bingham's reign did not start well, with only two wins in his first eight League games in charge, and he soon dipped into the £300,000 transfer fund pledged by Moores by paying Sheffield Wednesday £62,500 for his Northern Ireland compatriot Dave Clements. The 28-year-old left-sided midfielder had played for Bingham during his tenure as Irish boss and succeeded Howard Kendall as Everton captain. Howard made only two comeback appearances before his illustrious Goodison career, spanning seven years, 275 appearances and 30 goals, ended in February 1974 as part of a British record-breaking package that brought striker Bob Latchford to Goodison with a £350,000 valuation on his head. Birmingham, though, received only £80,000 in cash with Howard and left-back Archie Styles moving to St Andrews valued at £180,000 and £90,000 respectively.

Understandably, there was uproar from the fans and a stream of letters in the local press, critical of Bingham's decision to sell Howard who, despite being ruled out for much of that season, had been our best player up to his injury. Clearly, Howard could still have played a big role for Everton but Bingham felt his team needed an injection of goals and that Latchford was the man to provide them. But the only way Bingham could persuade Birmingham manager Freddie Goodwin to sell Bob was by parting with Howard. Obviously, he decided needs must and incurred the wrath of much of the blue half of Merseyside by trading Howard.

On a personal basis I was sad to see him leave. He was - and still is - a close friend and it left me as the sole Goodison survivor of the 1970 title-winning midfield trio. It has to be said, though, that Bingham's faith in Latchford, who had partnered Trevor Francis and Bob Hatton at Birmingham and hit 81 goals in three-and-a-half seasons, was certainly justified. He did add the much-needed firepower Bingham craved and went on to become a Goodison hero, although ironically he never won a thing with Everton apart from an enduring place in the hearts of the supporters.

Joe Royle, who had also been lauded by the fans for his striking abilities after joining the club as an apprentice more than a decade earlier, made only 11 senior appearances alongside Latchford before he moved on to Manchester City for £200,000 on Christmas Eve 1974. Joe had been troubled by back injuries but his contribution was underlined by the fact that he and Roy Vernon were the only players to score a century of League goals for Everton between Dixie Dean's Goodison departure in 1937 and Latchford's arrival. Latchford picked up Joe's banner. Originally wearing No 10 but later settling on the No 9 jersey, he was the club's standard-bearer for the second half of the 1970s, during which he won 12 England caps. In 13 appearances in his first season Bob hit seven goals and in an Everton career that lasted until he moved to Swansea in July 1981, he went on to amass 138 goals in 289 senior appearances, which make him the club's third highest all-time scorer behind Dixie Dean (383) and Graeme Sharp (159).

Prior to Latchford's signing, Henry Newton (£110,000 to Derby), Jimmy Husband (£80,000 to Luton) and Joe Harper (£120,000 to Hibernian) had already been sold by Bingham, who used Mick Lyons up front in his first full season of senior football with Gary Jones and George Telfer winning places during the second half of the campaign. We finished a much more respectable seventh in Bingham's first year at the helm, which was to prove my last full season as an Everton player. Although I started the first four games of the 1974-75 season - in which we won two and drew two - I knew the writing was on the wall and Martin Dobson's £300,000 arrival from Burnley, following Jim Pearson's £100,000 signing from St Johnstone, spelled the end of my active service in the team. Less than a fortnight later Billy called me into his office and said: 'I've had an offer for you from Sheffield Wednesday. Do you want to talk to their manager, Steve Burtenshaw?' I said I would, had a chat with Steve on the phone and arranged to meet him. We discussed terms, which paled by today's standards and meant I earned even less than I did at Everton! But I wanted to continue playing first-team football which meant I had to move. So I agreed the deal and I was transferred for £70,000.

I signed on the Thursday, trained with them on the Friday and made my debut for them in a 1-0 win at Bolton in the old Second Division the following day, September 14, 1974. That day Everton played a goalless home draw with Wolves, when fans paraded a banner in the Bullens Road Stand that proclaimed: '£70,000 - An Insult to Colin Harvey - The White Pele'. I was unaware of this until I travelled home with my Dad, who'd come to watch me accompanied by my mate Tommy Wright, who'd been forced to retire through a bad knee injury. Then the phone began to ring with people telling me that the banner had been unfurled at Goodison. I got the Football Echo and saw a picture of it. It was an unbelievable thing to happen and totally unexpected as far as I was concerned. I regard it as a wonderful honour and a much appreciated tribute from Evertonians.

I thought my departure to Hillsborough was the end of my Everton connection. I made 30 appearances for Wednesday that season but it wasn't a memorable one for the Yorkshire club, who finished bottom of the table and were relegated to the old Third Division. Everton, meanwhile, were rising. They finished fourth in the League, only three points behind champions Derby and qualifying for a return to Europe in the UEFA Cup. Yet, for what the season had held in prospect the outcome was an anguished anti-climax. Everton would have lifted the championship but for the fact they fell victim to one of the most bizarre doubles in the club's history, losing home and away to Carlisle. The Cumbrian club, whose Brunton Park pitch was famous for being grazed by sheep, had put the cat among the pigeons by finishing third in the old Second Division and winning a one-season term in the top flight. One of the clubs they displaced were relegated Manchester United and even more remarkable was that Carlisle began their promotion to the upper strata with three wins - at Chelsea and Middlesbrough and at home to Tottenham without conceding a goal - to go to the top of the League.

Managed by Alan Ashman, their team included sporting all-rounder Chris Balderstone, who batted for England against the West Indies the following summer, and John Gorman, later to become assistant to England manager

Glenn Hoddle. When Carlisle arrived at Goodison late in December they had added only three more wins to that opening burst and were languishing next-to-bottom of the table while Everton, with only one defeat in their opening 21 games, were setting the pace at the top with 28 points, one ahead of Liverpool, Stoke and Manchester City. Everton were odds-on to swamp the visitors and seemed destined for an expected victory thanks to an early Latchford goal that took them to half-time 1-0 in front. However, a scoring spree of three goals in six minutes early in the second half stunned Goodison. Latchford added a second in the 52nd minute but that two-goal lead was wiped out by two quick strikes from Joe Laidlaw. The agony was compounded for Bingham and his side when Les O'Neil scored a 65th-minute winner for Carlisle.

When the return fixture came round in March, Everton were back on top of the League and Carlisle were bottom. This time, surely, there would be no Cumbrian fairy story...but there was, and what a grim tale it was for Everton. Once again, the damage was done in the second half after a goalless opening 45 minutes. A 63rd-minute Laidlaw penalty followed by further goals from Dennis Martin and Frank Clarke gave Carlisle a 3-0 win. When I heard the result I found it hard to believe. It was Everton's heaviest League defeat of a season in which they had disappointingly gone out of the FA Cup at home to Fulham in the fifth round, after taking two games to beat Altrincham before winning at Plymouth, and had gone out to Aston Villa in a replay at the League Cup's first hurdle.

Having led the First Division for most of the time from late January to late March, Everton found themselves overtaken in the finishing straight and although a subsequent home draw with Burnley and a home defeat by Sheffield United were costly, it was the impact of those reverses to Carlisle that proved Everton's undoing. Carlisle, having sabotaged Goodison dreams, finished bottom and went back down. Less than 30 years later they had fallen right through the League system into the Conference, before making an immediate return by winning the play-off final against Stevenage. 'We should have won the championship but the home and away defeats by Carlisle cost us', Bingham reflected. 'I honestly thought it would have been the start of a golden era for us but we missed out. A good manager is also a lucky manager and perhaps, at the time, we didn't get the breaks.'

During November that season Everton had the chance to sign Peter Shilton from Leicester but Bingham, who had brought in Dai Davies in goal after starting the season with David Lawson, declined the opportunity in the belief that you could win the title with a capable, rather than an excellent keeper. Shilton signed instead for Stoke, at a cost of £325,000, later being recruited by Brian Clough for Nottingham Forest and proving a keystone of their amazing success at home and abroad. If Bingham had bought Shilton for Everton he might just have been the difference between frustrating failure and glittering triumph, as we were to experience a decade later with the great Neville Southall between the posts.

At the end of the 1974-75 season, with Wednesday relegated, my own career was approaching another crossroads. I was struggling with a hip problem and went to see the club specialist, who told me my hip was arthritic. 'What can I do about it?' I asked. 'Basically nothing, apart from taking anti-inflammatory tablets,' he replied. The summer of 1975 was warm and when we started pre-season training my hip was getting jarred on the rock-hard pitches and I was suffering. I started the season, in the old Third Division, but in October Steve Burtenshaw - later to join Everton - was sacked and Len Ashurst took over. But after playing on a Saturday it was Wednesday or Thursday before I could train properly and for somebody who'd prided myself on my fitness it was just too much. I played for Wednesday in a 3-0 home defeat to Port Vale on November 8 and decided it would be my last game. The club were three places off the bottom at the time - they ended up just avoiding relegation to the old Division Four - and I was doing neither them nor myself any favours. I felt it wasn't right for me to pick up my wages on that basis and asked them to terminate my contract, which had the rest of the season to run. Len kindly asked if I'd be interested in a coaching job at Hillsborough. I thanked him but told him that Maureen and I had decided we'd rather live back on Merseyside, or within striking distance. So in March I hung up my boots and looked to the licensing trade for a new direction in life. I had two uncles who had pubs at the time.

My Uncle Phil, who was married to my mum's sister Peggy, had a pub in Northwich, which were large premises with living quarters. It was ideal for training and learning the pub business. I'd go over on the Sunday, work all week and at the weekend Maureen, who was still living in Sheffield with my two oldest daughters Joanna and Melanie aged five and three, would drive over to see me. My uncle was determined that I would learn the trade backwards and my day consisted of getting up early, attending to all the little odd jobs, doing the bottling up, opening and closing the pub and checking the stock. It would be after midnight before I got to bed and at half-past six to seven in the morning the draymen would arrive with an order. I didn't enjoy it one bit. I remember one week realising I hadn't been out of the pub for four days so I made myself go out just to get some fresh air and thinking time.

In the spring of 1976 my uncle's pub was put up for sale and the brewery were going to get me a place in Liverpool. I was back in Sheffield for a few days with Maureen and the girls when one day in May the phone rang. It was Billy Bingham. What he said was like a drowning man being thrown a lifebelt. 'Would you like the job of youth coach at Everton?' Billy asked. I didn't have to think about it or what the wages were. The answer was yes. Bingham, the man who was far from my favourite person in the world when he'd sold me 20 months earlier, had come to my rescue - and was I grateful!

The vacancy had arisen because Ray Henderson had been appointed manager of Southport and Eric Harrison had moved up from youth coach to take charge of the reserves. Despite Bingham's signings of David Smallman (£70,000 from Wrexham), Bryan Hamilton (£40,000 from Ipswich) and Andy King (£35,000 from Luton), plus the first-team graduation of former apprentice centre-half Ken McNaught, the 1975-76 season was disappointing for Everton. They slipped to 11th in the League - a decline exacerbated by Bob Paisley's Liverpool winning the title - went out of the FA Cup in the third round at Derby and after beating Arsenal and Carlisle in the League Cup, they went out in a fourth round replay at Notts County.

Their UEFA Cup interest was brief too, although they were unlucky to draw AC Milan in the first round. They held the Italian club to a goalless draw at Goodison when a Latchford strike was disallowed and Mike Bernard was sent off for a foul on opposing captain Romeo Benetti. When Everton arrived in Milan for the second leg they found the city gripped by power and bank strikes and hit by a fierce electrical storm. Bingham and his players were in stormy mood after the events at the San Siro, the atmospheric stage for my first-team baptism as a teenager against Inter in 1963. This time East German referee Rudi Glockner was the villain in Everton eyes with a string of baffling decisions - including his rejection of penalty claims for fouls on Gary Jones and Jim Pearson - and climaxed his eccentric officiating by awarding a 67th-minute penalty to Milan for handball against Mick Lyons.

There was controversy at home, too, stoked by Everton's 3-0 mauling by Manchester City at Maine Road in February 1976, which according to reports was a dismal display by any standards. Furious Everton supporters gathered outside the ground to protest at what they saw as negative tactics and a dressing-room row sparked transfer demands from Gary Jones and Mick Buckley. A screaming back page Daily Mirror banner headline on the Monday proclaiming 'Bye Bye Bingham' angered the Everton manager to such an extent that he broke off communications with the media: 'You're persona non grata,' he declared, and ordered the Bellefield training ground gates to be closed. The press, gathering en masse outside and speaking to players as they drove out, were treated to tea, cakes and biscuits by a nearby resident who announced that she, too, had been upset by Everton's abject display. Her generosity spawned what has gone down in sportswriting folklore as 'The Doughnut Siege'. The following July, Jones was sold to Birmingham for £110,000, his fellow winger John Connolly joining him at St Andrews in a £70,000 move two months later. Midfielder Buckley saw out the Bingham era, eventually joining Sunderland in August 1978.

After my call from Billy I started back at Everton almost right away, in June 1976, and for the first few months I lived at my mum's house in Liverpool while Maureen and the children were in Sheffield, where our house was up for sale. I'd already got my junior coaching badges, something I started at Everton and completed at Sheffield, and the prospect of coaching youngsters appealed to me. I'd missed football and Everton in particular. Now I was back - on a Goodison odyssey I could never have dreamed of."

Pictured before the start of the 1983-84 season, a few months before being promoted to first-team coach at Everton.

Chapter Nine

The Road To A Grand Re-Union

Everton in the mid 1970s was a club that was all dressed up with nowhere to party, a giant unable to enhance its illustrious history. Littlewoods founder John Moores had stepped down as Everton chairman after two spells in the post - 1960-65 and 1972-73 - and was succeeded first by Alan Waterworth, then Bill Scott. But Goodison was still driven by the financial and business acumen of the remarkable self-made little man who remained on the club's board until his retirement in July 1977, his knighthood for charitable services following three years later. Some argue that the almost seamless link between Everton and Littlewoods was at best unhealthy and at worst sinister, citing examples of sportswriters, with hackles exploding, being summoned to the company's Old Hall Street headquarters to explain or justify articles that had upset the hierarchy. Yet it is indisputable that Moores, who died aged 97 in September 1993, still the club's largest shareholder, was one of Everton's most profound influences of the 20th century, his monetary support transforming their fortunes in the 1960s.

By the mid 1970s they continued to figure amongst the country's elite clubs. Yet, with the glitter of silverware glaringly absent since the 1970 championship triumph, attendances declined, amidst criticism of the team's functional play. It was a situation that contrasted painfully for Evertonians with the remarkable success across Stanley Park of Bob Paisley's Liverpool. Moores shared that pain. Harry Catterick, his first managerial appointment, had gone and into the seat of power had come Billy Bingham, the Northern Ireland wing star who had helped Everton land the title in 1963. The championship had come tantalisingly close for Bingham in 1974-75, only to see it slip through his fingers and by 1976 the tide of Everton's misfortune and under-achievement was about to engulf the loquacious Ulsterman as Moores and the rest of the board called time on his tenure in charge.

The long, hot record-breaking summer of 1976 was followed by a harsh winter for Everton - and the season that saw red and yellow cards introduced into the Football League also brought Bingham's exit from Goodison. In contrast it was the start of a new beginning for Colin Harvey, returning as youth coach to the club he had loved since boyhood:

"It was fantastic to be back and the feeling was even better because, in my first season guiding the youngsters, we reached the FA Youth Cup final for the first time in 12 years. We lost 1-0 on aggregate in the 1977 final against a Crystal Palace side who had Kenny Sansom and the nucleus of the squad under Terry Venables which sagged under the weight of the 'team of the 80s' label. I inherited a good squad from Eric Harrison, whose talent for guiding and developing youngsters was evident when he subsequently moved to Manchester United. I could also tap into the expertise of youth development officer Ray Minshull, a former Liverpool goalkeeper, north-west regional coach and, later, the Premiership's academy officer.

The youth team I took charge of included Mark Higgins, who would graduate to first-team centre-half and captain, and Joe McBride, a winger who was the son of Joe senior, a Scottish international, and who went on to score 11 goals in 70 senior appearances for Everton. Also in it was defender Pat Heard, who later had 11 first-team outings before joining Aston Villa in the £650,000 deal that brought John Gidman to Goodison in October 1979. The youth side also included Ross Jack, a Scot who later scored on his only first-team appearance - a 2-1 win at Middlesbrough in March 1979 - and after leaving Everton played for a host of clubs in England, Ireland, Scotland and Wales. Full-back Ray Deakin, who had to stop playing because of a knee injury, became a youth coach then recovered to resume his playing career with Port Vale and Bolton, was another member of our side. But the youngster whose name overshadowed all the others, simply because of the hype and publicity surrounding him, was Martin Murray.

Bingham had signed him from Dublin amateur club Home Farm in December 1975 after a multi-club pursuit of the 5ft 10ins, 17-year-old midfielder, who captained the Republic's Youth team. Manchester United and City, Aston Villa, Celtic, Wolves and Belgian side Anderlecht were among others on the trail of Murray, who played in Europe at the age of 16 and attracted the burdensome media tag of 'the new George Best'. It was ridiculous. He didn't even play in the same position as George. Home Farm's amateur status precluded any transfer fee but Murray's revelation that one manager had offered him £12,000 to move to England - even though regulations restricted him to £250 - sparked wild speculation and a Football League investigation after their refusal to accept his registration. Bingham stated publicly that Murray's televised claim was nothing to do with Everton, adding: 'We have acted strictly by the rules.' The League asked Everton and Murray to complete a questionnaire and six weeks after his signing their management committee relented and accepted the player's registration.

Murray was a good midfield player with a range of passing but my verdict when I first saw him was that he wasn't quick enough for the highest level. He was a nice footballer but as soon as the game got fast he disappeared. During the second leg of the 1977 Youth Cup final at Palace there was a melee on the field, punches were thrown and Martin broke his hand. I had to take him to hospital accident and emergency in London after the game.

Two-and-a-half years after he arrived, having played for Ireland Under 21s but without making an Everton first-team appearance in competitive football, he boarded the ferry back to Dublin in the summer of 1978, a disillusioned, homesick young man who was by then 19. 'I feel football here is a bit of a rat race and I just felt I wanted to go back,' said Martin, who rejoined Dublin club Home Farm. The following January, though, he was back. But in August that year at the start of the 1979-80 season, by which time I'd moved up to reserve-team coach, I had to take him to hospital again. He was the victim of a high, nasty tackle by a Leeds player in the opening Central League fixture at Elland Road. The challenge smashed his knee and he had to be carried off. Our physio Jim McGregor knew as soon as he examined him that the damage was severe. Martin underwent surgery, went home during his recuperation and was out of action for four months. But in January 1980, by which time he was married with a child, he announced he was quitting full-time football because of a heart condition.

Everton retained his League registration but allowed him to re-join Home Farm for a third time in March that year. He later joined Drogheda, helping them gain a UEFA Cup spot, and appeared for the League of Ireland against the Italian League. As a trialist he was even included in Brian Clough's Nottingham Forest squad for a pre-season tour in 1983, and played in four friendlies. But Clough decided against signing him and Martin returned to resume his career in Ireland where he eventually went into management.

Many years later, in 2004, I bumped into him when I was watching a game in Ireland and my mind went back to that chapter in his life. As he said: 'The publicity I got when I first arrived probably did me more harm than good, especially this idea that I was another George Best. But I had enough chances as far as going home and coming back was concerned. I made mistakes but I enjoyed my time at Everton.'

The 1976-77 campaign was to prove less then enjoyable for Bingham, for whom the writing was on the wall. The club's 11th-place finish in the old First Division the previous season had hardly made him the fans' favourite. Yet his £35,000 signing of teenager Andy King from Luton in April 1976 - which preceded the £15,000 sale of Dave Clements to New York Cosmos - and a 4-0 drubbing of QPR at Loftus Road on the opening day of the new season, transfer-seeking Latchford scoring twice, fired renewed optimism. A 2-2 draw with Manchester City in October lifted Everton to second place but after that it was down and eventually out for Billy, the patience of the club's 'Godfather' John Moores finally snapping after only two wins in the next 15 League games. That slump was punctuated by a League Cup run that included an emphatic 3-0 quarter-final conquest of Manchester United at Old Trafford, through two goals from Andy King and the other from Martin Dobson. In December, in a last, desperate attempt to halt the slide, he was allowed to spend £200,000 to sign Duncan McKenzie from Anderlecht and £180,000 to recruit Scotland captain Bruce Rioch to buttress his midfield.

They made their debuts together in a 4-2 defeat at Coventry City and were destined not to appear on a winning side under Bingham in the League. Even though McKenzie scored twice on an impressive home debut against Birmingham, it ended in a 2-2 draw. That was followed by a 4-0 Christmas crash at Manchester United before another 2-2 home deadlock, this time against Middlesbrough. In the cup competitions, though, it was a different story. Under Bingham, Everton had already reached a two-leg League Cup semi-final meeting with Bolton without conceding a goal, having beaten Cambridge, Stockport and Coventry prior to the 3-0 win at Manchester United. They began their FA Cup campaign under Bingham with another win - despatching Stoke 2-0 at Goodison. Less than 48 hours later, on Monday, January 10, Billy met the press at Bellefield to discuss the outcome of the fourth-round draw, which meant a trip to the winners of the Swindon v Fulham replay. It was the day, also, when many headlines marvelled at the technological breakthrough of Clive Sinclair's two-inch screen television, which went on the market for £175. That evening, though, Billy found himself out of the Everton picture when a club statement announced he had been sacked, with 18 months of his contract left.

Billy responded by saying: 'I've tried to do this job as well as I could. If you're with a big club you expect to be shot down but the timing of my dismissal is ironic because the team is just beginning to take shape. Now I have to leave it on the edge of the Wembley turf.' There was the little matter of overcoming Bolton before an appearance at the old Twin Towers was assured - but you knew what he meant. My relationship with Billy, overall, had been OK. I was upset that he'd sold me but I was deeply grateful to him for bringing me back to Everton. I'm aware of the stories of Billy being a tricky customer, but I have to say that my dealings with him when I left Goodison - and when I returned - were fine.

Eight days after his departure and with Steve Burtenshaw in temporary charge, Everton were held to a 1-1 home draw by Bolton in the semi-final first leg of the League Cup. The game drew a 54,000-plus crowd - surpassed only by Liverpool's visit later that season - with the Second Division side bringing 15,000 fans. The Bolton team included three future Evertonians in Peter Reid, Mike Walsh and Jim McDonagh as well as former Manchester United winger Willie Morgan. Duncan McKenzie headed Everton in front after 33 minutes but when David Lawson was penalised by referee Ken Burns for taking too many steps, Neil Whatmore smashed an 88th-minute equaliser after the free-kick had been played to him. That made Bolton favourites to face Aston Villa or QPR although Everton's cup attentions turned to the FA Cup in which goals from Latchford and McKenzie salvaged a 2-2 draw at Third Division Swindon to set up a Goodison replay.

In the League, though, as Everton hunted for a new manager, the alarm bells began to ring. Their only First Division games in January brought two defeats - 0-2 at Ipswich and 1-3 at home to QPR - leaving them 18th, only five points clear of a relegation place. During this anxious period for Everton a radio station reported on its main midday news bulletin that Ipswich manager Bobby Robson, having rejected past Everton approaches, was at that moment travelling from Suffolk to Merseyside to succeed Bingham. A telephone inquiry to Portman Road established that Robson was doing no such thing. He was at his office desk planning the next phase of Ipswich's pursuit of leaders and eventual champions Liverpool.

The man Everton did turn to was Gordon Lee, then managing Newcastle United, who was appointed on a reported £20,000 a year which, even with inflation, seems paltry today when the last data revealed Premiership managerial earnings ranging from £600,000 to £4 million-plus. Gordon is one of the most genuine people I have ever met in the game and I still see him today at charity and golf events. A son of the Black Country, he spent 11 years as a defender with Aston Villa, collecting League Cup winners and runners-up medals, before becoming Shrewsbury player-coach then taking Port Vale up to the old Division Three in 1971 in his first managerial job. Vale's FA Cup home clash with West Ham two years later revealed Gordon's back-to-basics approach to management and his dislike of anything fancy or superficial. 'Paint the visitors' dressing room with a pot of that non-drying stuff', he told Vale's handyman. 'Trevor Brooking, Bobby Moore and their London pals will be worried about getting their fancy suits stained and it might put them off their game!' If it did it didn't affect the outcome, West Ham winning 1-0. But Gordon moved on to Blackburn, leading them to the old Third Division championship in 1975 prior to taking over at St James's Park and taking Newcastle to the 1976 League Cup final.

Gordon is an uncomplicated man, down-to-earth and passionate about his football. He once asked me why cheese on toast was called Welsh rarebit! His football ethic was 'team, team, team'. He disliked the notion of superstars and incurred the wrath of Tyneside by selling Malcolm Macdonald to Arsenal. Gordon's management creed inevitably meant that he and Duncan McKenzie would be uneasy football bedfellows, Gordon once astonishing the media by telling them he didn't count a McKenzie goal that gave Everton a 2-1 FA Cup win at Cardiff. 'Why didn't he just stick it in the net instead of farting round?' Gordon said after the game. When a sportswriter offered the opinion that Duncan was a flair player, Gordon replied: 'That's something on the bottom of your trousers.'

Duncan was a showman player. To him, a flick was more important than a pass - and that was sacrilege to Gordon. Yet, somehow, Lee tolerated McKenzie and included him in his side on 52 occasions before selling him to Chelsea for £165,000 in September 1978. A player like Everton stalwart Mick Lyons, however, was right up Gordon's street. One day at Bellefield he declared: 'If you put Micky and Bobby Moore into that gym and throw a ball in there'd be only one winner...and it wouldn't be Moore.'

Gordon's first match in charge was the home FA Cup replay with Swindon on February 1, 1977 when late goals from Martin Dobson and Dave Jones gave Everton a 2-1 victory - the first time since before the First World War that Everton had come from behind in the final 10 minutes at Goodison to win a senior match. But the club's League position was perilous, fourth-from-bottom and without a League win since November. Said Gordon: 'I'm very excited at the prospect of managing what I call a Group A club - that is one with great tradition, style and ability. There are only half-a-dozen in the country. But I know two very different roads are looming ahead of us. One can lead to Wembley - maybe twice - and the other could lead to relegation and the Second Division. Whatever we do, we must avoid the second one.'

His first two League games in charge only added to the threat of the drop. A 2-0 defeat at his former club Villa followed by a 2-1 home reverse against Leicester extended Everton's alarming League sequence to 10 games without a win. However, the club's fortunes soon brightened considerably. Victory at Stoke, with £135,000 new signing Mike Pejic making his debut at left-back against his former club, began a run of only two defeats in the season's final 18 League games. That secured a respectable finishing position of ninth, which would have been surpassed if some of the eight draws in that closing sequence had been turned into wins.

The cups, too, brought an eventful climax to the season. Bob Latchford's only goal of the game at Burnden Park in the League Cup semi-final second leg - when McKenzie sent a penalty yards wide and the floodlights failed - booked a Wembley date with Aston Villa. Everton lined up at the Twin Towers - now lost to posterity - like this:

David Lawson; Dave Jones, Mick Lyons (captain), Ken McNaught, Terry Darracott; Andy King, Bryan Hamilton, Martin Dobson, Ronnie Goodlass; Bob Latchford, Duncan McKenzie. Unused substitute: George Telfer.

A dour battle ended goalless and in the Hillsborough replay Roger Kenyon, who had replaced the injured Martin Dobson, conceded an own goal which was cancelled out by a Latchford strike. There was no further score and the struggle stretched into another meeting at Old Trafford, the first time that a major English cup final had gone to a second replay.

Latchford put Everton ahead for the first time in the marathon battle, scoring from McNaught's header off a Goodlass cross, and that's how it stayed until the 80th minute. Then Chris Nicholl equalised with a spectacular 40-yard shot and within a minute Everton were behind when Brian Little, later to manage Tranmere Rovers, fired an angled shot past Lawson. There were only two minutes left when Lyons met a Goodlass corner to take the tie yet again into extra time. The then novel experience of a penalty decider was looming when, with a couple of minutes of the extra period left, a cross deflected off

Goodlass, beat Terry Darracott and Little pounced to win the trophy for Villa. The extended contest had generated receipts topping £500,000 from a total attendance of almost 210,000. With one chance of silverware gone, Lee and the players eyed another greater prize - the FA Cup. After a 2-1 fifth-round win at Cardiff, a 2-0 conquest of Derby set up a semi-final against Liverpool at Maine Road, Manchester.

Earlier in that month of April, Merseyside celebrated the astonishing and unprecedented feat of Red Rum, trained by Ginger McCain on Southport sands, winning the Grand National for a third time. Now, Mersey fans anticipated the fact that one of their clubs would be going to Wembley. But the semi-final was to be framed in infamy and anger in Evertonian annals with perhaps the most bizarre refereeing decision in the club's history.

Everton, stripped of the injured Latchford and King, went behind to a superb Terry McDermott chip but McKenzie equalised before half-time when he met Jim Pearson's cross. Even when Jimmy Case headed Liverpool back in front, Bruce Rioch restored equality in the 83rd minute with his first Everton goal, from a McKenzie cross. Just before Rioch struck, Lee had sent on Bryan Hamilton for Dobson and the Northern Ireland international was to figure in an incident that sparked a mystery that has haunted the club's followers down the decades. With time running out, Goodlass crossed from the left, McKenzie flicked the ball on and Hamilton diverted it past Ray Clemence, seemingly with his hip. Everton jubilation, though, was punctured by referee Clive Thomas, who disallowed Hamilton's effort. But to this day we don't know why. Did he think it was offside, even though there was no flag? Did he rule it out for handball? We may never know.

The Treorchy official awarded a free-kick to Liverpool, whose players were as baffled as Everton's. Indeed, the expression of disappointed acceptance on the faces of manager Bob Paisley and his players indicated that they had no quibble with the legitimacy of the 'goal'. Thomas's immediate after-match explanation was that 'there was an infringement of the rules'. Television evidence, though, failed to find it. In a later, considered comment on his action, Thomas said: 'From the angle of the cross there was no way Bryan Hamilton could have controlled the ball without the use of his arm. In no way could I say that from behind I could have seen the ball make contact with his hand or his arm. But I was 100 per cent certain that he couldn't have controlled it any other way. So I disallowed it for handball.' The infringement, therefore, was one he BELIEVED had occurred but had not actually seen. On such a tenuous basis Everton were denied a passage to Wembley and the course of football history was changed.

Reprieved, Liverpool won the replay emphatically 3-0 and although they lost to Manchester United at Wembley, they went on to lift the European Cup to add to their League championship. Their great win over Borussia Moenchengladbach in Rome came in the same week that the Orient Express arrived at Istanbul for the last time - and I couldn't help thinking that we should have de-railed Liverpool in that first FA Cup meeting at Maine Road.

To the credit of Gordon Lee and his crestfallen players, they shrugged off their deep disappointment by losing only one of their remaining eight League games to finish a respectable ninth. Centre-back Ken McNaught ended the eventful campaign with the proud record of appearing in all 58 of the club's games, the most domestic appearances by an Everton player in one season. Two months later Gordon, who had Mark Higgins breaking through, sold McNaught to Aston Villa for £200,000 and he went on to win League championship and European Cup medals with the Midlands club.

That summer - when 79-year-old John Moores resigned from the club board after 17 years saying, 'I feel I've done enough but I'll be here if Everton need me' - Gordon spent the income from the sale of McNaught to sign England winger Dave Thomas from QPR, as if to prove he would countenance flair players as long as they measured up to his yardstick. He also paid Blackpool £150,000 for Scottish goalkeeper George Wood and in the November brought in midfielder Trevor Ross from Arsenal for £170,000. Bruce Rioch re-joined Derby for £150,000 following the £12,000 summer departure of Bryan Hamilton to Millwall. Later, Bryan would return to Merseyside as player-manager of Tranmere.

During the closing weeks of the 1976-77 season, our youth development officer Ray Minshull asked me to go with him to give my opinion on a teenage defender about whom we'd had glowing scouting reports. Ray and I travelled to watch him play for Wales Under 15s against France at Colwyn Bay - and neither of us had any doubt about the lad's talent and potential. In June 1977 we signed him as an apprentice and less than 18 months later as a full professional. Kevin Ratcliffe was on his way to becoming one of the great Everton players and the most successful captain in the club's history, as well as being a notable skipper of Wales.

Gordon Lee's first full season in charge promised to be bigger and better for Everton but it was to be another of those bitterly frustrating campaigns that were such a feature at Goodison in the 1970s. A pre-season trip to Morocco for a tournament in Rabat in August 1977 highlighted the sparky relationship between Lee and McKenzie and also Gordon's less than comprehensive grasp on geography. 'So what do you think of Africa, Gordon?' asked Liverpool Echo reporter Alex Goodman as the Everton party checked into their hotel. 'Bloody hell', he replied. 'Are we in Africa? I thought we were in UEFA!'

Gordon was soon approached by Moroccan sports journalists, keen to talk to him about the Everton team. They spoke French, Gordon didn't so he called in McKenzie who did. 'Duncan, they want to know my best players so tell them it's big Latch, Micky Lyons and Micky Pejic,' said Gordon. McKenzie then turned to the local sportswriters and told them in French: 'The boss said his best players are Bob Latchford, Mick Lyons, Mick Pejic...and Duncan McKenzie!' Yet, despite Gordon's displeasure on hearing McKenzie add his own name, he selected him in both tournament matches against Czechoslovakia (drawn 1-1 with a goal from Latchford) and WAK Casablanca, which Everton lost 1-0. He was also in the line-up to start the season along with new signings Wood and Thomas. With the injured Latchford ruled out the side was:

Wood; Jones, Kenyon, Higgins, Pejic; Lyons, Darracott, King; McKenzie, Pearson, Thomas. Substitute: Goodlass.

But it was a far from happy curtain raiser. Newly-promoted Nottingham Forest came to Goodison and inflicted a 3-1 opening-day reverse, although immediate assessments were tempered by the shock impact Brian Clough's team were to have by surging on to win the title. A 1-0 loss at Arsenal the following midweek did nothing to reveal what was to follow...a 22-match unbeaten run in League and League Cup in which Bob Latchford revelled. The undefeated sequence ended dramatically with a 6-2 Boxing Day crash to Manchester United at Goodison, but Latchford kept on scoring.

It was a big season for Bob who for some time had felt unsettled at Goodison. With the financial terms of his original contract eroded by inflation and entangled in the web of the government pay code, he had lodged several transfer requests with former manager Billy Bingham. Keen to enhance his family's security, Bob even considered following the foreign path trod by Kevin Keegan, who had just quit Liverpool for German club Hamburg. 'The Irishman used to roll up Bob's written transfer requests and use them to light his cigars,' Bob Whiting reported drily in the Liverpool Daily Post. Jim Greenwood, Everton's former secretary and chief executive, revealed the bizarre circumstances in which Latchford lodged his first written transfer request. 'I was involved in many unusual situations during my 19 years with Everton but Bob Latchford must take the prize for the strangest transfer request', Jim recalled. 'One morning, as I was driving from home to start work at Goodison, I stopped at traffic lights in Litherland. Suddenly, there was a knock on my car window and I was shocked to see Bob standing there, clutching a letter. He duly popped it through my window before leaping back into his car and roaring off.'

But Latchford's feats on the pitch, leading to his first England cap against Italy at Wembley, meant that under the pay code his new international status allowed the club to negotiate a fresh three-and-a-half-year deal which he signed in March 1978. By then, Bob was well on the way to the first 30-goal League total in English football's top flight for six years. He was prolific from early in the season, hitting four in a 5-1 win at QPR which ended a club-record 288 matches without an Everton hat-trick, stretching back to November 1971 when Joe Royle and David Johnson each hit trebles in the 8-0 rout of Southampton. Latchford bagged another hat-trick in a 6-0 demolition of Coventry and hit doubles against Newcastle, Birmingham, Middlesbrough, Leicester and Manchester United.

Everton went out of the League Cup in the fifth round at Leeds, losing 4-1, after eliminating Sheffield United, Middlesbrough (after a replay) and Sheffield Wednesday - but Boro extracted revenge in the FA Cup. After beating Aston Villa 4-1 at home Everton were handed a fourth-round trip to Middlesbrough. Co-incidentally, both clubs flew out on a pre-match break to Jersey. But their planned three days in the Channel Islands stretched longer than planned as fog cut off Jersey and closed ports and airports. History was in the making with the possibility of the FA ordering the clubs to play the cup tie on a ground in St Helier. However, the January weather conditions changed in time for Everton and Boro to make a belated return home.

The trip, though, had been memorable, not least for the fact that Gordon Lee 'discovered' crab crunchers in a fish restaurant - 'I thought you were eating nuts,' he admitted - and named a member of the press, Colin Wood of the Daily Mail, as best trainer after a tough session on the sands of St Ouen's Bay revealed that his players had over-indulged during a night out the previous evening. 'You lot were a bloody disgrace this morning and I'm giving the yellow bib to Woody, who made a show of you all,' Gordon declared to a speechless first-team squad on the bus back to the hotel.

One Jersey resident was also left gulping in disbelief when, on a stormy evening, she saw a teenager emerge from the waves and walk along the promenade. 'Where on earth have you come from?' she exclaimed. 'Australia' came the instant reply. Exit one incredulous woman. The youngster was Craig Johnston, who paid his own fare from Down Under and made his Middlesbrough debut against Everton to help engineer Boro's 3-2 win and avenge their League Cup defeat the previous October. Three years later he would join Liverpool. Mick Lyons was on the mark in both cup competitions against Boro, the first Everton player to achieve that feat against the same club in one season. Andy King matched it against Newport County in 1982-83.

In the League, Everton were in a lofty position for much of the 1977-78 season and after four straight wins during the Easter period over Newcastle, Leeds, Manchester United and Derby, were second to pacesetting Forest until the completion of their fixtures. However, successive defeats - 1-0 at home to Liverpool and 3-2 at Coventry - signalled a downturn in fortunes. It left fourth-placed Liverpool four points behind with three games in hand.

Everton's final match was at home to Chelsea on April 29 and it's an occasion assured of a lasting place in Goodison annals because of Latchford's scoring feat. He needed only two more goals to reach a League total of 30 and land a £10,000 prize put up by the Daily Express and Adidas. On the corresponding Saturday 50 years earlier Dixie Dean had scored a hat-trick against Arsenal to complete 60 League goals in 1927-28 and set a record that will surely remain unassailable. Half Dixie's total is now a magical figure and the legendary Dean sent Bob his best wishes as he faced Chelsea. 'Latch' lined up in this 4-3-3 formation:

George Wood; Neil Robinson, Mick Lyons, Billy Wright, Mike Pejic; Mick Buckley, Andy King, Martin Dobson; George Telfer, Latchford, Dave Thomas. Substitute (not used): Dave Jones.

With 18 minutes of the game left and Everton leading 3-0, Latchford had still not scored. Then he connected with a Lyons header across goal and nodded the ball past Peter Bonetti for goal No 29. Just one to go...Lyons made it 5-0 and with 12 minutes left Goodison erupted when referee Peter Willis awarded Everton a questionable penalty for a push by Micky Droy. Latchford stepped up and with a less than full-blooded kick sent the ball beyond Bonetti and into the net before being engulfed in a sea of delirious blue-and-white clad supporters. Everton had won 6-0 and for the first time in the club's history three defenders - Lyons, Wright and Robinson, with his only goal for the club

- had scored in the same match. It was also a very rare instance of five different Everton players scoring in the same League game.

But it was Latchford, quite rightly, who dominated the headlines. 'To see the penalty go in was a terrific moment, a fantastic way to end the season', he beamed. 'The prestige and sense of achievement has thrilled and delighted me.' As for the big cheque - and in 1978 it was big - Bob ended up with just £192! The prize fund was split between the player, the Football League and the Professional Footballers' Association Benevolent Fund. Bob then decided to share his portion with team-mates and training staff but after a three-year dispute with the Inland Revenue, who wanted to tax him on £5,000, he ended up out of pocket!

His great finishing, though, ensured that Everton were 76-goal First Division top scorers in their 42 games. But Liverpool's win at West Ham, while Chelsea were being put to the sword at Goodison, followed by the Anfield club's subsequent win over Manchester City and draw with new champions Forest, pushed Everton into third place. Forest, who had beaten Liverpool in a replayed final at Old Trafford to win the League Cup, added the League championship with 64 points. They were seven ahead of Liverpool, who finished two points ahead of third-placed Everton with Arsenal and Manchester City three points further back on 52 apiece.

One of the stars of Forest's stunning success under Clough and Peter Taylor was goalkeeper Peter Shilton. The £250,000 capture from Stoke kept 20 clean sheets, with Forest conceding only eight League goals at home and 16 away. From the previous November they had also launched a record unbeaten League run that would span 42 matches until December 1978, when they lost 2-0 at Liverpool. They also emulated Liverpool in lifting the European Cup in consecutive seasons. It was amazing success and I just wonder what might have been if Billy Bingham had moved for Shilton when he had the chance. In saying that, I am not denigrating George Wood, who also kept 20 clean sheets in 49 League and Cup appearances in 1977-78 and during his first two seasons at Everton was an ever-present and won three Scotland caps. Big George soon became a great favourite with the fans. But he was given to goalkeeping eccentricities, both for Everton and Scotland, and after a dispute over a new Goodison contract and Lee's signings of Martin Hodge from Plymouth for £135,000 and Jim McDonagh from Bolton for £25,000, Wood was sold to Arsenal for £150,000 - the amount he'd cost from Blackpool - in the summer of 1980.

In 1978, the club's centenary year, Philip Carter, managing director of the Littlewoods Organisation, moved up from Everton vice-chairman to succeed Bill Scott as chairman. Carter, who had joined the board in 1975, would serve as chairman continuously until 1991 - the year he was knighted - through one of the most eventful periods in the club's history. He was Football League president from 1986 to 1988, a leading figure in football's television deals and the build-up to the formation of the Premiership.

The summer of 1978 was one that saw me change roles behind the scenes. When Gordon Lee's right-hand man Steve Burtenshaw left to take over as manager of QPR it meant Eric Harrison, who'd played for his hometown club Halifax, Barrow and Southport, stepping up to succeed him. I followed Eric as reserve-team coach after spending a very enjoyable couple of years as youth coach which, for me, was a valuable part of football's learning process. Prior to the start of the 1978-79 season Gordon paid Blackpool £325,000 to sign Republic of Ireland striker Mickey Walsh. Unfortunately for Walsh and Everton he managed only three goals in 29 senior appearances for the club - home and away against Irish club Finn Harps in the UEFA Cup and a League goal in a 1-1 draw at Aston Villa - and before the end of the season Lee swapped him for Peter Eastoe of QPR. Walsh later played for FC Porto and ended his career as player-manager of another Portuguese club, Rio Ave, before becoming an agent.

Another arrival in the summer of 1978 was midfielder or defender Geoff Nulty, for whom Lee paid Newcastle £45,000. Nulty had played for him at St James' Park but his career would last less than another two years before being ended by injury. Midfielder Mick Buckley (£70,000 to Sunderland) and Jim Pearson (£75,000 to Newcastle) went through the Goodison exit as the curtain went up on the new season.

Long before the mass foreign invasion of the 1990s, English football was agog with the arrival of Argentina's World Cup-winning duo Osvaldo Ardiles and Ricardo Villa at Tottenham. The government, whose anxieties then are felt by many today, were so worried that the floodgates might open that they imposed a ban on foreign imports from non-Common Market countries - and it became effective just a day after Southampton completed the signing of Yugoslav defender Ivan Golac.

Lee's line-up for the opening phase of the campaign was predominantly English, supplemented by one Scot and an Irish international. It read:

George Wood; Terry Darracott, Billy Wright, Roger Kenyon, Mike Pejic;

Martin Dobson, Andy King, Geoff Nulty; Mickey Walsh, Bob Latchford, Dave Thomas with the substitute role filled variously by Neil Robinson, George Telfer and Trevor Ross.

That summer the Philips company had created compact discs but Everton were about to make a record of their own - a club best 19-game unbeaten League run from the start of a season. The team won six of their first seven domestic and European games, although the victory at Chelsea through an Andy King goal on the opening day was soured by sickening after-match events. Many Everton fans required hospital treatment, some for stab wounds, when they were attacked by Chelsea supporters who had vowed vengeance after trouble following the previous season's final game at Goodison. It prompted Merseyside councillors to consider steps to ban Chelsea and Manchester United fans from attending Everton and Liverpool games after it was claimed they were among the worst behaved in Europe.

On the field, Everton's impressive start included an 8-0 League Cup trouncing of Wimbledon. Latchford scored five and Dobson three against The Dons, who were then in the old Fourth Division beginning their charge through the Leagues which would see them, less than a decade later, beat Liverpool to lift the FA Cup. Latchford's feat meant that he joined Jack Southworth, Dixie Dean and Tommy Eglington in the record books as the only players to score five or more goals for Everton in a senior match.

Everton had a comfortable start to their UEFA Cup campaign, winning 5-0 against Finn Harps in Donegal and by the same score in the return. The games provided some bizarre statistics. Apart from the fact that the scores were identical, in the 61st minute of both legs Harps substituted their goalkeeper through injury - Eddie Mahon replacing Joe Harper in the first game and Harper replacing Mahon in the second. And in both games the substitute keeper conceded a goal before touching the ball, and Everton sent on Mark Higgins as substitute for Mick Lyons in the 68th minute each time!

The season was little more than a month old when Lee sprang a double shock by spending £333,000 to sign England defender Colin Todd from Derby and selling Duncan McKenzie to Chelsea for £165,000, finally ending the uneasy - and sometimes humorous - professional relationship between manager and player. Todd had acquired a glowing international reputation as a centre-back. But Gordon's decision to play him in place of Darracott at right-back, and the fact that Todd was three months from his 30th birthday when he arrived, meant that Goodison never saw him at his best and a year later he moved to Birmingham for £300,000.

The Everton public's feeling for McKenzie was amply demonstrated when he returned with Chelsea in November, and his goal in the London club's 3-2 defeat was rapturously received by Goodison fans - Gordon Lee's comments are unrepeatable. Both Lee and the supporters, though, had been ecstatic a few weeks earlier when Andy King's only goal of the game secured a win over Liverpool that the fans, and all of us at Goodison, had yearned for since David Johnson's goal for Everton won the derby in November 1971. Of 15 League and FA Cup meetings, Liverpool had won eight, with seven drawn. Our seven-year itch to stem that tide had become unbearable.

At the time the two clubs were unbeaten after 11 League games and battling for the championship, with Bob Paisley's side on top four points ahead of us in second place. In a newspaper preview on the morning of the match that great Evertonian, Joe Mercer, wrote: 'Gordon Lee is a master of psychological warfare. He's certain to whip up his lads to go out and try to change that poor run against Liverpool. My greatest fear is that he'll try too hard and, for me, it all adds up to a stalemate.' The atmosphere on matchday intensified with a gathering of Everton legends as part of the club's centenary celebrations. Two former goalkeepers Ted Sagar and Gordon West were saluted by the fans and Dixie Dean received a standing ovation.

When the game got underway Joe Mercer's forecast was holding up until the 58th minute when a move launched in their own half by Kenyon and Wright was continued by Pejic on the left touchline. The full-back's cross was headed down by Dobson and when King fired on the half volley from just outside the box, the ball flew past Ray Clemence into the top corner of the net. Everton euphoria was clearly not shared by a police inspector who ordered King and BBC reporter Richard Dukenfield off the pitch at the end as the Everton hero was about to tell the world of his landmark strike! 'King Nets And Blues Rule Again', proclaimed the Football Echo headline, while millions of Evertonians re-lived the triumphant moment on Match of the Day later that night. 'That's it! Everton have beaten Liverpool, Andy King the scorer', declared commentator John Motson. 'Seven is his number, and seven years it is since it last happened...Liverpool's run of 23 League games unbeaten is over.' Evertonians were exultant, eager to crack the gag: 'We know where Queens Drive is in Liverpool, and now we know where Kings Drive is, too - in the back of Clemence's net!'

Liverpool, though, had the last laugh. Although our derby win reduced their lead to two points, they lost only three more League matches and won the title while we finished fourth. But Gordon and his players were still bubbling from their defeat of Liverpool when they flew to Czechoslovakia two days later for the UEFA Cup second-round return with Dukla Prague. They travelled with a 2-1 first-leg lead through Latchford and King. Mick Lyons, who'd missed the Liverpool game through injury was still out, with Kenyon continuing to deputise. Lee also dropped King to the substitute's bench and brought in the more defensive Trevor Ross.

With 10 minutes left, and after a magnificently defiant goalkeeping display by George Wood, it was still goalless in the Czech capital and Everton could glimpse round three...when their dreams crashed. In a classic example of a forward being caught out in a defensive situation, Dave Thomas attempted a fancy trick at the wrong time and in the wrong place - and Gajdusek accepted the opportunity by sending a brilliant shot through a crowded box and past the unsighted Wood. It put Dukla through on the away goal and Thomas admitted: 'I was to blame. I thought Gajdusek was closer to me when I tried to flick the ball over his head.'

Everton's 51-point, fourth-place finish in the League - behind Liverpool, West Brom and Nottingham Forest - followed a club record unbeaten run from the start of the season until Christmas week at Coventry. The defeat at Highfield Road also ended another club record sequence of 20 League matches unbeaten since the final match of the previous season. Lee was critical when the New Year's Day trip to Bolton was hit by a blizzard. The game, which should never have started, was abandoned at half-time with the score at 1-1 but not before Bolton's Peter Reid, later to become an Everton hero, had torn ligaments in his right knee which put him out for a year.

In February 1979 Forest boss Brian Clough crossed a threshold in football history when he signed Trevor Francis from Birmingham in British football's first £1 million transfer. Less than three months later Gordon Lee tried to bring Steve Daley to Everton from Wolves for a similar fee but the deal collapsed and the player eventually joined Manchester City for a then massive sum of £1.4 million. As well as Eastoe's arrival in March, Lee also paid Manchester City £150,000 for Brian Kidd. Between them they managed just three goals in 16 appearances through to the end of the season and Everton's seven draws in their final 13 games cost them dearly.

In the League Cup, the goal explosion against Wimbledon was followed by the narrowest of wins over Darlington before Lee's side went out 3-2 at home to Nottingham Forest, who went on to retain the trophy. There was instant disappointment in the FA Cup with a 2-1 third-round defeat at Sunderland and frustration on the terraces was reflected in a 4,000 drop in Goodison's average League attendance to a figure of 35,456.

Britain's political landscape was revolutionised shortly after the end of the season when Conservative leader Margaret Thatcher won the May 1979 General Election to topple James Callaghan's Labour Party and become the country's first woman Prime Minister. The Everton scenario, too, was much changing with David Jones joining Coventry City for £275,000 and three England internationals, Mike Pejic, Martin Dobson and Dave Thomas, also leaving the club. Lee reflected: 'The strength of the team was in what I called my Bermuda Triangle - the left-sided trio of Pejic, Dobson and Thomas. They were a very good unit but freedom of contract had arrived and I had to release them all. Then there was the American venture. Some lads decided to try their luck across the Atlantic, among them Terry Darracott, Roger Kenyon and Steve Seargeant. All were good, genuine players and the kind big clubs need. When things go wrong it's the local lads, and those brought up from the junior ranks, who have the soul to keep the ship steady. The loss of these players left me with a big hole to fill.'

As he left for Detroit Express, defender Steve Seargeant voiced the feelings of many in the 1970s about the state of our game. 'I'm sorry to be leaving Everton, but I'm not sorry to be leaving English football', he admitted. 'All you read about these days is hooliganism; people seem to want to go to games to fight. You don't get any of that kind of thing at matches in the States.' Steve later coached in the States and in September 2001 his son Christian became the youngest player to turn out for Everton's Under 17 youth academy side - at the age of 14.

Lee responded to the Goodison exodus by moving into the market in the summer of 1979 to sign defender John Bailey from Blackburn for £300,000, and midfielders Asa Hartford from Nottingham Forest for a club record £500,000 and Gary Stanley from Chelsea for £300,000. He also signed Eamonn O'Keefe from non-league Mossley for £25,000.

These summer signings followed Lee's earlier acquisitions of John Barton and Imre Varadi. Full-back Barton cost £27,000 from Worcester City, a record for a non-league player, while striker Imre Varadi had made only 10 League appearances for Sheffield United when Lee paid £80,000 for him in March 1979. When asked by the press from which nationality the largely unknown

Varadi was descended, Gordon provided one of his many unforgettable offerings. 'I think he's Uranian' he said, thus making Varadi the first player to be signed from another planet! The real answer is that Varadi's name came from his Hungarian father - his mother was Italian - and he is assured of a lasting place in Everton hearts for his 1981 FA Cup winner against Liverpool.

The re-vamped Everton side, without transfer-seeking Bob Latchford, began 1979-80 with two defeats - 4-2 at home to Norwich when Bailey made his debut at left-back - and 2-0 at Leeds. They then won 1-0 at Derby in what was Colin Todd's last Everton appearance - ironically at centre-back - before his move to Birmingham. Stanley made his debut in the next game - a 2-0 home win over Cardiff in the League Cup with Brian Kidd scoring both goals - and Hartford made his Everton entrance in the following match, a 1-1 home draw with Aston Villa when the line-up was:

George Wood; Billy Wright, Mick Lyons, Mark Higgins, John Bailey; Gary Stanley, Trevor Ross, Andy King, Asa Hartford; Peter Eastoe, Brian Kidd. Unused substitute: Geoff Nulty.

In October, another new face arrived when Lee again broke the club transfer record by signing right-back John Gidman from Aston Villa for £650,000. Latchford resolved his dispute with Everton after his hopes of a move abroad and talks with other English clubs collapsed. Lee swiftly recalled him yet despite his return, and the new signings, results were not forthcoming, although holding surging leaders Liverpool to a 2-2 draw at Anfield preserved honour. Goals from Andy King, scoring for the third consecutive derby, and Brian Kidd gained a point after Mick Lyons had lobbed an eighth-minute own goal past George Wood. The game made the record books for the wrong reason when Everton's Gary Stanley and Liverpool's Terry McDermott were sent off for fighting. They became only the second and third players to be dismissed in a Mersey derby - the only other one had been Everton's Alf Milward, also at Anfield, 83 years earlier in November 1896!

Just five wins in 23 games to the end of December left Goodison gripped by relegation fears and when Everton greeted the 1980s with a 1-0 New Year's Day home victory over Nottingham Forest it was a false dawn, although personally gratifying for 19-year-old winger Joe McBride. When Forest had come to Goodison the previous season he encountered Brian Clough in the corridor. 'Straighten your tie, young man,' Clough chided him, leaving the teenager speechless. Now Joe had the great satisfaction of playing a big part in beating Clough's team, thanks to a Kidd goal. Lee's side, though, had not won a League game since toppling Forest when they encountered Liverpool at Goodison on March 1, 1980. It ended in a 2-1 Everton defeat and Geoff Nulty's knee injury, sustained in a tussle with Jimmy Case, would end his career. The afternoon, though, was totally overshadowed by the death in Goodison's main stand of the greatest Evertonian of them all...the legendary William Ralph 'Dixie' Dean.

Dixie and Bill Shankly had attended the match as guests of my co-author John Keith, following a hotel lunch to launch publication of the Liverpool and Everton Official Annuals. In the taxi to Goodison 73-year-old Dixie revealed that the last Merseyside derby he'd been to he'd played in! When substitute Peter Eastoe scored Everton's 73rd-minute goal Dixie slumped in his seat and, shortly afterwards, was declared dead. Tears were shed for an icon that night. 'Bill's goalscoring was the greatest thing under the sun', proclaimed Shankly. 'He belongs in the company of the supremely great - like Beethoven, Rembrandt and Shakespeare.' An emotional Joe Mercer said simply, 'Bill Dean was bigger and better than life', while Liverpool manager Bob Paisley said: 'Dixie lived and breathed Everton. I knew him and I'm a better person for knowing him.'

Dixie's passing came during a sad nine-day spell for English football which also saw the deaths of Manchester United chairman Louis Edwards, former FA and Sheffield Wednesday chairman Sir Andrew Stephen and the formidable director general of the Football League, Alan Hardaker. Some 21 years later, on May 5, 2001, the day before the 73rd anniversary of Dixie's League record 60th goal in a season, an 8ft 2ins bronze statue of the great man was unveiled at the Park End of Goodison by Dixie's middle son Geoff.

A week after Dixie's death - the day after his funeral which stopped the traffic in his native Birkenhead - Everton had an FA Cup sixth round home collision with Ipswich. Bobby Robson's East Anglian visitors were third in the League and a vastly different proposition for Everton from their previous opponents Aldershot, Wigan and Wrexham. Now they were drawn at home in the quarter-final for the fourth consecutive occasion, providing a swift opportunity to avenge a 4-0 home drubbing by Ipswich only a month earlier when 20-year-old midfielder Gary Megson, who'd cost £250,000 from Plymouth, made his home debut. That defeat, in which dazzling Alan Brazil scored twice and was denied a hat-trick by the woodwork, had been greeted by a hail of stand seat cushions hurled by angry Everton supporters in a crowd of less than 32,000. They also demanded Gordon's resignation. Chairman

Philip Carter, though, stood by his manager and made available more money in addition to the £2 million that had recently been spent.

Ipswich, on a 16-game unbeaten run, made just one change for the Cup tie - Mick Mills replacing Kevin Beattie at left-back - from the team that had swamped Everton just a few weeks earlier. It included fine players such as Dutch duo Frans Thijssen and Arnold Muhren, Paul Mariner, Eric Gates, John Wark and, of course, Brazil. This time, though, Gordon Lee pulled off a tactical masterstroke. He switched John Gidman from right-back to a midfield role for the first time in his career and recalled Bob Latchford to partner Brian Kidd and Peter Eastoe in attack. It worked like a dream. Gidman delivered the cross from which Latchford headed a 28th minute opening goal and when Kidd smashed a 77th minute free-kick beyond Paul Cooper, most of the 45,000-plus crowd wildly acclaimed Everton's progress to the semi-final. A reply by substitute Beattie in the last minute was merely academic. 'The lads wanted to do it so much for the fans and the boss and we wanted to do it for Dixie Dean, too', declared jubilant captain Mick Lyons, who had been a pall-bearer at the great man's funeral. He added: 'The minute's silence for Dixie before kick-off inspired us.'

Everton's win, coupled with Liverpool's victory at Tottenham set up the prospect of a first all-Merseyside FA Cup final when the clubs were kept apart in the semi-finals - Everton paired with West Ham and Liverpool drawn against Arsenal. It was not to be. Liverpool ultimately lost to the Gunners after a record FA Cup marathon which spanned four games and two periods of extra time before Brian Talbot's only goal of the third replay at Coventry ended Anfield hopes of the Double. Amazingly in the middle of this series, they also met in the League which, hardly surprisingly, ended in a 1-1 draw at Anfield. It added up to five meetings between April 12 and May 1. The following day they paid Chester £300,000 to sign a certain Ian Rush, a boyhood Everton fan who was destined to haunt us.

Everton were leading Second Division West Ham 1-0 in the semi-final at Villa Park thanks to a Kidd penalty three minutes before the interval before a bust-up with Ray Stewart earned him his marching orders for violent conduct, bringing him an unwanted distinction. Having already been sent off against Wigan in round four he is believed to be the only player dismissed twice for his club in the same FA Cup run.

Stuart Pearson's equaliser 20 minutes from the end took the semi to a replay at Elland Road where Bob Latchford, replacing the suspended Kidd, equalised

Devonshire's extra-time goal with a great diving header from close range. A second replay beckoned until two minutes from the end when Frank Lampard Snr managed to connect with a Trevor Brooking cross to direct the ball over the line and break Everton hearts. It was a bitter pill to swallow for Gordon Lee, who had endured the agony of losing the 1977 semi to Liverpool and the second replay of the League Cup final to Aston Villa that same year. 'The only reason Lampard was there to score was because he was too knackered to get back to his defensive position,' Gordon lamented. Both Europe and the League Cup earlier that season had also been forgettable from an Everton standpoint. Dutch club Feyenoord won 1-0 home and away in the UEFA Cup first round. After eliminating Cardiff over two legs and Aston Villa in a home replay in the League Cup, Everton went out to a shock 2-1 defeat at Third Division Grimsby Town.

In the League, a sequence of five defeats in eight games after beating Forest on New Year's Day ended when Latchford scored his 100th League goal for Everton in a 2-0 home win over Stoke - but they were to collect only two more First Division wins in their remaining nine First Division games. With four games left, bottom-club Bolton were already relegated but Bristol City and Derby were only three points behind Everton, although Derby had only two matches left to play. Lee recalled George Wood in goal in place of Martin Hodge for the home clash with Southampton on April 26 and he kept a clean sheet in a 2-0 win. Goalless draws at home to West Brom and at Brighton ensured safety, despite a last-day 1-0 defeat at Nottingham Forest. It left 19th-placed Everton four points better off than Bristol City, who were relegated with Derby and Bolton.

That lowly League placing made the 1980-81 season a crucial one for Gordon and the club. Attendances were dropping and the pressure was heightening. It didn't help matters when another high-profile player, Andy King, left in a £425,000 move to QPR and Brian Kidd joined Bolton for £150,000. Goalkeeper Jim McDonagh's £25,000 arrival from Bolton was the prelude to George Wood's £150,000 transfer to Arsenal. Gordon tried to offset King's departure by signing Peter Reid from Bolton. Everton met the £600,000 asking price, as did Arsenal, but neither club could agree personal terms with Peter. Wolves were also in for him - but they failed to meet Bolton's valuation. The upshot was that Peter stayed at Bolton for another two-and-a-half years before finally joining Everton for a tenth of the originally agreed price!

Meanwhile, in the summer of 1980, Gordon Lee was well aware that in the looming new season it was results - or bust. To his great credit he didn't hide. He accepted an invitation to meet the fans publicly at Everton Supporters' Club headquarters on City Road, close to Goodison. The press were also in attendance on a night of great heat and passionate opinions. 'With regard to the team I had two options', Gordon recalled later. 'I could either go out and buy experienced 28-year-olds or try out some youngsters and live or die by their up-and-down form. So I brought in Steve McMahon, Graeme Sharp and Kevin Ratcliffe. And behind them were other youngsters like Gary Stevens and Kevin Richardson. I might have made the wrong decision for Gordon Lee yet I think things turned out right for the club.'

Consequently, his team for the opening match of the 1980-81 season was sprinkled with youth and inexperience. Ratcliffe was included at 19 after breaking through to make three senior appearances the previous season. McMahon, a former Goodison ball boy who'd also come through the ranks, made his senior debut four days before his 19th birthday, Megson was only 21 while 19-year-old striker Sharp was making only his second senior start since Gordon paid Dumbarton £120,000 to sign him four months earlier. The team that lined up to start the 1980-81 season at Sunderland was:

Jim McDonagh; John Gidman, Billy Wright, Mick Lyons, Kevin Ratcliffe; Gary Megson, Steve McMahon (sub: Peter Eastoe), Asa Hartford, Joe McBride; Graeme Sharp, Bob Latchford.

Not surprisingly, given all the changes, Everton lost 3-1 - Eastoe scoring the goal - and it was to be the only occasion that Latchford and Sharp played together. Eastoe was recalled and it would be another season-and-a-half before Sharp became a regular. After a win over Leicester and a draw with Nottingham Forest, Everton crashed 4-0 at Ipswich, the second successive season Bobby Robson's team had scored four against them.

The response by Lee's newly-fashioned side was a blistering one - six straight League wins with a goal tally of 19 for and only two against. Latchford hit a hat-trick against Crystal Palace and a brace at Coventry next-time out, both in 5-0 wins. The run also included a 2-0 win at eventual champions Aston Villa where McMahon played splendidly and skipper Mick Lyons scored his first goal for more than a season, Eastoe heading the other. The impressive League sequence was even more welcome because of an early exit from the League Cup. After a 5-2 aggregate second-round win over Blackpool - who had my good friend and former team-mate Alan Ball in charge in his first management job - we went out 2-1 to West Brom.

By early October, Everton were third in the First Division and celebrated becoming the first club to play 3,000 First Division matches with a 3-1 win at Brighton, whose boss Alan Mullery was moved to comment: 'Two months ago Gordon Lee was thinking he was going to get the sack...now he's got an excellent team playing exceptionally well.' Alas, after the feast came the famine and Everton won only six more League games through to the end of the season. The 2-1 defeat at Norwich in November was notable because it featured Latchford's 138th and final goal for Everton. He was subsequently troubled by hamstring damage, and his only further Everton appearance was as a substitute in the last match before moving to Swansea. At the time Bob's tremendous goal total from his 289 appearances put him second only to Dixie Dean in Everton's all-time scoring chart.

The build-up to Christmas that year was clouded by the killing of John Lennon on December 8 as the Beatles star was returning with his wife Yoko Ono to their apartment near New York's Central Park. Lennon was shot in the back by crazed fan Mark Chapman, the killer saying that voices in his head told him to kill the musical icon after asking for his autograph.

In the aftermath of Lennon's death football grounds reverberated to his song 'Starting Over', which was Britain's No 1, but on the pitch Everton never got started, losing 2-0 at home to Manchester City on Boxing Day and 1-0 at Middlesbrough 24 hours later. That saw them slide to ninth but the FA Cup brought unexpected New Year cheer. Everton were paired in the third round with Arsenal, who had reached three consecutive FA Cup finals and were aiming for a record fourth Wembley appearance in a row.

Terry Neill's Goodison visitors, though, had no answer to what the press called 'Lee's young lions'. Three minutes after the break Kenny Sansom - who played briefly for Everton 12 years later - diverted a Joe McBride cross past Pat Jennings into his own net. Everton deserved their piece of good fortune. They were the better team and secured a worthy win in the 89th minute when skipper Mick Lyons made it 2-0. 'Everton could point to the burning ambition and will to win of youngsters like Wright, Ratcliffe, McBride and McMahon', the Liverpool Echo enthused, adding: 'McMahon's partnership with Asa Hartford was a sheer delight at times.'

That win set up a titanic fourth round home tie against Liverpool, who were en route to winning the European Cup for the third time. But they couldn't cope with Everton that afternoon. It was the first weekend of the short-lived period when the FA scrapped red and yellow cards because they felt they were encouraging over-use by officials...and the referee happened to be every Evertonian's favourite Welshman, Clive Thomas! As it happened, he had a good game and Everton a brilliant one. Peter Eastoe opened the scoring after 17 minutes and when Imre Varadi made it 2-0 on the hour - receiving a meat pie in the face from one Liverpool fan - our supporters were ecstatic. Jimmy Case, a replacement for the injured Kenny Dalglish, pulled a goal back 14 minutes from the end but we were not to be denied a deserved win. Nobody was more delighted than skipper Mick Lyons, celebrating his first win over Liverpool at his 20th attempt.

'At the end I didn't want to be on the pitch - I wanted to be on the terraces with the fans,' exclaimed Mick. Liverpool manager Bob Paisley, a great admirer of Gordon Lee, took his side's defeat graciously. 'In all my years at Liverpool I have never known an Everton team that has been stronger than us, but in the first half they were stronger', he admitted. 'I hope now that Everton go on and win the Cup.'

The fifth-round draw sent Everton to Southampton in mid-February, the day before the first Football League game to be staged on a Sunday took place at Feethams where Fourth Division Darlington drew 2-2 with Mansfield Town watched by a crowd of 5,932 - three times their usual home attendance. The League gave the go-ahead for soccer on the sabbath because of the country's power crisis and three-day week, although the FA refused Cup ties to be played on Sundays. To comply with the law, admission for League games on a Sunday involved the sale of a single-sheet programme at the same price as normal admission, together with a complimentary admission ticket. Once inside, fans could buy the regular match programme!

Everton's trip to The Dell was strictly a tough Saturday away day against opponents lying fourth in the First Division and including in their ranks Kevin Keegan, signed the previous summer from Hamburg. But the visitors emerged with a goalless draw and in the Goodison replay the following Tuesday almost 50,000 fans, virtually twice the average League attendance, packed in and caused crushing problems on the terraces. Again, the 90 minutes remained goalless and the battle plunged into extra time. The clock had ticked into the 103rd minute when Eamonn O'Keefe broke the deadlock with the only goal of the tie and one that repaid at a stroke his meagre transfer fee from Mossley.

Everton's triumph over the Saints brought Manchester City marching into Goodison in the quarter-final. This time club secretary (and later chief executive) Jim Greenwood immediately declared the tie all-ticket and Goodison bulged with a capacity crowd of almost 53,000 on a rainy March day. City, floundering near the bottom of the First Division the previous autumn, which led to manager Malcolm Allison's sacking and John Bond's arrival, had climbed the table and had the better of the first half when they found themselves trailing two minutes before the break. Imre Varadi, having an extended run up front after Latchford's injury, crossed and Peter Eastoe beat Joe Corrigan. Yet City snapped back in the dying seconds of the half when Gerry Gow punished sloppy defensive play by grabbing an equaliser.

Everton were swiftly out of the blocks after the interval and within four minutes had regained the lead. Varadi was brought down, referee Peter Willis pointed to the spot and Trevor Ross stepped up to take it. Home fans were biting their nails, recalling the events of a week earlier at Crystal Palace when there was the rare event of Everton failing to score from two in-play penalties within a span of 12 minutes, Ross having one saved by Paul Barron and Steve McMahon sending another wide. This time, though, Ross's aim was true and Everton were back in front. That scoreline remained - thanks to a glaring Varadi miss and Corrigan's brilliant save from O'Keefe - until the 84th minute when Paul Power, later to join Everton, lobbed the ball into a goal vacated by the out-rushing Jim McDonagh.

In the dying stages Kevin Ratcliffe was sent off for butting Tommy Hutchison and the Goodison Cup dream was dismissed, too, the following Wednesday when City romped to a 3-1 victory in the Maine Road replay, Bobby McDonald scoring twice and Power again on target. Everton's reply was an irrelevant 89th minute Eastoe strike and as City marched on to Wembley - where they lost to Ricardo Villa-inspired Tottenham - our season fell apart. Five straight League defeats, in which we scored only one goal, followed the Cup exit. Overall, of our 12 remaining matches after our Cup defeat we won just one, ironically a 4-1 win over Middlesbrough that drew a meagre crowd of 15,706.

Graeme Sharp was promoted to the bench for the Middlesbrough game and had another taste of senior football as a 23rd-minute substitute for Gary Stanley on a day when Asa Hartford scored twice, his second from a penalty awarded after Sharp had been tripped. But 48 hours later Everton slumped to another 3-1 defeat at Manchester City, followed by a 1-0 home reverse against Stoke, when the match-winner was a certain Adrian Heath. The game drew an even lower attendance than the Middlesbrough match of 15,352 - at the time the club's lowest for a top-flight League game post war. It left Everton only two points ahead of third-from-bottom Wolves but a dour 1-1 draw at Birmingham ensured First Division survival. The goal, his 19th of the season, came from the much under-rated Eastoe.

Everton completed their programme with a goalless Molineux draw against Wolves, who also just beat the drop. The two clubs, though, were to tread very different paths in the years ahead. Although Everton finished 15th - four places better than the previous season - in points they were closer to relegation, just three ahead of third-from-bottom Norwich. And in 11 of the last 20 League games they'd failed to score. The club's average League attendance had slumped to 26,105 - the lowest post war - and clearly, the situation was intolerable for Everton. Two days after the final match at Wolves the club announced Gordon Lee's departure.

He took his dismissal as you'd expect him to - with dignity and honesty. 'I respect the decision of the directors', said Gordon. 'Our performances have not been good enough and the Everton fans deserve a successful team. I have done my best and I hope that some of the decisions I have taken will prove of benefit to this club in the years to come. I wish Everton well.'

That future was to be a switchback ride culminating in a fantastic voyage. My re-union with Howard Kendall was to prove unforgettable.''

At Goodison after receiving the Liverpool Echo's Dixie Dean Memorial Trophy for my contribution to Everton, summer 1984. From left to right: John Bailey, me, Howard and Adrian Heath.

Chapter Ten

Howard's Way

As the summer of 1981 beckoned, Everton chairman Philip Carter and his directors took a decision that was ground-breaking in the history not only of the club, but of English football itself. The sacking of Gordon Lee was unsurprising and expected. During four years and three months in charge Lee had come close to satisfying the club's yearning for a trophy, only to find fate kicking him in the face. Everton's move, though, to appoint one of the supporters' favourite sons as his successor was to prove, after anguish and angst en route, to be inspired as the club soared back to the glittering uplands of achievement. Under Howard Kendall they would reach unexplored horizons and experience unprecedented success domestically and in Europe, rising to challenge the national supremacy of Liverpool, the club across the road who were frequently conquering the Continentals.

Two days after Everton's final match of the 1980-81 season, in which they finished 15th, Lee was dismissed. "There was no recrimination from Gordon," recalled Everton secretary and, later, chief executive Jim Greenwood. "He just loved the club and felt it had been a privilege to be manager. Of course, he was disappointed but he accepted the club's decision with dignity. He never showed a hint of bitterness and through all the ensuing years he has continued to have great affection for Everton. He has always held up as a yardstick the way the Everton board of that period treated him." Forty-eight hours after Lee's departure, on May 8, the Kendall management era was ushered in, the former midfielder taking over on a four-year contract at the age of 34. That made him the youngest manager ever in the top flight of English football, a record that stood until Chris Coleman took charge of Fulham in May 2003, a month before his 33rd birthday.

The Everton hierarchy had been impressed with Kendall's record in coaching and management after he had continued his playing career with

Birmingham City - whom he captained - and Stoke City following his departure from Everton as part of the Bob Latchford deal in 1974. He was made player-coach of Stoke in February 1978 and the Potteries club returned to the old First Division in 1979, after which he was appointed player-manager of Blackburn and proceeded to do an outstanding job. In two seasons he guided them from the old Third Division, into the Second and missed out on promotion to the top flight only on goal difference.

Despite the managerial inexperience of Kendall - born at Ryton on Tyne on May 22, 1946, the same day that George Best was also entering the world in Belfast - he had done enough to win the call from impresssed Everton directors and the still highly influential Sir John Moores, whose word and financial muscle continued to carry massive clout. "There's been a lot of speculation about who would be our new manager, but Howard was our first choice and we're delighted to appoint him", chairman Carter declared. "He's always been an Everton man at heart." Just 19 days after Kendall's unveiling as manager Liverpool beat Real Madrid to add the European Cup to the already won League Cup. It spectacularly underlined the task facing the new manager of a club struggling in the shadow of Bob Paisley's record-breaking achievers across the green oasis of Stanley Park.

Kendall, though, was ready for what many saw as a daunting task. "It's a tremendous challenge when you look at our position", he said in a statement that brooked no argument. "However, it's one that I'm going to enjoy. I'm well aware that if you bring success to Everton there's no place like it and I feel greatly honoured to be offered the job. I've got a tinge of regret at leaving Blackburn but the pull of Everton was just too great. We're geared to win things and that's what we aim to do. Nothing has happened here, in terms of trophies, since 1970 and it will take a bit of time to put things right." How prophetic his words were to prove. Even before Kendall had got his feet under the desk his former manager Harry Catterick, who had signed him from Preston North End in March 1967, was demanding patience from the supporters. "I can only plead with the fans - for God's sake be patient and give the lad time", Catterick urged. "Howard's still learning and I know he can do a great job but he's going to need a lot of support and sympathy."

For Kendall, organising his staff and building his squad for the new season was top priority. Coach Eric Harrison and Geoff Nulty, who had joined the backroom team to assist Lee after his career-ending injury, were dismissed. Kendall went back to his former club Blackburn to appoint his Ewood Park coach Mick Heaton as his right-hand man. At 34 Heaton was the same age as Kendall and it meant that Everton's fortunes were in the hands of the top flight's youngest management duo.

Despite Kendall's knowledge and love of Everton built during his playing days at Goodison, Heaton - who died tragically after a road accident aged 48 in 1995 - recalled how the new manager was given an unscheduled reminder that on Merseyside colours can be very emotive. "On my first day in the job at Everton we went for a pub snack", said Heaton. "Howard was wearing a red shirt and suddenly this woman came over to us, yanked the shirt over his head and tossed it aside! The barmaid reminded him that Evertonians don't wear red, especially a new Everton manager! It was also a quick lesson for me in how seriously they take their football on Merseyside."

The man recorded as Kendall's first signing was Alan Irvine, an insurance broker playing as a winger for Scottish amateur club Queens Park, although his arrival straddled the eras of Lee and Kendall. "I had a choice of 23 clubs, including the Old Firm, Dundee United, Aberdeen, Manchester City, Leeds United and Sunderland among them - but Everton was the only one for me", recalled Irvine. "They tried to sign me the previous October but Queens Park wouldn't let me go. Gordon Lee tried to offer them money, strips, friendly matches, but they stood firm for months until finally agreeing to let me go. Although Gordon did the deal it turned out that I was Howard's first signing." Some 21 years later, long after hanging up his boots, Irvine would be brought back to Everton by another Everton manager, David Moyes, when he was appointed his assistant in March 2002.

Back in May 1981 Irvine hardly had time to pack his boots before jetting off with Everton to the Far East in the party for the end-of-season Japan Cup tournament. The squad, originally named by Lee, was rubber stamped by Kendall with the addition of Irvine and the new manager himself. Kendall's decision to retain his playing registration would have a spin-off during his first season. Apart from those ruled out by injury or international duty Gary Megson was the only omission from the players who had appeared for the first team late in the season, with Imre Varadi included after a proposed move to Benfica collapsed. On-loan goalkeeper John Turner from Chesterfield supplemented the party as cover for Jim McDonagh, who travelled directly to Japan after a tour with the Republic of Ireland. The squad was:

Goalkeepers: Jim McDonagh, John Turner.

Full-backs: John Gidman, John Barton, John Bailey.

Centre-backs: Billy Wright, Mick Lyons, Gary Stanley.

Midfielders: Trevor Ross, Howard Kendall, Asa Hartford, Paul Lodge, Eamonn O'Keefe.

Forwards: Graeme Sharp, Alan Irvine, Joe McBride, Peter Eastoe, Imre Varadi.

Kendall's first match in charge ended in a 2-2 draw with Japan in Tokyo on May 31, McBride and Eastoe the scorers, in front of a 25,000 crowd. Everton proceeded to defeat China 1-0 at Hiroshima through an O'Keefe strike - Kendall making an appearance as second-half substitute for Stanley - before losing 4-1 to Inter Milan at Nagoya in the tournament semi-final, Ross scoring the Everton goal.

For Colin Harvey the arrival of Kendall was a new landmark in a football career that five years earlier he feared was over as he began learning the licensed trade at his uncle's pub at Northwich while his wife Maureen and young children were still in Sheffield. His long-time friend and former team-mate confirmed 36-year-old Harvey as reserve-team coach. Kendall's backroom team was completed by the continuation of Graham Smith as youth coach, Ray Minshull as youth development officer, Harry Cooke as chief scout and John Clinkard as physiotherapist.

The summer of 1981 saw the nation thrilled by Ian Botham's heroics against the Aussies to inspire England's Ashes triumph and get itself all dressed up to celebrate the wedding of Prince Charles and Lady Diana Spencer. Everton fans had their own reasons to stir thanks to Kendall's spectacular sorties into the transfer market. A £750,000 bid for Bryan Robson from West Brom was rejected by Ron Atkinson who was then in his final weeks as Hawthorns boss before taking over at Manchester United.

He would soon do business with Kendall as part of the new Everton manager's seven-man transfer splurge for goalkeepers Jim Arnold (£175,000 from Blackburn) and Neville Southall (£150,000 from Bury), defender Mike Walsh (£90,000 from Bolton plus goalkeeper Jim McDonagh), winger Mickey Thomas (£450,000 exchange deal, with John Gidman joining Manchester United), strikers Mick Ferguson (£280,000 from Coventry City) and Alan Biley (£300,000 from Derby County) and midfielder Alan Ainscow (£250,000 from Birmingham). The newcomers were labelled 'The Magnificent Seven', a media tag which proved to be a gross exaggeration.

Mickey Thomas hardly had time to get used to his dressing room peg. After appearing in the opening 11 games of the season, he went out of the team injured in October. When Kendall pencilled in Thomas for a comeback game in the reserves at Newcastle he refused to play and demanded a first-team place against Manchester City. Kendall cracked the whip, slapped Thomas on the transfer list and within days sold him to Brighton for £400,000. "It was my first big test as Everton manager", said Kendall. "I had to stand firm. I had to show all the players that there wasn't one rule for one and a different one for others." One of Kendall's early signings, however, would become a legend, a giant of the club's history, and in the view of many, rank in the top three Everton players of all time alongside Dixie Dean and Alan Ball. For Neville Southall, though, it would not be a smooth path to greatness and at one stage he came within 90 minutes of being sent through the Goodison exit.

Another Everton luminary, Bob Latchford, joined Gidman and McDonagh as the first departures of Kendall's reign. There was a certain symmetry about Latchford's farewell, because it had been his arrival seven years earlier that took Kendall to Birmingham. The big centre-forward - who scored 138 goals in 289 Everton senior appearances - moved to Swansea for £125,000 in July 1981 to become one of manager John Toshack's burgeoning group of Merseyside 'exiles' at a club that had risen from Fourth to First Division in just four seasons. They included Dai Davies, Neil Robinson and former Liverpool players Max Thompson and Colin Irwin and would be joined early in Kendall's first season by Gary Stanley, who left Goodison in a £150,000 move to South Wales. Asa Hartford (£350,000 to Manchester City) was another departure early in Kendall's first season in charge which began with the famous 'hole in the heart' Scotland midfielder failing twice from the penalty spot in the curtain-raising game against Birmingham. Goalkeeper Jeff Wealands, penalised for moving too early to stop Hartford's first effort from 12 yards, saved his second attempt. Kendall's first line-up, with a club record-equalling five debutants, was:

Jim Arnold (d); Billy Wright, Mick Lyons, Mick Walsh (d), John Bailey; Mickey Thomas (d), Asa Hartford, Trevor Ross; Alan Ainscow (d), Alan Biley (d), Peter Eastoe. Unused substitute: Mick Ferguson.

It was a season which saw some major innovations in English football. One of them, sponsorship for a domestic competition inaugurated by the Milk Marketing Board's backing for the League Cup, would become a permanent feature of the national game. Another, the arrival of the plastic pitch at Queens Park Rangers' Loftus Road ground, would fail to stand the test of time. Although Luton Town, Oldham Athletic and Preston all followed by laying artificial surfaces, they not only proved unpopular but were banned by UEFA for their own competitions.

Another introduction for the 1981-82 campaign was the launch of three-points-for-a-win in English football - and on August 29 Everton duly secured their first three under Kendall, despite Hartford's double penalty failure. The Everton team received a standing ovation as they took to the pitch and the applause reached a crescendo when Kendall, now in charge of one of his former clubs against another, led his players out of the tunnel. A lost son of Goodison had returned. Yet an opening day crowd of little more than 33,000 was a sign of the times. Over the course of the campaign the club's average attendance dropped a further 2,000 to 24,673, with only four matches pulling in 30,000 or more. Those who turned out for the start of the Kendall era had plenty to cheer even though the game was only four minutes old when Toine Van Mierlo headed Birmingham into the lead. But Everton were soon level, Biley supplying the pass for Ainscow to score a debut goal against his former club. Hartford's profligacy from the penalty spot ensured a 1-1 interval scoreline but Eastoe's diving header early in the second half put Everton ahead. The outcome was settled two minutes from time when Hartford found Rod Stewart look-alike Biley to lob home.

Winning, though, was not a habit that came easily to Kendall's new-look team and their next four games brought 1-1 draws at Leeds and home to Brighton and defeats at Southampton (0-1) and Tottenham (0-3). Successive wins over Notts County and West Brom followed although events on the field were sadly overshadowed by the death of Bill Shankly. The charismatic Scot, who had become a great iconic figure of British football and a man beloved by Liverpool supporters, died at Liverpool's Broadgreen Hospital in the early hours of September 29, following a second heart attack. Football followers of all allegiances mourned the passing of a man who left an enduring, indelible impact on the game he adored. Sir John Moores, whose massive sphere of influence and involvement with Merseyside football included a large shareholding at Anfield, said of Shankly: "He MADE Liverpool FC. Before he became manager they were a very ordinary club. With Shankly in charge they became a great club, winning almost everything worth winning."

The rest of Kendall's first season was one of undulating fortunes for Everton. They climbed as high as fifth and fell to a low of 19th before ending the campaign with five wins and a draw from their final six games to finish eighth. Ironically, had the two points for a win system still operated instead of the newly-installed three points reward, Everton would have finished one place higher and qualified for the UEFA Cup.

The season saw an unfolding and contrasting tale of two strikers, Mick Ferguson and Graeme Sharp. Ferguson arrived from Coventry City having scored 51 goals in 127 League games and two years earlier was set to join Nottingham Forest for £800,000 before the deal fell through. "We needed to sign a big centre-forward to replace Bob Latchford and if you want a big man I rate Mick the best in the business," Kendall enthused. Sadly, injuries took their toll on Ferguson who made just 12 Everton first-team appearances, which brought him six goals. His first start did not come until October's League Cup clash with his former club Coventry when the bearded Newcastle-born striker scored with a diving header in the 1-1 first-leg draw. It was the start of a blistering spell of six goals in seven games, including the winner in the return leg at Coventry, a brace in the League win at Middlesbrough and another in a 3-1 Mersey derby defeat at Anfield.

But hamstring damage struck again and with Ferguson's big frame making great demands on his small feet he was also constantly troubled by ankle problems. It meant he started only two more First Division games in Everton colours before moving to Birmingham for £60,000 the following summer, following a loan period at St Andrews.

While Ferguson was passing through Goodison, Sharp was lighting the touch paper to a career that exploded with achievement. His strike in the 2-2 draw at Notts County in November was the start of a scorching sequence for the young Scot, which brought him 15 goals in 29 appearances. Sharp's strike against United in a 3-3 home thriller in April left Liverpool Daily Post reporter Ian Ross observing: 'Sharp's reputation as trainee thoroughbred centre- forward is obviously spreading. It appeared at times as if someone had put out a contract on the boisterous Scot. On this occasion the man given the thankless task of pulling the trigger was United centre-half Kevin Moran who harried, pushed and fouled his way through a torrid 90-minute confrontation with the youngster.'

Sharp was clearly going to play a big part in Everton's future as was another Kendall signing, Adrian Heath, who cost a club record £750,000 from Stoke City in January 1982, shortly before his 21st birthday. Heath had played alongside Kendall for the Potteries club - and just missed out on doing so for Everton. Between November and January, Kendall made six appearances in his team as the only player-manager in Everton history. Former Goodison ball boy Steve McMahon's 36 appearances was the most by any of the 27 players used by Kendall that season and he enjoyed a further 42 first-team appearances the following year prior to a £300,000 move to Aston Villa in May 1983. McMahon's subsequent £350,000 transfer to Liverpool saw him earn a unique place in the record books as the only man to play in the same team as the only two player-managers of Merseyside's big two clubs - Kendall and Liverpool's Kenny Dalglish.

Although Kendall's first campaign had been in the shadow of Liverpool's championship and League Cup double, it had been encouraging with Southall making his top-flight debut, teenagers Gary Stevens and Kevin Richardson emerging, Kevin Ratcliffe having 27 outings at left-back and the return of Mark Higgins after a triple left foot fracture the previous year. But it was farewell to long-serving Mick Lyons, who moved to Sheffield Wednesday. As if to underline his adaptability through an Everton career that brought him the captaincy, spanning 14 years, 462 appearances and 59 goals, the striker turned defender saw his last Goodison action for the club in goal! After scoring in the draw with Manchester United on Easter Saturday he donned the keeper's jersey in the final moments of the match after Southall had gone off injured.

Just five days earlier a British task force set sail for the Falklands after Argentina's invasion of the British islands. It precipitated a conflict that would last until the Argentinian surrender in mid-June at a cost of 255 British and 652 Argentinian lives. Britain's patriotic fervour was stoked by Aston Villa's surprise conquest of Bayern Munich to win the European Cup, thanks to the game's only goal from Liverpool-born Peter Withe. The England national side, though, came to grief in Spain after reaching their first World Cup finals since 1970, despite a shock qualifying defeat in Norway. Ron Greenwood's side went out at the second group stage even though they were unbeaten in five tournament games. Ultimate triumph went to Italy who beat West Germany 3-1 in the final.

Kendall's summer was a busy one. He stirred Merseyside emotions by taking advantage of the expiry of Kevin Sheedy's Anfield contract by signing the midfielder for £100,000. Liverpool had placed a £200,000 valuation on Sheedy and angrily rejected a £60,000 Everton offer for the 22-year-old, who cost £80,000 from Hereford. "There was no way I was going to stay at Liverpool," said Sheedy, who had already won Republic of Ireland Under 21 recognition but had started only three games for the Anfield club. Bob Paisley was fuming. "Howard Kendall made a dangerous statement midway through the season when he asked players whose contracts were due to expire to write to him", rapped the Liverpool manager, adding: "In time he might discover this can work two ways."

Although Liverpool initially sent the matter for a tribunal to fix the fee, the clubs agreed on the £100,000 compromise just 24 hours before the scheduled hearing. Sheedy's prospects at Liverpool were hampered by the development of his Republic of Ireland colleague Ronnie Whelan while at Goodison his career swiftly took wing. He was an instant success at Everton, appearing in 48 of the 51 League and Cup games in his first season, scoring 13 goals. Both club secretaries, Jim Greenwood and Peter Robinson, voiced their satisfaction that the Sheedy case had been settled amicably between Merseyside's great rivals, who had a common concern over their finances. Everton's balance sheet published in August 1982 revealed that they lost almost £100,000 on the previous season. Chairman Philip Carter reported a loss of £443,000 on the main football activities, a deficit reduced by development funds and income from other off-field activities. Liverpool, despite lifting the European Cup, the League Cup and League championship in the previous financial year, showed a loss of £150,000 although had a credit at the bank of £355,000 with substantial amounts owing. Their top earner was paid more than £70,000 and six others received more than £50,000. Everton's top earner was paid between £35,000 and £40,000.

Sheedy's move was the first transfer from Liverpool to Everton since Johnny Morrissey senior 20 years earlier and was swiftly followed by another when Kendall paid a further £100,000 to bring England striker David Johnson back to the club where he had launched his career. Also returning was Andy King, signed from West Brom in a straight swap for Peter Eastoe after pleading with Kendall for a second spell at the club he had left for QPR in September 1980. Another summer capture who, like Sheedy, would form a crucial part of Kendall's team jigsaw, arrived from Tranmere for £30,000. Derek Mountfield was only 19 when he crossed the river but he would become a key pillar of the most successful side in Everton history. Following the departures of Eamonn O'Keefe to Wigan the previous January and John Barton to Derby County in March, Kendall sold Alan Biley to Portsmouth for £100,000 and Joe McBride to Rotherham United for £50,000 in August.

New signings Sheedy, Johnson and King figured in a 2-0 defeat at Watford on the opening day of the 1982-83 season. The Everton team was:

Neville Southall; Brian Borrows, Mark Higgins, Billy Wright (captain), John

Bailey; Steve McMahon (Kevin Richardson), Andy King, Kevin Sheedy; Adrian Heath, David Johnson, Graeme Sharp.

Three days later at Goodison Everton rose magnificently to the challenge of European champions Aston Villa with an emphatic 5-0 win on a night when attendance concerns were starkly underlined. Only 24,000 spectators turned up to witness Everton's biggest opening home game victory for 61 years. A brace apiece from Heath and Sharp and a goal from King earned a standing ovation from the small crowd and ensured it was the first time since he became manager that Kendall had seen his side score more than three in a match. It was to prove a season similar to Kendall's first both in its inconsistency and in its seventh place finishing position - one higher than the previous campaign. But if the display against Villa and two more five-goal performances against Luton Town home and away were thrilling highs, there was no doubt about the low. It came on Saturday, November 6.

Four days earlier, television's brand new Channel 4 had broadcast the first episode of the Mersey soap opera Brookside, which was to run for 21 years. Goodison had its own compelling local drama when Liverpool arrived for the 127th League derby. Fortunately for Everton it lasted only 90 minutes. Before kick off the all-time scoreboard read: Everton 44 wins, Liverpool 44 wins, draws 38. When referee Derek Civil blew the final whistle to end one of Everton's most miserable afternoons, Liverpool were in front on the overall tally for the first time since the series began in 1894. Everton 0 Liverpool 5 was the day's scoreline and that, frankly, flattered the home side which had 28-year-old Glenn Keeley, on loan from Kendall's former club Blackburn, drafted in for his debut in place of Mark Higgins, who was dropped after a 3-2 defeat at Southampton. Keeley, who was in dispute with Blackburn, had not played League football since May and had last tasted First Division combat more than five years earlier. Sadly for him and Everton his re-introduction would last a mere 32 minutes. By then, boyhood Everton fan Ian Rush had put the visiting leaders ahead from Alan Hansen's sweeping run and pass while referee Civil bemused many observers with an offside verdict to disallow Kenny Dalglish's superb headed strike.

Then came the moment of agony for Keeley when he earned himself an unwanted place in the record books as one of the first victims of FIFA's new hard-line directive on so-called professional fouls. "Hansen played the ball through and it bounced awkwardly to give Kenny an advantage", said Keeley. "I knew I had to stop him and I grabbed his shirt, although I honestly expected just to be booked. When I was sent off I went straight to the dressing room and just sat on the bath in a state of shock. I only saw the last 10 minutes of that match and I can't remember a single thing."

Most Evertonians wished they had seen as little of the painful proceedings in which Rush added three second-half goals to his earlier strike - his first goals in eight games - to become the first player since 1935 to score four in a derby. Rush's feast against his fellow Welshman Neville Southall and Mark Lawrenson's goal nine minutes after the interval ensured it was the biggest derby win for 16 years and equalled the highest away victory in derby history. Everton, who were 11th in the table, went into the match with an undefeated home record spanning eight months - since Liverpool's last visit the previous March. Realities, though, were laid bare by this emphatic defeat in which Everton managed just one shot on target from six attempts, contrasting with 15 in 25 by Paisley's champions.

Keeley never appeared for Everton again although Alan Hansen insisted: "I don't think his sending off really had any affect on the result. On that performance I don't think any side would have lived with us." It was difficult to quibble with that assessment and, to his credit, a bitterly disapppointed Kendall didn't try. "We have players who are not capable of doing what is demanded at Everton", he admitted. "We will have to look at the problem and make a decision." Kendall's response was to make five changes for the home League Cup clash with Arsenal three days later. Higgins returned in place of Keeley, Jim Arnold was recalled in goal for Southall, Gary Stevens replaced Brian Borrows at right-back and Kevin Ratcliffe took over at left-back from John Bailey. Borrows never appeared for Everton again, moving on to Bolton for £10,000 the following March and later joining Coventry. The withdrawal of Southall, to give him a rest and time to recover from a toe injury before being loaned to Port Vale the following January, was to prove the making of the Welshman. He returned from the Potteries more confident and authoritative and was back in the side for the last four games of the season.

Gary Stevens, who scored in the 1-1 draw against Arsenal on his recall after the derby match calamity, believes that some good came out of Everton's massive defeat. "Many people have talked about the League Cup replay at Oxford the following season as the game which got the ball rolling for us", he said. "I think that moment came when Liverpool whipped us 5-0. A lot of the players who went on to be a part of the side which won the title were in the stand with me on that embarrassing day. It was hard to take but Howard thought long and hard about what to do, made a batch of changes and began to find the right balance. We built on that defeat and the Oxford result was a sign of the work that had been done in the months before."

The transformation, though, was long and painful. Everton lost 3-0 in the League Cup replay at Highbury and went down to a 2-0 defeat at West Ham in their next outing prior to a goalless home draw with Birmingham in early December, watched by a crowd of only 13,703. At the time it was Merseyside's smallest post-war top-flight attendance although this was lowered again late in the season when the 1-0 home win over Coventry attracted only 12,972. The Birmingham game in early December, in which Terry Curran made his debut on loan from Sheffield United, proved to be a watershed for two players and for Everton in general. Ratcliffe was dropped for Bailey to return at left-back and immediately asked for a move. However, events changed his fortunes almost instantly.

Kendall dropped skipper Billy Wright for being overweight, inspiring newspaper headlines which labelled the England 'B' and Under 21 defender as 'Billy Bunter'. Wright never played for Everton again - joining Birmingham on a free transfer the following June - and Ratcliffe came straight back in at Ipswich. Highly significantly, though, Ratcliffe returned at centre-back alongside Mark Higgins and the new partnership proved the bedrock of a 2-0 win for Everton. Ratcliffe became an outstanding player for Everton and Wales after landing his preferred role although, strangely, his transfer request was never rescinded. It was left forgotten, gathering dust in a drawer, while he and Everton marched on to glory.

Later that month, Kendall put in place another building block in his construction of an Everton team that was to lead the club to new heights when he paid Bolton £60,000 for Peter Reid. It was a tenth of the fee Kendall's predecessor Gordon Lee had been ready to pay for the midfielder two-and-a-half years earlier yet one that still needed the club to change banks to gain overdraft facilities to finance the deal.

"Many people will have no idea about the seriousness of the club's financial situation at that time", said former Goodison chief executive Jim Greenwood. "We'd had winger Terry Curran on loan from Sheffield United in December but when Howard wanted to sign him permanently we couldn't even raise the £100,000 required. We even considered selling our Bellefield training ground to raise cash. By the time of the March transfer deadline Howard still wanted to sign Curran, who'd enjoyed a good loan spell with us and had lifted the supporters. We managed to sort something out financially and Howard met Curran on the steps of Football League headquarters at Lytham just half-an-hour before the deadline. As far as we were aware everything had been agreed but suddenly there were obstacles. The lad was looking for something else linked to his personal terms and the proposed deal collapsed. You can imagine Howard's anger at missing out on a player he wanted right on the League's own doorstep! He was fuming. Eventually, though, he did sign him to make Everton one of Curran's 14 clubs."

Curran's £90,000 full transfer went through the following September but, ironically, he never repeated the form he had shown on loan. After a total of 28 Everton appearances and a single goal he moved on to Huddersfield after his contract expired in May 1985. For Peter Reid, however, a second chance to join Everton was irresistible. "When Howard came in to sign me I had no hesitation. I'd also spoken to Jack Charlton at Sheffield Wednesday but when Howard came in I just said: 'Give me the forms to sign'." Reid, who had joined Bolton as a 15-year-old after starring for Huyton Boys, was haunted by injury at Burnden Park and in moving to Everton he was joining the club his mother supported in a typical Merseyside family of split allegiances.

"My dad was a Liverpool fan and I followed him when I was a boy", said Reid. "In those days I used to admire Tommy Smith and I was made up to link up with Roger Hunt at Bolton. But Alan Ball at Everton also made a big impression on me as a youngster. My mother was the most intelligent member of the family and she was an Evertonian - so there was no problem about me going to Goodison! Another injury, though, set me back again and I didn't really get going until the following season." Reid was restricted to 10 senior appearances during the remainder of his first Goodison season in which Merseyside mourned the passing of pop legend Billy Fury, who died at the age of 42 on January 28, 1983. One of Billy's biggest hits was 'Halfway To Paradise' and although Kendall and his team were hardly in that heady state, they did restore some shattered pride at Anfield.

With Mark Higgins their fifth captain in a campaign which also saw Wright, Johnson, Heath and McMahon skipper the side, Everton gained some consolation for their drubbing by Liverpool. Without new signing Reid, they battled hard in the March return and prised a goalless draw in what was Bob Paisley's last Mersey derby before his retirement as Liverpool manager. Jim Arnold was one of Everton's heroes who played on despite being laid out concusssed in his goalmouth in the second half. His brave dive at Craig

Johnston's feet left Arnold seeing stars after receiving an accidental kick in the mouth. Although clearly groggy, Arnold insisted on continuing and added to his earlier saves to help his side to an impressive clean sheet and a point against their rivals, who ended Paisley's amazing 19-trophy nine-year reign with a championship and Milk Cup double.

Everton clinched the title for their neighbours when Heath and Sharp gave them a 2-0 Goodison win over Manchester United. It seems unbelievable in this Premiership era to reflect that the attendance for United's visit was a meagre 21,707 - and that was one of Everton's biggest gates that season. The city of Liverpool's almost 18 per cent unemployment rate was biting savagely at attendances. A golden era of Goodison success and bumper crowds was not far over the horizon although the opening five months of the 1983-84 campaign offered firm proof that it is darkest just before dawn.

Kendall's summer activities brought in another arrival who was to prove a key figure in Everton's resurgence although at the time the fans were baffled and critical. Through the Goodison exit went Steve McMahon. Although Kendall wanted him to stay, the cash-strapped club's failure to agree new contract terms with McMahon preceded his move to Aston Villa. McMahon's decision to reject a switch to Liverpool, where Joe Fagan had succeeded Paisley as manager, proved only temporary. Two years later he signed for another Liverpool boss, Kenny Dalglish, in a £350,000 deal.

Kendall put the income from McMahon's sale into a £300,000 swoop for Burnley's teenage midfielder Trevor Steven and Billy Wright's departure on a free to Birmingham was followed by another Kendall raid across Stanley Park. This time, in his third capture from Anfield in a year, he made the surprise signing of Alan Harper, a 22-year-old who had been at Liverpool for seven years. A reserve-team regular, he had won four Central League title medals without a sniff of first-team football. Unlike the Sheedy deal, which was bound for a tribunal until an eleventh-hour agreement, this one did go all the way to arbitration. Everton offered £10,000, Liverpool wanted £100,000 and the tribunal set a fee of £60,000 based on appearances.

Harper was to prove an inspired acquisition. Although never a star in the Goodison firmament he played a key, selfless role in Kendall's squad. He was a fetcher and carrier, the type of player that was, according to title expert Bob Paisley, crucial in a championship side. "You've always got to have one player in your side who's ready to carry someone else's suitcase to the station," Paisley once colourfully observed. Versatile Harper fulfilled that yardstick superbly in a five-year Goodison career. He left Liverpool as a defender but in 240 Everton appearances, in which he wore eight different numbered shirts, he played in every department of the side except goalkeeper. Harper and Steven made their senior Everton debuts together in the team that launched the 1983-84 season with a 1-0 home win over Stoke City. Kendall's line-up was:

Arnold; Harper, Higgins (captain), Mountfield, Bailey; Richardson, King, Sheedy; Steven, Heath, Sharp. Unused substitute: Johnson.

The game's only goal came from Sharp seven minutes before the interval in a match that drew Goodison's lowest opening-day attendance on record - 22,658 - as the era of live televised football began. Tottenham Hotspur v Nottingham Forest in October was the first live League match transmission. Football's television revolution had begun and with it the debate over live TV's affect on match attendances. Many pundits predicted catastrophe. If only they could have envisaged the situation less than two decades later with live matches beamed into people's living rooms like wall-to-wall carpet and yet with the Premiership turnstiles still clicking.

Everton's opening-day win was their only one in their first five games of the season. A 1-1 home deadlock with Birmingham had been sandwiched between away wins at Tottenham and Notts County with Reid scoring in both matches for his first Everton goals. The trip to Meadow Lane also saw a return in goal for Neville Southall after four clean sheets in the Central League. Jim Arnold, the man he displaced, never made another first-team appearance and joined Port Vale in August 1985.

Everton opened their Milk Cup campaign against lowly Chesterfield at Saltergate and emerged with a 1-0 first-leg win, thanks to a Sharp goal and some impressive goalkeeping from Southall. But before the return Everton crashed 1-0 at home to Luton, leaving them 15th, and the public pressure on Kendall was growing. On behalf of the Daily Express I contacted chairman Philip Carter for his response to the speculation about the manager's future.

The outcome proved to be pivotal in Kendall's career and Everton history. In an unprecedented move, Carter agreed to issue a personal statement in which he answered the big questions and, most significantly, offered total backing to Kendall. The statement said: "The rumours, accusations and criticisms currently circulating about Everton Football Club demand an answer. That is why I am taking the opportunity of this platform to present our case factually and honestly to try to correct some of the misconceptions. Broadly, the areas of concern - to us as well as our supporters I must stress -

cover home performances and attendances, finance and transfers. The first point I want to underline heavily is that we are not in any way complacent about our present problems. Indeed, we are most concerned.

But let me state unequivocally at the outset that our manager, Howard Kendall, has the fullest and absolute support of the board. He is a little more than halfway through a four-year contract with us and the board have not, and are not exerting any pressure on him whatsoever. If there is pressure on Howard it is self-induced because he is a professional and, like all good professionals, wants the team to do well. And we are right behind him.

There has been some misinformed comment recently that we are not in a position to support him in the transfer market - yet the facts are hardly mentioned. In the course of just a few months since the end of last season we have spent £500,000 on signing Trevor Steven from Burnley, Alan Harper from Liverpool and Terry Curran from Sheffield United. Before that, we paid £700,000 for Adrian Heath from Stoke. It is true that we did make an attempt to sign Charlie Nicholas but, then, most other clubs also decided that the price was either too high or financially out of reach.

Howard Kendall is constantly searching for new talent but he has to be satisfied that it would be right for Everton. If he does find a player he considers to be the right type he knows he can put the matter to the board and we will consider it. But suggestions that we have imposed some kind of ban on buying players are absolute nonsense.

As regards Goodison Park attendances and performances I think the two are inter-linked...and the figures tell a strange story. Compared with the attendances for our first five home games last season we are 25 per cent down. Yet we are more than 15 per cent up on last season's fixtures with the same clubs, Stoke, West Ham, West Brom, Birmingham and Luton.

On the field there has been almost a complete reversal of our early-season fortunes between this year and last year. While we opened our home programme last season with wins against Aston Villa and Tottenham and shortly after beat Manchester City, our first away League point did not come until our win at Swansea in mid-October. This year we have won two, drawn one and lost only one of our four opening away First Division games. But the fact that we have had disappointing home results means that our supporters were happier at this stage last season than they are now.

We are, I repeat, extremely concerned about our home attendances. Our average this season is now slightly below 18,000 and our financial break-even figure is 20,000, taking into account the club's other fund-raising activities. So we look forward anxiously to seeing an upturn in our attendances, coupled with improved Goodison results. We have every confidence the team will achieve that under Howard Kendall, in whom we have the utmost faith - I am stating that categorically."

Three days after Carter's declaration of faith in Kendall, Everton beat Watford 1-0 through David Johnson, which proved to be his last goal of his second spell at Goodison. He went out on loan to Barnsley the following February before moving to Manchester City a month later, his combined Everton record reading 103 senior appearances and 20 goals.

The Watford win, which raised Everton two places to 13th, was watched by only 13,571 spectators and thousands more voted with their feet for the second leg against Chesterfield in late October. The attendance of 8,067 was the lowest recorded for an Everton or Liverpool senior home game. The events of the match only heightened the mood of gathering crisis. An early strike from Adrian Heath and a 68th minute Trevor Steven goal put Everton 3-0 ahead on aggregate and seemingly cruising. However, the Fourth Division visitors shocked Goodison by pulling back two goals, from Brian Scrimgeour and an Alan Birch penalty, to give Everton an uncomfortable last few minutes to hold out for a 2-2 draw on the night.

The final whistle was greeted by jeers and boos and printed leaflets were distributed by angry, disenchanted supporters. The text of the sheets was: "Kendall and Carter out. Thirty thousand stay-at-home fans can't be wrong. Bring back attractive, winning football to Goodison Park." Kendall responded: "I've always said that supporters have the right to voice their opinions, however painful it is for the target of their criticism. I have to admit, though, that my pride was hurt when I read that leaflet."

Life was hardly any sweeter for Kendall shortly after that when he arrived at his Formby home after training to find that the words 'Kendall Out' had been painted across his garage doors and sprayed on a wall further down the road. "That made the situation very worrying because it was starting to affect my family", said Kendall. "After thinking carefully about the enormous pressures they were having to contend with I began seriously to consider packing it in." The pressure grew even greater with defeats at Leicester (0-2) and Liverpool (0-3), the latter being the first Mersey derby played on a Sunday and the first screened live on national television.

Four days later Kendall returned to Anfield as one of the guests at a Football

Writers' Association tribute dinner to honour Bob Paisley. During the evening a Liverpool fan stood up and, harking back to Johnny Carey's dismissal as manager in a London cab more than two decades earlier, shouted: "Howard...there's a taxi for you." Kendall's response was superbly controlled and dimissive. "It's nice to be amongst friends," he replied.

Everton were the League's lowest scorers with only seven goals from 12 matches and were languishing in 17th prior to Coventry's visit to Goodison in the Milk Cup third round on Wednesday, November 9. It is a date that became one of the most significant Everton history. On the morning of the match Kendall announced that he had promoted Colin Harvey from reserve-team coach to work with him and Mick Heaton as a first-team triumvirate.

"We've got to find a way to improve things and I've always had a tremendous regard for Colin's abilities", said Kendall. "It's something I've been thinking about for a while. In fact, when I was at Blackburn I tapped up Colin to join me but he wouldn't leave Goodison. He's an Evertonian through and through and all the players greatly respect him. I hope he brings to the first team the same fortune he's brought our Central League team this season - they've won all eight games without conceding a goal."

Heaton revealed some years later that he was ready to resign over Harvey's promotion. "When Howard told me of the decision to promote Colin I was ready to pack it in", he admitted. "I'd have done exactly that if I'd have been asked to step down to take the reserves. That's nothing against Colin, who's a good lad and a good coach. Howard talked me out of any thoughts of resigning and, anyway, we both felt we were in danger of the sack."

The pop charts were under assault from a group with a new Liverpool sound as Frankie Goes To Hollywood, fronted by Holly Johnson, began their rise to No 1 with their first single Relax. It was the last thing Kendall could do. The clash with Coventry - for which the 9,080 crowd was Goodison's lowest recorded for a game between top flight clubs -seemed destined to crank up the crisis, with Everton trailing to Dave Bamber's goal and only 20 minutes remaining. At that point Kendall withdrew Trevor Steven and sent Peter Reid into the fray. It was a move that plotted Everton's path into the next round...but the long-term effect was incalculable.

Reid drove the contest in the short period he was in action, Adrian Heath equalising in the 79th minute and Graeme Sharp heading a dramatic winner in injury time. "I needed a strong character in the middle to make things happen, which is why I bought Peter in the first place, but perhaps I didn't use him early enough," Kendall reflected.

The day after the win over Coventry, Kendall completed a 24-hour hat-trick of crucial decisions by signing Andy Gray from Wolves for £250,000. Press, pundits and public alike questioned Kendall's judgment in signing the injury-haunted Scotland centre-forward. They called it a gamble. Others dismissed it as a panic buy. It proved to be a brilliant signing. It is doubtful if any Everton player pro rata to his number of appearances has ever had the galvanising impact Gray had on his team-mates and supporters.

A year earlier Everton could not find the funds for Kendall to bid for Alan Brazil of Ipswich. His subsequent move for Steve Archibald was rebuffed by Tottenham. Paul Mariner, another target, was too expensive at £700,000 and Kendall rejected a chance to bring Bob Latchford back to Everton on a free transfer from Swansea. Kendall was not without his doubts about Gray, dogged by problems with both knees, when he watched him play for Wolves. One scouting report stated: "He's 'gone'. He's just going through the motions." The Everton manager, though, was swayed by Gray's appearances in more than 30 games in each of the previous two seasons.

Just before Gray's arrival a more exotic striker was in Everton's sights...Joao Batista Nunes de Oliveira, a Brazilian international known as Nunes. The Flamengo forward had some impressive credentials to warm the hearts of Everton fans - two goals in the 3-0 defeat of Liverpool in the 1981 World Club Championship, which earned him a car. The media ran stories that an Everton delegation was ready to jet out to sign Nunes, initally on loan, and make him the first Brazilian to play in the Football League.

Video evidence, though, deemed their trip unnecessary. While Kendall admired the tall striker's skills he felt he was not the type to ignite an Everton recovery in the demanding conditions of an English winter... especially as he was seen wearing gloves in the South American sunshine! So instead of the Copacabana it was to the Black Country that Everton turned to sign Gray, who made his debut against Nottingham Forest the following Saturday, less than three weeks before his 28th birthday. It was also Colin Harvey's first League game since his switch to first-team coach:

"I'd thoroughly enjoyed working with the reserves. It certainly helped develop your man management and psychology skills! First-team players were usually disgruntled when they dropped into the reserves. The worst one for that was Andy King. He'd never stop moaning. But you also had rising youngsters in the side. With them you had to point out and try to eradicate any mistakes - but at the same time always encourage them.

I'd been delighted when Howard had come back. We'd shared unforgettable experiences as players and although we didn't live in each other's pockets as team-mates - he lived in Formby and we lived in Liverpool at Gateacre - we remained firm friends. When Howard was at Blackburn he'd offered me a job there. But while I was grateful I turned it down for two reasons. The first was the fact that I was very happy being at Everton and, second, I would have incurred a financial loss in moving.

On his arrival at Everton, Howard confirmed that he wanted me to carry on working with the reserves and I was pleased to do so. Howard's first two seasons in charge brought quite respectable performances and finishing positions of eighth and seventh. In his third season, though, things got off to a bad start and the team was well beaten in the Mersey derby at Anfield in November. It was 3-0 but could have been more.

The following day Howard asked me if I'd move up to work with the first team alongside him and Mick Heaton, which I was delighted to do. My baptism in the new role was, to say the least, nail-biting. Coventry took the lead and we sent on Reidy and managed to get an equaliser through Adrian Heath. Sharpy got ligament damage during the match but stayed on and got that late, late goal.

The injury kept him out of the next three games but the day after the Coventry game Howard signed Andy Gray, who made his debut against Forest at home on the Saturday. We won 1-0. The winner came from Heath, who partnered the new signing in the absence of Sharpy, and Andy was just glad to be there. 'To be honest I was surprised and excited by the prospect of playing for Everton', said Andy. 'We were having a bad time at Wolves and I was having serious doubts about my ability to play at the top level. So I was delighted that Howard felt I could do a job for a club like Everton. I knew they needed a bit of character about the place and I think the enthusiasm of Peter Reid and myself helped the rest of the lads. I certainly believed it. Peter and I felt there was something about the team and we both thought: 'Right, let's give it a good go.' And that's what we did.'

The injection of Gray's passion and Reid's tenacity, however, did not bring an instant transformation of our fortunes. In fact, at Christmas the midwinter was bleak indeed. We lost the next two games - 1-2 at Arsenal and 0-2 at home to Norwich - but the Highbury match was highly significant. A pelvic problem, which sadly ended his Goodison career, ruled out club captain Mark

Higgins and Ratcliffe took over as skipper for the first time, Mountfield coming in alongside him at centre-back. Higgins made only three more Everton appearances and was forced to retire the following May. He made a comeback with Manchester United in December 1985, the Old Trafford club paying £60,000 insurance compensation. He made eight appearances for United before moving on to Bury, Stoke and Burnley.

Our defeat at Arsenal was followed by another a week later when Norwich won 2-0 at Goodison prior to a 2-2 draw at West Ham in the Milk Cup fourth round. We earned a replay with goals from Peter Reid and Kevin Sheedy, who proceeded to score in three consecutive matches to enhance his career on the left flank. The previous month he'd won his first full Republic of Ireland cap as a substitute against Holland and his consistency with us was underlined by his run of 76 consecutive appearances from November 1982 to March 1984, a sequence ended by an ankle problem.

Another of Kevin's goals gave us a 1-0 win at Manchester United which we followed by a 2-0 home win over West Ham in the Milk Cup replay, when Kevin again and Andy King were on the scoresheet. As if to illustrate the highs and lows of football Kevin sent a penalty over the bar in our next match - a 1-1 home draw with Aston Villa when Andy Gray scored against one of his former clubs - and we failed again from the spot a week later when King's penalty was saved by Peter Hucker in a 2-0 defeat at QPR. Things went from bad to worse. We could only draw 0-0 at home with Sunderland on Boxing Day and next day we lost 3-0 at Wolves, only their second win of the season and hardly an auspicious occasion for 18-year-old Darren Hughes to make his debut at left-back in place of Alan Harper.

The pressure on Howard was now massive. A radio reporter even broadcast that Mike England was taking over as manager, a totally erroneous announcement of which Howard was unaware until his wife, who thought the report was true, told him on his return home. He'd also encountered problems with the media in general and, as he said himself, he'd taken enough and went to see the chairman to offer his resignation. 'I decided to take the bull by the horns', said Howard. 'If I'd have parted company with Everton that day I'd have left with my dignity still intact because the decision would have been prompted by me.'

Fortunately for Howard and for Everton the chairman refused point blank to even consider Howard's departure. Philip Carter had been true to his word. He fulfilled the pledge he made in his public vote of confidence and his declaration that he had faith in his manager. We didn't know it at the time but Everton fortunes had bottomed out. After the Wolves debacle we were on the way up. Our next fixture was a home game with Coventry on New Year's Eve before which Howard had an important message for Neville Southall. He warned big Nev that if his form didn't improve his place was in jeopardy. Neville's response was to keep the first of eight clean sheets in our next 14 games in which we conceded only six goals.

Neville and I had our disagreements in training - he was always one to say what he thinks and never stand on ceremony - but he is without any doubt for me the best goalkeeper I've ever seen. Gordon Banks, Pat Jennings, Ray Clemence, Peter Schmeichel were all great keepers. None of them, though, in my book measures up to Neville. He was totally dedicated, working hard to maintain his towering standards. He was the best, most disciplined trainer I've had the pleasure to work with. Neville's reading of the game, his positioning and reflexes - amazing for such a big man - were unrivalled.

During his earlier days, Llandudno-born Neville had worked as a dish washer, hod carrier and bin man and as a person he was blunt and self effacing, shunning the trappings of stardom and often travelling on a bike to and from Bellefield for training! Yet he was a star in every sense in a fabulous 16-year Goodison career that embraced 750 senior appearances including 578 in the League - both club records - an all-time Everton best of seven consecutive clean sheets and 92 Wales caps. He won two championship and two FA Cup winners' medals, a European Cup Winners' Cup medal and finalist medals in the FA Cup (twice), Simod Cup and Zenith Data Systems Cup, although he was so little enamoured of the latter that he refused to collect his losers' medal.

Our goalless home draw with Coventry did us few favours. The fans were again chanting anti-Howard slogans - and we had an away game at Birmingham 48 hours later, our first action of 1984. I was interested to hear Andy Gray, talking years later, saying that while many people cited our Milk Cup tie at Oxford as the defining moment of our revival he felt the Birmingham match, watched by only 10,004 spectators, was the turning point of our fortunes. Andy said he vividly recalled Howard telling the players before kick-off at St Andrews: 'This is it. If it doesn't happen now I'm going to dismantle the team and make wholesale changes.'

We did, though, have to make an enforced change...thanks to match referee John Deakin. He felt there was not sufficient distinction between our silver-grey change strip and Birmingham's royal blue. Howard pointed out that we'd worn the silver-grey at Ipswich and Leicester without any problems but the referee at Birmingham felt that in the gloomy, wintry conditions there was a risk of the colours clashing. We had to go along with him and, before we knew it, a set of yellow jerseys was provided by Birmingham's youth coach Keith Bradley who'd spoken to the referee and gone into the kit room to find us an alternative. Howard joked afterwards that we should stay in yellow because we started 1984 with a 2-0 win, King and Stevens on target, against a Birmingham side which had Pat Van den Hauwe at left-back. The following September we signed him for £100,000.

That victory gave us a timely lift for our trip to Stoke in the FA Cup third round the following Saturday, a game which has gone down in Goodison folklore for an open window and a cast of thousands. The thousands were the army of Everton supporters who'd made the journey to the Victoria Ground, making up by far the majority of the 16,000 crowd, and the open window was in our dressing room.

Howard heard our supporters cheering and singing and opened the windows to let the players hear them. He felt, quite rightly, it would be a positive psychological move. 'That's how much they want you to win - if you can't do it for them today you'll never do it for anybody,' he challenged them. It was only later that we learned the cheering had been sparked by big Neville and Alan Harper taking penalties at each other on the pitch, to the great amusement of the fans! They just loved it and big Nev had them in uproar with his antics, which was typical of him.

We gave our fans a lot more to cheer that afternoon by winning 2-0, the goals coming in the last 24 minutes. Big Neville made an important save from Brendan O'Callaghan at 0-0 before Andy Gray put us ahead with a typical flying header. Andy flung himself almost horizontal only inches off the heavily sanded pitch to connect with a pinpoint Kevin Sheedy cross and Alan Irvine wrapped it up with an angled shot from a Heath pass.

A week later we were back at Stoke in the League. Adrian Heath scored against his hometown former club in a 1-1 draw and although we were fifth-from-bottom of the table, we were nine-points clear of the relegation places. Four days later, on Wednesday, January 18, 1984, came the famous Milk Cup game at Oxford, who were lying second in the old Third Division. It was an occasion to which Adrian made a crucial contribution. His ability to play in a slightly deeper role to allow for Gray and Graeme Sharp to partner each other up front was invaluable. Gray, though, was cup tied at Oxford and David Johnson, in what proved to be his last Everton appearance, came in to play up front with Sharp.

That game on the Manor Ground's sloping icy pitch, against giant-killing opponents who already in that season's competition had claimed the scalps of Leeds, Newcastle and Manchester United, will be recalled for as long as Everton exists. It looked ominous when Bobby McDonald put Oxford ahead and with 20 minutes to go Howard took off Johnson and sent on Kevin Richardson, releasing Adrian to push up front. With only nine minutes left we were still trailing when fate delivered a massive lift for our fortunes.

Peter Reid pressurised Oxford midfielder Kevin Brock after he had collected a loose ball deep in his own half. Peter's attentions were such that Brock unwisely attempted a back pass to his goalkeeper Steve Hardwick. Adrian, who must be credited with being so alert to the situation, second- guessed Brock's action and darted past Hardwick to curl in the equaliser before setting off on a dance of joy. Our fans sang with a blend of delight and relief to the rhythm of revival for Everton Football Club.

'Everyone tells me that if we'd lost that night I would have been sacked but I still don't know if that would have been the case or not', Howard reflected later. 'But I don't believe there was anything lucky about our equaliser. It was the product of good team play, of Peter forcing Brock into an error and Adrian demonstrating his sharp football brain.' From then on we were on a roll. After our Christmas defeat at Wolves to the end of the season, we lost only five of 36 games in three competitions and went to Wembley twice. We marched to the finals of both the FA and Milk Cups and after our earlier struggles near the bottom of the First Division table, we climbed back up to finish in seventh place. Such was the transformation that 33 of our total of 44 League goals were scored in the new year.

Our third-round win at Stoke in the FA Cup booked us a home tie against Third Division Gillingham. Obviously we were strong favourites - but they gave us a hell of a battle spanning three games. Gillingham's team included Tony Cascarino up front and Steve Bruce at the back. They held us 0-0 again in the replay, after extra time, and although we lost the toss for the second replay and had to go back to the Priestfield Stadium, this time we showed our quality. Two first-half goals from Kevin Sheedy and another from Adrian Heath gave us a 3-0 win and we were drawn against Shrewsbury Town, then in the old Second Division, in round five. A first-half goal from Alan Irvine, another from Peter Reid after the interval and an own goal by Colin Griffin five minutes from the end took us through comfortably to the sixth round.

Amongst our notable League displays was a 4-1 home hammering of Notts County, with Adrian Heath scoring a hat-trick, and a 1-1 home draw with Liverpool, in which Bruce Grobbelaar saved a Graeme Sharp penalty before substitute Alan Harper scored against his former club to equalise an early Ian Rush strike. We also drew 1-1 at home with Manchester United when 18-year-old Rob Wakenshaw replaced Terry Curran, who'd had a seven-game first-team run, and scored on his debut. The game also saw the debut of Ian Bishop, who replaced Wakenshaw. Both players showed plenty of promise but unfortunately opportunity didn't knock very often for them. Midfielder Bishop joined Carlisle for £15,000 in October 1984 but later joined Manchester City and West Ham - for combined fees of just below £1 million - and won an England 'B' cap. Striker Wakenshaw made only another four senior appearances before joining Carlisle for £20,000 in September 1985 and later playing for Rochdale and Crewe.

Our resurgence in the League was matched by our progress in the two domestic cups. After our dramatic Milk Cup equaliser at Oxford we won the replay at home 4-1, which booked us a two-leg semi final collision with Aston Villa. The first game was at Goodison in mid-February, the night after Liverpool had booked their place in the final by beating Walsall, and it was up to us to get through for the first all-Merseyside Wembley in history.

We went ahead after 29 minutes through a goal from Kevin Sheedy that took him by surprise as much as it did the 40,000 spectators. Kevin delivered a long cross from the left which, amazingly, eluded Everton and Villa players alike and trickled past goalkeeper Nigel Spink into the net. Villa's subsequent hopes of damage limitation by preventing us scoring again lasted until eight minutes from the end when Kevin Richardson seized on an attempted clearance and hammered in a low shot to make it 2-0. The congratulations from his team-mates had to be guarded because Kevin was wearing a plaster cast to protect a fractured arm. His other arm was the subject of Villa protests after a late incident when a Gary Shaw effort was heading for our net until Kevin blocked it. 'He got it away with his hand,' claimed Villa's boyhood Evertonian striker Peter Withe who, along with Steve McMahon and Kirkby-born Dennis Mortimer, was one of several players in their ranks with Merseyside connections. They also paraded winger Mark Walters, a player I later tried to sign for Everton before he joined Liverpool, while Paul Rideout, who later rejected a chance to join the Reds before coming to Goodison, was on the bench. Villa won the second leg 1-0 through a Rideout goal to see us through on a 2-1 aggregate.

The prospect of Everton and Liverpool meeting at Wembley for the first time in almost a century of rivalry had Merseyside agog and it made a far more attractive topic of conversation than the financial crisis of Liverpool City Council, of which Everton fan Derek Hatton was deputy leader at a time when Militant Tendency held sway. The miners' strike, which would last a year, had also just begun but dominating Merseyside thoughts was the looming collision of red and blue in front of the old twin towers, those wonderful edifices now sadly consigned to history.

From Saturday, March 24 through to the morning of the match the following day there was a mass Mersey exodus. Coaches, cars, vans and trains, draped in blue and red, set off for Wembley and, with typical Scouse wit, one wag had placed a poster on a south-bound motorway entrance which read: 'Will the last one to leave please switch off the lights.' The south was amazed at how rival supporters travelled and mingled together, especially with many from the same family having different football loyalties. Perhaps the only note of aggravation was shared by both blues and reds - the London price of 85p for a pint of beer was well in excess of the cost up north.

An estimated 70,000 Merseyside fans were among the 100,000 crowd to watch the teams do battle on a wet Sunday afternoon, the events watched live by the nation on ITV. With Andy Gray cup-tied the teams were:

Everton: Neville Southall; Gary Stevens, Kevin Ratcliffe, Derek Mountfield, John Bailey; Alan Irvine, Peter Reid, Kevin Richardson, Kevin Sheedy (Alan Harper 75); Adrian Heath, Graeme Sharp.

Liverpool: Bruce Grobbelaar; Phil Neal, Alan Hansen, Mark Lawrenson, Alan Kennedy; Sammy Lee, Craig Johnston (Michael Robinson, 90), Graeme Souness, Ronnie Whelan; Ian Rush, Kenny Dalglish.

It was our first Wembley appearance since 1977 and every Evertonian will always feel that we were denied what appeared a blatant penalty with the game only six minutes old. Adrian Heath chased a Graeme Sharp flick-on and, as Bruce Grobbelaar came out, hit the ball goalwards only for Alan Hansen to block it with his hand after it had come off his knee. It looked a sure-fire penalty to me but I can only assume that neither Portsmouth referee Alan Robinson nor his linesmen saw the incident. If they'd seen it then it must have been a penalty.

Liverpool improved greatly in the second half and, almost inevitably, Ian Rush began to make an impact. It needed some excellent goalkeeping from big Neville to prevent his fellow Welshman adding to the 35 goals he'd already scored that season, his latest coming four days earlier in Lisbon where Liverpool had crushed Benfica 4-1 to reach the European Cup semi- final. Although Liverpool twice had the ball in our net - through Alan Kennedy and Ronnie Whelan - they were both correctly ruled offside.

In the later stages of the match we lost Kevin Sheedy through injury. He'd come back after a three-game lay-off to play at Wembley but he began to struggle and Alan Harper replaced him. Kevin didn't play again that season, eventually undergoing surgery for snapped ankle ligaments. The final stretched into extra time without a goal and at the end of the 120 minutes the crowd gave another rendition of 'Merseyside, Merseyside' which they'd chanted throughout the afternoon. Pride for both sides was still intact as the fans sang and the two left-backs, John Bailey and Alan Kennedy, ran round the stadium with blue and red scarves tied together above their heads.

From every aspect a draw at Wembley was a fitting outcome - and it was on to Maine Road, Manchester for the replay the following Wednesday, again screened live on ITV. Our only team change was Alan Harper coming in for the injured Sheedy - Andy King taking over at substitute - while Liverpool paraded the same side. We started well, as we'd done at Wembley, but it was Liverpool who found the net for what was to prove the only goal. Midway through the first half Graeme Souness failed to control a Phil Neal pass but his mistake caught out everyone and he suddenly found himself with a shooting chance. To his credit, he took it well and sent a powerful left-foot shot that flew over Neville and dipped under the bar.

We did have our chances, notably through Kevin Richardson, Peter Reid and Adrian Heath, but we didn't make them count and Liverpool ran out winners to give Joe Fagan his first trophy as manager and the first of a treble completed by the League title and European Cup. Naturally, we were disappointed but were not downhearted. We lost only two of our remaining 11 League games, a run which saw Trevor Steven return to the team.

Prior to the Milk Cup final we'd booked an FA Cup semi-final place through one of Andy Gray's collection of amazing goals. We were drawn away at Notts County in the sixth round and although Kevin Richardson scored an early goal John Chiedozie soon equalised. It was 1-1 until the opening minute of the second half when Kevin Sheedy sent in a free-kick to the far post where Gray, only inches above the turf, flung himself to head the winner. Any closer to the ground and he'd have touched it with his nose!

That spectacular strike secured us a semi-final meeting with Southampton at Highbury. Although we had long spells of possession the better chances fell to them and Neville again distinguished himself in a tense contest. He was busier than his opposite number Peter Shilton but his prowess between the posts meant that after 90 minutes the game was still goalless.

For the first time in the first meeting in a semi-final there was extra time and we were only three minutes from the end of the additional period when Peter Reid's free-kick set up our winner. During the game Southampton had deputed a forward, Frank Worthington, rather than a defender to mark Derek Mountfield when he moved forward and that was probably their mistake. When Reidy sent the ball in Derek eluded Frank and got the vital flick to find Adrian Heath at the far post. His header past Shilton meant we were Wembley-bound for the second time in two months and through to our first FA Cup final since 1968.

I couldn't have agreed more with Howard after our win at Highbury when he said that he wanted time to stand still because the journey home was the best he'd ever experienced. All along our route out of London that night our fans were cheering us when they spotted the team bus and Howard told the driver to slow down so we could really savour it.

Our Wembley opponents were Graham Taylor's Watford, who beat Plymouth Argyle 1-0 in the other semi-final at Villa Park. They had finished 11th in the old First Division - four places below us - and were a committed, hard-working side who'd drawn 4-4 with us in a mistake-littered match at Vicarage Road in February, a game that was great for spectators but not for managers and coaches! But the confidence in our camp was sky-high in the build-up to Wembley and on the morning of the final Andy Gray and John Bailey opened their hotel room windows at our base in Beaconsfield and started to sing to the delight of a crowd gathering below! Hardly the sign of players taut with nerves and tension.

The Wembley teams produced the rarity of every player appearing in an FA Cup final for the first time. John Bailey, who'd missed our last two League games through suspension, was recalled to our side while Watford were without club captain Wilf Rostron, who was banned after being sent off in a League match against Luton. The line-ups were:

Everton: Neville Southall; Gary Stevens, Derek Mountfield, Kevin Ratcliffe (captain), John Bailey; Trevor Steven, Peter Reid, Kevin Richardson, Adrian Heath; Graeme Sharp, Andy Gray. Substitute: Alan Harper.

Watford: Steve Sherwood; David Bardsley, Steve Terry, Lee Sinnott, Neil Price; Les Taylor (captain), Kenny Jackett; Nigel Callaghan, Maurice Johnston, George Reilly, John Barnes. Substitute: Paul Atkinson.

We had a few early scares, the first of them with less than two minutes on the clock. A long throw from Lee Sinnott was flicked on by big George Reilly and John Barnes seemed certain to score, but he miscued and Neville saved. Then Neville blocked a Barnes shot with his feet and Les Taylor's 25-yard effort was deflected just wide by John Bailey's outstretched leg.

We had our own chances, though, with Kevin Richardson firing into the side netting and Graeme Sharp heading narrowly wide before we deservedly took the lead shortly before half-time. Watford's defence hesitated when Richardson sent in a cross from the left and when the ball came to Gary Stevens, he fired it in low and hard. Sharpy pounced by stopping the ball before unleashing a shot on the turn that flashed into the net off a post. Amazingly, a clairvoyant had predicted on an ITV programme that we'd score in the 37th minute - and the goal was timed at 37 minutes 18 seconds.

Six minutes into the second half we got our second goal. Trevor Steven, who was our man-of-the-match, delivered a menacing cross from the right which deceived Steve Sherwood. He managed to grasp the ball but as he fell backwards Andy Gray moved in to force the ball over the line. Television replays showed that Andy had made contact with the back of Sherwood's hands before heading the ball. But referee John Hunting deemed it a legitimate challenge and if we did get the rub of the green we deserved it - especially after our ill-luck at Wembley in the Milk Cup final.

Elderly Everton fans pointed out that Andy's goal was reminiscent of Dixie Dean's header against Manchester City in the 1933 final and, just like on that pre-war occasion, we emerged victorious as skipper Kevin Ratcliffe climbed the 39 steps to receive the FA Cup from the Duchess of Kent. At 23 he was the youngest winning captain since Bobby Moore 20 years earlier and our joy was in stark contrast to Watford's feelings. Their chairman Elton John wept at the crushing of his hopes of winning the Cup to crown the club's rise from Fourth to First Division. His newly-released record 'Sad Songs (Say So Much)' was so ironically appropriate.

Like many Evertonians, Howard Kendall and I felt very emotional when Kevin Ratcliffe held up the trophy because it was Everton's first for 14 years, since the pair of us had played together in the 1970 championship-winning side. The champagne that night back at our Beaconsfield hotel tasted wonderful indeed. We had recovered from a dismal winter to enjoy a glittering spring which also saw our youngsters win the FA Youth Cup. The team, captained by Ian Marshall, beat Stoke City on a 4-2 aggregate in the two-leg final. Although we didn't know it that joyful day at Wembley, it was the launch of the most successful period in Everton history in which we would taste unprecedented success domestically and in Europe."

*Pictured front left on each line-up, with my school Holy Name for seasons 1956-57 and 1957-58 (below).
The trophy above was the first and only trophy the school has won - ironically at Anfield!*

Above: My wedding day in Prestatyn, 1970.

Above: With my wife Maureen and daughters Joanne (left) amd Melanie. Notice the 1972 Olympics on the television!

Above: The family, from left to right: Joanne, her daughter Bethany, my youngest daughter Emma, me, Maureen and Melanie.

Above: On the journey back from the 1984 FA Cup final, with Melanie, Joanne and Maureen.

Left: With granddaughter Bethany at my testimonial against Bologna, 2003.

Below: With brother Brian prior to the Charity Shield at Wembley against Coventry, 1987.

Below left: Emma, who did not travel in 1984, finally gets her hands on the FA Cup, 1995.

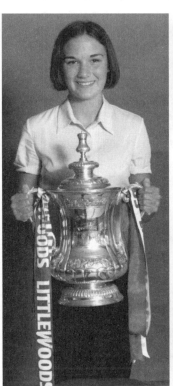

THE FOOTBALL ASSOCIATION

WINNERS WORLD CHAMPIONSHIP, JULES RIMET CUP, 1966

Patron: HER MAJESTY THE QUEEN
President: THE EARL OF HAREWOOD
Chairman: DR. A. STEPHEN

Secretary:
DENIS FOLLOWS, C.B.E., B.A.

Telegraphic Address:
FOOTBALL ASSOCIATION, LONDON, W.2

22 LANCASTER GATE, LONDON, W.2

Ref: AO/MB

9th May, 1967.

To Players

Dear Sir,

Representative Match - England v Young England

19th May 1967

    I have pleasure in advising you that you have been selected to play for the Young England team in the above match which will be played on the ground of Arsenal Football Club on Friday, 19th May, 1967, kick-off 7.30 p.m. Your club has already been informed of your selection.

    An itinerary for the match is enclosed herewith for your information.

    You will be entitled to a complimentary ticket for the final of the Challenge Cup Competition to be played at Wembley on 20th May, 1967, and this will be handed to you by Sir Alfred Ramsey at Headquarters if you propose to attend the match.

    Yours sincerely,

Secretary

C. Harvey Esq.

Above: My letter to confirm my place in the Young England team, 1967 and below training with England U23s with my Everton team-mates John Hurst (stood, second left) and myself and Jimmy Husband lying down at the front.

Above: In action during my one and only England cap in Malta during a European Championship qualifier in 1971. Also pictured in England action are my Goodison team-mates Alan Ball and Joe Royle.

Above: An England line-up pictured during a training session for the Home Internationals, May 1971. I was named as a substitute against Wales and Scotland but did not get on. Alan Ball has signed the picture along with myself.

Above: Scoring against Birmingham City at Goodison, February 1965.

Above: Being denied by West Ham goalkeeper Bobby Ferguson, November 1972.

Left: 'Here we go gathering cups in May'. Myself, Tommy Wright and Brian Labone, May 1966.

Below: Pictured with family after picking up my Dixie Dean award, 1984. Standing: Brian, me, Maureen and Brian's wife Judy. Front: My mum and dad.

Above: The bench during the FA Cup semi-final against Luton, April 1985. Having been told we could only have five people on the bench by an official, the instruction seems to fall on deaf ears.

Above: On the bench with Paul Power in 1990, wearing my No 6 shirt.

Above: Pushing a 'pile of pennies' (totalling over £1,000) with then Brookside actress Doreen Sloane in a charity fund-raising event at the County Court pub in Woolton, 1986.

Above: Helping to start the 'Walk For Life' around Stanley Park, summer 1987.

Above: Proudly leading out Everton in my first competitive game in charge, against Coventry in the 1987 Charity Shield at Wembley.

Above: With my first backroom staff at Wembley, 1987. Left to right: Graham Smith, Terry Darracott, Peter Reid and Mick Lyons.

Chapter Eleven

Glory And Glitter

The 1984-85 season will be recalled with relish whenever Evertonians reflect on the club's glorious achievements. It was a campaign when Howard Kendall and Colin Harvey experienced the heady delights of success both at home and abroad. But it was preceded for Harvey by a trip to the hospital theatre.

"One of my first assignments after the heady taste of Wembley was into hospital to have a hip replacement. The hip problem had forced the end of my playing career but after having the new hip I was up and about within 10 days. I had the other hip replaced four years later. By the time we were back for pre-season I was feeling fine and the mood in the camp was buoyant.

After friendlies in Switzerland and Greece we were back at Wembley to take on Liverpool in the Charity Shield which marked Paul Bracewell's competitive debut for us. We'd signed Paul from Sunderland for £250,000 just before the FA Cup final the previous May. Although he'd started as a youngster at Stoke during Howard Kendall's time there and had left the Potteries for Roker Park, he was born locally at Heswall. Howard had kept tabs on Paul and as soon as he became available he moved in. He proved a great acquisition for us in midfield and went on to play for England.

We won 1-0 at Wembley through a bizarre 55th-minute own goal. Graeme Sharp got in a shot that was well saved by Bruce Grobbelaar and Sharpy's follow-up attempt past the stranded keeper was cleared by Alan Hansen. But as Grobbelaar scrambled back to his line the ball hit the back of his boot and went into the net. Although the manner of the goal was crazy we were good value for our victory against a Liverpool side who were facing up to life without Sampdoria-signing Graeme Souness. Our midfield, with Bracewell enjoying an impressive introduction, won the battle with Liverpool's and we had chances to have won comfortably. It was only our third victory over

Liverpool in any competition in 31 meetings stretching back to 1971. So we enjoyed the moment without forgetting that the really serious stuff began a week later when the curtain went up on the League season. And what an opening act it was! With Kevin Sheedy still out after his ankle surgery our first match line-up against Tottenham was:

Neville Southall; Gary Stevens, Derek Mountfield, Kevin Ratcliffe, John Bailey; Trevor Steven, Peter Reid, Paul Bracewell, Kevin Richardson (Andy Gray, 68); Adrian Heath, Graeme Sharp.

Before kick-off our three trophies, the FA Cup, Charity Shield and FA Youth Cup, were paraded in front of the 35,630 Goodison crowd, our biggest opening-day home attendance since 1977. We took the lead through a 16th-minute Heath penalty - then, amazingly, lost 4-1. We kept getting hit on the break by Spurs, who went 2-1 up before half-time through goals from Mark Falco and Clive Allen. Our misery was complete when John Chiedozie added another two early in the second half. More anguish was to follow 48 hours later when we went to West Brom and lost 2-1. Heath again scored from a penalty but this time two minutes from the end.

Our performances were baffling. To be honest we didn't know whether our Cup win had just dulled the players a little and taken the edge off them or whether there was some other reason. What we did know was that we couldn't afford any more results like those. After being pre-season fancies for the title in many sections of the media we were already being written off as we languished pointless after two games.

Four days after losing at West Brom we went to Chelsea for a Friday night match, the first live televised game of the new season. We won 1-0, through a Kevin Richardson goal, which proved to be the launch pad for a great run of only one defeat in our next 20 League and Cup games which would help make it the most successful season in Everton's long history. How strange that two decades later, in 2004-05, Everton's fourth- place finish to secure a ticket to the Champions League qualifiers also came after a season which began with a 4-1 home defeat by a north London club, in this case Arsenal.

Our 1984-85 campaign was only a month old when we re-inforced the squad with the signing of Pat Van den Hauwe from Birmingham who, like Bracewell at Stoke, was a youngster at St Andrews when Howard was there. Pat arrived with a reputation as one of a band of Birmingham City hard men and earned the nickname 'Psycho'. When Howard announced his signing to the press in his office at Bellefield he held up a packet of uncooked bacon ribs and said:

'This is a snack for my new defender.' Joking aside, Pat didn't suffer fools gladly and I think he was proud of his unforgiving reputation.

It was only later that we discovered that Pat was given to pounding the roads near his Formby home before dawn to try to run off the excesses of the night before and in later life his personal demons threatened to overwhelm him. Having said that, he was also a very good player who was highly rated both by his team-mates and us on the backroom staff. He was naturally right-footed, but had impressed at left-back for Birmingham and it had always been one of Howard's firm beliefs that a right-footed left-back was better than a left-footed left-back.

While it was extremely tough on John Bailey, who ultimately lost his place to Pat, he proved a big success at Everton. Pat and John became good mates but when John left for Newcastle a year later we didn't half miss his banter in the dressing room. He's a great joker and a great character and served Everton well in his 222 appearances, in which he scored three goals.

Our squad - which was extended during the season by the signings of the versatile Ian Atkins (£70,000 from Sunderland) and striker Paul Wilkinson (£250,000 from Grimsby) - was formidable. Our last line of defence was, as I've said earlier, the best goalkeeper I've ever seen. Some of Neville's saves that season were incredible. There was the one to keep out Mark Falco's header at Tottenham and another stop at Sheffield Wednesday when a header at the near post was going in at the back post and somehow he got round to claw it out. His shot-stopping was as good as you'll ever see and in front of Neville the back four of Stevens, Mountfield, Ratcliffe and Van den Hauwe virtually picked itself. They were all terrific players and strong characters.

There was a tremendous balance about the whole side with Steven and Sheedy on the midfield flanks, Reid and Bracewell in the centre with Sharp up front alongside either Andy Gray or Adrian Heath. It was a team for all seasons, really. It was durable, physically and mentally strong and yet could produce the most creative football. It was also capable of switching styles and tactics, which was invaluable on our return to Europe that season.

Kevin Ratcliffe, the skipper, was one of the quickest centre-backs ever. He had great pace and after seeing him play for Wales Schoolboys in the 1970s, when I was youth coach, it was great to see him develop into such a fine player. At first Howard dabbled with the idea that Kevin might be better at left-back. I think Howard had a slight concern over his height because at just on six feet Kevin wasn't the tallest for a centre-back. But he had a great spring, superb pace and he was a fine reader of the game. I told Howard his best position was in the middle and that's where his qualities shone.

His centre-back partner Mountfield, who seized his chance after the pelvic injury to Mark Higgins, had a fantastic scoring ability for a defender. He rattled in 25 goals in 154 senior appearances for Everton, a ratio of a goal every six matches. On the basis of goals related to appearances that puts him alongside Steve Bruce and Stuart Pearce as the best goalscoring defenders of the modern era.

At right-back Gary Stevens was another player with an eye for goal. Including penalties he set a club record for his position by scoring 13 times. He was blessed with terrific pace and stamina. He could attack down the flank and yet he could always be relied on to to get back to his defensive role. A native of Barrow, he joined Everton as an apprentice, came through the ranks and went on to win 46 England caps.

The midfield has been compared to the 1970 title-winning one in which I had the pleasure of playing alongside Howard and Alan Ball. Well, the systems were different - we were a trio whereas the mid-1980s side was a quartet - and it's for others to deliberate on any way. There is no doubt, though, that the running and energy of Trevor Steven on the right and the left-foot skills of Kevin Sheedy on the left - both of whom contributed a fair share of goals - complemented perfectly the central midfield qualities of Peter Reid and Paul Bracewell. As Reidy remarked: 'Having two scoring wide men like Trevor and Kevin was great for Brace and me. We didn't have to get into the box. Our job was to get the ball and pass it to the others.'

Up front Graeme Sharp proved a prolific goalscorer, the second highest in Everton history after Dixie Dean. He was a typical British centre-forward yet he was quite a shy boy when he first came down from Scotland. He played for me in the reserves for a couple of years and it was a case of making him realise how good he could be. He scored goals mostly with his right but also with his left and he was very good in the air. Clearly, he also got a buzz from playing with his idol and fellow Scot, Andy Gray.

We produced several superb performances during the autumn of 1984 when we scored a club record 15 League goals without reply between Adrian Heath's winner in a 2-1 home defeat of Aston Villa on October 13 and a 4-0 win over Stoke on November 17. In between we beat Liverpool 1-0, Manchester United 5-0, Leicester City 3-0 and West Ham 1-0, a run that took us to the top of the table for the first time since February 1979.

The victories over Liverpool and Manchester United have earned permanent places in Goodison folklore. The first came on October 20 at Anfield, a stage where we hadn't won for more than 14 years. To be frank we'd had Liverpool up to our ears. The whole of Europe had been trying to match Bob Paisley's men and we had them on our own doorstep, getting their achievements rammed down our throats.

Eight days before the derby match the IRA very nearly succeeded in blowing up Margaret Thatcher and the rest of the British Cabinet when a 100lb bomb exploded in the Grand Hotel, Brighton, where the Conservative Party Conference was being held. The Prime Minister and her close colleagues survived but the bomb killed five guests and left dozens injured. Life, though, had to go on and Graeme Sharp brought smiles to Evertonian faces with a goal that has a permanent place in derby legend.

Thanks to both goalkeepers, Neville Southall and Bruce Grobbelaar, the game was goalless at half-time but three minutes into the second half, Sharpy latched onto a long ball out of defence from Gary Stevens. Sharpy takes up the story: 'Liverpool were one of the first clubs to use Adidas Tango balls while at Goodison we were using Mitre. So Howard got a sack of the Adidas ones so we could get used to them in training.

From Gary's long pass I knew I was never going to beat Mark Lawrenson for pace so I managed to get to one side of him and control the ball with my left foot. It sat up invitingly and I thought: 'Why not hit it?' I knew that if I connected properly and got it on target I'd have a chance of scoring. Bruce was off his line so I hit it from 25 yards. It sailed over his head and into the corner of the Anfield Road end net.' It was a fantastic strike and, as Joe Fagan conceded, one fit to win any game. Quite rightly it earned the accolade of Match of the Day 'Goal of the Season' and the belief that flowed from that win - our first in the League home or away over Liverpool since Andy King's only goal in October 1978 - was immense.

A week after that great fillip - with a 1-0 European away win against Inter Bratislava in the Cup Winners' Cup sandwiched between - we confronted Manchester United at Goodison. United arrived in third place, behind leaders Arsenal and Sheffield Wednesday. Ron Atkinson's side had lost only once that season but their total of 20 points was the same as ours and they were ahead of us only on goal difference. The goal difference between the sides that afternoon was emphatically in our favour - a 5-0 triumph over the title favourites that was thrilling to behold.

My co-writer John Keith reported in the Daily Express that during after-match celebrations in the Winslow pub, which stands in the shadow of Goodison, one fan intoxicated by the sheer power and precision of our performance proclaimed: 'If they'd worn yellow and green instead of royal blue they'd have called them Brazil.' That esteemed Evertonian Joe Mercer wasn't short on superlatives either. Joe declared: 'I've seen - and been part of - some terrific Everton displays. But that was the best-ever by this club.'

It was certainly a terrific performance which brought us our biggest League win since the 6-0 defeat of Chelsea in April 1978, when Bob Latchford reached a season's total of 30 First Division goals. Kevin Sheedy began the rout with a looping fifth-minute header that left him and Kevin Moran dazed after a clash of heads. Moran had to go off - he was replaced by Frank Stapleton to force a United re-shuffle - but Sheedy stayed on until 20 minutes from the end. By then he'd struck again, with a shot that Gary Bailey just couldn't stop. Another goal before half-time by Adrian Heath, who scored from a Trevor Steven cross, gave us a 3-0 interval lead. Groggy United held out without further breaches until the last 10 minutes but strikes from Gary Stevens and Graeme Sharp completed our nap hand of goals.

Wonderful though that display was I have to admit that I got more professional satisfaction three days later when we met United again, this time at Old Trafford in the third round of the Milk Cup, which we'd reached by beating Second Division Sheffield United on a 6-2 aggregate. I warned our players that United were a good side and after their mauling at Goodison would be bursting to restore lost pride. If the roles had been reversed we'd have been licking our lips at the swift opportunity for revenge.

But our lads went out and gave an unbelievable performance. United came out snarling. They were so fired up and some of the tackles that were flying in were X-rated! But far from basking in their 5-0 win our lads battled and scrapped to deservedly come out on top. A Graeme Sharp penalty just before the interval tied up the half-time score at 1-1 but an own goal from one of our former players, John Gidman, five minutes from the end gave us a 2-1 win and our just reward. Of all the great performances by Everton teams in the mid-1980s that display is the one that I recall with greatest pleasure.

In November 1984 top rock stars, responding to a call from Bob Geldof to help relieve the Ethiopian famine, formed Band Aid and recorded 'Do They Know It's Christmas', an iconic track which would send its message reverberating down the years. But there was no Christmas charity for opponents from our team who spread the goals around with eager abandon. Although none of our players scored a League hat-trick that season no fewer than eight of them scored twice in a match in a 16-game First Division sequence from mid-November. This prolific run began with a 4-0 home crushing of Stoke - Heath scoring twice, with Reid and Steven adding the others - which set a post-war club record of 10 consecutive wins in all competitions, our best run as a top-flight club in the 20th century.

Typical of football, though, we lost our next match three days later to Grimsby, then in the old Second Division. They came to Goodison in the fourth round of the Milk Cup and somehow won a game we dominated. In our previous Milk Cup game at Goodison, when we beat Sheffield United 4-0, we forced 15 corners to nil. Against Grimsby the corner count was 19-0 but we couldn't put the ball in the net. Then, a minute from the end, Paul Wilkinson headed a winner for Grimsby to knock us out, both literally and metaphorically. But before the end of the season Paul's role was to transform in the eyes of Evertonians from villain to hero. He joined us the following March and scored our winner against Liverpool - so I think we forgave him!

Our long-awaited return to Europe had begun with what many regarded as a soft touch re-entry to Continental competition. We were handed the short trip to the Republic of Ireland to face University College Dublin in the first round, first leg of the Cup Winners' Cup. A stroll in the park? Don't you believe it. They proved mighty stubborn opponents, packing their defence and keeping the door locked. A highly-frustrating 90 minutes for us ended 0-0. The only other side to prevent us scoring in a European match that season was Bayern Munich and UCD also became only the fifth League of Ireland club to hold a Football League side to a draw in Europe. The return was only slightly more rewarding. Again, the Irish side got 11 men behind the ball but this time Graeme Sharp, with a 10th-minute strike, found a gap in their defences for the only goal of the tie.

In the next round we made the trip to Czechoslovakia and came away with a 1-0 win over Inter Bratislava, thanks to an early goal from Paul Bracewell. We wrapped it up 4-0 on aggregate by winning the return 3-0, through goals from Sharp, Sheedy and Heath. That game saw John Morrissey junior, son of my former team-mate, make his senior debut as a substitute for Sheedy. John, an England youth international, had a total of only three outings for us but after a brief spell at Wolves became a key player for Tranmere in a superb Prenton Park career that spanned 14 years and more than 600 games.

The aggregate win over Bratislava secured only the second European quarter-final place in Everton history after reaching that stage in the 1970-71 European Cup - and we'd got there without conceding a goal. The draw paired us the following March with Fortuna Sittard. We went into the first leg at home with a two-point lead over Tottenham at the top of the First Division but without Adrian Heath and Graeme Sharp. Adrian had been carried off against Sheffield Wednesday in December, and his knee injury that day, when he was our leading scorer with 11 goals from 17 League games, cruelly ruled him out for the rest of the season which meant a return to the line-up for Andy Gray, who had been filling the substitute role.

Then in February, in the first minute of our fifth round FA Cup tie against non-League visitors Telford, Sharpy went over on his ankle and damaged ligaments which kept him out of four games, including our European duel with Fortuna. That meant a recall up front for Terry Curran in the previous match, a 1-1 draw at Manchester United. It was only his 14th start since his move from Sheffield United. Derek Mountfield scored our goal at Old Trafford in a game notable for both goalkeepers saving penalties. Neville stopped Gordon Strachan's spot-kick after only four minutes and Gary Bailey saved from Kevin Sheedy seven minutes from time.

Our clash with Fortuna was a night that belonged to Andy Gray, who scored a superb hat-trick on his European debut for Everton to give us an emphatic 3-0 win. They were his first Goodison goals of the season and his first treble for eight years since the final day of the 1976-77 season. The Dutch visitors had kept a clean sheet up to half-time but just three minutes after the interval Andy reacted quickest to score after goalkeeper Van Gerven could only parry Peter Reid's fierce drive from the edge of the box.

His second and third goals came in a two-minute spell that meant we'd already got one foot in the semi-final. He made it 2-0 in the 74th minute with a trademark strike. When Terry Curran crossed Andy bravely flung himself amidst the flying boots in the goalmouth to power a magnificent header into the net. Almost instantly he scored again, seizing on a Kevin Sheedy cross and firing past Van Gerven.

We completed the job in Holland a fortnight later with a 2-0 win. A superb 23rd goal of the season for Graeme Sharp after 15 minutes put us ahead on the night and a late strike from Peter Reid wrapped up a 5-0 aggregate triumph. It was a timely goal for Peter, who was named days later as the Player of the Year by his fellow professionals of the PFA, a richly deserved accolade, and we were well satisfied at reaching the club's first-ever European semi-final without conceding a goal.

Between the two games against the Dutch side, Goodison had been cloaked in sadness at the sad death of my old boss Harry Catterick in the most poignant of circumstances on an FA Cup afternoon. Wins over Leeds, Doncaster and Telford booked us a home quarter-final collision with Ipswich, who were struggling third-from-bottom of the First Division. But they didn't play like that at Goodison. With Harry Catterick, as always a keen Evertonian, watching from the stand we were only four minutes away from our first home FA Cup defeat since Fulham in 1975 when Derek Mountfield came to the rescue with an equaliser to make it 2-2.

We went ahead with a wonderful Sheedy strike after only five minutes. When Kevin curled a free-kick to goalkeeper Paul Cooper's right it was ruled out because the Ipswich 'wall' hadn't retreated the requisite 10 yards. It didn't faze Kevin one iota as he promptly sent the re-take into the net to Cooper's left. Ipswich, though, soon equalised through a rare error by big Neville, who allowed Kevin Wilson's 25-yard shot to squirm under his body. But there was nothing scrappy about Ipswich's second strike, a superb 32nd minute long-range volley by Romeo Zondervan.

Even though Ipswich were reduced to 10 men after Steve McCall's dismissal, we seemed to be heading for an exit until Mountfield slid in Pat Van den Hauwe's cross. Whether the tension of the match and the drama of our late goal affected Harry Catterick, who knows? But he suffered a heart attack, collapsed and died just after the final whistle, a tragic echo of Dixie Dean's death in the same Goodison stand five years to the month earlier.

With bitter irony, Tommy Eggleston, the man who was Harry's coach and assistant at Everton for more than a decade, was at Goodison as the Ipswich physiotherapist. Tommy was in the visitors' dressing room when he learned of the death at 65 of one of the great figures of Everton history. 'I wish I'd have known Harry was up there in the directors' box fighting for his life', Tommy was moved to comment. 'I would have liked to have got to him before he died but, regrettably, circumstances dictated otherwise.' It was also to be Tommy's last visit to Goodison. At the end of that season, after eight years as Ipswich physio and 50 years service to football, he retired to Wetherby, North Yorkshire and died at the age of 83 in January 2004.

Harry's passing, and the manner of it, was a great shock, especially to Howard Kendall and me. It was Harry who brought Howard to Everton as a player and I grew up in football under Harry's management. He signed players and built teams which gave the supporters great entertainment and brought us unforgettable success. As I've said earlier in this book, Harry had his critics but nobody can dispute the fact that he was a great manager and with his death an era had closed.

In the sad aftermath of Harry's death we had to be professional, as he would have wanted us to, by preparing for the FA Cup replay at Portman Road the following Wednesday. Although Ipswich had now drawn twice with us at Goodison that season - they'd held us 1-1 in the League in September - we'd gone there and won 2-0 in December through a brace of goals from Graeme Sharp and it was Sharpy who did the business for us again. Returning from injury, he scored the only goal of the game from a 75th-minute penalty which set us up for two semi-finals in four days. Our first was the trip to European Cup Winners' Cup favourites Bayern Munich, whose manager Udo Lattek declared: "This should be the final. Whoever goes through from this semi-final will win the Cup." He was proved correct...but not in the way he would have wished!

The first leg was played in front of a capacity 70,000 crowd at Munich's Olympic Stadium, but we had to face our big test without the injured Andy Gray - who'd scored twice in our 4-1 League win over Sunderland the previous Saturday - and Kevin Sheedy. Alan Harper and Kevin Richardson came in and Trevor Steven filled the gap up front whenever possible, but also helped form a five-man midfield whenever the situation demanded it.

It was a tight contest with chances sparse. Richardson cleared a Bayern effort off the line while big Neville denied Michael Rummenigge with a save low to his left and we emerged with a creditable and highly satisfactory goalless draw. Next up for us, three days later, was the FA Cup semi-final against Luton at Villa Park.

Luton's plan was to stop us playing and they certainly threw us out of our rhythm. Not only that but they took the lead before half-time when a terrific shot from Ricky Hill went in off a post. The score remained like that until four minutes from the end when we engineered another late rescue act, the free-kick skills of Kevin Sheedy evident once more. His bewitching left-foot curled a free-kick around the 'wall' and beyond the clutches of Les Sealey.

Luton looked devastated at coming so close and seeing victory snatched from them. We grew in strength and command in extra time before Sheedy worked his magic again, this time as supplier. With 114 minutes on the clock a foul by Brian Stein on Peter Reid gave Sheedy another free-kick opportunity. This time he picked out Derek Mountfield and the centre-back with the great scoring touch headed us to Wembley.

Our sheer delight at booking a ticket to our second successive FA Cup final - a habit that would continue for yet another season - was followed by a steely determination to beat Bayern in our Cup Winners' Cup semi-final return 11 days later. Between that and our win over Luton we hammered West Brom 4-1 at home - when, surprising as it sounds, it needed a brilliant first-half display by Neville Southall - and then won 2-0 at Stoke.

With Mountfield injured for both games Ian Atkins came in for two of his six Everton starts to help stretch our unbeaten run in all competitions to 23 and open up a 10-point lead over Manchester United. It was a great launch pad to send us into the Bayern game, which many Everton followers claim - and few would dispute - to be the greatest night in Goodison history.

With Mountfield fit again we paraded our strongest side and there were only a smattering of German fans in a crowd of just under 50,000. But if our task was difficult enough after the goalless first leg it became daunting when Bayern took the lead on 37 minutes. A Lothar Matthaus pass sent Ludwig Kogl through and although Southall stopped his shot he was helpless as Dieter Hoeness directed the rebound into the net for an away goal, and the first we'd conceded in Europe that season. It ended our British record sequence of seven consecutive European matches without conceding a goal, a run that spanned 11 hours, 7 minutes. But it threatened to be a crucial strike for Bayern who had that air of confidence bordering on arrogance as they went in at half-time. But they got a rude awakening when all the character and self belief of the players blew away Bayern in the second half.

Howard and I told the players to keep up the pace and tempo we'd shown in the first half and when we came out after the interval the noise level was the highest I've known at Goodison. It certainly lifted our lads - and it must have brought at least a wobble to German legs. Only three minutes after the break we were level when Andy Gray flicked on a long throw from Gary Stevens for Graeme Sharp to score at the far post. It was his 29th goal of the season and meant he had scored in every European round.

Gray was also savouring the mood of battle although we were relieved at Swedish referee Erik Frederiksson's leniency when, after taking stick all night from Hans Pflugler, Andy kicked out at his marker but escaped with a yellow card. The sight of one of his players having to go off for treatment to a bloodied nose after tangling with Gray was too much for Bayern boss Udo Lattek, who shouted from his bench to Howard and the rest of us: 'Kendall - this isn't football.' I won't repeat what we shouted back to him!

The fans were roaring us on but with only 17 minutes left and with Neville Southall proving his usual brilliant self in goal it was still 1-1 on aggregate and Bayern, armed with their away goal, were heading for the final. But that night, as on so many occasions, Andy Gray would have smashed through a brick wall and when Gary Stevens delivered another of his speciality long throws the combative Scot hurled himself forward to connect. Jean-Marie Pfaff fatally hesitated and Andy pounced to force the ball into the net to put us ahead for the first time in the tie. 'Gwladys Street must have sucked it in because I didn't hit it that hard,' said Andy. We clinched a legendary victory with a magnificent goal four minutes from the end by Trevor Steven. A link between Paul Bracewell and Gray sent Trevor racing from the halfway line clear of the defence to send a precise shot past Pfaff and leave us ecstatic.

Bayern, who had been undone by a fantastic team performance from us and a superb example of British centre-forward play by Gray and Sharp, were not amused. Their coach Uli Hoeness told Gray in the tunnel: 'That was not football. It was war. You are crazy men.' Andy's four-letter reply was delivered with as much ferocity as one of his trademark headers! To be fair to Bayern, their manager Lattek said as he left Goodison: 'On this showing Everton are the best team in Europe. They put us under pressure and, in the final analysis, were simply too strong for us.'

It had been an exhibition to behold, a sparkling performance that matched the bubbles in the champagne we cracked at the end amidst clouds of Howard's cigar smoke. 'Think pale ale, drink pale ale. Think champagne, drink champagne,' was one of Howard's favourite sayings. There was certainly nothing pale ale about the team's performance on that wonderfully atmospheric evening which saw us through to the club's first European final which would be against Rapid Vienna in Rotterdam on May 15. The heroic display by the players was put into perspective when Jock Stein, Alex Ferguson and John Greig came in for an after-match drink with us. Alex said: 'You played like a team of Glasgow brothers.' Praise indeed!

With two finals 'in the bank' our next job was to ensure a successful last lap in the championship. Our defeat by the odd goal in seven to Chelsea in late December dislodged us from the League summit - but it was also the launch pad for a fantastic run. Four days later, on Boxing Day, we went back joint top with Tottenham after a 2-1 win at Sunderland thanks to two goals from Derek Mountfield. It was the start of a magnificent 28-game unbeaten run in all competitions - including 24 wins - which swept us to the title.

Perhaps the defining victory, though, was our midweek win at Tottenham early in April. We went into the game on top with 63 points from 30 games. Tottenham were three points behind us having played a game more, but had won at Liverpool a fortnight earlier for the first time since the Titanic sank in 1912. They'd already beaten us 4-1 on that stunning opening day of the season and now, with home advantage and players like Ray Clemence, Steve Perryman, Ossie Ardiles, Clive Allen and Mark Falco, they were dangerous opponents. It was billed in the media as a title decider.

We struck first blood when a long kick by Neville caught out Paul Miller and Andy Gray scored with a first-time shot after 10 minutes, his ninth goal in 10 games. Trevor Steven doubled our lead five minutes into the second half but Graham Roberts thundered a 25-yard reply that put Tottenham right back in it. With only six minutes left it seemed they were certain to retrieve a point when Falco rose to meet a cross with the goal seemingly at his mercy. But with a save I believe was at least as good as the iconic Gordon Banks' stop from Pele in the 1970 World Cup, somehow Neville twisted and flung himself down to push away Falco's point-blank header.

Neville's piece of magic, which ensured we took all three points and sent us surging on to the title, was the talk of both dressing rooms. 'Our lads were amazed by the save which was world class,' said Tottenham boss Peter Shreeve. But Neville, with a typical, downplayed, deadpan response, brushed aside the welter of plaudits and insisted: 'I don't know what all the fuss is about - he put it straight at me!' There was more fuss the following month when the Football Writers' Association voted Neville their Footballer of the Year with PFA award winner Peter Reid runner-up.

Neville produced another outstanding display at Sheffield Wednesday in early May when a Gray goal gave us our 12th away League win to equal our post-war club record set by the 1969-70 side in which Howard and I played. But Liverpool's 4-3 win over Chelsea the same afternoon meant we still needed a point to clinch the championship when we met QPR at home 48 hours later on Bank Holiday Monday. It was carnival time at Goodison when a crowd of 50,514 - our biggest for 14 months - saw us go ahead with a first-half goal from Derek Mountfield. A late strike from Graeme Sharp, his 30th goal of the season, secured a 2-0 win and the club's eighth championship.

We'd won it with five games to spare and the players richly deserved their lap of honour. Two days later, when another brace from Mountfield to take his season's haul to 14 and a goal from Gray gave us a 3-0 win over West Ham, we received the Canon championship trophy.

Our captain, Kevin Ratcliffe, had been ruled out of the QPR game with a groin injury and although he returned at Nottingham Forest in our next match we were without Andy Gray, Graeme Sharp, Peter Reid and Paul Bracewell and with the Cup Winners' Cup final looming the following Wednesday we were taking no risks with their fitness. It meant a first start for Paul Wilkinson in a side that also included Alan Harper, Kevin Richardson and Ian Atkins with defender Darren Oldroyd making his only senior appearance for us - a two-minute stint as a late replacement for Richardson. We lost 1-0, to a goal from Garry Birtles which ended our 28-game unbeaten run, but our confidence was as high as the plane which flew us to Rotterdam the following Tuesday for the clash with Rapid Vienna.

We'd seen Rapid and had them watched just as Rapid boss Otto Baric had put us under the microscope. Even taking into account their Austrian international skipper Hans Krankl, we felt their team didn't match up to ours and that they were nowhere near as good as Bayern. But what we told the players and the press was very different. We had to keep the team sharp mentally as well as physically without allowing the chance of complacency creeping in. The line-ups in Everton's first European final were:

Everton - Southall; Stevens, Mountfield, Ratcliffe, Van den Hauwe; Steven, Reid, Bracewell, Sheedy; Sharp, Gray. Substitutes not used: Harper, Bailey, Richardson, Atkins, Arnold.

Rapid Vienna - Michael Konsel; Leopold Lainer, Reinhard Kienast, Heribert Weber, Kurt Garger; Peter Pacult (Hans Gross, 60), Rudolf Weinhofer (Antonin Panenka, 86), Peter Hrstic, Karl Brauneder; Hans Krankl, Zlatko Kranjcar. Substitutes not used: Joann Pregesbauer, Hermann Stadler, Herbert Feurer.

Referee: Paolo Casarin (Italy)

Everything turned out perfectly. We took an estimated 20,000 fans to Holland and their pre-match behaviour was a model of how supporters should conduct themselves. They were welcome wherever they went and even played impromptu football matches with Rotterdam police. The participants in the kick-abouts included chief officer Patrick Verwer who, 18 years later, became managing director of the Dutch Railways/Serco consortium running the

Mersey rail franchise. 'I was in charge of the police operation in Rotterdam for that final and when we played football with the fans in the town square they were great,' he recalled.

Security for the final was exemplary with a ring of steel around the Feyenoord stadium and, from every viewpoint, it was an occasion when football was the winner. So were we. Emphatically, as it turned out even though it was still goalless at half-time after a 38th-minute Andy Gray strike was ruled out for offside. In the 57th minute we deservedly took the lead when Graeme Sharp intercepted a back pass, rounded keeper Konsel and passed for ummarked Gray to score. We doubled our lead after 72 minutes. Sharp flicked on Sheedy's corner from the right, Mountfield ducked and Trevor Steven fired his 16th goal of the season at the far post. A sign of our dominance was reflected in the fact that Neville Southall's first real save was delayed until the 82nd minute. Yet with five minutes to go, Rapid got within a goal of us when Krankl scored after being put through by Gross.

Just before Krankl's goal a UEFA official asked Howard if he would attend a media conference immediately after we'd been presented with the cup. As he spoke, Krankl put the ball in our net and Howard told the guy to clear off and not tempt providence. Within seconds, though, Gray and Sharp combined to find Sheedy, whose shot into the roof of the net ensured victory and the first European prize in Everton history. Howard quickly shouted to the official to come back because we knew then victory was ours. Howard, rightly to be named Manager of the Year, lit another cigar and, naturally, was bursting with pride at his team while I got fantastic fulfilment from seeing players I'd coached collect their second trophy in a week.

Rapid boss Baric was fulsome in his praise for our side, saying: 'Even at our best we couldn't have lived with Everton. Their pace and aggression was frightening.' By necessity our European celebrations had to be muted because three days later we were to face Manchester United in the FA Cup final. So it was straight to the airport and a flight home for a quick turn round down to our pre-Wembley base at Beaconsfield. We had a few drinks on the plane and reflected on a glorious evening, none of us aware of a situation which would see UEFA fine Rapid Vienna £15,000 because some of fans let off rockets and smoke bombs in the stadium. It seemed incongruous given what was to happen a fortnight later, when UEFA chose a totally unsuitable and insecure venue for Liverpool's European Cup final against Juventus in Brussels.

FA Cup final day dawned warm and got hotter. It was exactly the weather we didn't need for our eighth game in 24 days, a demanding sequence which had begun with our European return leg against Bayern Munich and, excepting Darren Oldroyd's fleeting appearance, had involved just 14 players. We named an unchanged side at Wembley and went desperately close to scoring after only 10 minutes when Gary Bailey punched out a Gary Stevens long throw straight to Peter Reid. Peter fired first time from well outside the area and John Gidman just managed to deflect the ball onto a post and away for a corner. Shortly after that Reidy realised it probably wasn't going to be our day, that we were going to be victims of our draining schedule. 'I slid what I felt was a good ball through to Graeme Sharp who, unusually for him, failed to control it,' said Reidy. 'Andy Gray shouted to him: 'Hey, Sharpy get hold of it.' Sharpy replied: 'I'm xxxxxxx knackered, Andy.' When I heard that I thought to myself that if Sharpy was feeling knackered in the first few minutes then we really had a job on.'

The game was still goalless when Kevin Moran made an unwanted piece of Wembley history. The Republic of Ireland defender's scything 79th- minute tackle on Reid earned him the red card from referee Peter Willis, who pre-empted by several years FIFA's decreed punishment for denial of scoring opportunities. The County Durham official waved away pleas from Peter and the United players to re-consider his decision. Moran trudged off to become the first player sent off in an FA Cup final and, cruelly, wasn't even allowed to collect his medal at the end.

Moran's dismissal seemed to galvanise United as the game dragged into extra time. They survived an aberration by Bryan Robson, whose back header was heading for his own net until Bailey desperately scooped it away, and with 10 minutes of the extra period left United struck the winner. Norman Whiteside cut inside on the United right before curling a superbly hit shot with his left foot beyond Neville Southall and into the far corner of the net. Try as we did we just couldn't get back at United and when Mountfield's back header was saved by Bailey our dream died of matching Liverpool's feat a year earlier by winning a treble.

When we sat down and thought about it, the FA Cup final had been a match too far. We were half a yard short through sheer fatigue. The players had been magnificent to achieve what they had. They received a rapturous salute from the fans who lined the streets of Liverpool to welcome back the most successful side in Everton history with one banner proclaiming: 'Two Will Do'. But we still had something else for them to cheer. On the Thursday after the Cup final we had the little matter of the Merseyside derby at Goodison to occupy our minds.

We were without Derek Mountfield, Paul Bracewell and Peter Reid through injury while Trevor Steven and Graeme Sharp were away on international duty. It meant a home debut for Paul Wilkinson in a side that also included Ian Atkins, John Bailey, Kevin Richardson and Alan Harper. Liverpool, too, had their absentees with Mark Lawrenson, Gary Gillespie, Paul Walsh and Alan Kennedy missing but Joe Fagan still paraded a line-up including that terrific strike force of Ian Rush and Kenny Dalglish.

But it was our night, Wilkinson getting the game's only goal in the 68th minute to claim the unique distinction of scoring Goodison winners against both Everton and Liverpool in the same season, following his decisive late header for Grimsby that knocked us out of the Milk Cup the previous November. Watched by Goodison's biggest crowd of the season, more than 51,000, the win was our third over Liverpool that campaign following our victories in the Charity Shield and at Anfield - and we hadn't conceded a goal against them. It completed our first League derby double for 20 years and since the introduction of three-points-for-a-win set a record for the former First Division of 90 points, a total equalled by Liverpool in 1987-88.

Howard Kendall, who had joined the elite band of people who have played in and managed championship-winning sides, celebrated by heading up to Glasgow next morning to receive his Manager of the Year Award. And typical of Howard it was a journey with a difference. He asked our coach driver if he was available and booked the team bus to take him and some press friends to Scotland for the presentation! For the record, he's still one of only nine to have achieved title triumph as player and manager. The others are Ted Drake, Bill Nicholson, Sir Alf Ramsey, Joe Mercer, Dave Mackay, Bob Paisley, Kenny Dalglish and George Graham.

Because of our fixture pile-up we still had two League games left - at Coventry the following Sunday and at Luton two days later. We had several injured absentees at Highfield Road and lost 4-1. Coventry's win meant Norwich were relegated and when we went to Luton we had nine of the first-team squad missing through injuries and international calls. The situation meant that Jason Danskin, Derek Walsh and Neil Rimmer, who was substitute, had their only senior Everton outings while it was one of only a few appearances for Darren Hughes, John Morrissey junior and Rob Wakenshaw. Perhaps not surprisingly we lost 2-0.

It had been an amazing season, the most successful in the club's history, and the statistics make remarkable reading.We played 63 games in the various competitions, scoring 125 goals, and our 43 victories set an English club record that still stands. We used only 25 players, with three of that total making only one appearance, another having only one start and one substitute outing and another one start and three substitute appearances. So, effectively, we used 20 players in the marathon campaign which must say something about today's obsession with rotation. Neville Southall was ever- present, Kevin Ratcliffe and Trevor Steven played in 61 games, Derek Mountfield amd Gary Stevens in 58, Paul Bracewell and Peter Reid in 57 and Graeme Sharp in 55. The team matched our 1969-70 side's feat in beating all their League opponents at least once during the season - the only times it had happened in the top flight since before the First World War - and the 13-point margin over runners-up Liverpool was then a record in the three-points-for-a-win era.

It was satisfying, too, that our goals were spread through the squad. Graeme Sharp top-scored with 30 in all competitions with Kevin Sheedy next on 17. They were two of six players to reach double figures and eight of the squad scored twice in matches. We were named European Team of the Year while World Soccer magazine voted us World Team of the Year.

Our glow at this welter of plaudits and the deep satisfaction at winning the championship and Cup Winners' Cup swiftly translated itself into exciting anticipation of our looming challenge in the European Cup. There was a real sense among the players and backroom staff that we could become champions of Europe. As the captain Kevin Ratcliffe declared: 'We couldn't wait to get out there onto that stage and compete with the best.

We believed we were as good, if not better, than Liverpool as our results had indicated and nobody in Europe frightened us. There's no doubt that we were good enough to win the European Cup, even in those days when it was harder to win because every round was knock-out. If we had done what a massive impact that would have had on the club.'

My own view concurs with Kevin's. At that period I felt we were the best team in Europe. We'd beaten two of the great European forces in Bayern Munich and Liverpool and even without the comfort zones of today's Champions League system - in which you can lose several games and still win the trophy - I felt we were a match for anyone, capable of beating anyone. We had a squad filled with international quality and experience with an average age only in the mid-20s. The players had demonstrated their mental and physical toughness and durability, Howard was a proven manager, I felt great fulfilment in charge of the coaching and Mick Heaton dovetailed into a balanced backroom set-up. I had faith in my coaching abilities and I concentrated on developing the players as a unit - especially when we didn't have the ball.

Alex Ferguson's comment likening us to a band of Glasgow brothers suggests that we'd got it right. Everything was primed, everything was set for our assault on Europe's greatest prize which could have changed the face and finances of Everton for years to come. Alas, our 'honeymoon' period was brief before tragedy intervened with the horror of the Heysel disaster, the second devastating blow for our national game in less than three weeks.

Earlier in the month fire had broken out in the main stand at Bradford City's Valley Parade ground, killing 56 spectators, which was a grim prelude to that appalling evening in Brussels at the European Cup final between Liverpool and Juventus, which cost 39 lives and injured hundreds. Such events transcend football which, like the Heysel match itself, was rendered irrelevant by the grief and human tragedy which still has repercussions today. Our hearts went out to all the bereaved and injured.

We felt, too, for Joe Fagan, who had decided in advance of that awful night to make Heysel his last match in charge of Liverpool. What a dreadful farewell it was for him. Suddenly, the close season was cloaked in a pall of tragedy and UEFA's ban on English clubs meant we were out of Europe, only days after dreaming of a new Continental campaign. Now we had to get down to our plans for a new, solely domestic season.

Howard had been an admirer of Leicester's Gary Lineker for some time and the media had speculated that we would make a move for him. Howard felt that while Graeme Sharp, Adrian Heath and Andy Gray were superb strikers they didn't pack the pace of Lineker, who'd finished the season as the First Division's joint-top scorer with Chelsea's Kerry Dixon on 24 goals. He'd scored 29 in all competitions - not bad in a team that finished 15th in the table. Our initial offer of £400,000 was rejected by Leicester, who valued Gary at £1.25 million, both clubs well aware that it would go to a tribunal who decided on a fee of £800,000 with a sell-on clause.

Our capture of Lineker spelled the end of Andy Gray's brief but eventful Goodison career and he returned to Aston Villa, his first English club, for £150,000. Andy's 18-month partnership with Graeme Sharp, in which he scored 22 goals in 68 senior appearances, will be remembered as perhaps the most swashbuckling in Everton history and he had a personal chemistry with which fans passionately identified.

Consequently, when the news broke that he was leaving Everton the radio phone lines and newspaper letters columns were filled with shocked supporters, who even launched a petition trying to get him to stay. There was criticism not just for selling Andy but that we'd sold him too soon. The fact is that in Gary Lineker we'd signed the country's hottest striking property and, given that, there was no way Andy wanted to stay because, quite understandably, he wanted regular first-team football.

Andy was typically forthright about it when he said: 'It did disappoint me that Howard felt he needed to bring in Gary to make the side better. But I understood - and I was old enough and experienced enough to be aware that these things happen. Howard told me he was bringing Gary in and that I'd start the new season in the reserves. After the season I'd had, and all we'd won, I couldn't accept that. Howard had to make a decision and Gary's 40 goals in his one season at Everton suggest he was right. But the lack of trophies suggest that maybe he was wrong. I left on a high, though, and nobody could think badly of me. So maybe it was meant to be.'

Andy did have a persistent knee problem and it's purely hypothetical to speculate on what might have happened had he stayed. But Andy's point about us not winning a trophy in 1985-86 touches a raw nerve because it was sheer painful frustration for everyone at the club to finish runners-up to Liverpool in both the championship and FA Cup.

The curtain went up for us back at Wembley against Manchester United in the Charity Shield. Our team was:

Southall; Stevens, Mountfield, Ratcliffe, Van den Hauwe; Steven, Reid, Bracewell, Sheedy; Sharp and Lineker.

Our substitutes included Adrian Heath, back after a nine-month absence with knee ligament damage, and goalkeeper Bobby Mimms, a £150,000 buy from Rotherham with our previous reserve keeper Jim Arnold moving on to Port Vale. Although it didn't compensate for our Cup final defeat by United, our 2-0 win was satisfying. Trevor Steven put us ahead in the first half and Adrian Heath celebrated his comeback with the clinching 82nd-minute goal after replacing Lineker. With the Charity Shield retained we made a mixed start in the League, losing our opener 3-1 at Lineker's former club Leicester, and although we won our first home game - Heath's brace ensuring a 2-0 victory over West Brom - we were then held to a 1-1 draw by Coventry.

Lineker scored his first goal for us to give us a 1-0 win at one of his future clubs Tottenham. He followed up with a hat-trick in a 4-1 defeat of Birmingham, then a brace in our 5-1 win at Sheffield Wednesday, taking his haul to six in three games. Ian Marshall, a versatile 19-year-old who had come through our junior sides, found opportunity knocking for his debut at the back in place of knee casualty Derek Mountfield and we also lost Achilles victim Peter Reid for 31 games between September and February.

Marshall played in nine of our first 14 games before we opted for the experience of Pat Van den Hauwe alongside Kevin Ratcliffe. In a season when our defensive selection was far from stable Gary Stevens and Alan Harper also appeared in the middle while midfielder Kevin Richardson made 30 senior appearances. Another defender, left-back John Bailey, got the chance to resurrect his career with an £80,000 move to Newcastle in October with Neil Pointon arriving for £50,000 from Scunthorpe, memorably making his debut in a 6-1 home thrashing of Arsenal when he outshone Kenny Sansom and earned a standing ovation.

Manchester United scorched into the season by winning their first 10 League games and the Daily Mirror unwisely declared that it was Old Trafford's title. We lost a thrilling derby 3-2 to Liverpool at Goodison when Kenny Dalglish, who had taken over as player-manager in the dreadful aftermath of Heysel, scored after 20 seconds and began a worrying trend for us of being hit by early goals. We conceded in the first minute five times in 16 games with Dalglish's swift strike being followed by Bournemouth's Colin Clarke (11 seconds), Southampton's Glenn Cockerill (11 seconds) and Chelsea's Kerry Dixon, who scored in the first minute in two Milk Cup matches, the second of them a fourth-round home replay which we lost 2-1.

Chelsea also beat us by the same score in the League at Stamford Bridge in October when Neville Southall was sent off for two bookable offences - dissent and handling outside his area. Kevin Ratcliffe went in goal and kept a clean sheet in his 31 minutes emergency duty. Neville's ban a fortnight later, ending his two-year ever present run, gave Bobby Mimms his debut in a 1-1 draw at Manchester City.

Our title prospects looked a bit gloomy by the time we lost at West Ham in early November. It left us in seventh place, 17 points behind leaders United. Even second-placed Liverpool were 10 points behind Ron Atkinson's side. We'd actually beaten United 4-2 at Old Trafford in September in the Screen Sport Super Cup - the hurriedly arranged competition for English clubs who'd been denied their places in Europe - and beat them again, 1-0, in the return at home. It was inevitable that United's First Division pace would slacken and gradually their lead was eroded. When they came to Goodison on Boxing Day we gave a brilliant display to come back from a goal down, after Frank Stapleton scored, to win 3-1, the fourth time we'd beaten them that season. Graeme Sharp scored twice and Gary Lineker got the other to top the Christmas scoring charts with 19 goals. We'd won at Coventry the previous Saturday, which was the start of an 18-game unbeaten run in the League, FA Cup and Screen Sport Cup.

Peter Reid made a happy return to action on February 1 by scoring the only goal of our home clash with Tottenham. It was only his fifth League goal on his 83rd First Division outing for Everton but it put us top - by a point from United - for the first time since winning the championship the previous season. With our strongest line-up since September, with only Mountfield missing from our recognised first-choice side, we hammered Manchester City 4-0 at home in our next League game to take us three points clear of United and complete a 20-point turn-around since November. It was a freezing night but Lineker was hot. In fact by then he rivalled Ian Rush as the hottest scoring property in Europe and hit his third hat-trick of the season - two for us and one for England - to take his Everton goal total to 29. But for fine saves from City keeper Eric Nixon, our winning margin would have been greater. Unfortunately, we lost Kevin Sheedy with a knee injury during the match but he made a headlines by being back in our squad just 19 days after keyhole cartilage surgery and made his return to action four days after that, in our home FA Cup quarter-final replay with Luton.

Following our emphatic defeat of City we went to Anfield to face Liverpool. It was goalless until the 74th minute when we broke through in bizarre style and from the most unlikely source. Kevin Ratcliffe picked up possession some 25 yards out and unleashed a speculative shot. Meat and drink to Grobbelaar we thought...until the Zimbabwe international allowed the ball to squirm away from him and into the net. Not even the shot's slight deflection off Lineker could explain Grobbelaar's costly error which brought Kevin his first goal for more than three years and only the second - and last - in a wonderful career that spanned almost 500 senior appearances.

The Anfield crowd were still trying to come to terms with that shock when we clinched a great win four minutes later when Lineker pounced for his 30th Everton goal. It was a result that maintained our three-point lead over

Manchester United at the top and took us eight points clear of third-placed Liverpool. It put us firmly in the driving seat and I'm told that after the game Alan Hansen told Dalglish it was the worst Liverpool team he'd played in. Be that as it may, Kenny and his squad must take great credit for their tremendous response to what must have felt like a crushing loss. Liverpool licked their wounds and then went on a stunning run in which they won 11 and drew one of their last 12 League games to pip us to the championship.

In the FA Cup we reached the quarter-final by beating Exeter, Blackburn Rovers and Tottenham. Our 2-1 win at White Hart Lane was secured by goals from substitute Adrian Heath, who'd replaced the injured Kevin Ratcliffe, and Lineker, his 32nd of the season to bring up the 50-partnership with Sharp. Heath scored as a sub again against Luton - this time having replaced Neil Pointon - and after an earlier goal from Sharp it sealed our comeback from 2-0 down to earn a home replay. A Lineker goal at Goodison was sufficient to take us through to our third consecutive semi-final.

Luton, though, struck a major blow to our hopes of retaining the title and gave Liverpool the first real scent of success in their bid to overtake us. We went back to Kenilworth Road's plastic pitch but despite being without the injured quartet of Ratcliffe, Reid, Steven and Heath, then losing Sheedy with a torn hamstring, we seemed to be heading for victory. Kevin Richardson put us ahead after the interval, his shot taking a massive deflection off Steve Foster, and we were leading up to nine minutes from the end.

But we went down to two late Luton goals, Foster heading home and then turning provider for Mike Newell, a striker I'd later sign for Everton. Our 18-match unbeaten run was over. Liverpool, who trounced Oxford 6-0 at Anfield the same day, went level with us at the top on 66 points and Howard Kendall still believes that was the afternoon that cost us the championship.

Four days later fate dealt us another major blow when Neville Southall fell into a pot hole on Dublin's Lansdowne Road pitch when he was on duty for Wales against the Republic of Ireland, leaving him with a dislocated ankle and ligament damage. To lose for the remainder of the season the man I rate the best keeper I've ever seen was an Easter present we could have done without - and that's no disrespect to his deputy Bobby Mimms. But Neville had that special authority and charisma, plus an understanding with his defence that comes only from playing week in, week out.

Bobby came in and helped set what was then a new club record of six consecutive League clean sheets. The sequence stretched to 10 hours 28 minutes - but when it ended it effectively shattered our title dreams. Our midweek game at Oxford at the end of April was goalless until the last two minutes. Then Oxford caught us on the counter and Les Phillips nipped in to head their winner. What made it particularly galling was that, for once, Gary Lineker was guilty of some remarkably uncharacteristic misses. He later told us that he'd left behind his battered but 'lucky' old boots and tried to break in a new pair at the Manor Ground. If only he'd stuck with the tried and tested pair we may have gone on to keep a grip on the title and Gary's name might have earned more reverence in Everton folklore than it seems to have done which, given his prolific season's performance, seems grossly unfair.

The Oxford result was only our second defeat in 27 games but with Liverpool winning at Leicester the same night the destiny of the championship went out of our hands and into Liverpool's. They led with 85 points from 41 games, West Ham were second with 81 points from 40 games and we were third with 80 points from 40 games. All our frustration exploded into a 6-1 home hammering of Southampton three days later when Lineker - complete with old boots - rifled his third Everton hat-trick, Graeme Sharp hit his 24th goal of the season and Derek Mountfield and Trevor Steven added the others. But Dalglish's goal at Chelsea the same afternoon gave Liverpool a 1-0 win and made them champions, with Kenny becoming the first player-manager to win the title.

We still had a chance to get one over them in the little matter of the first all-Merseyside FA Cup final, the appetite for which had been whetted by our Wembley encounters in the Milk Cup final and Charity Shield. Forty-eight hours after beating Southampton we secured the runners-up spot by beating West Ham 3-1 at Goodison, Lineker scoring twice and Trevor Steven converting a penalty. With the FA Cup final looming on the Saturday - which we'd reached by beating Sheffield Wednesday 2-1 after extra time through goals from Alan Harper and Graeme Sharp in the semi-final at Villa Park - we left out Mountfield, Reid, Sharp and Bracewell against West Ham.

They had had an assortment of injuries so Peter Billinge came in for his only League appearance for us and Warren Aspinall, who'd done well on loan at Wigan, made his senior debut as a substitute. Lineker's brace against West Ham took him to 39 Everton goals for the season and 30 in the First Division, only the second player along with Ian Rush to achieve that total since Bob Latchford in 1978. Even more impressive was the fact that his haul didn't include a single penalty and Gary was full value for his double honour of being voted Footballer of the Year by the football writers and Player of the Year by the PFA.

We earnestly hoped he would add an FA Cup winners' medal to those awards when we met Liverpool in our third consecutive final and our sixth Wembley appearance in little more than two years. The teams were:

Everton - Mimms; Stevens (Heath, 72), Ratcliffe, Mountfield, Van den Hauwe; Steven, Reid, Bracewell, Sheedy; Sharp, Lineker.

Liverpool - Grobbelaar; Nicol, Lawrenson, Hansen, Beglin; Johnston, Molby, MacDonald, Whelan; Rush, Dalglish. Substitute: McMahon.

The first half belonged to us. We were well on top and the only criticism was that we should have been ahead by more than Lineker's 40th goal of the season. We also felt we should have had a penalty when Nicol fouled Sharp but Alan Robinson, the referee who had rejected our penalty claims for Hansen's handball in the 1984 Milk Cup final, waved away our appeals.

We were still in control when the second half got underway and when Grobbelaar and Beglin had a 'handbags' spat it looked as though the occasion was getting to Liverpool. Had we kept them out a bit longer it might have done but when Whelan and Molby combined in the 57th minute Rush beat Mimms to equalise. Even then it needed a great tip-over by Grobbelaar from a Sharp effort to prevent us regaining the lead before Johnston put Liverpool ahead with 63 minutes on the clock.

We were still in with a shout until seven minutes from the end, by which time we'd brought on Heath, an extra attacker, in place of Stevens. But a superb Whelan pass set up Rush for his second goal of the game to clinch the Double for Liverpool and leave us in double despair. Our 3-1 defeat was only the third we'd suffered in 30 games in all competitions - yet we'd ended up empty-handed. It was a bitter pill to swallow for all of us.

In what had seemed like a good idea at the time it was arranged that us and Liverpool would return to Merseyside together for a joint tour. The fact is that after congratulating Kenny and his team we just wanted to go home and shut the door! We went through with the plan - apart from one man. Peter Reid couldn't face it and bowed out of it, saying: 'I shook hands with every Liverpool player, but there was no way I was getting on that bus for the drive round the city. I just couldn't have handled it. Instead, I was well away from it all in a pub in Manchester.' I know how he felt. We all did. But a year later we could smile once again as more glitter arrived at Goodison.

Making myself heard with stand-in captain Dave Watson, 1988.

Chapter Twelve

Into The Hot Seat

The 'Hand Of God' loomed large in English football during the summer of 1986, Diego Maradona's unpunished act of cheating helping to down England in the World Cup quarter-finals in Mexico. The fact that they were pushed through the exit by a fantastic second goal from the Argentinian, after a run that left half the England team in his wake, tended to be lost in the collective recollection of a bitter injustice to the boys of St George.

Everton were being hit by the hand of fate. A series of blows threatened to end their championship hopes before the 1986-87 season. They had already come close to losing manager Howard Kendall in the first stirrings of a trail that would see him leave Goodison and Colin Harvey step up from coach and complete a unique journey from fan to manager, with a celebrated playing career sandwiched between.

Even before Everton had completed an agonising season of finishing second to Liverpool in League and FA Cup in 1986 it seemed that Kendall was on his way out. In the closing weeks of the campaign Barcelona rang him with the news that Terry Venables was leaving the Nou Camp and that they wanted Kendall to take over. Kendall, excited, flattered and keenly interested in a reign in Spain, informed his chairman Philip Carter of Barcelona's overtures and kept him updated on developments. Carter accepted that if there were no unforeseen problems, Kendall would be leaving.

A top level Barcelona delegation, including club president Jose Luis Nunez, met Kendall in London and the Everton manager signed a provisional contract to take over at the Nou Camp when, as expected, Venables left that summer. Carter's response was to tell Colin Harvey that Everton wanted him to succeed Kendall and to prepare for an impending handover of managerial power. Alas, a few weeks later Venables announced he was staying at Barcelona, who lost to Steaua Bucharest on penalties after a mind-numbing goalless draw in the

European Cup final in Seville.

Kendall's provisional contract with Barcelona - which he still has "to remind me of what might have been" - was now null and void. But what we didn't know then was that his departure and Harvey's succession was merely delayed for a year until another Spanish club came knocking. However, it was far from the end of discussions with Barcelona. The World Cup finals involved four Goodison players - Gary Lineker, Gary Stevens, Trevor Steven and Peter Reid - and Lineker's feat of scoring 40 goals in a season for Everton and his top-scoring display for England in Mexico alerted a host of European clubs to his predatory talents.

Barcelona, though, had made overtures for him several months before. Venables was a fervent admirer of Lineker and the Spanish club made an inquiry about the player direct to Kendall, who revealed the development to his chairman Carter. The asking price of £2.8 million - with a third of the £2 million profit due to Leicester - was readily agreed. Everton, naturally, were not desperate to sell Lineker, who had three years of his contract remaining. But when the inevitable leaks about Barcelona's interest reached the player he was keen to talk to them. His displays in Mexico, crowned by six England goals, made Barcelona desperate to land Lineker and Kendall saw no sense in trying to keep hold of a player excited by the lure of Spanish football, who had agreed an eight-year deal at a £250,000 annual salary.

Thus, in successive close seasons, Everton had sold two star strikers, who went about their craft in very different ways. A year earlier had seen the departure of Andy Gray, a typically British centre-forward, who thrived on crosses and put his head where the boots fly. He wore his passion on his sleeve and he was adored by the Gwladys Street faithful. Lineker was a much cooler customer, composed and calculating. Lineker seemed detached from almost everything but his job of putting the ball in the net, which he did not only frequently but as the product of lightning pace.

Yet this perceived aloofness - and probably the fact that his bounty of goals failed to deliver a trophy - denied him the terrace hero worship which to this day still envelopes Gray. Gray and Lineker share the same birthday - November 30 in 1955 and 1960 respectively - and both went on to become high-profile television performers with Sky and the BBC. Yet the contrast in their playing styles could not have been more marked.

While Lineker's departure left Kendall on the receiving end of public criticism for the second successive summer, the Everton boss prepared a tactical response to overcome the sale of the prolific England marksman. To capitalise on Lineker's speed and finishing Everton had tended to knock the ball long, down the centre and over the top, at the expense of utilising the wide skills of Kevin Sheedy and Trevor Steven, whose scoring rate had dropped. Kendall felt that now Lineker had gone the time was opportune to feel the width and the quality of his side in the forthcoming 1986-87 season. But when the curtain went up his squad had been ravaged by injuries.

Goalkeeper Neville Southall was still unfit from his ankle damage the previous season and the other casualties were Gary Stevens, Derek Mountfield, Neil Pointon, Pat Van den Hauwe, Paul Bracewell and Peter Reid. Of Everton's England World Cup quartet only Trevor Steven started the season - along with Graeme Sharp, who'd played for Scotland in Mexico - but Kendall had made several sorties into the market to fortify his squad. The biggest expenditure was the £900,000 club record signing of Kirkdale-born former Liverpool reserve centre-back Dave Watson from Norwich. Other arrivals were England Under 21 winger Neil Adams from Stoke, 22-year-old Wigan midfielder Kevin Langley and Manchester City's veteran and versatile skipper Paul Power. The newcomers were to play their part in a remarkably rewarding campaign. Colin Harvey recalls:

"A few months earlier, in April the previous season, we had a League game at Watford when our chairman Philip Carter stopped me in the corridor and said he wanted a word with me. We went into the Watford boot room and he said: 'I presume you're aware that it looks like Howard will be leaving us.' I told him that Howard had made me aware of the situation. The chairman then told me: 'If Howard goes we want you to become the new manager.' I said I'd be delighted to accept. Howard had asked me to go with him to Barcelona but my instinct was to stay at Everton and by the time the new season came round the issue had gone away, anyway.

So the thoughts of Howard and I were dominated by how best we could introduce the new signings into a team stripped by injury of so many key players, many of whom were long-term casualties. The big story, of course, had been the sale of Gary Lineker whose 40-goal season with us had been overshadowed by the fact that we didn't win anything. I think, also, it had been difficult for the fans to relate to him because, unlike Andy Gray, he was very undemonstrative and you could never imagine him losing his temper or getting over-excited. I always got the feeling with Gary that he treated football as a job he was exceptionally good at rather than one he enjoyed. I often wondered if he was really a football fan whereas Andy was in the great tradition of Everton No 9s, a line adored by the supporters.

Although Gary was sold to Barcelona we didn't sign a replacement. We relied on Graeme Sharp, Adrian Heath and Paul Wilkinson up front. But then we got hit by that massive injury pile-up. Paul Bracewell, whose last appearance had been in the previous May's FA Cup final, was ruled out for the whole season, Gary Stevens and Peter Reid were out until December and big Neville didn't return in goal until late October. We played pre-season games in Holland and Germany and we had to send Pat Van den Hauwe home from the tour with an ankle problem. He also contracted a virus that ruled him out of action until January.

Journalist Ian Hargraves, who'd been covering some of our games for the Liverpool Echo, was also flying home so Howard and I asked him to keep an eye on Pat. Ian had a journey to remember, including an argument between Pat and customs officials at Manchester Airport! Apparently, they asked Pat to open his case for inspection, which he did. Then he demanded that as they'd put him to that trouble they should re-pack his case and close it for him! I think he came close to being arrested. Ian, an educated, amiable man, was totally embarrassed and, reflecting on his Van den Hauwe experience, memorably remarked: 'It was like guiding a rabid dog home.'

Pat subsequently had a few more problems in his life, some of them splashed across Sunday tabloids, but I understand he's now fit and well and living in South Africa. I always had a lot of time for Pat. I got on with him and he was good company. Above all, he was a very good player and in my view it's a pity he opted for Wales instead of England when he had the choice of which British country to play for. He was certainly England calibre and highly talented at left-back and centre-back.

Given our number of casualties in the summer of 1986, our Wembley starting line-up to face Liverpool in our third consecutive Charity Shield included only five players who had appeared in the FA Cup final three months earlier. The team was:

Bobby Mimms; Alan Harper, Ian Marshall, Kevin Ratcliffe, Paul Power; Trevor Steven, Kevin Langley, Kevin Richardson, Kevin Sheedy (Neil Adams, 56, Paul Wilkinson, 82); Adrian Heath, Graeme Sharp. Unused substitutes: Fred Barber, Warren Aspinall, Mike Stowell.

The five who had started in the FA Cup final were Mimms, Ratcliffe, Steven, Sharp and Sheedy and when Adrian Heath scored 10 minutes from time it seemed victory was in sight before that goal plunderer of Everton nightmares, Ian Rush, equalised two minutes from the end.

The Wembley game provided a swift lesson for Neil Adams who became, as far as I'm aware, the first Everton substitute to be substituted. Howard sent him on for his debut, with certain instructions, as a 56th-minute replacement for Kevin Sheedy. Eight minutes from the end Neil saw some activity on the bench and asked Adrian Heath: 'Who's going off?' 'You are,' Adrian replied. Howard felt that the lad wasn't doing what he'd been asked to do so decided to make an example of him by taking him off and sending on Paul Wilkinson for the last few minutes.

Neil took the message on board and he and the other new signings who - Dave Watson apart - were far from star names, did well for us that season. The likes of Adams and Langley were sound players without being top drawer. It was a big step-up for them but they really dug in and responded. Our play was more functional than in previous years, not as spectacular as in some earlier seasons. We were more compact and with Lineker gone the goals, once again, were spread through the team. Sheedy and Steven scored 32 between them whereas the previous season they'd scored a total of 19.

Paul Power made a magnificent contribution. Howard picked him up for a song. Considering he'd paid a mere £65,000 for the Manchester City skipper it must go down as one of his best signings. Paul was 32 when he joined us but was super fit. He was a natural athlete, a leader, the type of player you want. And when he had to pack up he stayed with us as a coach.

Despite all the upheaval we made a good start in the League and didn't lose until our eighth game, a 2-0 reverse at Tottenham which ended the First Division's last unbeaten run. It left us third on 15 points, two behind Norwich and four behind leaders Nottingham Forest. We lost a few slices of local pride, though, by losing to Liverpool in two cup competitions. We'd both reached the final of the Screen Sport Super Cup, held over from the previous season, but we lost on a 7-2 aggregate, with Ian Rush scoring five in the two matches.

After helping Liverpool to a 3-1 win at Anfield the Welshman exposed the naivety and inexperience of our reserve centre-back Peter Billinge in the second leg at Goodison. We'd signed Peter from South Liverpool and, with Dave Watson cup-tied, he played in both legs alongside Kevin Ratcliffe. Kevin told us later that Rushie had said: 'This lad doesn't know what day it is. I am going to 'do' him with the old tying the lace trick.' Sure enough, during the game at Goodison, Rushie started tying his boot lace. 'What's up?' asked

Peter. 'I'm just doing my lace up,' said Rushie. Peter took half a step away as one of the Liverpool players knocked the ball over the top and Rushie was on it in a flash to score. I'm glad to say that Peter survived the experience. He left us a couple of months later, going on to have more than 200 League outings for Crewe, Coventry, Port Vale and Hartlepool.

We lost again to Liverpool at home in the Littlewoods Cup quarter-final, which we'd reached by beating Newport on a 9-1 aggregate - Paul Wilkinson scoring five in the two legs - Sheffield Wednesday 4-0, with Wilkinson scoring twice, and Norwich 4-1. Our Littlewoods tie with Liverpool was the fourth time we'd played them since Dave Watson's arrival and he'd missed out on facing his former club on each occasion. Twice he'd been cup-tied and now, for the second time, he missed out through injury. It was the night Liverpool's Jim Beglin suffered a horrific broken left leg after a challenge from Gary Stevens and we lost to the only goal of the game scored - surprise, surprise - by that boyhood Everton fan Ian Rush late on.

In the FA Cup we beat Southampton 2-1 in the third round - our 24th home game in the competition without defeat since February 1975 - then won 1-0 at Bradford when our £840,000 new signing Ian Snodin from Leeds scored his first goal since choosing to join us rather than Liverpool. Both ourselves and Liverpool had agreed the fee with Leeds and I think personal terms were more or less identical. But what I think swayed Ian's decision in our favour was that Kenny Dalglish wanted him to play on the right while Howard saw him as a central midfielder, which was where the lad wanted to play. He was a highly talented player and desperately unlucky not to add full England caps to his Youth, Under 21 and 'B' appearances. Ian showed he was also a very capable performer at full-back and after being named in the England squad to face Greece in 1989, was forced to withdraw through injury. Opportunity, sadly, never knocked again.

We went out of the FA Cup to new First Division arrivals Wimbledon on a totally forgettable Sunday afternoon at Plough Lane. The team fashioned by Dave Bassett, who was succeeded by Bobby Gould at the end of that season, had climbed from non-League football to the top flight in a decade, an amazing climb. Our first encounters with the Crazy Gang brought us the happy outcome of a League double. Our 2-1 away win in September was followed by a 3-0 victory at Goodison in December, which marked substitute Peter Reid's first senior action since England's fateful World Cup clash with Argentina six months earlier.

But when we faced the Dons in the FA Cup we were well beaten. Even though Paul Wilkinson put us ahead early on, we failed to deal with their aerial threat. They outpowered us and we lost 3-1. It was our first defeat in the competition outside Wembley for almost four years - since losing 1-0 to Manchester United in March 1983 - and just to make things worse our bus broke down on the motorway on the way home.

In our League games against Wimbledon they'd been trying to play a bit of football but when we played them in the Cup they reverted to what they were good at...powerful route one football and challenging for every ball. They had a collection of players perfectly suited for that in-your-face physical style and gave a lot of teams problems. They went on to finish sixth in their first season in the top flight and a season later produced one of the greatest shocks in FA Cup history by beating Liverpool at Wembley. I often reflect on the fact that but for the ban on English clubs Wimbledon would have competed in Europe. I wonder how Real Madrid, Barcelona or any of the Continent's other elite clubs would have set about the task of taming the Crazy Gang! It would have been football's ultimate chalk and cheese.

The vacuum caused by the European ban on English clubs saw the introduction of yet another competition: the Full Members Cup. It was devised for teams in the top two divisions who were full members of the Football League as it was then constituted. Frankly we could have done without this concoction but after beating Newcastle 5-2, featuring Graeme Sharp's first career hat-trick, in front of a 7,530 crowd - which was then Goodison's lowest post-war senior attendance - we faced Charlton at home in the quarter-final. John Ebbrell made his senior debut for us in that game at the age of 17 and the match seemed like the longest ever. We drew 2-2 after extra time and then lost 6-5 on penalties, a shoot-out memorable for Neville Southall's only Everton goal in his 750 senior appearances!

We were just grateful to be out of the competition, which was a meaningless intrusion into what was still a 42-match League season. But with the funding stream of Europe having been switched off clubs were keen to maximise any financial potential although poor attendances for these competitions underlined what the public thought about them. It was probably incumbent on Everton to take part, given that our chairman, Philip Carter - who was knighted in 1991 - was Football League president from 1986 to 1988 and played a leading role in the formation of the breakaway Premier League, which became known as the FA Premiership.

The Full Members Cup game against Charlton was played on March 3 and already by that stage of the season Trevor Steven was our only ever-present, underlining just how deep the injuries had cut into our squad. Paul Wilkinson's goal against Charlton was his 13th in 16 starts but it turned out to be his last prior to his £200,000 move to Nottingham Forest. Through the arrivals door came striker Wayne Clarke in a £420,000 move from Birmingham, a deal that included £120,000-rated 20-year-old Stuart Storer also joining us. Storer never made a first-team appearance and was sold to Bolton for £25,000 some 10 months later. But Clarke, signed to help fill the gap during Sharp's absence with Achilles damage, proved a key man in our championship win.

Wayne, one of five footballing brothers including Allan and Frank, wasn't the quickest but he was an impressive technical player with good touch and control. His five goals in his 10 outings for us that season, including a hat-trick in a 3-0 win over Newcastle, were crucial. His first was a wonderfully spectacular strike to give us a 1-0 win at Arsenal. Goalkeeper John Lukic sent an attempted clearance straight to Wayne who controlled the ball, looked up and, seeing Lukic towards the edge of his box, clipped it first time over his head from 35 yards into the top corner.

It was, as Howard said afterwards, the kind of result that wins championships and coming on the same afternoon that Wimbledon were gaining a shock win at Anfield, it meant we had slashed the gap on leaders Liverpool from 10 points to three in 10 days - and we had two matches in hand. They had 67 points from 35 games, we had 64 from 33. The Wimbledon result was the second of three consecutive League defeats for Liverpool - sandwiched between a 1-0 reverse at Tottenham and 2-1 loss at Norwich - to swing the title battle powerfully in our favour.

The previous November we'd drawn with Liverpool in a dismal goalless live televised Sunday game at Goodison and although we lost the April return at Anfield, we remained in the top spot we'd reached earlier that month. Kevin Sheedy scored a great free-kick in our 3-1 defeat by his former club but made a two-fingered gesture to the Kop, who had been giving him stick. Adrian Heath also made a gesture and their actions would have a direct legacy for me during the close season.

We had four games left after that derby defeat, winning three and drawing one. Fate, for once, was kind to us because as we lost Clarke with a shoulder injury sustained in the last minute of our next game - a goalless home clash with Manchester City - Sharp was fit to return against Luton after three months and 14 games out. Liverpool's defeat at Coventry while we were drawing with City meant that we could secure the title 48 hours later on Bank Holiday Monday when we faced Norwich at Carrow Road, backed by massive support from travelling fans.

Many spectators hadn't even settled into their seats when Pat Van den Hauwe scored the most memorable goal of his career with a mere 45 seconds on the clock. Paul Power delivered a corner and, after Trevor Steven and Sharp had shots blocked, Pat blasted a fierce shot that flew into the roof of Bryan Gunn's net. It was to prove the game's only goal, Van den Hauwe's only one of the season and one of only three he scored in his Everton career. But it ended Norwich's 35-game unbeaten home run in the League and made us champions.

Given the circumstances we'd had to battle through that season, we were absolutely delighted. Howard's cigar and champagne time had deservedly come again! We'd turned the tables on Liverpool, who on the same afternoon were saying farewell to Ian Rush. He scored his 39th goal of the season in the 1-0 home defeat of Watford before throwing his boots into the Kop and departing for what would be only a one-season stint at Juventus.

Our 86-points total was identical to our tally the previous year when we'd finished runners-up to Liverpool, who this time were nine points behind us. Our ninth title win meant that the championship had come to Merseyside for the sixth consecutive season and for the 10th time in 12 seasons. We celebrated with a 3-1 home win over Luton, when Steven's two penalties put him level with Adrian Heath and Kevin Sheedy as our co-top scorers with 16 goals in all competitions, with Sharp on 13 and Wilkinson 12. Before the game, the original championship trophy was presented to Kevin Ratcliffe by Philip Carter in a very pleasurable duty as League president while the Today sponsors trophy was handed to Kevin by Bobby Robson.

We rounded off the campaign with a 1-0 home victory over Tottenham, with Derek Mountfield scoring late on. Tottenham were later fined £10,000 for fielding an under-strength side as they prepared for the FA Cup final against Coventry five days later. The FA's halving of their fine on appeal was scant consolation for their shock 3-2 Wembley defeat. But even before we'd won the title I was one of only a handful of people privy to a secret that would have shocked many Evertonians - that Howard Kendall was set to leave.

Even though the opportunity to take charge at Barcelona had shimmered into view for Howard a year earlier and then disappeared, his biting frustration at the European ban and his desire for new frontiers left him itching for something different. His chance came about six weeks before the end of the season when he received a call that would lead to his Goodison departure, not to a European glamour club but to one in northern Spain that operated a Basque-only player policy.

Howard was at home in Formby when Fernando Ochoa, general secretary of Athletic Bilbao, rang to tell him that he had arrived in Liverpool and was desperate to speak to him. They duly met and Ochoa told Howard that they saw him as the man to revive their club, then struggling in the Spanish League. Howard agreed to fly to Madrid for a secret meeting with Bilbao officials after our end-of-season tour to New Zealand, Australia and Hawaii. Howard still had two years remaining on his Goodison contract and Everton's response was to offer him a new four-year deal, which I understand matched Bilbao's financial package. But I knew Howard had itchy feet. He wanted something new, something different. The idea of throwing off administrative duties, which were part of English management and becoming a tracksuit boss again strongly appealed to him. So I was not totally surprised when he decided to accept Bilbao's offer.

When I came back from our tour I went on a family holiday to North Wales still uncertain about what was happening. Maureen, our youngest daughter Emma and I were staying at my Auntie Peggy's caravan in Prestatyn. Our eldest girls, Joanne and Melanie, stayed at home with my dad because of their exams. It was Thursday, June 18 and we'd gone out for the day. When we got back we found a note which had been pushed under the door, apparently by a contact of one of the Everton directors who knew where we were staying. It was still the era before mobile phones and the note asked me to ring the chairman, Philip Carter, on a stated number.

I found the nearest phone box and rang him. He told me that Howard was definitely leaving the club and would be attending a press conference the following day. He said: 'We're offering you the manager's job. Will you accept?' 'Yes, please,' I gulped. We came home and I went to see the chairman at his Wirral house to tie up all the details prior to a press conference at Goodison on Sunday, June 21, to formally announce my appointment on a four-year contract. From supporting Everton since boyhood I was now manager at the age of 42.

Back home with Maureen and the family I reflected over a couple of cans of Guinness that becoming manager wasn't something I'd set out to do. My great ambition had been to play for Everton, which I'd not only achieved but also won championship and FA Cup medals. Then the coaching came along and I thoroughly enjoyed that aspect of the game, which gave me great fulfilment and satisfaction. I didn't give the manager's job much serious thought because until that last year I didn't expect Howard to leave. To be honest, I didn't want him to go and I told him so in our chats about the situation. It was certainly a challenge for him and over the years not many English managers have worked abroad. But he'd made up his mind to go and I was going to have a damned good go at the manager's job. I had to pick up the mantle, although while Howard drove a Mercedes the gear change for me was from Ford Sierra to a club-provided Scorpio.

Howard's departure pre-empted Mick Heaton leaving the club to take charge of non-League Workington, later re-uniting with Howard at Manchester City. Terry Darracott was appointed as my assistant with Peter Reid becoming player-coach, Mick Lyons taking over the reserves and Graham Smith became youth manager following Ray Minshull's retirement. From my initial conversations with the chairman I understood that if I wanted to sign a particular player the money would be there. I have to say that through my entire period as a manager I never once encountered a situation where funds for transfers were refused.

One of my first jobs as manager was to accompany Kevin Sheedy and Adrian Heath to an FA disciplinary summer hearing in London, where they had to answer charges of making obscene gestures to the Anfield crowd after our Mersey derby defeat in April. The incidents were not reported by the referee or linesmen but were captured on film to prompt an FA inquiry. Although both players were found guilty of bringing the game into disrepute, they escaped with a caution and a warning as to their future behaviour. I thought the verdict, taking into account their previous good conduct, was very fair indeed. I was relieved, too, because I didn't fancy Kevin and Adrian being suspended at the start of my first season as a manager when we already had an injury pile-up.

My first signing was goalkeeper Alec Chamberlain, who cost £80,000 from Colchester in July 1987. Fred Barber had joined Walsall the previous year and I needed cover for Bobby Mimms, who started the season in the absence of knee casualty Neville Southall. The second player I brought in was Scotland international Ian Wilson, a £300,000 September signing from Leicester. I moved for him because Kevin Sheedy was hit by Achilles problems. I saw Ian as a squad player, a 'steady Eddie' who'd provide balance on the left flank.

Then, like now, left-footed players were not in abundant supply. As Chamberlain and Wilson arrived we accepted a £130,000 offer from Manchester City for Kevin Langley, who'd made 23 appearances, scoring three goals, in his year at Goodison.

We began our pre-arranged, pre-season programme still with a host of injury absentees which made our physio, John Clinkard, one of the busiest men at the club. My first game in charge was a friendly against Linkoping in Sweden which we won 4-1 through a brace from Graeme Sharp and strikes from Ian Marshall and Ian Snodin. And my first official game as manager provided me with the proud pleasure of leading out the players at Wembley for the Charity Shield against shock FA Cup winners Coventry. We were without Neville Southall (knee), Gary Stevens (virus), Pat Van den Hauwe (groin), Ian Snodin (groin) and Paul Bracewell (shin and ankle). The team was:

Bobby Mimms; Alan Harper, Dave Watson, Kevin Ratcliffe (captain), Paul Power; Trevor Steven, Adrian Heath, Peter Reid, Kevin Sheedy (Neil Pointon, half-time); Wayne Clarke, Graeme Sharp. Substitutes unused: Derek Mountfield, Alec Chamberlain, Ian Marshall, Neil Adams.

Given our problems it was pleasing that in front of the ITV cameras we won 1-0 through a Wayne Clarke goal just before half-time. I was glad, too, that it was our record fourth consecutive Charity Shield without defeat. But because it was an occasion rewarding the previous season's championship feat, I didn't feel it belonged on my management CV.

After two games in the La Coruna Tournament - losing on penalties to Benfica after a goalless draw and going down 2-1 to Sporting Gijon in which Chamberlain made his debut - we opened the new League campaign with a 1-0 home win over Norwich. A Paul Power goal secured the points on a day when we were without seven first teamers. Knee casualties Peter Reid and Adrian Heath had swelled the absentee list and our line-up was:

Mimms; Van den Hauwe, Watson, Ratcliffe, Pointon; Adams, Steven, Harper, Power; Clarke, Sharp. Substitutes unused: Mountfield, Marshall.

We completed our opening three games unbeaten after drawing 1-1 at Wimbledon and playing out a goalless draw at Nottingham Forest before we came crashing down to earth in the spectacular venue of Real Madrid's Santiago Bernabeu Stadium.

With English clubs banned from European competition it was a prestige midweek friendly between the champions of Spain and England watched by a 75,000 crowd. Sadly, we had eight first-team men unavailable and Emilio

Butragueno, the striker nicknamed 'The Vulture', picked us off with two goals in the first half-hour during which Hugo Sanchez also scored and Alan Harper conceded an own goal.

To give him some experience of a really big stage I sent on John Ebbrell in place of Wayne Clarke for the second half and with 61 minutes gone Paul Power reduced the deficit. Real simply turned up the heat with Sanchez swiftly hitting his second of the night and Michel making it 6-1. As well as Real's second-half goals they hit our post and bar and had three shots cleared off our line. All we got from the night was a superb glittering silver salver, which is on permanent Goodison display, and a powerful reminder of what the elite of Europe could do.

I told the players to absorb lessons from our pain in Spain and use it as a launch pad to bounce back, which they did by thrashing Sheffield Wednesday 4-0 at Goodison three days later with Steven and Clarke sharing the goals equally. Next time out, though, we lost 1-0 on QPR's plastic pitch which meant we'd won only one of our eight games on artificial surfaces. That record worsened when, after a goalless home draw with Tottenham, we lost 2-1 on the plastic at Luton, a game that saw Neville Southall return in goal for his first game of the season.

Back on grass at Goodison, Wayne Clarke scored his second brace in three home games to give us a 2-1 win over Manchester United, move us to seventh in the table and leave third-placed Liverpool as the only unbeaten top-flight club. An Ian Wilson goal on his debut gave us a 3-2 win at home to Rotherham in the Littlewoods Cup second-round first leg before a mixed bag of results. They included a 2-1 home defeat by Coventry - on the weekend that the British and European golf team won for the first time on American soil to retain the Ryder Cup - followed by a 4-0 win at Southampton, by which time we had used 20 players in our first 12 games.

Our hero at The Dell was Graeme Sharp, who scored all the goals and became the first Everton player to hit four or more in a game for nine years, since Bob Latchford's five against Wimbledon in the League Cup in 1978. Sharp was also the first to score four times away from home for Everton since Latchford at QPR a decade earlier. A goalless Littlewoods Cup return with Rotherham to take us through to the third round was marred by another injury to Southall, who tore back ligaments during the game. But Mimms came in to help us beat Chelsea 4-1 at home when Heath's brace was matched by Sharp, which meant he had scored six goals in two consecutive League games.

Mimms stayed in goal when we drew 1-1 at Newcastle a week later, the day after the worst storm to hit Britain since 1703. Winds of more than 110 miles per hour left 22 people dead, felled 15 million trees and caused £1.1 billion of damage to property. Some 48 hours after that natural disaster came a financial hurricane when panic selling saw the stock market suffer its worst crash in history with £50 billion -10 per cent - wiped off shares in London on Black Monday. But we profited by three points the following Saturday when Southall returned in a 2-0 home win over Watford, although the fans let it be known that the entertainment value left a lot to be desired.

They were happier four days later. We went to Anfield in the Littlewoods Cup and ended Liverpool's 12-game unbeaten run from the start of the season. Their new attacking alliance of John Barnes, Peter Beardsley and John Aldridge had more than compensated for the loss of Ian Rush. They'd surged to the top of the League even though they'd played two or three games fewer than other clubs after a collapsed sewer under the Kop forced them to postpone their first three home matches. But we matched them that night at Anfield, in my first derby as manager, to win 1-0. Only six minutes remained when Peter Reid, who'd earlier won applause by catching a dog that invaded the pitch, unleashed a superb pass to find Gary Stevens. He let fly with his left foot and the ball deflected past Bruce Grobbelaar off Gary Gillespie to give us our first win in eight meetings with Liverpool.

There was a 44,000-plus crowd at Anfield and another 12,000 at Goodison watching on closed-circuit television. It was the third Mersery derby in history to be beamed to the other ground by this method - following the 1967 and 1981 FA Cup ties - and we'd won all three. But Liverpool got swift revenge. The following Sunday we went back to Anfield in the League, without Adrian Heath who was banned after being sent off at Newcastle, and lost 2-0. John Barnes set up both goals for Steve McMahon in the first half and a second-half blinder from Peter Beardsley. The result took leaders Liverpool nine points clear of us in seventh - with three games in hand.

But that Anfield result was our only reverse in a 15-match sequence in all competitions stretching from our defeat to Coventry in September to our Christmas trip to Old Trafford, where we lost 2-1 after squandering good chances, with Peter Reid guilty of an amazing miss. We were in fifth place yet such was Liverpool's remarkable form that they had now opened up a 16-point lead over us and a 10-point advantage over second-placed Nottingham Forest. Liverpool were producing some terrific performances and their 5-0 hammering of Forest late in the season was hailed by Sir Tom Finney as the finest display he'd ever seen.

After our defeat at United I tried to bring in Mark Walters from Aston Villa. He was out of contract and we were ready to pay the £500,000 asking price. We met the player at Haydock and agreed personal terms. But Graeme Souness was also after him for Rangers. He contacted Mark and sent down an air ticket for him to fly to Glasgow and meet him. At the time whatever finance Souness wanted at Ibrox he got. It was like a kid in a sweet shop. Mark said that he'd go to meet Souness out of courtesy but I knew that the way money was flying around up there at the time he'd sign for them. I knew he wouldn't come back and join us.

I was disappointed because he would have given us something extra. He was quick and would have given us an outlet. He'd have been a break-out man for us. We were a steady, methodical side and Mark would have injected extra pace. Mark was the first black player to join Rangers and Souness also signed their first Catholic (Maurice Johnston) and first Jewish player (Avi Cohen), although I'm sure that the only consideration in Souness's mind in each case was whether they were good players. That was the only yardstick for me, too, but I do think that if we'd landed Mark Walters, as a by-product his presence might have prevented the small lunatic fringe indulging in the racism that sadly reared its head at Goodison in the late 1980s and 1990s, including the disgraceful incident of John Barnes having bananas thrown at him. People tend to forget that Everton's first black player was Cliff Marshall back in the 1970s. But Cliff, who I still see around Merseyside today, made only seven first-team appearances whereas a high-profile signing like Mark Walters would have had a major impact.

The new year of 1988 launched us into a series of games against Sheffield Wednesday that is etched in the Goodison record books. Between January 1, when we lost 1-0 in the League at Hillsborough, to January 27 we played Wednesday five times. The reason for this glut of games was the FA Cup third-round draw which gave us an away trip to Wednesday. Peter Reid's late equaliser earned us a 1-1 draw after Kevin Ratcliffe had to go off with a torn groin muscle that ruled him out for the rest of our injury-blighted season. Player-coach Reid took over as skipper for the replay, which was just as tight as the first encounter. A spectacular volley by Graeme Sharp cancelled out Lee Chapman's goal and it ended 1-1 after extra time.

We won the toss for the second replay to be staged at Goodison but again it finished 1-1 after extra time, Chapman equalising after Trevor Steven had put us ahead. The tie had now run for five-and-a-half hours without a resolution but just to underline how plain daft football can be we went to Hillsborough for the third replay and played Wednesday off the park. We were 5-0 up at half-time - which was how it finished - and my dad couldn't believe it. He'd gone by coach but there was massive traffic congestion en route to Sheffield and, along with many other fans, he didn't get into Hillsborough until the end of the first half to find he'd missed all the goals.

Graeme Sharp hit a classic hat-trick - the third of his career - with a right-foot shot, a left-foot strike and a header. It's the only post-war FA Cup treble scored by an Everton player. Adrian Heath and Ian Snodin scored the others on a night that marked Paul Bracewell's return as a substitute for his first senior action in 20 months, since the 1986 FA Cup final.

Discounting the tie against Bolton way back in 1887-88, when Everton were disqualified over player eligibility, the series of games against Wednesday is the longest FA Cup marathon in the club's history and will remain so following curbs on the number of replays. It also meant that next to Liverpool, who've faced Everton on 20 occasions in the FA Cup, Wednesday are the club's most common opponents having met them 19 times. We had another drawn-out battle in the fourth round which we went straight into the following Saturday at home to Middlesbrough. Graeme Sharp popped in another goal but Boro, then lying third in the old Second Division, came back to draw 1-1 and earn a midweek replay to try to decide who would take the prize of a fifth-round home duel with Liverpool.

The second game was goalless until Dave Watson headed us in front after 67 minutes, only for Boro to equalise through Tony Mowbray in the dying seconds. So into extra time we went and after Boro had gone ahead through Alan Kernaghan I thought we were on the way out. We were into injury time after the extra half-hour. Referee Keren Barratt had checked his watch and signalled to a linesman and I thought that was it. Then a Boro move broke down, Adrian Heath got possession and he lofted the ball forward for Trevor Steven of all people to snatch a last-gasp equaliser and make it 2-2 with a rare header. It was a dramatic climax to a thrilling match.

We won the second replay at Goodison 2-1 through Sharp's sixth FA Cup goal of the season and an own goal by Tony Mowbray. It meant we had taken seven games - one more than is needed to win the Cup - to reach the fifth round, a new post-war top-flight record. It also completed a demanding sequence of nine cup games in 10 matches between January 9 and February 9 because we also had to face Arsenal in the semi-final first leg of the Littlewoods Cup and Luton Town in the Simod Cup third round.

As was the case in so many games in my first season we were depleted when we faced Liverpool in a live TV Sunday tie in round five. Kevin Sheedy, Kevin Ratcliffe, Wayne Clarke, Derek Mountfield and Ian Wilson were all ruled out and then we lost Peter Reid with thigh damage after just 21 minutes, Bracewell going on. To be fair, Liverpool were without casualties Mark Lawrenson, Ronnie Whelan and Gary Gillespie and the game was never a classic. The only goal came 15 minutes from the end, Ray Houghton heading home a John Barnes cross.

To go out of the FA Cup is always disappointing, to do so in a Mersey derby made it worse. That's why the outcome of our home Littlewoods Cup first leg against Arsenal - for which my daughter Emma, then aged 8, was our team mascot - was agonising. I desperately wanted to bring silverware to the club. At every other level - from an 11-year-old schoolboy appearing alongside 15-year-olds to playing for Everton, being a coach then assistant to Howard - I'd been a winner and I wanted to continue that in management. I felt the Littlewoods Cup offered us a great chance of doing that after we'd reached the semi-final by adding Oldham (2-1) and Manchester City (2-0) to our earlier defeats of Liverpool and Rotherham.

Arsenal went ahead through Perry Groves after only 10 minutes but when Tony Adams challenged Graeme Sharp in the 80th minute referee George Tyson awarded us a penalty and an equalising chance. Trevor Steven placed the ball on the spot but, to my anguish and that of every Evertonian, sent his kick over the bar - his second penalty failure from four attempts that season - and Arsenal collected a 1-0 win. I still joke with Emma that she didn't bring us an ounce of luck that Sunday afternoon and that I blame her!

Seriously, though, we started brightly in the return at Highbury when we were without Kevin Ratcliffe, Peter Reid, Kevin Sheedy, Derek Mountfield and Ian Wilson in Dave Watson's first full game as skipper. We did have a bit of fortune when Neville Southall conceded a penalty for bringing down Martin Hayes, but the Arsenal man followed Steven's first-leg example by blazing his kick over the bar. It was still 0-0 at half-time but four minutes into the second half our hopes began to unravel. Michael Thomas increased Arsenal's aggregate lead to 2-0 and during the move that led to the goal Pat Van den Hauwe collided with David Rocastle and had to be stretchered off.

Alan Harper took over and then Adrian Heath, who I'd sent on in place of Ian Snodin, reduced the overall arrears to 2-1 with a 69th-minute goal. But fate frowned on us again when Steven was forced to limp off, reducing us to 10 men. Two Arsenal goals in the last 19 minutes, from Rocastle and Alan Smith, gave them a flattering 3-1 win on the day and a 4-1 aggregate passage to the final, where they surprisingly lost 3-2 to Luton.

Between the two legs against Arsenal we lost 2-1 to Luton in the Simod Cup, a new name for the competition that had begun as the Full Members Cup. We were without a batch of senior players but Paul Bracewell made his first start since the 1986 FA Cup final. His prolonged ankle and shin problems, which necessitated several operations including one in America, stemmed from a tussle with Billy Whitehurst at Newcastle on New Year's Day 1986. It wasn't Whitehurst's fault. He was just such a big guy and I grimaced as Paul went into a fateful tackle with him and came off the worse.

The Simod game also marked Kevin Sheedy's return from a two-month injury absence and Neville Southall was captain for a game watched by a mere 5,204 spectators, the lowest post-war home attendance at either Everton or Liverpool. Phil Jones, a 17-year-old right-back who later played for Wigan, made his debut and his only start for us and I included Gary Powell and Eddie Youds in my squad for the first time, naming both on the bench. Powell, a striker who came from Wirral, never made an appearance for us. He moved on to play for Welsh clubs Rhyl and TNS. Centre-back Youds, who had 10 first-team outings for us, went on to have a good career with Ipswich, Bradford, Charlton and Huddersfield.

It's amazing to reflect that during my first season as manager - when the League programme was cut from 42 to 40 games - we played in eight different competitions, admittedly some of them only single matches, yet still a total which included 21 cup games. In addition to the League, FA, Littlewoods and Simod Cups and the Charity Shield, we beat Bayern Munich 3-1 at Goodison in the League's Mercantile Credit Centenary Challenge, lost on penalties after a 2-2 draw with Rangers in the Dubai Super Cup and played two games at Wembley in the Football League Centenary Festival - beating Wolves and losing to Manchester United.

In the game against Rangers for the unofficial British championship we dominated and were leading 2-0 through goals from Dave Watson and Kevin Sheedy, who won the man-of-the-match award presented by Brazilian star Carlos Alberto. But Rangers player-manager Graeme Souness came on and changed the game. He made a huge impact. Rangers equalised through goals in the final nine minutes from Robert Fleck and Ally McCoist and went on to win the penalty decider 8-7. It demonstrated once again what a fine player Souness was. In my book he ranks alongside Roy Keane and Bryan Robson as the best midfield players of their type in post-war British football.

One of the highlights of a deeply frustrating initial management campaign for me came in March when we faced Liverpool at Goodison in the return League derby. The wonderful season Kenny Dalglish's side had enjoyed had seen them equal the Leeds United record of 29 top-flight games unbeaten from the start of a season, which has since been surpassed by Arsenal's unbeaten 38-match campaign in 2003-04.

Liverpool came to Goodison intent on overhauling that Leeds total and their only defeat up to that stage had been against us at Anfield in the Littlewoods Cup. The live televised Sunday game was staged just days after the Bank of England pound note ceased to be legal tender and was replaced by the pound coin. But the match brimmed with that enduring Mersey derby currency of passion and commitment and I'm delighted to say the only goal was struck for us by Wayne Clarke.

Only a quarter of an hour had gone when Liverpool goalkeeper Bruce Grobbelaar fumbled a clearance, succeeding only in pushing the ball towards Clarke, who gleefully accepted the opportunity to toe-poke it into the bottom corner. Dave Watson and Pat Van den Hauwe were magnificent for us at the heart of a defence that repulsed all that Barnes, Beardsley and company could throw at them and, backed by the usual efficiency of Neville Southall, denied Liverpool another entry in the record books. The Clarke family were doubly represented at Goodison. Wayne's brother Allan, a member of the Leeds side that set the record, was in the Main Stand working for a radio station and was beaming at the outcome. Said Wayne: 'He wanted a car park pass and the winning goal - and I obliged with both.'

After that great result we strung together an unbeaten eight-match run that lifted us into third place going into our final game at home to Arsenal. The visitors handed a debut as a substitute to an 18-year-old striker called Kevin Campbell, who much later in his career would answer a crisis call by Everton. That day, though, we were guilty of a last-day flop and lost 2-1 even though Dave Watson had given us the lead. Arsenal hit back before half-time from Michael Thomas and Martin Hayes and, typical of our season, we were down to 10 men when Pat Van den Hauwe limped off with ankle damage after we'd used our two substitutes Alan Harper and Kevin Sheedy. The defeat pushed us into a finishing position of fourth with 70 points from 40 games, three behind Nottingham Forest with runners-up Manchester United on 81 and champions Liverpool on 90, equalling our record total in 1985 but from two fewer games.

Even though Ian Rush was playing for Juventus, we found there was no escape from his habit of scoring against us. We went to Leeds to play in a joint testimonial for John Charles and Bobby Collins and lost 3-2. Guess who scored a hat-trick. Yes...Rushie! He'd come over to guest for Leeds and I distinctly remember one of his goals that night for the quality of the reverse pass from Michel Platini over our defence for Rushie to pounce on.

My verdict on our season was that it had been frustrating and disappointing, even though to finish fourth today is a cause of celebration. I felt we were capable of beating anybody if we were at, or close to, full strength. But I told the players repeatedly at our team meetings - some of them quite heated - that if we'd reproduced our home form in away games we'd have been up there with Liverpool. Sadly, we weren't able to do that often. We were stretched to the limit and I remember late that season, due to injuries to Graeme Sharp and Wayne Clarke, I had to parade what must have been our smallest-ever strike force of Trevor Steven (5ft 8ins) and Adrian Heath (5ft 6ins). Yet they both scored and we beat Portsmouth 2-1.

One other major factor that was clear as I took stock of my first season was our lack of a cutting edge. We'd conceded four goals fewer than in the title year 12 months earlier to set an Everton record - the 27 we let in was the lowest in a League season in the club's history. But our scoring output was well down: 53 League goals compared to 76 in 1986-87. So I knew I had to bring in new blood, including a proven striker, especially as several players left that summer following the sales earlier in the year of Bobby Mimms (£400,000 to Tottenham) and Ian Marshall (£100,000 to Oldham).

As well as Mimms, we also sold another goalkeeper, Alec Chamberlain, who joined Luton for £150,000. That meant that the unenviable role of being understudy to Neville Southall would be taken over by Mike Stowell, who we'd signed on a free from Preston some years earlier. Although he would have only one senior outing for us - and that in the Simod Cup - he later joined Wolves and as well as being called into the England 'B' squad, he broke the Molineux goalkeeping record, set by England's Bert Williams, by making 448 appearances for the club.

The season had not long ended when Derek Mountfield, who'd lost his regular place due to Dave Watson's arrival and Pat Van den Hauwe's impressive response to playing centre-back when needed, joined Aston Villa for £450,000. We also sold Alan Harper to Sheffield Wednesday for £275,000 while Paul Power, forced to retire from first-class football because of knee trouble, joined our coaching staff.

I tried to sign defender Steve Bould from Stoke but he chose Arsenal and we had the same disappointing outcome with striker Paul Stewart who, instead of being Goodison-bound, left Manchester City in a £1.7 million move to Tottenham. I also flew to Sweden to watch Barcelona's Mark Hughes in action. He'd gone out from the Spanish club on loan to Bayern Munich and I'd been alerted by news that he wanted to return to England. He was a class striker any manager would be interested in but he said that if he did come back here he would return to Manchester United which he did, re-joining them for £1.5 million in July 1988. Some 12 years later he did arrive at Everton - on a free from Southampton.

When you're operating in the transfer market you have to be philosophical and patient and you have to get used to being linked with almost every player who's available - and many who aren't! Paul Gascoigne was one of a host of names linked and we might have landed him in an exchange deal if Peter Reid had decided to accept an offer to join Newcastle. But Peter opted to sign a new Everton contract although, as things unfolded, he left the following February for QPR after I'd dropped him. It was the first time he'd been omitted, when fit, since October 1983 and he felt it was time to move.

Kevin Sheedy was another player whose Goodison future was uncertain. Kevin, who played for the Republic of Ireland in that summer's European Championships in West Germany, including their memorable win over England, asked me to transfer list him. He said he preferred playing in the centre of midfield - where he'd operated during part of our 1986-87 title season - rather than the left of midfield. I thought the left side was his best position and the one on which he'd built his deserved reputation.

Kevin angrily denied a report that came out of the Republic camp quoting him saying he would never kick a ball for Everton again. He was insistent he'd never said any such thing. Anyway, we had a chat and I agreed to place him on the list. I was still prepared to pick him, though. Why cut off your nose to spite your face? In our opening eight games of the season he came on once as a sub and started the other seven before I left him out following our 2-1 defeat at Wimbledon in October. Then he got a series of injuries, first on international duty and then in our reserves, and it wasn't until late December that he was back in the first team - playing on the left side.

I was delighted the following month when there was a knock on my door and it was Kevin. We had another chat and he said he wanted to come off the transfer list. I was very happy to oblige and he started all but three of our remaining games. To be honest, it would have needed a terrific offer to persuade me to part with him, anyway, because he had a bewitching left foot - as good as anyone's in English football at the time.

I also had to make a decision that summer about Gary Stevens. He wasn't enjoying his football and consequently wasn't producing his best. We had several chats and one of the reasons for his dip in form was his personal life. It had included a publicised divorce from his childhood sweetheart and a second marriage. His private life was all over the newspapers. 'I can't seem to stay out of the wrong end of the papers and it's getting to me', Gary admitted. 'I'm usually easy going but I've become short tempered and that's just not me. The spark's gone out of my game and it's been significant to me that I've done my best when I've got away from it all on England duty.'

Gary had two years left on his contract and I told him I wanted him to stay. He'd come through from a kid with us and at his best he was a tremendous right-back. At the same time I could appreciate his problems and the difficulties of living in a media goldfish bowl. So I agreed to let him go and he was soon on his way to Rangers for £1.25 million.

Around the same time Ian Snodin pledged his future to us by turning down a £600,000 return to his native Yorkshire with Sheffield Wednesday and I was glad to see our squad bolstered by four more signings. In came midfielder Stuart McCall from Bradford for £850,000, his Scottish compatriot Pat Nevin from Chelsea for a tribunal-fixed £925,000, England Under 21 full-back Neil McDonald from Newcastle for £525,000 - also fixed by a tribunal - and Tony Cottee, who cost us a club record £2.2 million from West Ham. It was a toss-up between us and Arsenal who would get Cottee and the speculation was that he would stay in his native city. In fact, Tony fancied the challenge of leaving London and moving north.

Over the years Tony's had his critics but the fact is that in five of his six seasons at Goodison he was our top scorer and overall he totalled 99 goals in 240 Everton appearances. I accept that perhaps Tony wasn't a team player like Graeme Sharp, Adrian Heath and Andy Gray. He probably was more goal-minded than team-minded but some of the greatest-ever strikers have been single-minded and selfish. I bought him to score goals because that's what we needed and that's what he gave us. Tony was the best around at the time and, with hindsight, I've no regrets at all about bringing him to Everton.

Pat Nevin, a Scotland internatiional, was a clever player who'd done well for Chelsea both in wide and central attacking positions and I felt he would give us a variety of options. His contract at Stamford Bridge had expired but while we offered an admittedly unrealistic £300,000, Chelsea valued him at an over-the-top £1.7 million. We'd have been willing to pay a bit more but Chelsea's price was ridiculous and we hoped they'd come back with a more sensible figure. They didn't. So the matter went to the lottery of a transfer tribunal. My opposite number, Chelsea's Liverpool-born manager Bobby Campbell, must have had a persuasive tongue because the fee was set at £925,000 - the biggest fee set by a tribunal in the system's 10-year history.

I decided to go for Stuart McCall to inject more combative spirit into our midfield. He also had vision, passing ability and a good engine and was deservedly called up by Scotland, going on to win 40 caps in a long career. It wasn't easy trying to replace Gary Stevens who was, after all, England's right-back and blessed with great pace. I went for Neil McDonald, who was a good footballer but a bit slow. He didn't quite have the speed we needed in that position and our defence for the start of the new season had also been stripped of the pace of captain Kevin Ratcliffe, who was still out from the groin problem he sustained in the FA Cup tie at Sheffield Wednesday the previous January and had to undergo pre-season hernia surgery.

Our new physiotherapist Chris Goodson, who arrived from Wigan that summer to replace Oxford-bound John Clinkard, had plenty to occupy him. Even before a ball had been kicked in pre-season we were without Stuart McCall and Peter Reid, both with thigh injuries, and ankle casualties Paul Bracewell and Pat Van den Hauwe as well as Ratcliffe. I switched Ian Snodin to centre-back alongside stand-in skipper Dave Watson when we began our warm-up programme in the Philips Cup in Berne, Switzerland and kicked off with a 2-1 win over Cruzeiro through goals from Watson and Sharp. The game marked the debuts of Cottee, Nevin and McDonald and was memorable for the continuous samba beat of the Brazilian side's fans and the exotic dancing girls amongst their contingent. It was certainly different from Scunthorpe on a wet night in December!

The Sharp-Cottee combination brought us both goals in our second match, a 2-2 draw with Torino, before we lost on penalties. We then travelled across

Switzerland to the upmarket ski resort of Chur to play in a game celebrating the local club's 75th anniversary. It was in this beautiful situation, in the shadow of the Alps, that I had to remind the players who was boss and that if I gave them any licence they had to accept it responsibly.

I told them that they could go out for a drink as long as they behaved themselves when they returned to the hotel. Around one o'clock in the morning I heard shouting and singing downstairs in the hotel lounge. I have a high boiling point but I'd reached it then. So I got out of bed, went down and gave them a piece of my mind. 'Get to bed', I roared at them. 'All of you. Now!' I have to say that the impact of my outburst was instant. They all put their glasses on the table and silently went to bed - and that included senior professionals like Graeme Sharp. I had to smile later when Ian Snodin, recalling the incident, said: 'Colin was clearly very angry and we went upstairs doing our impression of mice!'

Next day I warned them that if there was any repeat they'd be grounded. Mind you, being on the ground was where two press members of our party would have liked to have been on the morning of the match. Mike Ellis of the Sun and my co-author John Keith, covering the tour for the Daily Express, went off to attend a barbecue in the mountains. On the way down, as they sat in open, one-man cable chairs, the power failed and left them swinging in space thousands of feet up. Both of them tended to suffer from vertigo, which didn't make them feel any more comfortable! After about five minutes - but what seemed to them an eternity - the current was switched on again. They completed their descent but still felt a bit dizzy by the time we kicked off our 6-1 win in the scenic Ring Strasse Stadium, a game in which John Ebbrell, Stuart McCall and Pat Nevin scored their first Everton goals.

We continued our pre-season programme with a 1-0 win against a Drogheda select side, a 3-0 victory at Tranmere in Ronnie Moore's tesimonial before a 2-0 defeat by Real Madrid to open a new stadium at Santander, when Seve Ballesteros kicked off the match. Bill Scott, a golf-loving Everton director, a former chairman and a lovely man was like a starry-eyed kid when he found out that Seve was going to be there and I think meeting him meant more to Bill that day than the match! We completed our warm-up games in Spain by meeting Howard Kendall's Athletic Bilbao side in a match to mark the 75th anniversary of the club's San Mames Stadium, the ground known as 'The Cathedral'. It was anything but cathedral-like that night as 38,000 passionate fans saw a meaty match which we lost by the odd goal in five, Sharp and

Cottee our goalscorers.

Our season about to unfold would begin on a high, feature fluctuating fortunes, fuel expectancy of a trophy and then be enveloped in a tragedy that would change the face of English football forever. Shortly before the start of the season the club's annual accounts highlighted the game's slender financial margins with a profit of £141,000 reported for the previous year, with the wage bill slightly down at £2.24 million.

The curtain went up with a home clash against Newcastle. With Ratcliffe and Van den Hauwe ruled out I included debutants Cottee, Nevin, McCall and McDonald in this team:

Southall; McDonald, Watson (captain), Snodin, Pointon; Nevin, McCall, Reid, Steven (Sheedy, 81); Sharp, Cottee. Unused substitute: Heath.

It was a wonderful start. Cottee scored with just 34 seconds on the clock, the earliest goal in our opening home game since the war. He proceeded to add another two - in the 31st and 63rd minutes - to become the first Everton player to score an opening-day hat-trick since Jimmy Dunn against Birmingham in August 1931. Tony's treble was also the first on an Everton debut since Fred Pickering started with a hat-trick against Nottingham Forest after his signing from Blackburn in March 1964.

Graeme Sharp added another goal to give us a 4-0 win in front of a 41,000-plus crowd, whose expectancy level had soared. The only gloom on our sunny day was the loss of Trevor Steven, who'd been passed fit to play after Achilles trouble but had to be carried off when it went on him late on. He left the ground on crutches and was out for seven games. Cottee later remarked that his hat-trick was the best and possibly worst start he could have had because it set such a massively high personal bench mark. But I didn't expect a hat-trick every match! That would have been ridiculous.

After a 1-0 defeat at Manchester United in the Mercantile Credit Centenary Trophy - a tournament involving the top-eight clubs from the previous season - Cottee struck again at Coventry when Sheedy's return for Steven was our only change. That win was as much down to Neville Southall as to Cottee's finishing. He was brilliant and his heroics included a first-half penalty save from Brian Kilcline.

A 1-1 draw with Nottingham Forest in our next match was costly because Pat Nevin suffered knee ligament damage which forced him to miss 15 games in a three-month spell. With Steven also out I brought in Adrian Heath - who'd scored against Forest after replacing Nevin - on the right flank for our trip to

Millwall where we lost 2-1, the only encouraging note being sub Van den Hauwe's first senior action of the season. It was the start of a bleak run which saw us win only once in eight League games and slump to 15th, our lowest position for four-and-a-half years.

What made it even more frustrating was that during that period I was away recovering from my second hip replacement operation, leaving Terry Darracott to manfully hold the fort. I went in for surgery following our home game with Southampton on October 8 after our defeat at Wimbledon led me to shake up the team. The outcome was a 4-1 win, Cottee scoring twice with Dave Watson and Trevor Steven, on his comeback, also on target. I dropped Neil Pointon, Neil McDonald and Kevin Sheedy, recalled Pat Van den Hauwe at left-back, switched Ian Snodin to right-back and welcomed back captain Kevin Ratcliffe, after a 10-month absence, along with Steven.

Although I was still recovering from my hip surgery I insisted on attending our 1-1 draw with Manchester United at the end of the month which, coincidentally, was the first match of ITV's £44 million four-year deal for screening live top-flight games - very much an indication of things to come. Cottee scored our goal that day but Neville Southall was man-of-the-match and was earmarked for interview by the ITV team. They soon wished they had picked someone else as they were given a harsh lesson in the fact that Neville did his talking on the pitch and not in front of a camera, that he would never use two words when one would do. 'Neville was a fantastic goalkeeper with so many attributes, but doing interviews wasn't one of them,' reflected presenter Jim Rosenthal.

My decision to go to the game was just as foolish. I sat with my crutches on the steps of the directors' box but I shouldn't have gone. It was too soon after the operation and it caused complications. I was ordered by the specialist either to go back into hospital for a fortnight or stay in bed at home. So my recovery, unlike my first replacement when I was out on crutches in 12 days, took five weeks. Finally, I returned for our 1-1 draw with Norwich on November 19 and I'm glad to say the operation, like my first one four years earlier, was successful. I was soon back in full fitness training, often solitary sessions, which I still go through at a gym today.

During my recovery period we took the decision to sell Adrian Heath to Espanyol for £500,000, his departure following Trevor Steven's return from injury. We received an inquiry about Adrian from the Barcelona-based club and as we'd signed Tony Cottee, and also had Graeme Sharp and Wayne

Clarke as well as Trevor Steven who could play up front, we decided to open negotiations. Adrian, or 'Inchy' as he was nicknamed because of his size, felt a bit miffed that we'd signed Cottee and that was quite understandable from his point of view. Although he could have stayed with us he felt that the realistic decision for him to make was to move on. He always felt he was the best of Graeme Sharp's batch of attacking partners and there's no doubt that he made a great contribution to the most successful period in Everton history. His 1984 Milk Cup goal at Oxford, one of 94 he scored in 307 Everton appearances, is guaranteed a permanent place in Goodison folklore. It symbolises the remarkable transformation in the club's fortunes at that time although Adrian picks as his most memorable strike his FA Cup semi-final winner over Southampton a few months later.

We also saw a couple of changes in our goalkeeping back-up to Neville Southall with Mike Stowell going on loan to Port Vale and Jason Kearton, a 19-year-old Aussie who just walked into Goodison asking for a trial, signing as a professional. He went on to make eight first-team appearances for us before carving out a career with Crewe that spanned more than 200 games.

By the time I resumed full daily duties after my operation the team had already embarked on a 10-match unbeaten League run between late October and the end of December. But hardly had Heath left than we were facing up to the loss of Sharp. He underwent hernia surgery in early December and we were without him for 12 matches, beginning with the Mersey derby. But I did have a great boost just before the trip to Anfield when four key members of our squad, Southall, Ratcliffe, Watson and Sharp, pledged themselves to the club by signing long-term contracts. Southall signed a seven-and-a-half-year deal, the others four-year contracts, while Kevin Sheedy followed suit shortly after by agreeing a new three-year agreement after withdrawing his transfer request. Wayne Clarke made his first start of the season in place of Sharp at Liverpool and hit a 52nd-minute penalty, his second in successive derby outings, to cancel out Ray Houghton's opener.

We finished the year with a 3-1 win over Coventry at Goodison. Paul Bracewell, back after six operations since his ankle injury almost three years earlier, was on the scoresheet after Sheedy had struck twice. That result put us fourth in the table with 30 points from 18 games, two ahead of Liverpool who were one place behind us. It also meant that since the Everton revival began in January 1984 we'd amassed 400 points, more than any other top-flight club, in five calendar years.

We opened 1989 with a 2-0 defeat at Nottingham Forest to end our unbeaten League run. Trevor Steven had the chance to put us ahead with a penalty but sent his kick wide - his fourth failure in 12 attempts over a season-and-a-half. It was the start of a seven-match League sequence without a win, underlining the inconsistency which, with all the injuries, blighted my time in charge. We fell as low as 11th and didn't have another League victory until March 11, a 1-0 home win over Sheffield Wednesday.

By then Peter Reid had left us for QPR, Neil Adams had gone on loan to Oldham while the injury curse had cruelly struck down Snodin, who was hit by hamstring damage only hours after his form in just 22 outings at right-back had been rewarded with a place in the England squad. His call-up came in the morning and in the evening he was forced to withdraw after being injured in our 4-0 FA Cup fourth-round replay win over Plymouth. It was cruel because Ian had quickly become the best right-back in the country. But the injury ruled him out of all but four of our remaining 23 games that season and although he finally did travel with England for the World Cup qualifier in Albania in March, he didn't play and never won an England cap.

In the Littlewoods Cup that season we comfortably saw off Bury over two legs on a 5-2 aggregate before Oldham held us to a 1-1 draw at Goodison. A late Tony Cottee double saw us win the Boundary Park replay 2-0, only our second victory in our 10th outing on a plastic pitch. But in round four we came a cropper at Second Division Bradford, a tie which gave Stuart McCall a swift return to his former club. It wasn't a happy one for him or us. We just couldn't cope that night with Bradford's 6ft 4ins striker Ian Ormondroyd. Although he didn't score he had us all over the place with his height and we lost 3-1, Dave Watson's 85th-minute goal for us being purely academic.

We were also back in the Simod Cup which, although it was a much-derided competition, took us all the way to Wembley. We went in at the third-round stage at home to Millwall on a chilly Tuesday night in December. Perhaps not surprisingly it failed to excite the public and the paltry attendance of 3,703 set a 20th-century low for a home first-team match involving Everton or Liverpool. I took the opportunity to rest Neville Southall and Mike Stowell, back from his loan spell at Port Vale, made his only senior Everton appearance and kept a clean sheet in our 2-0 win through a Cottee strike and an own goal by Terry Hurlock. The meagre attendance prompted the headline 'Silent Night' in the Liverpool Daily Post and our chief executive Jim Greenwood reported a slender profit of £14,000.

Our dubious reward was a quarter-final trip to Wimbledon in January and when we faced them the 'Crazy Gang' had full momentum, having chalked up seven straight wins. They were a huge, powerful side. Every set piece was a physical test, there was a venom in their every tackle, they were always in your face. There were no frills. But what they did they did extremely well. So we were pleased to go to Plough Lane and win 2-1 with Wayne Clarke scoring both our goals. We would also have the even greater pleasure later in the season of ending their hold on the FA Cup, which they'd lifted after that sensational win over Liverpool the previous May.

In the Simod Cup semi-final we beat QPR 1-0 at home, a game that drew a massively improved attendance of just over 7,000! Our goal came from Pat Nevin, a rare header from an Ian Snodin cross. So we were through to Wembley to face Nottingham Forest in the final and although it was in a competition widely sneered at I wanted to win it. They always say your first one is the hardest to win and I was desperate to put a trophy on the table.

It was not to be. A contest that gave the 46,000-plus fans more than their money's worth was locked at 2-2 after 90 minutes. Tony Cottee, making his first Wembley start, gave us a great boost by scoring after only eight minutes at the end of the stadium he'd stood as a young fan watching West Ham beat Arsenal nine years earlier. But Brian Clough's side equalised through Garry Parker on the half-hour after we'd failed to prevent Lee Chapman flicking on a Tommy Gaynor corner.

We were back in front, though, early in the second half through a great strike from Graeme Sharp, who smashed in a volley off Kevin Sheedy's long ball. Forest responded with a 67th-minute equaliser that caught us cold. With a lightning counter Parker raced from his own half with our defence awol and although Paul Bracewell, very impressive on the day, tried to stay with him he couldn't prevent Parker firing past Neville Southall to make it 2-2.

Sutton's late save off Cottee's snap shot sent the game into extra time and it was Forest who took the lead for the first time, just two minutes into the additonal period, when Chapman scored. Back we came to tie the score at 3-3 when Cottee got his second of the game with a downward header from a Pat Nevin cross. I thought we'd won it with five minutes left when Sutton palmed Sharp's shot into the air. The ball struck the bar but instead of falling to Cottee it bounced straight into the keeper's arms. With time running out, a cross from Forest substitute Franz Carr found Chapman - who'd looked clearly offside when the move began - and the striker scored a close-range winner to add the Simod Cup to Forest's previously won Littlewoods Cup.

The FA Cup also took us to Wembley but in starkly contrasting and poignant circumstances. The trail began at Second Division West Brom in round three. We drew 1-1 through a Kevin Sheedy penalty in a game that marked the end of an Everton era. It was the 50th and final occasion that the acclaimed midfield quartet of Trevor Steven, Peter Reid, Paul Bracewell and Sheedy started in the same side. Their record together was highly impressive: 35 wins, 10 draws and only five defeats.

Steven missed the replay with a groin injury while Reid made only two further appearances before his move to QPR. I left out Peter after we'd lost 3-1 at home to Arsenal in the League - our fourth consecutive defeat by the team who would dramatically pip Liverpool for the title. I felt that Peter's edge had been blunted, that he wasn't quite the influential player he had been. But he left behind wonderful memories and a career record at Goodison of 234 appearances and 13 goals.

The Goodison replay with West Brom was goalless and heading for extra time until Sheedy struck again with a superb volley four minutes from the end. That booked us a trip to face Plymouth. Amazingly, we had our first fully-fit senior squad for more than four years stretching back to December 1984. Sharp was back after a 12-game absence following hernia surgery and Steven and Van den Hauwe also returned after injuries although that happy state of affairs was all too brief.

Strangely, we gave a less-than-convincing display against the mid-table Second Division side, and Sheedy again came to our rescue by firing home a 79th-minute penalty to earn us a 1-1 draw after Sean McCarthy had put the home side ahead. We won the replay emphatically 4-0 with Sheedy again on the scoresheet - his fourth in as many FA Cup games - Sharp striking twice and Nevin registering his first senior goal for us. It extended our record of not having lost a home FA Cup replay since our defeat by Leeds in 1965, but there was a sour aftermath. Plymouth's Kevin Summerfield fractured his right leg in a first-half tussle with Sharp and their captain Tommy Tynan, a former Liverpool junior, accused Graeme of going over the top. Video film of the incident, though, showed that Graeme had gone for the ball.

In the fifth round we were drawn at Barnsley, a tie which provided a landmark in the Yorkshire club's history. The game drew a crowd of 32,551, the first time Barnsley had recorded English football's biggest attendance of the day. Among our supporters packed into Oakwell was my daughter

Melanie, who went with a friend to every cup tie home and away that season. She was a fervent Evertonian and always followed football. Now, as a journalist on the Daily Record in Glasgow, she goes to see Celtic as often as she can. My youngest daughter Emma watches Everton home games regularly and my eldest daughter Joanna also follows the game. Barnsley were in the old Second Division at the time and we managed a 1-0 win - Sharp scoring after 15 minutes - and it took us back to Wimbledon in the sixth round for a live televised Sunday duel.

A few weeks earlier they'd drawn with us 1-1 at Goodison in the League when Vinnie Jones was sent off for butting Kevin Ratcliffe, his second successive Goodison dismissal. The previous season he'd got his marching orders for kicking Peter Reid and although it wasn't a full-on head butt on Kevin he definitely made contact. It was something you didn't want to see on a football field and the referee was right to send him off. In the tie we overcame the disappointment of Hans Segers saving Sharp's early penalty to secure a deserved 1-0 win and it was Stuart McCall's first goal since September that took us through. After 28 appearances without scoring he tucked one away in the 59th minute to secure our semi-final ticket .

Our League form was erratic and in the midweek following our success at Wimbledon we went to Newcastle on a snowy night in front of a crowd of only 20,000, and lost 2-0. Dave Watson was missing through injury so I moved Pat Van den Hauwe to centre-half where he had a few tangles with Mirandinha and eventually got booked. The Brazilian scored for Newcastle in the first half and Liam O'Brien added the other shortly after the interval on an evening when our attitude just wasn't right. It was a case of 'after the Lord Mayor's Show' and we were poor. I was far from happy with the fact that we hadn't won an away League game since November and my reaction was to drop Cottee for the first time. He'd scored only twice in his last 17 outings and I demoted him and McCall to the bench for our Easter home game against Millwall and brought in Nevin and Clarke.

That was disappointing, too. We went behind to a Teddy Sheringham goal after 85 seconds and in a game of 46 free-kicks - 29 awarded against Millwall - we drew 1-1 thanks to a second-half Sheedy penalty. I recalled Cottee, in place of groin casualty Sharp, for our trip to Middlesbrough two days later. Although he scored, along with Nevin and Sheedy, we were held 3-3 before a welcome 4-1 home victory over QPR the following Saturday. It was only our second League win in 12 games since the turn of the year. Cottee scored again, his 16th of the season, and Peter Reid, returning to Everton on April Fools Day, won't want to remember his return because it was his backpass that led to Cottee's goal.

The other goals came from Clarke, a Sheedy penalty and Steven, his first since Boxing Day. It was the first time that season QPR had lost by more than one goal and it left us with three games before the semi-final. The first of them was a home friendly against Athletic Bilbao in Kevin Ratcliffe's testimonial, which we won 1-0. Sheedy scored, enabling us to 'get even' for our pre-season defeat by Howard Kendall's side in Spain. More importantly, a crowd of more than 13,000 in a season when our League average was less than 28,000, generated receipts of around £50,000 for Kevin.

Ratcliffe, though, was banned under the totting-up system for our next match, which was at Arsenal. Dave Watson was also out - with a hamstring problem - so Neil McDonald and Pat Van den Hauwe were the centre-backs. Sharp was still out injured - as well as being banned - and hamstring casualty Ian Snodin was also missing. It was hardly the best way to face the future champions and we suffered another blow when Steven limped off in the second half to give John Ebbrell his second taste of League football as a substitute prior to making his England Under 21 debut in the end-of-season Toulon Tournament. We lost 2-0 to goals by Lee Dixon and Niall Quinn, our fifth straight defeat by George Graham's very strong and capable side.

For our last outing before the FA Cup semi-final - a Monday night home game against Charlton - I dropped Cottee to substitute for the second time in five games. I'd expected more from him in some of the games. After all, Joe Fagan once dropped Kenny Dalglish so I don't think Tony could complain! I brought in Wayne Clarke to team-up with Sharp who, like Ratcliffe, was back from suspension. It was an eventful night for both. Kevin conceded an own goal in our 3-2 win - only our third in 14 League games and one in which Neville Southall was brilliant - while Graeme headed his 100th League goal on his 257th top-flight appearance. That was an impressive ratio for a player who wasn't just an out-and-out goalscorer. He was a team player in every sense and when we were defending corners he'd come back and get in some terrific clearances. He was a good, all-round footballer and in my opinion was the best Scotland centre-forward of his era, deserving far more than the dozen caps he won for his country.

Also on target against Charlton was Kevin Sheedy, taking his sequence to five goals in six games including the friendly against Bilbao. Pat Nevin's

58th-minute offering received a standing ovation from most of a meagre 16,000 crowd in a season when only three clubs - Liverpool Manchester United and Arsenal - had average attendances topping 30,000. Pat beat two defenders and exchanged passes with Sharp before dinking the ball over Bob Bolder. 'That was brilliant...probably the best goal I've seen all season,' enthused watching Scotland manager Andy Roxburgh.

Nevin also scored our next goal five days later at Villa Park in the FA Cup semi-final against Norwich. But Saturday, April 15, 1989, will forever be ringed in black for the events that unfolded before the other semi-final at Hillsborough involving Liverpool and Nottingham Forest. Around the world the very name Hillsborough signifies tragedy after the disaster at the Leppings Lane end, where fans were crushed to death, cost 96 lives, injured more than 2,000 and changed football irrevocably. The human misery rendered football irrelevant and the eternal flame that burns outside Anfield's Shankly Gates ensures that the memory of those who perished will endure.

They say that losing a semi-final is the worst feeling in football and, conversely, there aren't many better feelings than winning one. So when the final whistle went at Villa Park and we'd beaten Norwich 1-0, through Nevin's 26th-minute goal, the joy of our players was unbridled. I knew where my dad was in the stand and I spotted him jumping up and down with delight, as indeed I was. The players almost danced off the pitch in jubilation, totally unaware of the grim events in Sheffield. As they got back to the dressing room I was outside, hearing the first reports about Hillsborough where the match had been abandoned after six minutes.

In a couple of minutes I'd gone from eleation to deep sorrow. I went back into the dressing room, which was absolutely bouncing and being showered with champagne, and said to them: 'Lads, I've got something to tell you. People have died at the other semi-final.' Giving the players that news was like sticking a knife through a balloon. The atmosphere was punctured by the realisation that something tragic had happened at Hillsborough and the awful reports started to come in. It was hard to comprehend. I invited members of the press into our dressing room and by the time our bus left to head back to Merseyside we knew that a full-scale disaster had occurred.

The bus journey home was a muted affair. I just sat at the front with my own thoughts. By then our win seemed like something from another dimension. It didn't matter any more. I kept thinking: 'It could have been us.' My daughters had been at our match and they had friends who were Liverpool fans and they were anxious about them, hoping they were alright. On the Sunday night, with Merseyside grieving, I went with my family to a specially held mass at Liverpool's Metropolitan Cathedral.

Ironically, only four days before the disaster, UEFA had granted the FA's application for the return of English clubs to European competitions from season 1990-91, with a later decision delaying Liverpool's re-entry for an extra season. But the fences that had been called for in the wake of the Heysel Disaster four years earlier would be dismantled after Hillsborough with Lord Justice Taylor's report into the disaster paving the way for the all-seat stadia we have today. That had to be the right direction for football to go. It's just very sad that it took a disaster to make it happen. I know many people regretted the end of terracing but having lived through that era and having seen the packed, swaying crowds at Gwladys Street and the Kop I'm amazed there were not many injuries to spectators.

Even though the FA rather speedily announced the day after Hillsborough that the Cup final would be played on May 20, a week later than scheduled, we didn't really know if it would go ahead at all. The FA also set a date of May 7 for the semi-final to be re-staged at Old Trafford but Liverpool chairman John Smith, quite justifiably in my view, accused them of being insensitive in their haste and some Liverpool players expressed doubts as to whether they would play in it.

I honestly didn't think there would be a Cup final and I'd have fully sympathised if the competition had been cancelled. Some of our players agreed with some of the Liverpool players in the view that it shouldn't have gone ahead. In fact, many people thought the competition should be scrapped as a mark of respect to the Hillsborough victims. Others thought it should go ahead for the same reason. You could understand both opinions.

Our next match was a week later, at Tottenham. Before we left Bellefield for London on the Friday lunchtime our players asked if the bus could make a detour so they could lay a wreath at Anfield, where the pitch had been transformed into a garden of remembrance. When we got there the emotion was tangible. It was a remarkably moving sight. We lost 2-1 at Tottenham and after the Simod Cup final against Forest we prepared for a unique Mersey derby. Fate had decreed that Liverpool's first competitive game after Hillsborough would be against us at Goodison on Wednesday, May 3.

Kenny Dalglish and his squad had played at Celtic the previous Sunday to swell the Hillsborough disaster fund by £300,000 and before we met them both clubs had voluntarily dismantled their perimeter fences. Perhaps fittingly the game, which was screened live on ITV, finished goalless on a night when everyone's thoughts were far removed from football.

Before the game both chairmen, Philip Carter and John Smith, walked together onto the pitch and supporters of both clubs paraded 95 intertwined red and blue scarves (signifying the death toll at that stage). Liverpool supporters carried a banner declaring: 'LFC fans thank EFC fans. We never walked alone.' Our chairman captured the public mood when he said: 'There are many families within our city with divided loyalties when it comes to football. But in present circumstances we are united in such adversity as only, perhaps, Liverpudlians can be.'

By now Liverpool's re-staged semi-final was on and they duly beat Forest 3-1. The Old Trafford capacity was reduced to 50,000 but the clubs returned 12,000 tickets and the attendance was only 38,000, a powerful indication that many thought it should never have been played. But it meant we were meeting Liverpool at Wembley for the fifth time in five years, this time though in poignant circumstances. My opposite number Kenny Dalglish said: 'You can't pick and choose your opponents but if we could have chosen anybody to play in this final it would have been Everton. They have made their own contribution to the city of Liverpool. They have helped a lot of people. It's a fairytale final, really. We've been through so much and I'm so pleased that both clubs from this city are going to be playing each other.'

We went into the final on the back of three straight wins which saw us climb to finish eighth. For some clubs that would have been satisfactory but not at Everton, especially after the first, second, first placings immediately preceding my term as manager. That was a hard act to follow, in some ways a hiding to nothing. I never hid behind the injuries. I had money to spend and spent it. So I had to hold up my hand and say we hadn't quite done it.

After losing 1-0 at Norwich, two goals from Graeme Sharp gave us a 2-1 win at Manchester United, our first away League win since November. The Old Trafford attendance of 26,722, which seems barely believable today, was the lowest for the fixture since 1961-62. We followed up with a 3-1 home win over West Ham and finished our League programme with a 1-0 Goodison victory over Derby on a night that marked two firsts. John Ebbrell made the first of his 207 League starts for the club and our win was secured by the first and only League goal Ian Wilson scored for us.

Having taken the decision to go ahead and play the FA Cup final everyone was rewarded with perhaps the most thrilling, as well as the most emotional meeting in Wembley history. It was our 11th appearance there in little more than five years and Ratcliffe's 10th with Everton, all as captain. He was now setting a record of leading the side in four FA Cup finals. With the exception of Ian Snodin I was able to field my strongest line-up which was:

Southall; McDonald, Watson, Ratcliffe, Van den Hauwe; Nevin, Steven, Bracewell (McCall, 60), Sheedy (Wilson, 78); Sharp, Cottee.

The Liverpool line-up was:

Grobbelaar; Nicol, Ablett, Hansen, Staunton (Venison, 90); Houghton, McMahon, Whelan, Barnes; Aldridge (Rush, 73), Beardsley.

Liverpool scored early doors - John Aldridge on his 100th appearance for the club putting one away from a Steve McMahon pass after just four minutes - and overall they were the better side and deserved to win. But what came in between was breathless, dramatic stuff on a sun-kissed afternoon brimming with new entries for the record books.

We managed to get to half-time without conceding again and after Neville Southall had managed to turn around a John Barnes shot deflected off Neil McDonald I decided to make a change in midfield, where we'd been losing the battle. Paul Bracewell, who'd done ever so well to regain a place after his injury nightmare, was visibly tiring so I sent on Stuart McCall and his energetic, combative qualities had an immediate impact.

With 17 minutes left and us still trailing by that early goal, Liverpool took off Aldridge and sent on the bogey man, the figure that still sends a chill through Evertonian hearts...the dreaded Ian Rush. Even so, we kept him at bay while at the other end forcing Bruce Grobbelaar to deal with a Graeme Sharp header. Then, with seconds remaining, Grobbelaar could only palm out a Dave Watson cross-shot from the right and McCall stepped into the scramble and fired our equaliser to ensure extra time.

We were only five minutes into the additional half-hour when the almost inevitable happened. Rush took a cross from Steve Nicol, checked inside his Wales friend and team-mate Kevin Ratcliffe and put Liverpool back in front. Still we came back. Eight minutes after Rush's strike we were level once more and again it was McCall who scored, volleying Alan Hansen's clearance into the net from 25 yards. As well as crowning a great personal display that played him into the Scotland team McCall had also become the first substitute to score twice in an FA Cup final. Alas, he would be alone with that record for a mere two minutes before you-know-who struck again.

Barnes delivered a cross to the near post and Rush connected to send a header into the far corner beyond Neville Southall. As well as clinching a 3-2 Liverpool win it took Rush's goal total against Everton to 21 in 23 appearances, surpassing Dixie Dean's previous Mersey derby record of 19. It also meant he had equalled the record of Blackburn's William Townley in the 1890s and Blackpool's Stan Mortensen in 1948 and 1953 by scoring four FA Cup final goals - all against us I might add! Three years later, against Sunderland, Rush added a fifth to carve his own niche in Cup statistics.

At the end of a pulsating 120 minutes, in which there hadn't been a single booking by Warrington referee Joe Worrall, a lot of fans ran onto the pitch because, in the post-Hillsborough climate, the Wembley fences had been taken down. I accept that they shouldn't have invaded the playing area but in the circumstances the fans were in no way threatening. It was more a release of exuberance, pride and emotion after what they'd witnessed. I was proud of my players but I'd rather we'd played a stinker and won. So, once more, I was striving to find that elusive team chemistry that would bring us a trophy,which is why I was busy in the transfer market again in the summer of 1989."

On the bench with Howard second time around, 1991.

Chapter Thirteen

Painful Departure And Swift Return

As the new season of 1989-90 beckoned, Colin Harvey's third as Everton manager, he mounted a dragnet at home and abroad in pursuit of the players who might be able to inject that crucial extra ingredient to deliver silverware for the Goodison cabinet.

"In common with most managers, I didn't land all the players I targeted and certainly not everyone I was linked with. I was interested when the news broke that Gary Lineker was leaving Barcelona. I made inquiries but it was no surprise when he re-joined Terry Venables at Tottenham for £1.2 million. I was also keen to sign Norwich midfielder Mike Phelan. I had talks with him, we agreed on everything and he seemed happy. Then he rang to tell me he'd decided to accept Alex Ferguson's offer to join Manchester United. As United had also signed Neil Webb, I asked Alex if he'd be prepared to sell Bryan Robson. His answer was firmly in the negative. If he'd said yes we were prepared to offer Robson a lucrative contract although not quite the staggering sum at that time of £200,000 a year which was speculated on.

The tables were turned with Martin Keown, who I wanted to bolster us at the back. Alex was confident of signing him from Aston Villa, even going public to say he believed the player was keen to play for United. But he signed for us for a tribunal-fixed fee of £750,000. Martin, as he later proved with Arsenal and England, was top class. When he became available I decided to move so that, with captain Kevin Ratcliffe and Dave Watson, we'd have three quality centre-backs. I faced competition from Nottingham Forest and Derby as well as United but I was delighted when Martin, on the eve of his wedding, rang to say 'I do' when asked if he'd accept our offer. Keown's arrival paved the way for our acceptance of Tottenham's bid for Pat Van den Hauwe. I'd transfer-listed Pat at his own request and he went for £575,000 - a handsome profit on the £100,000 we'd paid for him.

To boost our attacking armoury and provide competition for Tony Cottee and Graeme Sharp, I signed Mike Newell from Leicester in a £1.1 million package deal that took Wayne Clarke, valued at £450,000, in the opposite direction. It was a homecoming for Liverpool-born Mike who had been a junior at Anfield before playing for Crewe, Wigan and Luton - for whom he scored a hat-trick against Liverpool - prior to joining Leicester.

I added to our midfield options by signing Swedish international Stefan Rehn from Djurgaarden for £400,000. He became the first foreigner to play for Everton although his career with us would be brief. We were contacted by an agent who told us about Rehn, who was playing for his country in Stockholm in a tournament that also involved Brazil and Denmark.

I went over with our reserve-team coach Mick Lyons to watch him. Before the game we went into a little room and inside we found Pele, Michel Platini and Michael Laudrup. Mick, quick as a flash, got the autographs of all three on a piece of paper - which, incidentally, he proceeded to lose! We had to go back to the stadium next day and found that he'd left it in the bar. The detour to recover his prized signatures meant we had to catch a later flight home.

Rehn, the reason for our trip, played well against Brazil and we were interested. But we bumped into Arsene Wenger at the game. He was then coach of Monaco and we learned that he, too, was on Rehn's trail. We had a chat with Arsene and he told us he was going to go in for Rehn. We assumed it was a done deal and that the player was heading for Monaco until a week or so later our chief executive Jim Greenwood got a call to say that Monaco couldn't sign him because of UEFA's 'three foreigner rule' that applied at the time in Europe. So that opened the door for us. Unfortunately for him and us his move didn't work out. Stefan was a nice footballer but couldn't adapt to the pace of the English game. He came to see me several times and told me he just couldn't adjust to life on Merseyside or the English style of football.

During his time with us he dropped down from Sweden's full team to the Under 21s and helped them beat their England counterparts 1-0. Rehn started only two games for us and made four substitute appearances. In the last of them, against Millwall, we sent him on and then took him off and he returned to Sweden the following January to join IFK Gothenburg for the same £400,000 fee we'd paid for him.

In stark contrast, I also signed Norman Whiteside for £750,000 from Manchester United, a player Alex Ferguson was willing to sell. Norman had played a lot for United as well as becoming the youngest player to appear in a World Cup finals when he appeared for Northern Ireland aged 17 in 1982. But he was still only 24 and although I was aware he'd got a knee problem, and that he'd had his first cartilage operation at 16, I decided that to get someone of his calibre was a gamble I had to take. Some of the things he could do on a football field were terrific and we were victims of his shooting power in the 1985 FA Cup final, when he scored the only goal.

However, other things he did made you cringe. To say he could look after himself is an under-statement. Off the field he was quiet and polite but he was like a different person on it and, in that respect, was reminiscent of his United colleague Mark Hughes. For some reason when Norman went on the field not so much a red mist but more a thick fog of aggression would descend on him, as I was to discover in his first few months at Goodison.

My fifth summer capture was Raymond Atteveld from Haarlem, the Dutch club that provided Ruud Gullit with his launch-pad to stardom. Once again, we'd been alerted to Ray by an agent. We invited him to train with us for a week, played him in a couple of behind closed-doors friendlies and decided to pay the modest fee of £250,000. He was physically strong and, without being top quality, did reasonably well for us playing both in midfield and at right-back in his 66 appearances over a three-year span.

We were well into the season when I made another signing, bringing in winger Peter Beagrie from Stoke for £750,000 in late October because I felt we needed more width in the squad after selling Trevor Steven, Neil Adams and Ian Wilson. Steven was a player I didn't want to lose but with the money-go-round at Rangers he rejected our offer of a new contract and headed up the road to join Gary Stevens at what was then the biggest spending club in British football. It needed an Anglo-Scottish Tribunal to decide on the transfer fee which they set at £1.525 million - at the time the highest-ever fixed by a tribunal.

In my opinion Rangers still got a hell of a good deal and when I said we'd been short changed on Trevor's value it prompted a verbal spat with the Football League. They were quick to point out that the UEFA compensation method had a ceiling of only £772,000. I wasn't arguing with that. I just felt the fee the tribunal set was too low for a player of Trevor's ability. Adams moved to Oldham for £100,000, Wilson joined Besiktas for £200,000 while in September Paul Bracewell signed for Sunderland for £250,000.

Our new players had an exotic build-up to the 1989-80 campaign with a winning four-match pre-season Far East tour. It began with a 3-1 win over

Manchester United in Kobe, Japan, a game memorable for Norman Whiteside's spectacular strike against his former club. We followed up with a 3-1 victory over Japan's national side in Nagoya after which we were presented with an eye-catching Mikado Doll, which is still on view today in Goodison's trophy room. A 3-0 win over Thailand in Bangkok was followed by a goalless draw against Malaysia in Kuala Lumpur, from which we emerged victorious 4-2 on penalties.

We began the season on the wrong foot, losing 2-0 at Coventry when Newell and Whiteside made their competitive debuts, but then embarked on a sequence that took us top-of-the-table with Newell blazing into his Everton career like a house on fire and forcing his way into the England squad. He celebrated his home debut with a 97-second goal against Tottenham - when Kevin Sheedy was also on target in our 2-1 win - and scored again in our 3-0 Goodison defeat of Southampton with McCall and Whiteside adding the others. Tony Cottee, who had lost his place to Newell, didn't even make the bench against Southampton. I omitted him from the 13 after fining him two weeks wages for his failure to turn out as selected in a midweek reserve game at Coventry. Ironically, Graeme Sharp had to go off and have stitches in his knee after tangling with Jimmy Case. So Cottee was back in for our next game, a 1-1 draw at Sheffield Wednesday when a last-minute equaliser by Dalian Atkinson denied us the League leadership. I substituted him after 77 minutes and with Sharp back he didn't start again for seven matches.

Newell, meanwhile, was scoring goals, creating chances and was a real work horse - a good pro. He gave his utmost in training and in games. You knew exactly what you were getting from him. Newell scored in our 3-2 win over Manchester United - when Sharp bagged his 12th goal in 20 senior outings against the Old Trafford side - and fired our goal in a 1-0 win at Charlton, which put us top for the first time in my managerial career. Rehn made his debut at Charlton in place of hamstring casualty Whiteside and had his only other Everton start in our next outing, a 2-0 Littlewoods Cup win at Leyton Orient before Whiteside returned to face Liverpool at Goodison.

Liverpool had just parted with John Aldridge, sold to Real Sociedad for £1.1 million, but they still paraded Ian Rush. We struck first through Newell but Liverpool levelled when John Barnes headed in before the break. Like many derbies the result could have gone either way until Rush struck twice in as many minutes to heighten his Goodison billing as 'public enemy number one'. First he finished a Barnes cross and then seized on a Beardsley pass and scored with a shot that looped in off Neville Southall. It raised his goals total against us to 23 and saw Liverpool dislodge us at the top.

Despite Newell's seventh goal of the season in his ninth appearance, to celebrate his first England squad call-up, we lost 2-1 at Crystal Palace next time out. A less-than-impressive home display saw us draw 2-2 with Leyton Orient to take us into the Littlewoods Cup third round on a 4-2 aggregate. Early on we lost Kevin Ratcliffe with a torn groin muscle that would keep him out for nine games and propel Martin Keown into the team. Up front, Graeme Sharp's goals had dried up so I dropped him and recalled Cottee as I juggled to find the most potent attacking combination. It was a case of how best to utilise Newell, who didn't naturally link with others but was a grafter who chased things down, had a good turn and got shots away.

We then embarked on a four-game run that took us back to the top of the table and into the fourth round of the Littlewoods Cup. We won 2-1 at home to Millwall before a 3-0 Goodison defeat of Arsenal crowned a special week for a man destined to play a massive role in Everton's future. Lifelong fan and actor Bill Kenwright, known to millions for his role as Betty Turpin's son Gordon Clegg in Coronation Street, had just secured the proudest role of his life - being appointed to the Everton board. The Arsenal game was the first he attended as a director and the man who has idolised Dave Hickson since he watched him as a starry-eyed schoolboy was thrilled to see us play Arsenal off the park and end their run of five straight wins over us.

John Ebbrell switched from midfield to right-back in place of hamstring casualty Ian Snodin and with Ratcliffe and Pointon also absent Dave Watson was the only regular in our back four. But it was a superb display against the reigning champions, perhaps the best of my management career. Pat Nevin scored twice, his first double for more than five years. He struck first five minutes before half-time but his second, late in the game, was a gem. Taking a Cottee pass he showed great control to glide past John Lukic and fire the ball into the roof of the net. In between Nevin's two, Neil McDonald scored his only goal of the season and what made the day even sweeter was that with Liverpool losing 4-1 at Southampton we went back to the top.

Newell scored twice in our next game - a 3-0 Littlewoods Cup win over his former club Luton - to take his goal tally for us to nine in 13 appearances. Yet, remarkably, he didn't score again until the final game of the season...late October to May without a goal to his name! It was extraordinary. Cottee's first goal of the season clinched us a 1-1 draw at Norwich which kept us on top until we were dislodged by Liverpool's win over Tottenham 24 hours later, never to taste such high life again.

The following Sunday, Guy Fawkes Day, November 5, we came down to earth with a bang, crashing 6-2 at Aston Villa, our heaviest defeat since losing 5-0 to Liverpool seven years earlier and the first time an Everton side had conceded six since losing 6-2 at home to Manchester United on Boxing Day 1977. We got taken apart that day when the only fireworks we could offer were damp squibs. It's by no means an excuse to say that Villa were developing into quite a good side at the time and went on to finish runners-up to Liverpool. They were a powerful side with some good players. Gordon Cowans put them ahead with only six minutes on the clock followed by two more first-half goals from Ian Olney and David Platt. Platt and Olney scored again after the interval and the big Danish defender Kent Nielsen made it a painful 6-0. That was still the scoreline with seven minutes left before Cottee put the ball in the net and Paul McGrath followed with an own goal.

I took off Norman Whiteside at half-time after he'd collected his sixth booking in his 13th Everton appearance as well as receiving another yellow card on Northern Ireland duty. It meant he was facing a three-match ban under the totting-up process, although an Achilles injury meant he was ruled out of our next nine games anyway. I took him off not only to prevent him being sent off but also because some of the ways he got himself booked were ridiculous. He'd go lunging in when there was no need or reason to do so, and for a manager watching it made you want to tear your hair out.

I sent on our new signing Peter Beagrie for his debut in place of Whiteside while Graeme Sharp came on for Dave Watson, who damaged his hamstring in the first half, and Stuart McCall took over as skipper. The loss of Watson only increased the threat from Ian Ormondroyd, who'd gives us trouble in the League Cup tie at Bradford the previous season. He caused havoc in the air, he was winning everything and Villa kept on picking up the second ball. We couldn't get on the bus and away from Villa Park quickly enough.

It was a bit of a traumatic afternoon for Beagrie to be pitched into his debut. He had great talent, he could beat players, had a good engine on him, worked hard and soon after joining us won England 'B' caps. He could also be infuriating, especially for a striker trying to anticipate the cross coming in. It was difficult to read when he was going to put the ball into the box. He'd have the opportunity to do it and then check back while the strikers were making their runs. He liked that trick. It was something he sorted out and I'm pleased for Peter that it's been a long one. He's played more than 700 games for nine clubs under 20 managers who've had the pleasure of watching Peter's trademark scoring somersault.

Peter felt that he, and not McGrath, should have been credited with our second goal after making his debut on that dismal afternoon at Villa but the records have registered it as an own goal. In fact, he was fated not to score under my management. He had to wait 14 months before his first Everton goal arrived on his 31st appearance. The length of his career hasn't surprised me because he's always been a very fit lad and seldom got injuries. He's a good trainer, a good type and a very sensible lad if we except the pre-season escapade in Spain in 1991. Peter hitched a lift on a motor bike back to the team's San Sebastian hotel and ended up lacerating his arm when he was thrown into a plate glass window as the rider crashed the machine!

Four days after our defeat at Villa the Berlin Wall, which had stood since 1961 symbolising a divided Europe, was torn down to signal the end of the Cold War between east and west. But the demolition that concerned me was the dismantling of our hopes of challenging near the First Division summit as we began a bleak sequence of results. Just to underline the perils and fluctuating fortunes of management came the news that Howard Kendall had been sacked by Athletic Bilbao following three defeats in six days. Within a month, he had a new job as successor to Mel Machin at Manchester City.

We lost 1-0 to Chelsea and drew 1-1 with Wimbledon prior to our Littlewoods Cup fourth-round trip to Nottingham Forest, a venue that's brought much misery to Everton over many years including our 3-2 FA Cup defeat as holders back in 1967. Things were not about to change. The game was goalless until the 83rd minute when Sunderland referee George Tyson penalised and booked Neville Southall for time-wasting and from the free-kick Lee Chapman scored to knock us out. Our players were calling Tyson a cheat so I went on the field to usher them off the pitch. As I passed Tyson I said to him: 'They're calling you a cheat - and, by the way, you are.'

Almost inevitably, I was charged by the FA with bringing the game into disrepute and when the case was heard I was fined £1,500. The referee said in his report that I'd peppered my remarks with a few 'f' words, which I did not. A timing of Neville with the ball showed that he'd held it for 12.43 seconds so the referee wasn't a cheat. But I think it was officious, which I have found to be a trait of many North East referees. I accept that refereeing is a difficult job and one I wouldn't want to do. I've always tried to think about that, and the pressure referees are under, when I've seen decisions I haven't agreed with. What angers managers and players is that some referees will blow up for things like that and others won't. And I doubt if Neville would have been penalised if the game had been at Goodison.

To compound matters we were back at Forest three days later in the League amid reports that our players had trashed the dressing room and that Forest were going to leave it in that state. It was ridiculous. The players had done no such thing and when we returned the dressing room was in pristine condition. The result, though, was the same. We lost 1-0 to a Nigel Clough penalty awarded for Martin Keown's lunge on Steve Hodge. We'd won only twice at Forest in 26 years and the defeat saw us slide to 12th.

In view of Newell's goal drought after his early-season torrent I dropped him for our next five matches and recalled Tony Cottee. We beat Coventry 2-0, lost 2-1 at Tottenham and then entertained Manchester City in Howard's first match in charge, in which he gave debuts to newly-signed Peter Reid and Alan Harper. The word 'entertained' is really a misnomer because it was a grim, goalless affair and certainly not something to set before the nation watching on live television. There was one isolated, noteworthy incident when a Beagrie shot hit the outside of a post.

It was now Christmas and we'd won only one of our last eight League games, scoring only seven goals - and one of those was an own goal. But Stuart McCall unwrapped a present for us with a 25-yard Boxing Day strike at Derby which gave us a 1-0 win, only our second away League victory of the season. We then lost 1-0 at QPR before Norman Whiteside celebrated his New Year's Day return from Achilles surgery with a goal in our 2-1 win over Luton, which our last outfield ever-present Kevin Sheedy was forced to miss with an ankle problem. Graeme Sharp got our other goal - only his second of the season - in a game for which I dropped Cottee and brought back Newell as I grappled with our scoring problem.

The start of the FA Cup took us to Middlesbrough where we played out a goalless draw. The midweek replay also ended all-square at 1-1 after extra time, Sheedy scoring our goal. For the second replay at Goodison I dropped Beagrie for the first time since his debut and recalled Pat Nevin. We got through with a 1-0 win thanks to a last-minute goal from Whiteside, who was displaying his scoring touch on his return. He'd scored twice in our previous game - a 2-2 draw at Southampton - and after a double from Sheedy gave us a 2-0 home League win over Sheffield Wednesday, we had to travel to face them at Hillsborough in the FA Cup fourth round.

Cue Whiteside again. He scored twice to set us on the path to a 2-1 win and take us into the fifth round for the eighth consecutive season. It took Whiteside's goal haul since his comeback to six in seven games, underlining that although he was a midfield player, he retained that finishing instinct that had led him to launch his career as a striker. He had the ability to arrive in the box from open play as well as set pieces and was a good all-round footballer. He had top-class touch and technique, his qualities hampered only by a lack of pace and his irrtitating tendency to kick people.

We went into the Mersey derby at Liverpool on a seven-match unbeaten run from the start of the year. We'd played with three centre-backs at Hillsborough - Ratcliffe, Watson and Keown - and I stuck to that with Sharp operating as a lone striker. For once, Rush didn't score but John Barnes and Peter Beardsley, from a penalty, did before Sharp pulled one back just before the interval. That 2-1 scoreline is how it finished watched by a then lowest post-war derby crowd - 38,730 - on a day of postponements.

On the morning of our next match, a home League fixture with Charlton, a wartime bomb was discovered half-a-mile from Goodison. But it was dealt with in time for the match to start on schedule and it was Whiteside who extinguished Charlton's hopes of a point by scoring the winner, following a goal just before the interval by the recalled Cottee. I'd dropped Dave Watson for the first time, pairing Ratcliffe and Keown at the heart of defence, but we missed him and I brought him straight back for our next FA Cup engagement - a fifth-round trip to Joe Royle's Second Division Oldham.

It meant another outing on plastic although artificial surfaces were on the way out after the League outlawed them in the top two divisions from the start of the 1991-92 season. Sharp and Cottee gave us a 2-0 interval lead and we were on top when referee Tony Ward gave a penalty on the hour after Roger Palmer had fallen over Neville Southall. Andy Ritchie scored and not long after Palmer equalised to set up a replay. After the match I said to Ward: 'That wasn't penalty. Have a look at it on television tonight.'

In those days the original referee also had charge of the replay and I spoke to Ward, a London-based official, hours before the game at Goodison. 'Now you've seen the incident on television what do you think?' I asked him. 'I'd still have given a penalty,' he replied. I just walked away. I'd have thought a lot more of him if he'd admitted at least some doubt about it. Mind you, he was quite right to send off Whiteside in the replay. For no reason at all

Whiteside, who'd already been cautioned, had a kick at Mike Milligan early in the second half. He almost cut him in half. Whiteside's dreadful disciplinary record with Everton read: played 24, bookings 8, dismissals 1.

All the talking in the world had no affect on him. Whatever you said you couldn't get through to him and I'm sure Alex Ferguson had the same problem. Norman would be playing well and behaving himself then you'd see this aberration occur and you'd say to yourself: 'Why has he done that?' With 10 men for most of the second half in the replay we reached 90 minutes without a goal being scored. Then Ian Marshall put Oldham ahead in the 101st minute, before we were rescued by a Kevin Sheedy penalty.

Prior to the second replay we lost 3-1 at Wimbledon, Sheedy's strike taking him past Whiteside as our 11-goal top scorer at that time. For our third meeting with Oldham - played on a Saturday - it was back to the Boundary Park plastic. We were without Dave Watson, who'd had a bang on the head, and the suspended Whiteside. I think it's fair to say that it wasn't a game for Neil McDonald's scrapbook. After Cottee had given us the lead McDonald made two mistakes that effectively knocked us out. His backpass allowed Palmer to equalise and after we'd been unlucky to have another Cottee strike disallowed for a foul on the keeper, we went into extra time.

The additional period was only three minutes old when McDonald brought down Marshall to concede a penalty. Big Ian got up and sent his spot-kick past Southall to give Oldham a 2-1 win. The exit was bitterly disappointing and public and media criticism of me and the team was rising. But to the credit of the players they responded with a run of only one defeat in nine games, starting with a goalless draw at Manchester United. We were still without Watson at Old Trafford, Newell was unavailable after undergoing a knee probe and I dropped McDonald and recalled Neil Pointon for his first outing since November after undergoing knee surgery.

Whiteside also returned in place of John Ebbrell and I named an unchanged side for our home game with Crystal Palace a week later. Sadly, our biggest League win in 19 months was watched by only 19,274 people, which at that stage was Goodison's lowest League attendance of the season. We won 4-0 with Sharp getting the show on the road after five minutes with his 106th League goal for the club, equalling Bob Latchford's post-war Everton record. Cottee bagged a brace and Whiteside rounded things off with his 11th goal of the season four minutes from the end. We followed that with a 2-1 win at Millwall, with Cottee and Pointon on the mark, and climbed to fourth with a

3-1 win over Norwich when Cottee's double took his goal burst to eight in nine games and Sharp's strike made him Everton's most prolific post-war League scorer with 107 goals in 289 appearances.

As Watson returned for our trip to Arsenal at the end of March we lost Kevin Ratcliffe with a heel injury and early in the second half Martin Keown went off with a hamstring problem. McDonald came on at right-back and I moved Ian Snodin, who I'd made captain in Kevin's absence, to centre-back. Despite the re-organisation we prevented Arsenal adding to Alan Smith's goal. Unfortunately, we couldn't hit the target and went down 1-0.

But we came back with another four-goal show, this time avenging our League and Littlewoods Cup defeats by Nottingham Forest. We were without Ratcliffe and Keown, then lost Snodin in the opening 20 minutes with more hamstring problems. It was the fifth time in two years he'd been hit by right hamstring damage and he'd had another absence through problems with his left hamstring, forcing him to miss 32 matches. His career was cruelly haunted by it. Before the end of the live TV game we also lost Pointon, with a groin injury, but two goals apiece from Cottee and Whiteside, who were now 13-goal top scorers, saw us through to a 4-0 win - Forest's biggest defeat since their 5-0 hammering at Liverpool two years earlier. We were stripped of Watson, Ratcliffe, Snodin, Keown and Pointon for our next fixture, the visit of QPR. Yet we still came out on top, but only after Neville Southall had performed more heroics

I brought in 20-year-old Manchester-born reserve centre-back Mark Wright for his debut and what proved to be his only Everton appearance before moving on to Huddersfield. Wright was at the heart of an emergency back four alongside Neil McDonald with Ray Atteveld and John Ebbrell in the full-back berths. Despite the disruption we were heading for a 1-0 win through Cottee's 71st-minute penalty when, in the dying seconds, debutant Wright fouled Danny Maddix to concede a penalty. But Southall proved the man for the moment by saving Simon Barker's spot-kick and securing our three points. It was Neville's second penalty stop in 10 days following his save from Kevin Sheedy for Wales against the Republic of Ireland.

In a situation like that I'd have taken Neville every time. He made outlandish saves his stock in trade. The big man was a giant between the posts and his pride and passion would be powerfully demonstrated twice in the coming months. Sharp, too, had an eventful game. He was involved with defender Brian Law for our penalty and after we'd conceded that late one ourselves he correctly told Neville which way to go for Barker's kick.

With Watson back in for Wright, but still with six first-teamers missing we drew 2-2 on Luton's plastic. Top scorer Cottee hit his 15th of the campaign with Sharp getting our other goal. We came back to Goodison to beat Derby 2-1 in Southall's 400th Everton appearance. It was our eighth straight home League win. Ray Atteveld scored the first of his only two Everton goals with a cross-cum-shot that beat goalkeeper Martin Taylor and Sheedy, who'd come on for the injured Beagrie, won it for us late on with a superb volley.

After that win we were lying third with 58 points from 35 games, seven behind Aston Villa and eight adrift of leaders Liverpool. But successive defeats - 1-0 at Manchester City, when Sharp's season was prematurely ended by a knee injury, and 2-1 at Chelsea, where Newell made his first start since January - knocked us down to fifth. We'd have stayed in that position with a win over runners-up Villa in our final match. We were without Sharp, Snodin and Beagrie and I dropped Whiteside, Sheedy and Atteveld to recall Nevin and Ebbrell. Kevin Ratcliffe returned after nine games out and in a terrific game Newell scored his first goal since October.

Villa striker Tony Cascarino made a piece of history by becoming the only opposition player to score for both sides in an Everton match. He put us ahead with an own goal on the half-hour then scored a Villa equaliser early in the second half. Newell then put us ahead, Gordon Cowans levelled again for Villa before Tony Daley put them ahead. I sent on Sheedy for Ebbrell and he earned us a 3-3 draw and a finishing position of sixth with a penalty eight minutes from the end. We'd improved on the previous year but I was deeply disappointed that a season that started with so much promise dipped so badly in the middle, before improving markedly near the end. It was a soft-centre campaign which, frankly, was unacceptable.

Four days after the Villa game we flew out for an end-of-season Far East tour and as we were about to leave Neville Southall said he wanted a move. The big man was clearly unhappy that we hadn't won any silverware but nobody was as unhappy about that as I was. As far as I was concerned Neville was the best goalkeeper in the world. There was no way I wanted to lose him and I turned down his request. As it happened, he was staying behind on Wales duty along with Sheedy for the Republic of Ireland and Stuart McCall with Scotland, who were both involved in the World Cup finals in Italy that summer. On the tour we beat the China Olympic side 2-0 in Beijing and lost 3-2 on penalties after a 2-2 draw with a Hong Kong Select before winding down with five days in Hawaii.

While we were there I got a call from Terry Darracott back home to say that Andy Townsend was available at Norwich. I thought he'd be a good acquisition and I told Terry to speak to him and tell him to delay any decision on his future until I got back. We still didn't have mobile phones so basic communications were still problematical. Terry did contact him and Andy said he'd be interested at the prospect of joining us. But by the time I returned home he'd already decided to sign for Chelsea for £1.2 million. I also pondered a move for Millwall's Terry Hurlock. I asked about him because although he wasn't the silkiest of footballers, he was a 100 per cent committed player who could be the heartbeat of a team. I inquired about him and was told he wasn't available. Some time later they sold him to Rangers.

Although I didn't know it the summer of 1990 was to be my last as manager and I made two more sorties to bring in full-back Andy Hinchliffe and midfielder Mike Milligan. Andy had a lovely left foot and, later in his Everton career, his deliveries for Duncan Ferguson were a big feature of Everton's play. He went on to win England caps and had many qualities. He was a magnificent athlete, quick and strong but, given that, he wasn't as physically imposing or aggressive as he should have been in the position he played in and he didn't seem to like heading a ball. But he was still a classy defender and I signed him in a £900,000 deal from Manchester City, which comprised a £600,000 payment with Neil Pointon moving to Maine Road.

Milligan cost us a total, with appearance-linked clauses, of £1 million from Oldham, managed by my pal and former Everton team-mate Joe Royle. I'd been alerted to Milligan when Oldham knocked us out of the FA Cup the previous season and, of his midfield type, he was the best outside the top flight at the time. He'd starred in Oldham's run to the Cup semi-final and they'd had a good season in the Second Division. He was a busy, aggressive player and he was someone I felt would offer us something a bit different from what we had. I thought he was capable of making the jump to the top flight but although he went on to win a Republic of Ireland cap he just lacked the ability to make that step up. He didn't have enough quality on the ball and he made only 24 appearances before re-joining Oldham a year later.

That summer, knowing how unsettled Neville Southall was, I also went partly down the road of signing Egypt international goalkeeper Ahmed Shobeir after being tipped off about him by our Northern Ireland scout Jim Emery. Jim had seen him play in the World Cup and been impressed by his displays against Holland and the Republic of Ireland. Shobeir was voted the tournament's third-best keeper so I got on his trail and went as far as agreeing a £300,000 fee with his Cairo-based club Al-Ahly. Shobeir, who was 28 and had won 60 caps, was keen to join us. But the thing became snarled in red tape and work permit problems forced the deal to collapse.

Another Goodison departure with Pointon that summer was reserve goalkeeper Mike Stowell. He ended four-and-a-half years at Everton, in which he'd made one senior appearance and been out on loan six times, by making a tribunal-fixed £275,000 move to Wolves. There were changes, too, on my backroom staff. My former team-mate Jimmy Gabriel, who'd coached at several clubs in America before becoming assistant manager at Bournemouth, came in as first-team coach in place of Terry Darracott after a 23-year absence from Goodison. Terry had switched to the role of chief scout to succeed Harry Cooke, who retired after 51 years at Everton.

We also appointed a new physiotherapist in Les Helm, who joined us from Shrewsbury to succeed Chris Goodson. I wanted a stricter regime in our medical room and Terry Darracott and I had received a lot of good reports from players and other people who had worked with Les or been treated by him. Asa Hartford, for instance, spoke highly about him. I made contact with him and we arranged that he'd come for a talk about the prospect of becoming club physio. We knew he was a keen fitness fanatic but Terry and I got a bit of a shock when he arrived at Bellefield on a mountain bike!

Les was duly appointed and he did a terrific job. The treatment room was run almost on military lines. There was no skylarking or playing the wounded soldier in Les's room. It was his domain and what he said was law in there. I think that's something I'd recommend at every club. I'm glad to say that Les worked at Everton right up until his retirement in the new millennium and that our paths were to cross again.

We had a sound pre-season programme in the summer of 1990 with four wins in Ireland over Cork, Athlone, Swindon and Linfield, a 2-2 draw at Fulham in a joint testimonial for Peter Scott and John Marshall, a 3-1 win over Galatasaray in Istanbul, a 2-1 win at Tranmere in Johnny King's testimonial and a 2-2 draw at Celtic. But we started the new campaign without three players. Ian Snodin suffered a recurrence of his hamstring problem in his first pre-season outing since surgery in April. As fate would dictate, he would never play under my management again and would spend most of the next two seasons on the sidelines. We were also without ankle casualty Peter Beagrie and Tony Cotttee, who had a stomach virus.

Neville Southall, who'd signed a seven-and-a-half-year contract only in December 1988, followed up his verbal request for a move at the end of the previous season with a written request on the eve of the new campaign. I told him that we'd listen to offers but they'd have to be huge ones to even consider letting him go. His feelings clearly spilled over onto the field in bizarre fashion in our first game.

Kevin Sheedy, a player I greatly admired but with whom I had difficulty communicating on a personal basis, also asked for a move. I appreciated his ability and the great goals he'd scored for us. He could conjure them out of nothing. I wouldn't say we had a clash of personalities but there was something not quite right between us. We'd never quite hit it off and I'm sure Kevin would say the same. I suppose you have to put it down to the complicated business of human relationships. Kevin was duly transfer-listed and I named him and Kevin Ratcliffe on the bench for our opening match at home to Leeds, for which our line-up was:

Southall; McDonald, Keown, Watson, Hinchcliffe; Nevin, Milligan, McCall (Sheedy, 60), Ebbrell; Newell, Sharp. Unused subsitute: Ratcliffe.

It proved a traumatic afternoon. Chris Fairclough and Gary Speed put Leeds 2-0 up by half-time after we'd given a dreadful display and also missed a penalty when McDonald put his kick wide. We went in at the break to a chorus of jeers from our fans who were then astonished by the next turn of events, although I was one of the last to learn what had happened.

The home dressing room at Goodison is huge. You could hold a dance in it. When we got back in I had a few words with the players - not shouting but trying to sort things out - and then told them to get ready to go out for the second half. I had no idea that Neville had left the dressing room early, walked out onto the pitch on his own and sat against a goalpost. I still knew nothing about it as we went 3-0 down to much-travelled former Everton forward Imre Varadi and lost McCall with knee ligament damage.

I was still unaware of what happened at half-time as our re-jigged team, with Sheedy replacing McCall and John Ebbrell switching to centre midfield, staged a very creditable fightback. Pat Nevin pulled a goal back then Ebbrell scored his first Everton goal and instead of being trampled on we went down fighting 3-2. I still wasn't happy with the result. In fact it was heart wrenching. But I was encouraged by our players' battling attitude.

It was only when I got back to the media interview area that I discovered about Neville's one-man show. With the cameras rolling, television commentator Clive Tyldesley posed the question: 'What's your view, Colin, of Neville Southall's half-time sit-in?' 'What was that?,' I replied, baffled. Cut! The cameras stopped and Clive told me what had happened. I was flabbergasted. Later I saw the incident on TV and the Sunday and Monday papers were full of it. I had a word with Neville on the Monday and I think he did it because he was frustrated by our performance. He said it wasn't meant as a protest or demonstration and I didn't see it as that either.

Neville always wore his heart on his sleeve. He was and remains a very committed person and I think he'd felt badly about conceding two goals in the first half. I told him I could understand his feelings but that it was unacceptable to do what he did in public and I'd be fining him a week's wages. That was the end of it as far as I was concerned but after we'd lost our next two games - 3-1 at Coventry and 1-0 at Manchester City when our former striker Adrian Heath scored the goal - some fans targeted Neville in our next home match. Those three straight defeats had left us bottom of the table for the first time since September 1959 and rubbing salt in the wound was the fact that Liverpool were top with a 100 per cent start.

When we faced Arsenal at Goodison one banner bore the words, aimed cruelly at Neville: 'Once a bin man, always a bin man.' The people responsible should be ashamed of themselves. Apart from the fact that it was highly disrespectful to bin men it was grossly unjust on Neville, whose heroics for the club far outweighed his personal eccentricities.

Four days before the game we had another unwanted distraction when Sheedy and Martin Keown were involved in a bust-up in a Southport hotel after we'd all gone out for a Chinese meal, a club tradition going back several years. When we got so much money collected from players' fines we'd use it to pay for a squad-bonding Chinese meal, to thrash out any problems and help build team spirit. The kitty also covered the cost of taxis to ensure the players got home safely. As I left that day after the meal I told them: 'Make sure you don't get into any bother and don't get into any trouble with the public.' Little did I think they'd get into trouble with themselves over something that apparently was quite petty. It proved the truth of the old adage that if things can get worse they will!

In the cold light of day Sheedy and Keown apologised and, like Southall, they were both fined. But I left them out of the Arsenal game the following Saturday when we were also without Peter Beagrie, who'd undergone ankle surgery. Naturally, I was feeling low after our first three results and the other distractions hadn't helped. So in the dug-out that day I wore a No 6 jersey, to remind me of the shirt I wore with pride during my playing days.

Our display against the third-placed visitors from Highbury showed significant improvement. Perry Groves put Arsenal ahead in the second half but Mike Newell equalised with his first goal of the season. He scored again, along with Sharp, in our 2-2 draw at Sunderland before we took on pacesetting Liverpool at Goodison. The derby was played in pouring rain and Liverpool ran all over us in the first half. Like the Leeds game we went 3-0 down before making a real fight of it.

It wasn't a happy afternoon for Ray Atteveld. He conceded the free-kick from which Peter Beardsley opened the scoring, conceded the penalty for John Barnes to give Liverpool a 2-0 interval lead and was booked early in the second half. Beardsley made it 3-0 for Liverpool with 21 minutes left, but Andy Hinchcliffe drove in his first Everton goal and an 85th-minute header from Stuart McCall hit the bar and Glenn Hysen before going in. It set-up a hectic climax but we couldn't find an equaliser and Liverpool went away with a 3-2 victory, having equalled their best start to a top-flight season of six straight League wins. Our fortunes were in stark contrast. Our nine games without a win since April was the worst sequence for more than 13 years and we were languishing third-from-bottom with only two points.

We had a welcome goal glut in our next match, Tony Cottee hitting a hat-trick in a 5-0 win at Wrexham in the Rumbelows Cup second round, first leg in what was his first start of the season after a stomach virus. He was on target again twice next time out when at last we collected our first League win of the season, a 3-0 defeat of Southampton in which John Ebbrell was our other scorer. The Nottingham Forest hoodoo continued to haunt us as we went to the City Ground and lost 3-1, stretching our dismal record there to only two wins in 27 years. Our Rumbelows return with Wrexham brought another big score with Graeme Sharp hitting his fourth hat-trick for the club. He scored all three goals with his left foot and our 6-0 win was completed by strikes from Cottee, Ebbrell and McDonald. The attendance, though, was only 7,415, the lowest at Goodison in a major competition since the 1890s.

In our next game Goodison witnessed its first goalless draw for almost a year when Crystal Palace were the visitors. We were without the injured Sheedy, Whiteside, Milligan, Snodin and Beagrie, and in the second half lost Hinchcliffe with knee damage and Ratcliffe, who had to be taken off to have stitches above his left eye. It was not the most edifying 90 minutes to mark what was to prove my last home game in charge. We drew 1-1 at Luton, Nevin getting our goal, which left us still third-from-bottom as a prelude to our Rumbelows Cup trip to Sheffield United. The promoted Yorkshire club were propping up the table with three points and no wins from their opening 10 League games but the events of Bramall Lane that wet Tuesday night, October 30, 1990, were like something from a nightmare.

It was goalless at half-time but everything just fell apart after the interval. With an hour gone Dave Watson was sent off by London referee Alf Buksh for a professional foul on Brian Deane, the red card sanction for such offences having been ordered by FIFA edict. With Watson gone our defence was weakened and within five minutes of his exit Carl Bradshaw put United ahead, although in our view it was offside and the goal shouldn't have stood. Ten minutes from the end Deane hit a second United goal although that, too, looked offside. Nevin, who'd gone on for Cottee, pulled one back but with 10 men we couldn't add to that and we were out.

I had a feeling I was out, too. That this was a watershed moment. Our belief that both United goals were offside could not mask the reality of our performance which, added to our struggles in the League, was painful to watch. Being a lifelong Evertonian as well as manager made that pain even worse. The buck stopped with me. I was the man in charge - and that was it. I felt so bad I didn't go home that night. When the team bus got back to Bellefield I rang Maureen to tell her I was spending the night at the training ground. I just sat there and thought about the season we'd had, that I was into my fourth season and although we'd come close twice, we hadn't won anything. I was soul searching. Our coach Jimmy Gabriel kept me company for a while, offering his valuable opinions on certain things, but when he went home I just stayed there all through the night, sleeping only fitfully.

Next morning the staff came in and I was due to do a presentation at a five-a-side tournament when I got a phone call at Bellefield asking me to go to a meeting at Goodison. At that moment a chill ran down my spine, not because I knew I'd be losing my job but because I felt I'd let down the club and myself. I drove to the ground and the chairman Philip Carter and another director Desmond Pitcher were waiting to see me. It was very professionally done. Phil Carter said they couldn't allow the situation to continue, they had to do something and that they were dispensing with my services. My response was: 'You're in charge and I fully accept that.'

I didn't ring Maureen right away. I drove to a spot near Crosby lighthouse to spend an hour or so by myself reflecting on what had happened. My overwhelming feeling was one of great disappointment, not primarily over being sacked but at not doing the job I'd been entrusted with. I had the opportunity and I'd failed. I'd spent around £10.5 million in the transfer market and recouped almost £7 million, losing some players I wanted to keep. Yet that successful chemistry had eluded me. Soon I went home to break the news. Maureen and the family were very supportive, as I knew they would be. 'Worse things happen at sea,' was a phrase I recall.

The following day our late parish priest, a lovely Irishman and long-time Evertonian called Father Brean, called at the house and had me laughing. He came in and said: 'Well done, Colin. You've done a tremendous job getting that club off your back!' Jimmy Gabriel took over as caretaker-manager and I was delighted for him and the club when they beat QPR 3-0 the following Saturday to climb out of the bottom three for the first time that season.

The previous afternoon, on the Friday, I went to Bellefield to collect my personal belongings in a bin bag and while I was there Mary, the secretary, said there was a call for me. When I picked it up Bill Kenwright was on the line. He'd rung the house and Maureen had told him where I was. Bill offered his commiserations over my sacking and then said: 'Would you be interested in coming back. We're having talks with Howard Kendall about returning as manager and he said that he'd like you to come back as first-team coach. What do you think?' My first response was to say no. It had come out of the blue. But after thinking about it overnight I changed my mind and when Howard rang me I said I would be interested.

Joe Royle had been the media favourite for the job but the following Tuesday, November 6, a press conference at Goodison was given the shock news that Howard was back as manager with me as his right-hand man. Less than six months earlier Howard had declined the opportunity to be interviewed for the England manager's job to succeed Bobby Robson after the World Cup. Now he had left Manchester City to begin a second spell at Goodison, enthusing: 'When you talk about a love affair with City you are talking about a marriage with Everton.' And here was I, a week after being sacked as manager, re-appointed at Everton alongside Howard.

I can't speak for Howard - and would never do so - but with hindsight, I shouldn't have gone back. There were too many ghosts. I was going back to coach and work with players I'd managed only a week earlier. It was a strange situation. I think I should have made a clean break. It wasn't difficult to work again with Howard. After all, our relationship had been built over a 23-year period. Yet something was missing. A little bit of the magic between us had been lost. We'd gone our separate ways in management and had different experiences. We'd both changed a bit, too. Different things had occurred in our lives. Even though I will always be a fervent Evertonian, I didn't feel right going back - and I shouldn't have done so.

Apparently the board, when they were talking to Howard about returning as manager, said they wanted to make sweeping changes and one of his first tasks was the unenviable one of sacking Mick Lyons, Terry Darracott, Graham Smith and Paul Power. In came new chief scout Brian Greenhalgh, youth coach Jim Barron and youth development officer Ray Hall.

With that strange irony football regularly conjures the first game of my re-union with Howard was a League game back at Sheffield United, which finished goalless. The first home game under the new set-up also saw the points shared, McCall heading our goal in a 1-1 live televised draw with Tottenham which came just four days before Margaret Thatcher resigned as Prime Minister to be succeeded by John Major.

We needed a major change in fortune following a 2-1 defeat at Wimbledon and a 1-0 home defeat by Manchester United and it was provided by a blistering right-foot McCall volley for the only goal of our Goodison meeting with Coventry. But in our next League outing we lost 2-0 in a Sunday live TV visit to Leeds and then lost 1-0 at Norwich, when Eddie Youds made his senior debut as substitute for the injured Martin Keown.

That left us fifth-from-bottom but a run of five straight wins - including a 2-1 New Year's Day success at Chelsea - lifted us to 12th in the League and into the fourth round of the FA Cup after knocking out Second Division Charlton 2-1. Non-league Woking gave us a stiff test in our next tie, which was switched from their ground to Goodison. The only goal of the game came in the second half from Kevin Sheedy's left-foot volley and Woking headed back south with their pride intact and around £90,000 richer from their share of the gate receipts paid by 34,000-plus spectators.

That narrowest of wins earned a fifth-round collision with Liverpool at Anfield. We'd lost there 3-1 only eight days earlier in the League but this time held out for a goalless draw in which Steve McMahon suffered serious knee tendon damage in a tackle on John Ebbrell and we were denied what looked a blatant penalty for Gary Ablett's challenge on Pat Nevin. The events of the following Wednesday, February 20 have a permanent place in Merseyside football folklore. Some have called it the greatest-ever Mersey derby. Others claim it rivals the 6-4 Cup classic against Sunderland in 1935 and our 3-1 European Cup Winners' Cup semi-final win over Bayern Munich in 1985 as Goodison's most memorable match.

It was a fantastic contest with an unforgettable sequence of events. Four times Liverpool took the lead - through Peter Beardsley twice, Ian Rush and John Barnes - and on each occasion we came back to equalise. Graeme Sharp had scored twice only for Rush to put Liverpool back in front at 3-2 and I must say I thought we were going out when, with four minutes left, we sent on Tony Cottee in place of Nevin as a last throw of the dice. We were into the last minute when Cottee cracked in an equaliser and, amazingly, we were into extra time. A brilliant, curling shot from Barnes restored Liverpool's lead but again we weren't finished and Cottee was the hero once more with his second rescuing goal to ensure a final scoreline of 4-4.

We won the toss for venue for the second replay a week later but by then Kenny Dalglish had sensationally resigned as Liverpool manager. Ronnie Moran was in caretaker charge for the third Cup meeting, which was in total contrast to the earlier extravaganza. The only goal came from former Liverpool reserve Dave Watson, the first time he had scored against the club he had left for Norwich in November 1980. That put us through to the sixth round in which we suffered the anti climax of losing 2-1 at West Ham, a massive disappointment after overcoming Liverpool.

Howard responded to that setback by signing Polish winger Robert Warzycha from Gornik Zabrze for £500,000 a few days later. He injected pace and width but his goals were rare, scoring only eight in 86 appearances during three years at Everton. Strangely, four of his goals came in his first six appearances, including one on his debut at Leeds in a 3-3 draw in the first leg of the northern area final of the Zenith Data Systems Cup, the latest title of a competition that had previously interrupted the fixture calendar as the Full Members Cup and the Simod Cup.

A 3-1 win over Leeds in the second leg took us to Wembley for the national final against Crystal Palace in which Warzycha also scored to cancel out a Geoff Thomas goal. It was 1-1 at 90 minutes but two goals from Ian Wright and another from John Salako in the extra period gave over-physical Palace a 4-1 win. Palace were reminiscent of Wimbledon. Keown had to be taken off for four stitches in a cut mouth and Mike Newell also had to be substituted after taking a blow to the head. It was our fifth consecutive losing final at Wembley and, true to type, Neville Southall refused to receive his losers' medal, saying: 'A Zenith Data losers medal! What do I want one of those for?'

Palace's aggressive, combative style was evident again later that month of April when we went to Selhurst Park and drew 0-0 in the League in which Dave Watson was stretchered off after an accidental clash of heads with Gary Thompson. Howard commented after the match: 'You don't arrange a date with your wife or girlfriend after playing Palace - you need smooth lips for that.' He may well have been thinking of an occasion in our playing days when Howard caught Johnny Giles in a game against Leeds with the result that their players went looking for him. They got him, too, and Howard had to go on a date that night sporting a big, fat lip!

Our preceding game, a 2-2 home draw with Chelsea, ensured our safety from relegation and after a closing unbeaten six-match run - four of them draws - we finished ninth. Give Howard his due, we'd been well down the table and needed some pulling round but I wasn't enjoying it like I had in the past. I'd managed the club and I just found it a strange experience being back as first-team coach. I still loved the club, though, and I stuck at it.

By the time we kicked off the 1991-92 season we had several new players as well as a new chairman. Philip Carter, who'd been knighted two months earlier in the Queen's Birthday Honours List, resigned after 13 years at the helm and was succeeded by Dr. David Marsh. A year earlier Dr. Marsh had gained the prestigious honour of being named captain of the Royal and Ancient after twice winning the English amateur golf championship and twice captaining the Walker Cup team.

The new players were Peter Beardsley, who made a headline-grabbing £1 million move across Stanley Park from Liverpool; Mark Ward, who followed Howard from Manchester City for £900,000; Alan Harper, who also returned to Goodison from Maine Road for £300,000 and goalkeeper Gerry Peyton from Bournemouth for £80,000. Howard had also tried to sign Dean Saunders from Derby. The Wales striker was wanted by a number of clubs but the attraction of linking up with his compatriot Ian Rush at Anfield proved irresistible and he signed for Graeme Souness for £2.9 million.

Graeme Sharp's illustrious Everton career ended when he and Mike Milligan joined Joe Royle's Oldham for £500,000 and £600,000 respectively, and were soon joined there by Neil McDonald, who moved for £500,000. The highest-priced departure was Stuart McCall. The Scotland star, whose midfield role would be taken on by John Ebbrell, was sold to Rangers for £1.2 million after some memorable contributions to the Everton cause.

The new season saw the first FIFA change to the offside law in 65 years, ruling that from now players level with defenders would be onside, and we opened our programme with a 2-1 defeat at Nottingham Forest when even our goal came courtesy of home defender Stuart Pearce. Our line-up was:

Southall; Harper, Keown, Watson, Ratcliffe; Warzycha (Nevin, 73), Ebbrell, Sheedy, Ward (McDonald, 83); Beardsley, Cottee.

Although we beat Arsenal 3-1 in our first home game, with a couple of goals from home debutant Ward and the other from Cottee, it was our only win in the opening eight games to leave us fourth-bottom. The sequence included a 3-1 defeat at Liverpool, who were blasted in front by David Burrows, later to play for Everton, after just 48 seconds. Saunders - wouldn't you bet! - added another before the interval and Ray Houghton made it three in the second half, before Mike Newell scored a consolation goal. It was to prove the last of his 15 League goals for Everton before Howard sold him to Blackburn for £1.1 million in November, the same month Maurice Johnston arrived from Rangers for £1.5 million after becoming the first Catholic to play for the Glasgow club. I'm sure Howard would agree that Johnston's signing was far from a success. He scored 10 goals in 39 appearances and after two years at Goodison returned north of the border to join Hearts on a free transfer. As Howard said, every manager makes mistakes.

Our season started to pick up with our 1-0 win at Manchester City in September, thanks to a Beardsley goal, and the England striker followed that with a hat-trick to give us a 3-0 home win over Coventry. When he hit one of the goals in our 2-2 draw at Chelsea it was his eighth in six games and he became the first Everton player to score in six consecutive matches since Bob Latchford in 1975. Then it was Cottee's turn to mark his name on the scoresheet. To celebrate his 100th top-flight appearance for the club he hit a hat-trick in a 3-1 home win over Tottenham - his first League treble since his dramatic debut against Newcastle in 1988.

In October, Matt Jackson made his debut at right-back after his £600,000 move from Luton but as he came in Kevin Ratcliffe was ruled out to undergo knee surgery. Everton's most successful captain would make only one more appearance - his 494th in a Goodison jersey - before being freed and eventually joining Cardiff while our defensive resources were re-inforced by the signing of Liverpool's Gary Ablett for £750,000. Howard also agreed a

£425,000 fee with Liverpool for Barry Venison. But the player declined to cross Stanley Park and joined Newcastle, where he was joined in March by Kevin Sheedy, who ended his 10-year Everton career on a free.

We went into 1992 tenth in the table after a home 1-1 draw with Liverpool - ending our run of five straight defeats in League derbies - thanks to one of Maurice Johnston's goals. In January, Dave Watson was installed as club captain following the announcement that Ratcliffe was available for transfer, but before the month was over we had nothing to play for except pride and aiming for the highest possible League position. We'd been bundled out of the Rumbelows Cup by a 4-1 fourth-round defeat by Leeds and after beating Southend in the FA Cup we lost 1-0 at Chelsea in round four. There wasn't even the small matter of the Zenith Cup to anticipate - we'd gone out of that 2-1 at Leicester in the northern area quarter-final.

One of the forgettable experiences during our remaining League programme was playing a goalless draw against Wimbledon at Selhurst Park watched by a mere 3,569 spectators, the lowest top-flight League attendance for an Everton match. Mind you, less than a year later for the same fixture the crowd was even smaller at just 3,039 - which is in the record books as the lowest top-division attendance since the war. We won only four of our final 19 games and finished in limbo in 12th place. In football terms we were just treading water. We beat Chelsea 2-1 in our last match through goals from Beardsley (penalty) and Beagrie. Amidst the disappointment of the season it had been a personal triumph for Beardsley, who scored 20 goals for the first time, and was an ever-present in all our 50 games.

The 1992-93 season heralded a revolution in English football. The elite breakaway FA Premier League, which had been muttered about for many years and carefully planned for several, finally became a reality ushering in an era of massive television money for the game. By a sheer co-incidence, highly fortunate for football, satellite television had also arrived on the scene. Three months before the season began the Premiership clubs agreed a £304 million five-year joint television deal with BSkyB and the BBC guaranteeing each club £1.5 million per season.

Money was certainly needed. A year earlier Everton, once called 'The Mersey Millionaires', for the first time in decades had a bank overdraft. It stood at more than £1.3 million. And as the Premier League curtain went up the club revealed it had lost £2 million on the year and were £3.6 million in the red, blaming rising costs on increases in players' wages.

Three new players arrived that summer - midfielder Barry Horne for £675,000 from Southampton, striker Paul Rideout for £500,000 from Glasgow Rangers and Belgrade-born forward Predrag Radosavljevic - thankfully known as 'Preki' - for £300,000 from American Indoor Soccer League side St Louis Storm. Pat Nevin crossed the Mersey to Tranmere for £300,000 following Ray Atteveld, who joined Bristol City for £250,000, and Sheedy out of Goodison.

One of the major consquences of the Premiership's formation was the invasion of foreigners attracted by the new rich pickings at the top level of the English game. When it began that summer of 1992 there were 491 British and Irish players and just 30 foreign nationals. By 2004, almost a decade after UEFA was forced to abolish restrictions following the Bosman ruling, the respective figures were 293 and 247. It meant that foreign players comprised 45.7 per cent of the total.

Before these mass imports began Robert Warzycha - or 'Bob the Pole' as he became known - seized his own enduring niche in the record books. He'd started the season on the bench in our 1-1 home draw with Sheffield Wednesday, when Horne scored on his debut and this Everton team lined up:

Southall; Jackson, Watson, Ablett, Hinchcliffe; Ward, Horne (Warzycha, 69), Ebbrell, Beagrie; Rideout, Beardsley. Unused substitutes: Johnston, Kearton.

For our second game at Manchester United Warzycha was in the starting line-up and became the first foreigner to score in the Premiership when he struck the 80th-minute second goal in our impressive 3-0 win. Beardsley and Johnston scored the other two. A 1-1 draw at Norwich followed by a 1-0 home win over Aston Villa, the day after Goodison Park's 100th birthday on August 24, put us second in the table. But we were held goalless at home by Wimbledon before our unbeaten start was ended by Tottenham, who beat us 2-1 at White Hart Lane. Then Manchester United gained swift revenge for our early win at Old Trafford by coming to Goodison and winning 2-0 four days before the national economic crisis of Black Wednesday, when sterling crashed out of the European Exchange Rate Mechanism.

Our performance against United made it a black Saturday for us but we showed dramatic improvement against Blackburn at Ewood Park in what was Warzycha's best Everton display. The moustachioed Pole had been dropped by Howard, along with Maurice Johnston after our defeat by United. But when Mark Ward broke his right leg after a challenge by Mark Atkins that brought him a booking, Warzycha found himself thrust back into action as an

11th-minute substitute.

A minute later Alan Shearer, Blackburn's £3.3 million signing from Southampton, won and converted a penalty but Warzycha's pace tormented the home defence and he set up an equaliser for Tony Cottee and a goal for John Ebbrell before half-time. Even though Paul Rideout's shoulder injury meant he was unable to continue in the second half, Matt Jackson went on at right-back, Alan Harper switched to midfield and Peter Beardsley pushed up.

Neville Southall had a distinguished evening with a series of terrific saves but was finally beaten again by Shearer, who fired a 74th-minute equaliser. But in the last 10 minutes Warzycha set off on another right-flank raid and set-up Cottee to secure us a 3-2 win. Sadly, such positive occasions were to be conspicuous by their absence. By the end of October we'd won only three of our opening 14 League games and had dropped to third-from-bottom.

In the Coca-Cola Cup we beat Second Division Rotherham on a 3-1 aggregate then drew 0-0 with Wimbledon at home in the third round, for which Cottee was dropped and scored a reserve-team hat-trick the same night! His pride had clearly been wounded and he publicly blasted Howard on the morning of our 3-1 home defeat by Manchester City, which he watched with his family from the stand. Criticising the manager in the media is not the wisest course to take and banished Cottee started only one of our next 16 matches. Beardsley's only goal of the game at Selhurst Park took us through our Coca-Cola replay with Wimbledon but after a 2-2 fourth-round home draw with Chelsea, we went out 1-0 in the replay.

By the time we went into the Goodison derby with ninth-placed Liverpool early in December we had won only four of our 17 League games and were fourth-from-bottom of the table. Yet we made it a memorable night for our anxious fans in front of the live TV cameras with a 2-1 win in the first Mersey derby played on a Monday. Our side included Billy Kenny, a 19-year-old midfielder who'd made his debut in the Coca-Cola Cup against Rotherham two months earlier. He signed a new two-and-a-half-year contract before the derby and his future looked rosy. Kenny's talent earned him England Under 21 recognition but his career would sadly hit the buffers over off-field problems. He made only 23 appearances for us, scoring one goal, before being released in 1994 and joining Oldham.

Also in our line-up was a certain David Unsworth, a powerful defender, also 19, making only his fourth senior start following his goalscoring debut as a substitute at Tottenham the previous April. Although he was replaced at half-time by Peter Beagrie to allow us to revert to a back four from a five-man system, Unsworth went on to make 350 appearances and scored 40 goals in two spells at Everton.

Liverpool took a 62nd-minute lead through a Mark Wright header but almost immediately Johnston, with a left-foot shot deflected in off a post, equalised with his second consecutive derby goal. It was his first League appearance since October and however harsh the judgment that Goodison history delivers on Johnston, they can't take his derby goals away from him.

With six minutes left Gary Ablett, making his 13th derby appearance but first against Liverpool, played a one-two with Peter Beardsley for the England striker to fire past goalkeeper Mike Hooper and clinch our first win in nine League derbies since March 1988. It was the first time since the war that an Everton side had come from behind to win a Mersey derby and Beardsley's goal put him alongside David Johnson as the only players to score and net winners for both clubs. That superb derby win failed to kick-start our season as we'd hoped although the second part of the campaign was more productive than the first. We won only six League games in the opening half of the programme but managed nine subsequent victories.

We ended 1992 with a 4-2 defeat at QPR when Stuart Barlow, a local lad whose great asset was his turn of pace, scored his first League goals for the club on a day when the headlines were dominated by the dismissals of Neville Southall and Paul Rideout. Southall, who had been sent off at Chelsea during the 1985-86 season, got his marching orders from referee Gerald Ashby after 18 minutes - and with the game goalless - for handling outside the area. Ironically, it was the match in which Neville overtook Brian Labone's club record of 533 senior appearances and his early bath on his 206th consecutive League appearance meant a debut as sub for reserve keeper Jason Kearton. He was on the receiving end of an Andy Sinton hat-trick with Gary Penrice scoring QPR's other goal. But even before half-time we were down to nine men after Rideout's 44th-minute dismissal for violent conduct - or, as referee Ashby said, for 'flicking a foot at Darren Peacock.'

There was no joy, either, in the FA Cup. Our next action was a goalless third-round trip to face Wimbledon and we lost 2-1 in the replay, when Kearton made his first start and home debut in place of suspended Southall. The Australian managed to make contact with John Fashanu's 35th-minute shot but couldn't keep it out and we went two-down shortly after the interval through a Robbie Earle goal. Dave Watson pulled one back but for the second consecutive year by January we had only League position to play for.

Successive League wins for the first time in almost a year - 2-0 at Crystal Palace and 2-0 at home to Leeds - took us to 13th place, level with Graeme Souness's Liverpool on 29 points. We made it three in a row by beating Wimbledon 3-1 at Selhurst Park when the 3,039 crowd set a Premiership attendance low. It was the sixth time we'd met Wimbledon that season after being paired with them in the FA and Coca-Cola Cups. Tony Cottee scored twice and our other goal came from Ian Snodin, his first for five years. But we then slumped into a run of four straight defeats. We lost 1-0 at home to Norwich, 3-1 at Sheffield Wednesday - when Southall was again sent off for saving Paul Warhurst's shot outside the area - 2-1 at home to Tottenham and 2-1 at Aston Villa, when Southall's ban ended his club-record run of 212 consecutive League appearances.

Martin Keown, one of the best signings I made for Everton, missed the defeat by Norwich with a dead leg and two days later was on his way back to his first club Arsenal for £2 million. The England defender's contract with us was due to end in the summer of 1993 and after Howard had met the player and his agent they failed to agree new terms. So when George Graham came in with such a massive bid sadly we had no real option but to accept, especially given the club's financial situation.

As Keown was departing, Howard signed former England full-back Kenny Sansom on a free from Coventry, but his stay was brief. After his debut in the defeat at Sheffield Wednesday he made only another seven appearances before joining Brentford on a free in March along with goalkeeper Gerry Peyton. Alan Harper was also released, later playing for Luton, Burnley and Cardiff before returning to join the youth coaching set-up at Goodison.

The defeat at Villa left us fifth-from-bottom, only four points above the relegation zone with the bottom three all having games in hand. We climbed clear with a three-match run that saw us draw 2-2 at home to Oldham, beat Blackburn 2-1 at Goodison and win 1-0 in a live TV match at Coventry through a goal from Mark Ward, back in action after his leg fracture. Although we then lost 2-1 at Chelsea, we responded with a 3-0 home win over Nottingham Forest in mid-March when Andy Hinchcliffe scored his only goal of the season and Tony Cottee hit two, taking his goal tally to eight in 11 games since his recall in January. Before kick-off Neville Southall was presented with a cut-glass football to mark his achievement in becoming the club's all-time appearance record holder, a total he would extend to 750 before his departure to Stoke in February 1998.

We lost the Mersey derby at Anfield in cruel circumstances. Substitute Barlow failed to take any of three clear chances and the game was heading for a goalless draw until Ronny Rosenthal gave Liverpool victory with a goal 40 seconds into injury time. Four days later, though, a right-foot volley from Barlow, a great headed goal from Cottee and another strike from Jackson gave us a 3-0 win over Ipswich, a game in which Paul Holmes made his debut after his £100,000 move from Birmingham.

Easter Saturday saw us win 2-1 at Middlesbrough when Dave Watson scored his only League goal of the season and Preki scored his first Everton goal after going on as substitute for Barlow. A small Bank Holiday crowd of less than 20,000 for the Easter Monday visit of QPR saw eight goals scored - but the visitors scored five of them, helped by Les Ferdinand's second hat-trick in 48 hours. It was the first time we'd conceded five at home since Liverpool went nap in November 1982. Our goals came from another Cottee header, Barlow and Preki, who scored as a sub for the second successive match and earned promotion to the starting line-up for our final four games.

We played out goalless draws at Southampton and home to Arsenal - which guaranteed our Premiership safety - before losing 2-0 at home to Sheffield United in front of the live TV cameras. It was a dismal way to end our Goodison season, especially in front of a crowd of just over 15,000. Neil Moore, who'd had his senior baptism as a substitute in the Coca-Cola Cup against Rotherham earlier in the season, made his League debut against the Yorkshire club as a half-time replacement for Barry Horne. We wound up the season with a trip to Maine Road to face Manchester City. We went into the match in 15th place, City in sixth.

During the week leading up to the game Paul McCartney's classic Yesterday officially became the most played record ever and our display was like something from our brighter yesterdays to end a tortuous season. It was a day of goalkeepers as well as goals. City's first choice Tony Coton was injured in the pre-match warm-up so Martyn Margetson took over between the posts and was beaten three times in the first 32 minutes. Matt Jackson opened the scoring with six minutes on the clock and Peter Beagrie doubled Everton's score after 19 minutes. Peter Beardsley added a third after Preki's shot hit the woodwork before David White pulled one back for City.

City boss Peter Reid withdrew Margetson at half-time and sent on Andy Dibble, but he was soon beaten by a cracking 20-yard shot from Preki to make it 4-1. With 63 minutes gone the game's fourth goalkeeper entered the fray. We had to take off Neville Southall, who had a back problem, and send on Jason Kearton. He had to pick the ball out of the net following Keith Curle's 73rd-minute penalty but we made it 5-2 with another long-range strike, this time from Beagrie for his second of the game. Howard Kendall, back at the club he used to manage, had an egg thrown at him by a spectator but the result and display applied a finishing flourish to what had been an angst-ridden campaign. It ensured us 13th place - nothing to sing and dance about but a damned sight better than the plight we'd found ourselves in earlier in the season. What we couldn't know then was that only twice in the ensuing decade would Everton finish higher than that.

The following season would be even more traumatic for the club, which was £4 million in the red and its ownership in the melting pot following the revelation that the Moores family were ready to sell their £2.5 million majority shareholding. The Moores patriarch and Everton benefactor Sir John, the man who founded Littlewoods and built it into the largest privately-owned company in Britain, died at the age of 97 early in the 1993-94 season, which only deepened the uncertainty over the family's holdings.

From a football point of view Howard Kendall, who had sold Peter Beardsley to Newcastle for £1.5 million to raise funds to buy a target man, was still searching when the curtain went up on the campaign. He'd tried for Brian Deane, Niall Quinn and Duncan Ferguson, and had a look at Bayern Munich's Scotland international Alan McInally and St Etienne's Danish forward Miklos Molnar during our pre-season programme...all without success. So we kicked off the season with no new players and without Andy Hinchcliffe (Achilles), Barry Horne (foot) and Billy Kenny (stomach strain). This was our line-up in a 2-0 win at Southampton:

Southall; Holmes, Watson, Jackson, Ablett; Ward, Snodin, Ebbrell, Beagrie; Cottee, Rideout. Unused substitutes: Warzycha, Barlow, Kearton.

Beagrie's 10th-minute goal was the first of the Premiership season and Ebbrell was our other scorer, equalling his single goal in the whole of the previous campaign. Our first unchanged side since the previous November came out on top 1-0 at home to Manchester City and our third game was a Goodison duel with Sheffield United. We hadn't beaten the Yorkshire club in the League since 1975 but we ended that sequence in style. Watson and Snodin had to drop out injured but Hinchcliffe returned and Graham Stuart, who'd joined us for £850,000 from Chelsea 48 hours earlier, made his debut in a 4-2 victory. Tony Cottee, who'd signed a new three-year contract, hit a brilliant hat-trick and linked well with Paul Rideout. His fifth Everton treble took him past his double century to 201 career goals in 451 appearances.

It was the club's best start since 1978-79, when we also won our opening three games, and took us to the top-of-the-table for the first time since October 1989 until we were overtaken by Liverpool on goal difference the following day. After that early season high it was, I'm afraid, downhill. We lost our next three games - 1-0 at Newcastle, 2-0 at Arsenal and 1-0 at home to Aston Villa - before a Cottee goal gave us a 1-0 win at Oldham watched by Brett Angell, who'd been signed on a month's loan from Southend. He was an unused substitute a week later when we had a morale-boosting home win over Liverpool when Neville Southall celbrated his club-record 33rd derby appearance with a clean sheet in a 2-0 win.

Ward put us ahead in the first half, which prompted the bizarre incident of Liverpool keeper Bruce Grobbelaar slapping team-mate Steve McManaman for his failure to clear Hinchcliffe's corner which led to the goal. Cottee, on his 200th Everton apprearance, wrapped up a richly deserved win four minutes from the end. Southall's knee ligament injury, sustained in a collision with Ian Rush in the derby, ruled him out of our Coca-Cola Cup trip to Third Division Lincoln. Jason Kearton deputised and although he conceded three we came out on top thanks to Rideout 's first hat-trick in English football for nine years and another goal from Cottee.

Our next match, at home to Norwich in the Premiership, was an absolute debacle and after beating Liverpool in our last home outing the attendance of only 20,531 was alarmingly low. At least the stay-at-home fans were spared the anguish that afternoon. Every time Norwich attacked they seemed likely to score and ended up 5-1 winners. The damage was done by Efan Ekoku, who had stood on the Goodison terraces as a Liverpool fan watching us lose 5-0 in the Mersey derby in November 1982. Strangely, Rideout had put us ahead before Ekoku levelled just before the interval. He proceeded to run riot with three more goals after the interval and Chris Sutton deepened our agony with a fifth. Brett Angell tasted his only action of his loan spell when he went on as a sub and the fact that Rideout and Hinchcliffe both hit the woodwork did nothing to ease our concern over our performance. Little did we, or visiting manager Mike Walker know as Norwich drove away from Goodison that September day, that he would be back in January as Everton boss. That would form a new and brief chapter in the club's history but a massive one closed in the early hours of the following morning when Sir John Moores, the Goodison 'godfather', died in his sleep.

A week after the Norwich defeat two Tottenham goals in the final two minutes by Darren Anderton and Darren Caskey plunged us to a 3-2 defeat at White Hart Lane after a Cottee penalty and a Rideout goal had put is in sight of victory. We completed an 8-5 aggregate win over Lincoln with a 4-2 win in the Coca-Cola return at Goodison and after a 2-2 home draw with Crystal Palace in round three we won the replay 4-1, the notable feature of the two matches being the fact that Dave Watson scored three of the goals!

In the Premiership, though, our wins were few and far between. We could only draw 1-1 at rock-bottom Swindon and lost 1-0 to Manchester United before a welcome 2-0 victory at Ipswich, through goals from Barlow and Beagrie. But then we went down 2-1 at Coventry, lost 3-0 at home to QPR - with Bradley Allen following Andy Sinton and Les Ferdinand by bagging a hat-trick against us - drew 1-1 at home to Leeds and then 1-1 at Wimbledon.

Our Coca-Cola hopes were ended in the fourth round by Manchester United, who came to Goodison and claimed a 2-0 win through goals by Mark Hughes and Ryan Giggs. We might have had a shout if we'd converted a penalty early in the second half, but Peter Schmeichel plunged to his right to save Tony Cottee's spot-kick.

Four days later, on Saturday, December 4, we had a home game against Southampton. Cottee's first-half goal was enough to win the game and put us 11th in the table. But as the 13,667 spectators were making their way home there were developments within Goodison. At 5.34pm a club statement was delivered to the Goodison press room announcing that Howard Kendall had resigned. As Howard later made clear, he quit on a point of principle. Howard had brought in £3.5 million from the sales of Martin Keown and Peter Beardsley and he wanted to sign a target man to increase our scoring threat. When the board refused to sanction a £1.8 million deal with Manchester United for Dion Dublin, he felt his position was untenable and resigned. You couldn't blame him for that. If he felt his authority had been undermined he had to take the course of action he felt was right. Dublin was a more than useful player in attack or defence, going on to win four England caps and commanding transfer fees dwarfing what Howard would have paid. He left Old Trafford to join Coventry for £2 million in December 1994 and four years later he cost Aston Villa £5.75 million.

In the wake of Howard's departure Jimmy Gabriel was again appointed caretaker-manager and I felt it was best that I followed Howard out of the door as quickly as possible. The next day I spoke to the chairman, David Marsh, and told him that as I had worked in harness with Howard I should go immediately. I said I'd be grateful if the club would pay off my contract to the end of that season and I'd leave there and then. He told me there would be a new manager in place soon and that would be his decison. I asked the chairman several times but I got the same answer so, reluctantly, I had to wait during what was a dismal, miserable period. Everyone was deflated about what had happened.

The media homed in on Joe Royle and Peter Reid as candidates to succeed Howard while Jimmy himself said publicly that he, too, would like to be considered. Sadly, performances became dire and the Christmas period was a nightmare. We experienced the longest barren run in our history, including six consecutive games without a goal. We lost 1-0 at Manchester City, drew 0-0 at Sheffield United, lost 2-0 at home to Newcastle, 2-0 at home to Sheffield Wednesday, 2-0 at Blackburn and 1-0 at home to West Ham.

In our next match we lost 4-2 at Chelsea, with our first goal from Cottee early in the second half ending a club-record sequence of 10 hours 41 minutes without scoring since Cottee had scored against Southampton in Howard's last game. The Chelsea defeat was the last before the shock appointment of Mike Walker as manager. Jimmy's last act as caretaker was to pick the team for our third round FA Cup trip to First Division Bolton, which Mike watched and was drawn 1-1. I asked Mike right away for a quick decision on my future and I waited a fortnight for his response. His first game in full charge was a 6-2 home hammering of Swindon followed by a 3-2 extra-time home defeat by Bolton in the FA Cup replay, when they came back from two goals down - both of ours scored by Stuart Barlow.

The following day, January 20 - the same day that Sir Matt Busby died at the age of 84 - Mike asked to see me. He told me that he appreciated how I'd welcomed him to the club but that I didn't figure in his plans. I gladly accepted that and left Everton for the third time in my life at the age of 49. I thought it would also be the last time and I certainly didn't have a General Patton moment in thinking I would return. But return I did, more than three years later, with the grandiose title of Director of Youth Coaching. It was a very different yet deeply fulfilling role and one that brought me into contact with an amazing school kid called Wayne Rooney. "

Back working with the youth lads at Everton, including future England international Francis Jeffers.

Chapter Fourteen

How It Happened For 'Baby' Wayne

Colin Harvey is to hyperbole what Long John Silver was to tap dancing. So when Harvey draws on his vast reservoir of 40 years in football and proclaims that Wayne Rooney can become better than Maradona, his assessment carries powerful authority. From the moment Harvey walked across Everton's junior pitches and rubbed his eyes in astonishment at his first sight of the youngster, he has been awe-struck at Rooney's progress and prodigious record-breaking feats for Everton, England and Manchester United. "Wayne's the best young player I've ever seen, the best Everton have produced, and he can become one the greatest English players of all time," says the man who proved to be Rooney's football father figure during his formative years prior to his explosion onto the game's biggest stages.

"Until Wayne came along the best youngster I'd ever seen was Alan Ball. I later teamed up with Bally at Goodison and he did it all for Everton and England, winning 72 caps, the World Cup and championship medals. He was the best Everton player in my opinion and my experience. Obviously, older generations cite Dixie Dean as the finest-ever to wear the blue shirt and nobody can argue. His achievements were phenomenal. But due to the passage of time there are fewer eye-witnesses of Dixie's greatness and I felt that if Wayne had stayed at Everton he had all the qualities to become the greatest Everton player in living memory. He has fantastic ability. I rate him so highly and, like all Evertonians, I was desperately disappointed when he left Goodison in that amazing £27 million move to Manchester United in August 2004." It was seven years earlier, on a summer's day in 1997 shortly after Harvey had begun his second stint as Everton youth coach, that he first clapped eyes on Rooney - and the memory will live with him forever:

"I was in charge of the Under 19s and Under 18s but I used to go to the club's youth training complex at Netherton every Sunday morning to take in a couple of games involving the Under 16, 15 and 14 sides just to keep tabs on the next batch of players who were coming through. Wayne, who attended Our Lady and St Swithin's Primary School, was nine-years-old when he was signed for Everton by the club's youth director Ray Hall in 1994 and went on to score 99 goals in a season for the Under 10 team.

Everton scout Bob Pendleton, a retired train driver, spotted Wayne as an eight-year-old playing at the Jeffreys Humble playing fields in Long Lane, Liverpool on the border of the city's Aintree and Fazakerley districts. At the time Wayne was playing for Copplehouse Under 10s in the Walton and Kirkdale Junior League and what Bob saw made his jaw drop in sheer incredulity at the boy's talents. As Bob recalled: 'I was once told by a friend that you'll find a talent like Wayne's once in your lifetime - if you're very, very lucky! So sit back and enjoy it.' Not surprisingly he'd also been spotted by Liverpool, who invited Wayne to their Melwood training ground. The lad duly turned up there - wearing his Everton kit! Bob Pendleton made sure Wayne's football allegiance followed the obvious channel.

Wayne played his first recorded game at the age of seven when he went on as a substitute - and scored - for an Under 11s team from the Western Approaches pub in Storrington Avenue, Liverpool. As well as playing for Copplehouse he also appeared for East Villa and Pye FC, with whom he won a Golden Boot after top-scoring in the BT Challenge Cup competition. After scoring freely and winning a league and cup double in his first year at De La Salle School, he concentrated on playing for the Everton Academy.

Wayne had also made a massive impact for the Liverpool city's schools team, breaking the scoring record for Liverpool Schools FA Under 11s in the 1996-97 season, which he still holds. He scored 72 of the team's 158 goals, overtaking the previous highest total set by Steve Redmond, later to become a Manchester City defender.

One anecdote about 'baby' Wayne sums up the lad's abilities. Apparently, during a Liverpool Schools game he was getting vocal encouragement and conflicting instructions from the touchline from his father, Wayne Senior, the team manager Tim O'Keeffe and his assistant Jim Milne. Wayne was in the middle of the field deep in the opposition half and was urged both to take on his man and to pass the ball wide! He did neither. He simply unleashed a shot from more than 30 yards that flew into the net. That's Wayne for you.

But all I knew about this lad called Rooney was from other people. And it was all in glowing terms. Over the years, though, many people have told me many things about youngsters, how they were going to be world beaters and what have you. Sadly, in 99 per cent of cases, this is not borne out in reality, due to many factors. Sometimes the lad does not make progress from one level to another, he may lack the commitment or he may be found wanting physically. There are many reasons why rich promise is never fulfilled. I'd even met Wayne's mother Jeanette before I'd seen or met Wayne. Sid Benson, one of the club's scouts, introduced me to her and she left me almost speechless by exclaiming: 'I used to have so and so pictures of you all over my so and so bedroom wall!'

Sid himself told me enthusiastically that this kid had scored hundreds of goals and that he was the best thing since sliced bread and all that. Experience teaches you to treat such talk with great caution. But I was there at Netherton as usual one Sunday in August 1997 when there was a break in the Under 16s game because of an injury. I happened to glance over to where the Under 11s were playing. As I looked, this kid got the ball on the halfway line, went past four opponents and lashed it into the net! That was my first sight of him - he was still a couple of months away from his 12th birthday. So I left the Under 16 match, which wasn't a good one anyway, and went to see more of this lad in the Under 11 team. Any thoughts that what I'd seen was merely a freak were soon dispelled. Wayne did remarkable things on a regular basis. He was stronger than the rest of the kids and I did wonder whether he would develop and whether the others would catch him up physically. I've seen it happen so often. But not with Wayne. He developed and maintained his strength. I just looked at him and thought: 'Blinkin' heck...if he carries on like this he's going to be a world beater.'

So I kept my eye on him. He was being looked after in the Under 11s by Dennis Evans, a Wirral schoolteacher who was a very good coach. I was in charge of the Under 18 and 19 sides with Alan Harper looking after the Under 17s. After a while I decided I'd include Wayne in the squad for a couple of Under 19 games in the FA Academy League because he was so far advanced he was head-and-shoulders in ability above others of his age and many who were much older than him.

At the start of the 2000-2001 season, when Wayne was still only 14, his uncle took him on holiday and he got back in the early hours of Saturday, the day of our first Under 19 match that year. I'd wanted him to come with us but as we were going overnight to play Chelsea in London I couldn't take him. Instead, Alan played him in the Under 17s home game against Birmingham.

When I spoke to Alan after the matches he told me: 'We got beaten 4-1 but Wayne scored an absolute blinder. He stood out from everyone on the field.' That was it. I said to Alan: 'Right, I'll definitely take him next week for our match down at Leicester.'

I named Wayne as one of the substitutes. We were losing 2-0 with about 20 minutes to go so I said: 'Wayne, get warmed up and we'll send you on.' Nick Chadwick was up front and at that level he scored goals for fun. He'd rattle in 30 a season. But he was having one of those games when nothing was going right for him. So I took off Nick and put Wayne on. Well, within a minute he'd made three chances and a couple of openings for other people. The next minute he got the ball on the left some 30 yards out, worked it onto his right foot and bent a shot into the top corner of the net.

Everyone just stopped. Our lads had heard about him but they were stunned. He was still 14, remember, and he was up against lads of 19, some going on 20. So he was giving away five years or more. But he was no stick insect liable to be physically overwhelmed. Wayne could look after himself even then and from that stage he was with our Under 19s all the time. We went on to win our Academy League Group that year, finishing with 61 points from our 28 games, nine ahead of Manchester City.

I had him in the Under 19s for the next two seasons when normally he'd train two nights a week. But during our run to the FA Youth Cup final in 2002 he trained with us on Tuesday and Wednesday mornings which he was allowed off by his school, De La Salle. They were brilliant about it. I think the fact that Wayne was a conscientious pupil was a big factor in the school's attitude towards his football and his parents brought him up the right way. He comes from a down-to-earth family. Even in training Wayne would light up the place. He'd produce something magical and Alan Harper and I would exclaim to each other: 'Goodness me...never seen him do that before!' But whatever he did was never at the expense of sheer hard work. He'd always apply himself.

I realised what a fantastic talent we had on our hands and I often used to give him a lift to his home in Croxteth, or to his grandmother's, after we'd got back from games. I'd have a little word in his ear and give him some little bits of advice about whom he was knocking around with. I'd remind him to keep his feet on the ground and that he must continue to work hard at school. Wayne was very receptive to things like that. He'd listen and take it all on board. He wasn't an introvert but very much a quiet, self-contained lad. That was until he stepped onto the field. That was - and is - his playground. Once he got on there he knew exactly how good he was. I also told him I'd pay to watch him play!

I used to look forward to going in to see him train and wonder what he would come up with. Wayne very kindly said publicly that I'd helped make him a better player. Well, I take no credit for that. I agree with one of the sayings of Bill Shankly, that it's not coaches who make players - but mothers and fathers. It's an inborn talent. All coaching can do is bring out skills and help their natural expression. Even if Wayne was having a bad game he would still do three or four things in a match that would take your breath away. He'd do something that would make your heart beat a little bit faster. He's scored goals right through his young life, at primary and secondary school and also for Liverpool Schoolboys.

Wayne also scored eight times in our run to the 2002 FA Youth Cup final. That was played over two legs against Aston Villa in the April, less than three weeks before the new manager David Moyes named him in the first-team squad for the first time as an unused substitute in the Premiership match at Southampton. He would have been in the squad before that during the latter days of Walter Smith's management. Walter wanted to include him but there were major problems because Wayne was still at school and special dispensation was required.

Walter and his assistant Archie Knox came to watch our Under 19s game against Bolton, which had been switched to a Monday because of youth international calls. Wayne scored a goal and made another early in the game. Then he got the ball in his own half and looked as if he was going to play it to a team-mate to his left. But no. Although the ball was under his feet he just lashed it - and his shot hit the crossbar. He has this great ability to strike a ball out of nothing. He'd seen the keeper on the edge of the box and the ball crashed off the bar and over his head. I'd seen David Beckham do something similar from his own half but while Beckham lined up his shot, Rooney appeared not even to assess the situation before shooting. He obviously had done - but he must have done so in a split second. I'd been telling Walter and Archie about Wayne and showing them videos of him. Then they saw with their own eyes, in spectacular style, what he was capable of! But any plans they had to call him up disappeared when Walter was sacked just 10 days before Wayne left school at 16 in March 2002. So it was left to David Moyes to hand him his promotion to the senior stage.

I can empathise and understand to some degree what it must be like for Wayne to come to terms with his sudden transformation from unknown schoolboy to international star. In no time he has seen his earnings zoom from £50 to £15,000 a week with Everton and then a reported £55,000 a week with United, plus lucrative shirt and boot deals that have led to projections that his career earnings could surpass a mind-boggling £100 million. Wayne's world has been turned on its head. When I was 18 I had the shock of being thrown into my first-team debut in the European Cup against Inter Milan. It caused a stir and a lot of headlines. But the media machine then and now is incomparable, as are the rewards. TV coverage, the insatiable appetite of newspapers and the coming of the Premiership mean top players are now living in a goldfish bowl, even though they are being rewarded with riches beyond the dreams of footballers only a few years ago. So those close to Wayne, the club, his family, and his agents - who have already been involved in unfortunate, negative publicity - must look after him and guide him because he's the best young player I've ever seen.

He became England's youngest-ever international and the youngest goalscorer ever for club and country. He can become one of the greatest players English football has seen. It's a hell of a tall order but he has the talent to do it and the ability to be a great, long-term England star. He's got all the attributes. As well as his strength he's got pace, he's good in the air and he's a tremendous athlete. He's two-footed, although he's weaker on his left side and should work on that to make his armoury even more potent.

His top-scoring displays for England in the 2004 European Championship made the whole world sit up, prompting comparisons with the young Pele and Maradona and the glowing appreciation of Sir Tom Finney, who called him 'a sensation'. But what Wayne did in Portugal - and there's no doubt for me that he was England's player of the tournament - didn't surprise me because I know what he can do. He can become as good as Maradona. Even better. I think he's the best talent since Maradona and I've always rated the Argentinian a better all-round performer, even than Pele.

Even if Wayne's having a poor game there will be occasions when he'll either create a chance for himself or for someone else. He will always have an impact some time in a match. That was superbly illustrated in United's win at Anfield in January 2005. It was far from Wayne's most effective performance and he had only two shots - yet one of them produced the game's only goal and secured a crucial win for his club. I feel that if Wayne hadn't suffered that fateful broken metatarsal after 26 minutes of the European Championship quarter-final against Portugal we'd have gone on to beat them instead of going out agonisingly on penalties.

Wayne's disciplinary record has made plenty of headlines, which is not surprising when you reflect on the fact that during his all-too brief Everton first-team career he received 20 yellow cards and one red in his 77 senior appearances which, incidentally, brought him 17 goals. Then, after joining United, he made the wrong headlines by throwing down his black armband - worn in memory of the late Emlyn Hughes - when he was substituted on England duty in Spain in November 2004. Wayne was taken off for his own good because he'd already received a yellow card and then incensed the home players with a wild challenge on Carlos Marchena. But I'm certain that it was just sheer frustration on Wayne's part. In no way would he have been disrespectful to Emlyn, whose funeral had been that very day.

Probably frustration and provocation were the main factors in his clash with Tal Ben Haim at Old Trafford the following month when he raised his hand and slapped the Bolton player. It led to Wayne being charged by the FA with violent conduct and being banned for three matches. He was also criticised for his celebrations after scoring at Anfield and was said to have taunted the Kop. Well, I'm sure he took a lot of stick from Liverpool fans on his first return to Merseyside and surely, at the age of 19, he's entitled to celebrate his goal - and rival supporters should be big enough to take it.

I agree with Sir Alex Ferguson when he said: 'Young boys do have a sense of adventure about them that older players don't have. Experience teaches many things and, unfortunately, you can't put the clock forward for a boy of 19. But he's going to have to accept the responsibility of being the most talked about player in Britain. Aggression has to be channelled, but forwards are explosive players and you don't want them to lose that explosive nature. That's what makes them tick. Pele had that, the great players show that spark. Maradona got sent off in the World Cup finals. If you take that devil, that heart out of them, you don't have the same player.'

I do not believe discipline will be a continuing headache for Wayne with United or England because, like fine wine, he will mature with age. In the two years he was playing for me in the Under 19 and FA Youth Cup teams I recall him getting just one booking, and it's clear to me nothing is wrong with his temperament. Sure, he's competitive, he's enthusiastic and he's a winner. But he never sets out to hurt anyone. He is by no means a serial, pre-meditated offender. I am certain that his catapulting onto football's big stage at Everton was linked with his bookings ratio. When he was sitting on the bench and the game wasn't going Everton's way his frustration became intense. So when he was thrown into the action he was wound up, which may explain some of his bookings - and goals - after coming off the bench.

Wayne is very much a team player and some of the cards he's collected have been the result of him getting involved in situations on behalf of his colleagues. Perhaps all these factors lie behind the statistics showing that Wayne collected most of his Everton bookings, plus his sending off, in away games. But as he matures as a Premiership, European and international player and settles into the status that has been thrust upon him with one of the top-three clubs in world football, I am convinced Wayne's disciplinary transgressions will reduce. My overriding advice to him would be: 'Kill teams with your talent, not your temper.' When it comes to talent, he's got it to spare. Wayne, in fact, has that almost indefinable quality. He's box office. He has that aura about him. He makes people stand up in their seats. And he doesn't do things at a slow pace. He collects the ball and he's immediately off into his stride. He takes the crowd with him.

There has been a great debate about Wayne's best position. He's been used wide right and left and in midfield as well as up front. My view is that he's an out-and-out striker. He's not the type to be the main striker. But he'll get 15 to 20 a season and if you've got a goalscorer alongside him you're going to get an attacking return of up to 40 goals a season from them. He's already filled a few roles for United but I think you'll see him settling into a central role, playing off the main striker. What a start he made for United. Some 96 days after his injury in Lisbon he illuminated his delayed United debut with a stunning Champions League hat-trick against Fenerbahce, via his left foot, right foot and then a Beckham-style free-kick. You couldn't script it!

Wayne's not going to get a lot of tap-ins. But he'll score goals with his head, he'll score blinders from outside the box - as we've already seen - and he will score in the box. But not the Jimmy Greaves-type goals, nor the one-touch side-foot speciality of Bob Latchford. I went to watch one of Wayne's first games for the Everton reserve side at Southport's Haig Avenue ground when I got a tap on the shoulder. It was Peter Robinson, the highly-respected former Liverpool chief executive. I said to Peter: 'Wayne reminds me of Kenny Dalglish.' Peter replied: 'Oh, no. He's quicker than Kenny!' Of course, Kenny's brilliance stemmed from a razor-sharp football brain. It's an old football adage that the first few yards are in your head and Kenny was such a cunning, crafty player who was always thinking several moves ahead. I think

Wayne has those visionary qualities, too.

You could say he's a speeded-up version of Kenny, and there are other similarities. While Kenny scored his fair share of goals his attacking partner, a certain Ian Rush, was the main scorer. I see the ideal role for Wayne as supporting a regular marksman. But, above all, Wayne is a footballer. He can drop back and probably be your best midfielder. He can even go in goal! I've seen him. He might not be the tallest but he's got good hands, he's athletic and brave. I've seen him stand between the sticks in training for people to take pot shots at him and he's made unbelievable saves.

The great thing for United and England is that he will get even better. It sounds frightening but he's by no means the finished product and every upward curve his career takes will make it that much harder for Evertonians to swallow. After all, on the day Wayne was born his father bought him an Everton jersey. He grew up steeped in the club and many Goodison fans feel betrayed that he left, especially over the timing of his departure. I felt it would have been more beneficial for Wayne and Everton if he stayed and developed. But circumstances conspired against such a scenario. His fantastic European Championship made him the hottest young footballer in the world and Newcastle's apparent move for Rooney forced United's hand, when it was understood they were planning to wait another year.

Sir Alex revealed: 'As soon as Wayne became available I knew we had to sign him. I spoke to David Moyes several times. I said: 'If he ever becomes available, don't let me down.' The word came back to me when he was 14 that there was a boy at Everton. We could have got him then but he wouldn't leave and he wouldn't leave at 16, either. I can understand that. He is a local boy. But the European Championship changed his mind. Once they decided to sell him we couldn't afford not to get him.'

The fact that United and other clubs moved in for Wayne when he was only 14, because even then his talent was raising eyebrows throughout the football world and the scouting jungle drums were beating loudly, I don't think has been fully appreciated. But Wayne's boyhood Goodison allegiance and his family's dyed-in-the-wool commitment to the club ensured that he rejected all their overtures and signed for Everton.

When Wayne did join United it came during a summer of dire forecasts for Everton on-and-off the field. His departure followed what had been in 2003-04 statistically the worst season in Everton history, ending in a 5-1 trouncing at Manchester City. Yet Everton's response under David Moyes the punters, the public and the pundits. The media, too, was baffled as to how Everton could lose their greatest talent in Wayne Rooney yet produce the club's best-ever Premiership start and go on to finish fourth.

I think the answer to the riddle lies in their goalless draw at Manchester United in August, which ended a run of nine consecutive Everton defeats by United since December 1999. Tim Cahill, who at £2 million from Millwall has proved a wonderful buy, made his debut and David Moyes hit on a five-man midfield system. It also included Leon Osman, a player whose graduation through the ranks had been hampered by serious injury. As well as being solid and adding protection to the back four, the new formation meant that players could get forward to support lone striker Marcus Bent, who has also impressed since his £450,000 move from Ipswich. Both Australian international Cahill and Bent have proved shrewd signings by David who, later in the season broke an eight-year old club record by paying Southampton £6 million for James Beattie. So the accidental by-product of Rooney's departure was a system that sent Everton's season soaring.

When Wayne left the media hype went with him and I'm sure the rest of the Everton players felt something like, 'it's not about Wayne now, it's about us...let's dig in and show what we can do.' As for Wayne, even though he's a Manchester United player, given his lifelong affinity with Everton I bet in his heart he still roots for the Blues and will have been delighted at the club's renaissance. His first return to Goodison with United for the FA Cup fifth-round tie in February 2005 sparked something approaching hysteria amongst Everton supporters and he had to run the gauntlet of boos and barracking for almost the entire 90 minutes. Yet Wayne conducted himself impeccably and was denied a goal only by Nigel Martyn's brilliance.

On his second return he was on the losing side when Duncan Ferguson's only goal of the game in April gave Everton three precious Premiership points before Rooney scored on his third visit in United's 2-0 win in the opening match of the 2005-06 season.

One thing's for sure. Television commentator Clive Tyldesley's plea to the gallery to 'Remember the name - Wayne Rooney', as the lad wheeled round and unleashed a crashing strike beyond David Seaman to destroy Arsenal at Goodison in October 2002 was quite superfluous. How on earth could you overlook him!"

At Bellefield just short of my retirement.

Meeting the press again following my return with Howard, November 1990.

Chapter Fifteen

Takeover And A Great Escape

Everton, for so long one of English football's ships of state, was plunged during the 1990s into the most perilous and turbulent voyage in its history, a decade when there was a long-running battle for control on the bridge and a remarkable flow-through of personnel on deck. It was a period when the team became grimly familiar with the bottom half of the table, with two last-day escape acts to beat relegation. There were even moments of pantomime, such as the mercifully shortlived attempt to replace the club's time-honoured 'Z Cars' theme with an appalling Scandinavian version of 'Bad Moon Rising' - a gross offence to Goodison tradition as well as the iconic recording by Creedence Clearwater Revival. When Everton finished sixth in the old First Division at the end of Colin Harvey's last full season as manager it was a position that would be matched only once in the next 14 seasons, and not surpassed until the team under David Moyes completed the voyage to fourth and a ticket to the Champions League qualifiers in 2004-05.

The death early in the 1993-94 season of Sir John Moores - the man whose interest-free £56,000 loan to the club in 1960, and shrewd business skills were the building blocks of the modern Everton - had been preceded the previous May by the news that the Moores family wanted to divest itself of its controlling 40.2 per cent stake in the club.

Onto the stage stepped two rival contenders for control of Everton. In one corner, self-made businessman Peter Johnson, who owned and rescued Tranmere and built Park Foods, a company embracing a hamper empire that had sprung from Christmas tontines in working class areas of Merseyside. In the other, theatre impresario and former actor Bill Kenwright and his consortium which included Cheshire building company owner Arthur Abercromby, business consultant and writer Professor Tom Cannon, Michael Dyble, a partner in a Manchester advertising agency and Tony Tighe, owner of a public relations agency. While Kenwright was a fervent, lifelong Everton fan who idolised former centre-forward Dave Hickson - "Dave taught me how to dare," he revealed - Johnson's affiliations had been to Liverpool, a fact that without any justification aroused suspicion amongst some of the Goodison faithful and which would come back to haunt him.

The late Sir John's shareholding had passed to his two sons, John Junior and Peter, and daughters Lady Betty Grantchester and Janatha Stubbs. A claim aired in the media that Sir John had stipulated that the family's Everton holding should pass only to 'a true Blue devoted to the club' was refuted by John, who said his father's wish was that the club should be run on a sound financial basis and be successful. The power battle between the rival camps and discussions with the Moores family stretched almost the entire 1993-94 season, a football soap opera that might have reminded Kenwright of his Coronation Street acting days. It lasted until the eve of the club's critical final League game with Wimbledon, when victory was crucial to prevent the club plunging to relegation for the first time since 1951.

A little more than three weeks before Tony Blair and Gordon Brown dined together at London's Granita restaurant to shape the future of the Labour Party and, ultimately, the country, Peter Johnson and Bill Kenwright came to an accord over the ownership of Everton. On Friday, May 6 it was revealed that Johnson's £20 million investment had won the day with the board ready to accept his bid. He would pay £10 million for the existing 2,500 shares and underwrite a further 2,500 at the same price.

The events that occurred on the Goodison pitch the following afternoon were as crucial to Everton's future as the outcome of the protracted power battle off it. Everton, at the end of Mike Walker's first four months in charge, went into the game in the bottom three of the Premier League table and staring at the abyss of the drop after taking only five points from the previous 30, and scoring only four goals in those 10 games. Wimbledon were sixth and managing director Sam Hammam had promised manager Joe Kinnear and his players a trip to Las Vegas if they won. What unfolded was a drama of such stomach-churning, heart-pounding, nerve-jangling proportions that surpassed anything that might have been created for one of Kenwright's stage shows. The Everton match programme declared:

"Decision day has arrived. Quite simply, the club's membership of the Premier League is at stake. For 40 years the name of Everton has featured in the top division of English football. We are proud of that record and want it to

continue. So much has happened since that April day at Oldham in 1954 when John Willie Parker, Dave Hickson and Tommy (T.E.) Jones scored the goals which restored the Blues to the First Division stage. New generations of supporters grew up along the way and now the children of the 1950s are the parents of the 1990s. The future of the club will be with their children. This is a vital day for all Evertonians."

Some 31,297 spectators packed into three-sided Goodison, the Park End stand having been demolished two months earlier prior to re-building. The lock-out attendance was Everton's biggest League crowd, excepting Liverpool and Manchester United visits, for almost four years. Others climbed trees in adjacent Stanley Park for an unorthodox view of the hand fate would deal Everton. Hammam greeted "my close, personal friend" Bill Kenwright on the Goodison staircase while media representatives arrived at the ground to the revelation from the Wimbledon camp that their team bus had been set alight outside their Merseyside hotel the night before the game.

The heat, though, was soon on Everton who found themselves 2-0 down in 21 minutes. Anders Limpar handled with only four minutes gone and although Neville Southall touched Dean Holdsworth's penalty, he could not prevent the ball crossing the line. The distress levels for Everton and their fans reached a new intensity when Dave Watson and David Unsworth failed to clear a Warren Barton free-kick and Andy Clarke's follow-up shot was diverted into the net off Gary Ablett. The trap door was opening.

Four minutes later, though, Everton pulled a goal back thanks to a generously awarded penalty by Darlington referee Robbie Hart when Limpar went down in the box. It was their first penalty since January, when Tony Cottee had scored against Swindon in Walker's first game in charge. This time, however, Cottee declined the chance to take the penalty, prompting Southall to stride forward, pick up the ball and head for the spot! Graham Stuart, ironically brought up in Wimbledon, persuaded the goalkeeper to let him take it even though from the only other penalty of his career, during his Chelsea days, he had sent the ball soaring over a Stamford Bridge crossbar.

Unsworth, who would later prove a master from 12 yards, turned his back and prayed as Stuart stepped up. To Everton's good fortune Stuart sent his kick into the net to the right of Hans Segers as the Wimbledon goalkeeper dived the wrong way. "I thought it was crazy to have a goalkeeper taking a penalty", said Stuart. "I wasn't nervous because I thought things couldn't get any worse. I just picked a corner and tried to keep the shot on target."

The significance of Stuart's goal could have been wiped out 10 minutes later when Holdsworth headed over. Limpar and Ablett combined to provide a cross which Paul Rideout just missed at the far post before Holdsworth failed again to hit the target, this time from a Marcus Gayle centre.

The strains of Ottilie Patterson's 'We Shall Not Be Moved' blasted defiantly from Goodison's public address system during the interval but Everton's removal from the top flight still looked likely, especially when Segers turned another Stuart shot over the bar in the opening minute of the second half. There were chances at both ends but the score remained Everton 1 Wimbledon 2 until the 67th minute when Barry Horne took possession and smashed a spectacular 25-yard strike into the Gwladys Street net. It was his first goal since the opening match of the previous season!

Now one more goal was required for a hope of Premier League salvation. Nine minutes and few fingernails were left when Stuart collected the ball some 20 yards out and played a one-two with Cottee. As the ball came back to him Stuart prodded it forward under challenge and the tamely hit shot crept under the clutches of Segers and into the net as Goodison went delirious with joy. With Ipswich's draw at Blackburn and Southampton's 3-3 draw at West Ham it meant that Sheffield United, who lost 3-2 at Chelsea, were relegated with Oldham and Swindon. Everton were safe, in 17th place.

In a court case three years later the Dutch goalkeeper, along with Bruce Grobbelaar and his Wimbledon team-mate John Fashanu, was acquitted of conspiring to fix matches. Segers explained later in a book entitled 'The Final Score - the inside story of soccer's trial of the century': 'Stuart was on the edge of the box, maybe just inside it, when he hit a shot that took a deflection off another player's leg so that the ball changed direction completely. The pitch was uneven, as you would expect at the end of the season, and the ball hit a bump and spun beyond my control as I dived.'

The outcome for Everton was beyond price. Relegation at that juncture could have been catastrophic. Peter Johnson said afterwards: "The Premiership is the best place to start. Relegation would have meant one lost year at least." In July 1994 the formalities of Johnson's takeover were confirmed at an extraordinary shareholders meeting when, after relinquishing the Tranmere chair, the former Liverpool season-ticket holder was unanimously elected to the Everton board and installed as chairman.

Kenwright remained on the board with the Moores family retaining a presence with the election as a director of Lady Grantchester's son Christopher

John Suenson-Taylor. "The fact that Peter Johnson's original offer was vastly increased because of our consortium's bid can only benefit Everton", said Kenwright. "With Peter being a Liverpool fan we've had a lot of banter and I asked him why he wanted to buy Everton. His reply was that he wanted to win the European Cup. That'll do for me."

The dream never remotely materialised. By the end of the following October the team hadn't won another game following the great escape - the worst start to a season in the club's history. In the process they crashed out of the Coca-Cola Cup at the first hurdle on a 4-3 aggregate to Portsmouth, the second leg, a 1-1 draw at Fratton Park marking the debut of Duncan Ferguson, on loan from Rangers.

On November 1 they ended their appalling sequence with a 1-0 home win over West Ham - their first clean sheet since April - then played a goalless draw at Walker's former club Norwich. But Johnson had seen enough and sacked him on November 8 with the team rock-bottom of the Premiership with eight points from 14 games. Walker, who a year earlier had been bathed in plaudits for Norwich's victory over Bayern in Munich and subsequent UEFA Cup knock-out of the elite German club, had the shortest reign of any Everton manager. He was in charge for 35 games of which only six were won, 18 lost and 11 drawn with 35 goals scored and 59 conceded.

Johnson turned to Oldham boss Joe Royle to solve the crisis. Unlike Walker, the former Goodison and England centre-forward was steeped in the club and he was widely regarded as a man destined to manage Everton. One of the shining moments of his playing career had been to score one of the goals in Everton's 2-0 win over Liverpool at Anfield in March 1970 that was instrumental in making Harry Catterick's side champions.

Royle brought with him his long-time coaching colleague Willie Donachie and, as fate would have it, his first game as boss was a Mersey derby against Liverpool at Goodison. Royle's blueprint and subsequent tactical policy was an aggressive and compact midfield pressing game, harrying the opposition into mistakes and making swift attacking breaks. Significantly, Royle recalled John Ebbrell to face Liverpool after the England 'B' and Under 21 international had missed 10 games after being dropped by Walker and then being out injured. Andy Hinchcliffe, too, was brought back after being axed by Walker and both he and Ebbrell found their careers re-ignited in a midfield that earned the soubriquet the 'Dogs of War'. With Barry Horne on the right, Ebbrell and Joe Parkinson in the middle and Hinchcliffe on the left, with

Anders Limpar also featuring, Royle's warriors seized instant reward with a 2-0 defeat of Liverpool.

Duncan Ferguson opened the scoring in the 57th minute with his first Everton goal, a rocket header off a Hinchcliffe corner. Ferguson's aerial threat and physical presence played a key role, too, in the second goal near the end. The towering Scot rose with David James as a cross came in and the Liverpool goalkeeper succeeded only in punching the ball onto Ferguson. When it bounced down Rideout pounced to clinch a victory that sent morale soaring and lifted Everton off the bottom for the first time in more than two months. Royle's galvanised side proceeded to win 1-0 at Chelsea and 3-0 at home to Leeds and before the turn of the year Ferguson's move from Ibrox was made permanent for £4 million. In January, Royle also signed defender Earl Barrett from Aston Villa for £1.7 million.

As Everton made the long climb to safety and a finishing place of 15th - a run that included a 1-0 home win over Manchester United and a goalless draw in the return derby at Liverpool - the FA Cup provided an exciting diversion. Derby, Bristol City, Norwich and Newcastle were beaten without conceding a goal to set up a semi-final collision with Tottenham at Elland Road. The London club were hot favourites to reach Wembley and set up a so-called 'dream final' against Manchester United. Royle utilised the hype and criticism of Everton's style as a psychological incentive to his own team.

Their response was to outplay Tottenham with skill as well as spirit. Jackson's 35th-minute header off a Hinchcliffe corner set Everton on the path to only their second victory at Elland Road in any competition since 1951. Graham Stuart doubled their lead early in the second half, knocking in the rebound after Ian Walker's save from Rideout, before Tottenham ended Everton's clean sheet record through a dubious penalty, awarded for Teddy Sheringham's fall over Dave Watson and converted by Jurgen Klinsmann.

But a remarkable sequence of events unfolded to provide the enduring memory of the match. As Rideout was about to return following touchline treatment for a knee injury, Daniel Amokachi, who had been warming up, burst onto the pitch without the go-ahead from the Everton bench. Royle, who admitted to being puzzled as to what was the Nigerian's most effective role, was a stunned spectator as Amokachi secured his own niche in Everton folklore with two goals in the last eight minutes to secure a 4-1 victory. They were Amokachi's first goals under Royle's management - his first since his home debut against QPR the previous September when the London club were managed by Gerry Francis prior to his move to Tottenham!

As the mass of Evertonians packed into Elland Road chanted 'Amo, Amo', the Everton manager offered the memorable observation: "It was the best substitution I never made." Royle, who had twice tasted defeat in FA Cup semi-finals with Oldham, could not resist a post-match swipe at the media, declaring:"Sorry about the dream final, lads!"

It certainly turned out to be a dream final for Everton which they went into, once again, as the underdogs of war against championship runners-up Manchester United. The Wembley line-ups were:

Everton: Southall; Jackson, Watson (captain), Unsworth, Ablett; Limpar (Amokachi, 69), Horne, Parkinson, Hinchcliffe; Rideout (Ferguson, 50), Stuart. Substitute unused: Kearton.

Manchester United: Schmeichel; G. Neville, Bruce (captain) (Giggs, 46), Pallister, Irwin; Butt, Keane, Ince, Sharpe (Scholes, 72); McClair, Hughes. Substitute unused: Walsh.

United had the majority of possession but were hit by a lightning 29th-minute raid which was to prove decisive. Limpar's run allowed Matt Jackson to swing in a low cross, which was met by Graham Stuart. His shot came off the bar and Paul Rideout headed his 16th goal of the season. His previous headed strike had been the winner at Ipswich less than a fortnight earlier, which ensured Everton's Premiership survival.

Injury to Rideout meant Ferguson's introduction five minutes after the interval and semi-final hero Amokachi replaced Limpar after 69 minutes. Everton defended superbly to protect their lead. Watson was magnificent, winning the man-of-the-match award while Southall, the only Everton survivor from the 1985 final defeat by United, produced a superb 75th-minute double save from Paul Scholes before plunging to his right five minutes later to keep out a Gary Pallister header.

Referee Gerald Ashby's final whistle completed a triumph that would have seemed fantasy in the grim grip of midwinter and one that installed Gary Ablett in the record books as the only player to gain FA Cup winners medals with Everton and Liverpool. "Beating relegation was the battle when I arrived, but to win the Cup as well is the icing on the cake," beamed Royle.

Skipper Dave Watson, having completed his collection of domestic honours after a title win with Everton and League Cup triumph with Norwich, thrust the trophy into the air and declared: "I'm delighted we've got this cup because I've followed Kevin Ratcliffe as captain and that's like following Frank

Sinatra." Heroic Southall, praised by United boss Alex Ferguson for his display on his 650th Everton appearance, became the first player to win two FA Cup winners medals with the Goodison club. But with characteristic earthiness, the big Welshman stopped media interviewers short by saying: "We're only a pub team." Under Royle, Everton had lost only six of 34 League and Cup games, keeping 18 clean sheets, but that Wembley glory was to prove the high-water mark of his Goodison management.

With a return to Europe in the Cup Winners' Cup beckoning Royle moved to bolster his squad after the departures of Ian Snodin to Oldham on a free, David Burrows to Coventry for £1.1 million, Brett Angell to Sunderland for £500,000 and Stuart Barlow to Oldham for £450,000. Royle signed defender Craig Short in a £2.65 million deal with Derby that took £300,000-rated Gary Rowett in the opposite direction and after unsuccessful attempts to land Stan Collymore and Chris Armstrong, he lined up Manchester United winger Andrei Kanchelskis. A £5 million deal was agreed and announced in July, but its completion took another five weeks due to the Ukrainian's former club Shakhtar Donetsk claiming payment under a 'sell-on' clause.

Everton finally agreed to pay an extra £500,000 but the delay meant the player was ineligible for the opening two rounds of Everton's first European venture in a decade. As it happened he would have been ruled out of the first round anyway after dislocating his right shoulder and rupturing tendons in a 3-2 home dfefeat by his former club Manchester United, which kept him on the sidelines for seven games.

Back at Wembley Everton toppled champions Blackburn in the Charity Shield. The game's only goal was a spectacular angled left-footed strike from Vinny Samways, a player who appeared only rarely under Royle and whose name was not even listed in the match programme.

Everton returned to the Continental stage with a 6-3 aggregate defeat of KR Reykjavik but when an eligible Kanchelskis might have inspired a different outcome, they went out in the second round to Feyenoord, losing 1-0 in Holland after a goalless Goodison draw in the first leg. The value of Kanchelskis was underlined a fortnight after Everton's European exit when he crowned a powerful performance by scoring both their goals in a sweet 2-1 win over Liverpool at Anfield.

But Everton bowed out of the Coca-Cola Cup at the first hurdle, drawing 0-0 at Millwall in the second round, first leg before losing 4-2 after extra time at Goodison in October. During the same month Duncan Ferguson began a three-month sentence at Glasgow's Barlinnie Prison for head-butting Raith player John McStay in 1994 during his period with Rangers. He was released early - in late November - and with the remaining seven games of a 12-match ban frozen he returned to action as a substitute against West Ham in December after a 20-match absence. But on the day of Ferguson's prison release Rideout sustained an injury at Goodison that wrecked his season and shattered his Everton career. He was involved in a clash of heads with Des Walker in a 2-2 draw with Sheffield Wednesday. He was rushed to hospital and spent seven-and-a-half-hours in casualty after tests revealed a cracked palate. He also required 32 stitches to gum and lip lacerations. Although Rideout returned in the 4-0 Boxing Day win over Middlesbrough, he was still struggling to hit top form. He made only a further four starts that season and after undergoing Achilles surgery was never again a regular starter through to his departure to Chinese club Huan Dao Vanguards in 1997.

Everton's hold on the FA Cup was broken in shock circumstances. They were taken to an Edgeley Park replay in the third round by Second Division Stockport and after Port Vale had drawn at Goodison in the next round, they stunned Everton with a 2-1 win in the replay. "We were so bad we made Vale look like Real Madrid," thundered angry Royle, who did at least have some satisfaction in the League. He added full-back Marc Hottiger to his squad by paying Newcastle £700,000 and Everton's completion of the double over Middlesbrough with a 2-0 March win at the Riverside took them to sixth in the table, their highest position since September 1993.

Frustratingly, their finishing position of sixth meant that they missed out on a European ticket by one place, trailing fifth-placed Arsenal by two points. It was their highest finish in six years and their points haul of 61 was their best since 1988, when they totalled 70 and finished fourth. The other satisfying factor was that Everton's average League attendance of 35,424 was their highest for 17 years and the fifth highest in the country.

The crowd average climbed above 36,000 the following season - but it was one that Royle was destined not to complete as Everton manager. His preparations for the 1996-97 campaign included the £3.5 million arrival of Gary Speed from Leeds and the £1.5 million signing of goalkeeper Paul Gerrard from his former club Oldham. Everton missed out, though, on Stan Collymore when the player chose Liverpool after both clubs had made £8.5 million offers for the Nottingham Forest striker, and made a ludicrous £12 million bid for Blackburn's Alan Shearer when he was already heading to

Newcastle for a then world record £15 million. In October, Everton paid a club record £5.75 million for Middlesbrough's Nick Barmby. Out went Paul Holmes to West Brom for £80,000, Gary Ablett and Barry Horne to Birmingham for £390,000 and £280,000 respectively and Daniel Amokachi to Besiktas for £1.75 million.

The season opened in upbeat fashion with a 2-0 home win over Newcastle watched by a sell-out 40,000-plus crowd. Ferguson, once said by Royle "to be a legend before he's become a player," was saluted by the manager as "awesome" after a devastating display, forcing a penalty fired home by David Unsworth and setting up a debut goal for Speed. He followed up with two goals of his own in a 2-2 draw at Manchester United but before September was out he was sent off at Blackburn for the third time as an Everton player. The 1-1 draw at Ewood Park was Everton's seventh senior match without a win, equalling the worst run under Royle.

In their next outing they crashed out of the Coca-Cola Cup in the second round to York, occupying 18th place in the Second Division. The first leg had been drawn 1-1 but Royle's side lost 3-2 in their first-ever visit to Bootham Crescent, going out ignominiously on a 4-3 aggregate. It was their third consecutive exit to lower division opposition at that stage of the competition following Portsmouth (1994) and Millwall (1995). A 4-2 Boxing Day defeat at Middlesbrough was the first of six consecutive League losses - equalling the club's worst run - and in the midst of that sequence First Division strugglers Bradford won 3-2 at Goodison in the FA Cup fourth round. There were after-match chants of 'Royle Out' from fans and when the staff and players reported for training at Bellefield on the Monday they were met by graffiti carrying a similar message daubed on the wall.

In the next match after the Bradford debacle Royle axed Southall and brought in Paul Gerrard for the trip to Newcastle. It was the first time the iconic Wales goalkeeper had been dropped in 15 years since November 1982. He also dropped record buy Nick Barmby and brought in his Danish signing Claus Thomsen. But the changes failed to halt the losing trend and Royle's side crashed to a 4-1 defeat, their sixth in a row in the League.

Royle's relationship with the press became strained and by transfer deadline day, Thursday, March 27, after losing 2-0 at home to Manchester United, Royle wanted to sign the Norwegian pair Tore Andre Flo and Claus Eftevaag from SK Brann Bergen for £2.85 million to beat the deadline. Then, when Flo pulled out of a move for contractual reasons, Royle hoped he could land

Danish international Eftevaag for a much reduced fee. The plan was blocked by chairman Peter Johnson and the outcome was a statement by Royle which said: "I have been disappointed by recent results and our current League position. Having spoken to the chairman it has been agreed that we part company by mutual consent." He later added: "In the end it was an amicable decision but I'm just very, very sad about it all." Royle's record in charge was: played 118, won 46, drawn 38, lost 34.

Five days later on April 1 Dave Watson's qualities of leadership on the field were given broader horizons and responsibilities when Johnson appointed him caretaker player-manager for the final seven, crucial matches. The challenge was heightened by the fact that for his first match in charge, the trip to Aston Villa on April 5, he had just 10 fit outfield first-team players plus Southall, who had regained his place under Royle. Earl Barrett, the last ever-present that season, and Barmby had joined the long list of casualties. It meant that Watson had to fill the bench with two 18-year-olds in John Hills and Michael Branch and 17-year-olds Richard Dunne and Michael Ball. Gerrard was named as substitute keeper even though he, too, was injured. Everton lost 3-1 at Villa Park which meant that they had taken only nine points from 45 with just two wins in 15 League games.

Everton had to sweat on their fate until three days before their final game when Blackburn's goalless draw with Middlesbrough ensured Goodison's Premiership survival after the club's third relegation struggle in four seasons. The relief was tangible when Chelsea came to Goodison to bring down the curtain on another angst-ridden campaign. Watson, with eight players unavailable, called up Hills, Royle's £90,000 signing from Blackpool, for his first start. Danny Cadamarteri, aged 17 years, seven months, made his debut as second-half replacement for Thomsen while Gavin McCann and Adam Eaton were on the bench for the first time.

It was a distinctly downbeat finale to the season and Watson's short tenure in charge. Chelsea, despite having goalkeeper Frode Grodas sent off after 21 minutes for bringing down Ferguson in a scoring position, won with 10 men. Dennis Wise and Roberto Di Matteo put them 2-0 ahead before the interval and although Barmby beat substitute keeper Kevin Hitchcock 13 minutes from the end, the London visitors secured a victory that meant Everton finishing 15th, just two points clear of relegation.

Johnson had promised a "world class" replacement for Royle and top of his list was Barcelona's Bobby Robson, the third occasion the former England and

Ipswich boss was wanted by Everton. The arrival at the Nou Camp of Ajax coach Louis Van Gaal gave Johnson hope that he could land Robson, who was also being pursued by Celtic. The wait went on...and on. It lasted six weeks until Robson announced he was staying at Barcelona in an upstairs role supervising new signings. "I've had contact with Everton but because of my contract and because I want to stay here for another year I've really had to say 'no' to Goodison and to Celtic," said Robson.

Myriad names and many of the usual suspects appeared in the media as contenders for the Everton job, including John Toshack, Bryan Robson, Arigo Sacchi and Martin O'Neill. Then, in mid-June, a firm candidate did emerge - none other than Andy Gray, whose contribution to the glory days of the mid-1980s established him as a supporters' folk hero and who had now opened up a new career as a Sky TV pundit. There were also rumours that Gray's former boss Howard Kendall was to return as general manager in harness with the former centre-forward.

Protracted talks with Gray were held and just when his appointment was expected to be rubber-stamped he announced that he was not going to occupy the manager's seat. "In my heart I wanted to manage Everton but, increasingly, my head has been telling me different things", said Gray. "To take the job, then let the supporters down would have been too much to bear." Money was not a factor between Everton and Gray, who signed a new Sky contract shortly afterwards. But Johnson was angered at his apparent U-turn and rapped: "I'm aghast that the man has behaved like this. You can gather I'm upset."

Some seven years later Gray offered a new slant on the affair when he told BBC Radio Merseyside: "I met Peter Johnson and a couple of directors on the Wirral and we talked for hours about the Everton manager's job. I was never actually offered it but I was asked what I would do in certain hypothetical situations if I was manager. If I'd been offered the job I'd have signed a contract. But I went away without anything being settled. Sky made me another offer and I also had to think about how often I would see my daughter. The more I thought about it the more I realised the Everton job would not be the right thing for me."

Gray's decision led to the appointment of Howard Kendall, Act Three. Everton's most successful manager was back in charge for the third time. "I'm just delighted to be back", beamed Kendall, who brought with him Viv Busby, who had been his assistant at Sheffield United, and his former player Adrian Heath, who left the manager's job at Burnley to return to Goodison.

During Everton's managerless limbo period Johnson signed defender Slaven Bilic for £4.5 million from West Ham, a move that had been initiated by Joe Royle before his departure. It would prove one of the most costly episodes in Everton's transfer history, who, on his arrival, was Britain's most expensive defender. A former law trainee, Bilic spoke four languages and clearly had a head for figures, too. Kendall revealed later that Bilic's contract stipulated that only one other player at the club could be better paid and if a new signing was paid more, the Croatian would receive an automatic wage rise.

The figures of his Everton career, however, were alarming. He made just 32 appearances and in his first season - during which he captained the side at Newcastle - he was sent off three times and booked on eight occasions. An FA Cup tie at Bristol City in January 1999 proved to be Bilic's last for Everton as he struggled with hip and pelvic injuries. But it took another 14 months to settle the insurance and contractual issues and it is believed Everton received a pay-out of less than £1 million.

Marc Hottiger had returned to his native Switzerland before Kendall took charge again at Goodison. His first signing was Irish midfielder Gareth Farrelly from Aston Villa for a tribunal-fixed fee of £700,000, rising to an appearance-linked £900,000. One goal he was destined to score was almost beyond price for the club.

 Another arrival was winger John Oster from Grimsby, for a fee rising to £1.5 million depending on appearances, and defender Tony Thomas from Tranmere for a basic £400,000 rising by a further £250,000 linked to appearances. Kendall also recruited midfielder Danny Williamson from West Ham for £1 million cash and David Unsworth moving to Upton Park.

Johnson authorised £15 million moves to land Paul Ince, Stefan Schwarz and Fabrizio Ravanelli but they proved fruitless, the Italian striker's decision not to to join Everton taken in theatrical circumstances. Ravanelli's limousine arrival at Goodison with a retinue of three minders and agents, the player peering from behind a pair of stylish shades, would have done Frank Sinatra proud. Given the reported demand of his advisors for £2.5 million a year wages it was not surprising that talks broke down and the 'White Feather' floated off from Middlesbrough to join Marseille. "I found him to be a true professional", said Kendall. "He asked about our facilities and training methods. I felt he could have made a big impact and been a valuable asset for the club. The deal broke down because of the personal terms. The money could not be found and I regret not landing him."

Prior to the start of the 1997-98 season Everton announced a new three-year, £2 million sponsorship deal with One-2-One. But when the curtain went up at the opening game against Crystal Palace the mood of the fans was clear. 'A hamper is for Christmas, Everton is for life' was the message one banner delivered to Johnson. The result and peformance did nothing to lighten the mood with Palace winning 2-1, Ferguson scoring Everton's goal four minutes from the end. Kendall named this opening day line-up:

Southall; Thomas (Branch, 46), Watson, Bilic, Phelan; Oster (Short, 88), Speed (captain), Thomsen (Barmby, 63), Farrelly; Stuart, Ferguson. Unused substitutes: Gerrard, Barrett.

Thomas, Bilic, Oster and Farrelly made their Everton debuts in that defeat and Danny Williamson came in for his first appearance in a re-shuffled side at home to West Ham a week later when goals from Stuart and Watson secured a 2-1 win. But in their third consecutive home game Everton were outclassed by Manchester United 2-0 and when they went to Bolton for the first match to be staged at the Reebok Stadium on September 1 the world was reeling from the death of Diana, Princess of Wales, after a Paris car crash the previous day.

An impeccably observed pre-match period of silence was followed by a goalless draw, although one incident would have a profound effect on both clubs. Bolton forced the ball into the Everton net but, as the home side celebrated, a linesman ruled that the ball had not crossed the line. The significance of that decision would become massively apparent on the last day of the season but Kendall was insistent that it was a correct one - for the wrong reason. "Yes, the ball did cross our goal line before it was cleared", he admitted. "But Neville Southall was fouled in the melee so it shouldn't have been given anyway."

At the end of the month, struggling Everton took on pacesetting Arsenal at Goodison. Arsene Wenger's side, who went on to win the championship and FA Cup, were unbeaten and looked to be cruising to victory after goals from Ian Wright - his 15th against Everton - and Marc Overmars gave them a 2-0 interval lead. But in a remarkable recovery in the opening 10 minutes of the second half Michael Ball cut the deficit by heading his first goal for the club and Danny Cadamarteri fired an equaliser and took the scoring pair into the record books. It is the only instance of two 17-year-olds scoring for Everton in the same game and the only time it has happened in Premiership history. Ball was four days short of his 18th birthday while Cadamarteri was aged 17 years and 351 days.

A fortnight later, though, it was a very different story. Everton crashed out of the Coca-Cola Cup 4-1 in the third round at Coventry. Kendall was so ashamed of the performance that he ordered the players to applaud their travelling fans. Craig Short was so angry that he had to be restrained by Bilic. In the days leading up to the Highfield Road debacle, Neville Southall and Dave Watson were told they could leave on a free transfer when their contracts expired at the end of the season.

Southall, omitted from the Coca-Cola tie, was recalled for Everton's next match - the Goodison derby with odds-on favourites and seventh-placed Liverpool. By now, Kendall's side were in the bottom three and the response of supporters was to issue printed leaflets calling for Peter Johnson's head. A Neil Ruddock own goal just before the interval broke the deadlock and recalled Cadamarteri had the blue half of Merseyside in raptures 15 minutes from the end when he seized possession from Bjorn Tore Kvarme, surged forward in a 35-yard run and fired past David James to clinch a 2-0 win. It was Cadamarteri's fifth goal in his last six starts and came a week after his England Under 18 debut. Although he went on to win England Under 21 recognition he never fulfilled the rich promise that flowed so gloriously on that October afternoon and after 60 starts, 61 substitute appearances and 15 goals he joined Bradford City on a free in February 2002.

Southall, in his 42nd and last derby in all competitions, did not have a shot to save. The result made it three straight derby wins for Kendall - after victories in December 1992 and September 1993 - and meant that Everton had had four managers since Liverpool last won a derby. The sequence was extended at Anfield the following February when a right-foot stike from Duncan Ferguson gave Everton a 1-1 draw, stretching their unbeaten League derby run to a post-war best eight games.

Local pride, though, was one thing. Premiership survival quite another and three successive defeats at the hands of Southampton, Blackburn and Aston Villa put them bottom of the table in late November. Kendall moved into the transfer market, signing full-back or midfielder Mitch Ward and centre-back Carl Tiler from Sheffield United in a package deal comprising £500,000 cash plus Graham Stuart, and paying £800,000 for Norwegian goalkeeper Thomas Myhre from Viking Stavanger.

Myhre's arrival signalled the end of Southall's amazing Goodison career. His 750th and last appearance was, sadly, in a 2-0 home defeat by Tottenham which extended Everton's losing run to five straight League defeats. The following month Southall went out on loan to Southend United. He later joined Stoke on loan before his move was made permanent in March when he became player-coach at the Britannia Stadium.

Shortly after Myhre's debut in a goalless draw at Leeds - which ended the run of defeats and included a penalty save off Gary Speed by a certain Nigel Martyn - chairman Johnson was reminding Everton shareholders at the club's annual meeting of the extent of his transfer market investment. He pointed out that since he had won control in 1994 the club had spent £26.7 million net on new players compared to Liverpool's £20.7 million and Manchester United less than £500,000. The obvious riposte from the Everton faithful was to point to Everton's record and their woeful position in the table. Before the turn of the year Kendall swooped for French striker Mickael Madar on a free transfer from Deportivo La Coruna.

For the home game with Bolton in Everton's last action of 1997 Kendall made Duncan Ferguson captain for the first time on his return from a three-match ban. The big Scot did not disappoint. He responded with his first Everton hat-trick - every goal a header - in a 3-2 win on a day that Kendall was without 13 professionals through injury and suspension and fielded a team containing four teenagers: Dunne, Oster, Ball and Cadamarteri. In addition, 16-year-old Francis Jeffers was on the bench two days after going on as a half-time substitute at Old Trafford to become the second youngest player, after Joe Royle, to appear in a competitive match for Everton. The record was lowered in April 2005 by James Vaughan, who went on as a substitute against Crystal Palace and scored at the age of 16 years, 271 days.

Kendall was named Manager of the Month for January and the day before the 2-2 draw at Barnsley, he sold Gary Speed, the man he had made the new captain at the start of the season. The Wales international midfielder asked for a move and joined Newcastle for £5.5 million. Speed followed Andy Hinchcliffe through the exit. The England international full-back or wing-back joined Sheffield Wednesday for £2.75 million.

Others moving out were defenders John Hills, who returned to Blackpool for £60,000, Jon O'Connor, who joined Sheffield United in a £1 million package deal that took former Liverpool midfielder Don Hutchison to Goodison, Earl Barrett on a free to Sheffield Wednesday and midfielder Claus Thomsen, who joined AB Copenhagen for £500,000. Kendall brought in Chester midfielder Matt McKay for £250,000, although he never made a first-team appearance, and spent £1.5 million on striker John Spencer from QPR following a month's loan. Peter Beagrie also returned to Everton on a short loan from Bradford.

A week before his goal at Anfield, Ferguson was sent off in a 2-1 home defeat by Derby for elbowing Paulo Wanchope. It was his fourth dismissal in 108 Everton appearances, which meant he would be banned for three games after the derby. But when his suspension was over Ferguson was then ruled out of the home clash against Aston Villa due to a knee injury. The team duly crashed to a 4-1 defeat, which left Everton just one place and two points above the relegation zone.

Kendall pointed out that he had up to £20 million worth of talent unavailable. Highlighting the massive duty rota was the fact that Beagrie, who went on as substitute for Oster, became the 34th player used by Kendall during the season, a total surpassed in Everton history on only three occasions - in 1888-89, 1919-20 and 1998-99 when 35 were used.

A Madar goal prised a point in a 1-1 draw at Tottenham - when Gavin McCann made his first start - followed by a precious 2-0 home win over Leeds through goals from Ferguson and Hutchison. After a goalless draw at Wimbledon, Madar scored his fourth goal in his last five starts to clinch a 1-1 home draw with Leicester. But a 3-1 Paolo Di Canio-inspired defeat to Sheffield Wednesday and a 4-0 hiding at Arsenal - their heaviest defeat of the season coinciding with Arsenal clinching the championship - dumped Everton into the bottom three with their Premiership fate hinging on their final match - a Sunday duel with Coventry.

In the week leading up to that encounter on May 10, a Kop banner at Liverpool's home clash with Arsenal proclaimed: 'Agent Johnson: Mission Accomplished'. The sinking feeling felt by Everton fans was demonstrated by a city centre cinema publicity poster for the movie Titanic which had the head of the ship's captain obliterated and replaced by Kendall's.

The build-up to the Coventry game reached hysteria level. Memories of the last-day escape against Wimbledon only four years earlier filled the airwaves and the headlines. Recriminations about the running of the club reached boiling point and the public spleen aimed at Johnson and his associates, including director Cliff Finch, led to stringent security measures not only for the match but also in the preceding days. After he had flown back from his Jersey-base to his Wirral home police were stationed in nearby roads monitoring movements just in case the supporters' anger metamorphosised into something more menacing.

As a journalist and broadcaster I was asked by Johnson to offer advice on a message he wished to deliver to supporters at the Coventry game. When my taxi approached his home the day before the match we were stopped by a police patrol checking why we were there. Such was the mood of menace in the air during the countdown to another day of Everton destiny.

Kendall cited the Premiership's worst disciplinary record of 80 yellow cards and five red, plus a massive injury list, as huge obstacles thrown in Everton's path, saying: "I believe I'm the right man for the job. Everyone's aware of the difficulties this season but if I didn't believe things could improve dramatically I would understand the finger being pointed. I don't want to talk about the possibility of relegation but I wouldn't resign."

Kendall's decision to drop Slaven Bilic and John Oster after the Arsenal drubbing and recall Gareth Farrelly along with Mickael Madar turned out to be crucial. This was his team:

Myhre; Short, Watson, Tiler; O'Kane, Barmby, Hutchison, Farrelly (McCann, 88), Ball; Barmby; Madar (Cadamarteri, 50), Ferguson (captain). Substitutes unused: Gerrard, Bilic, Beagrie.

Everton's fate was not entirely in their own hands. If Bolton won at Chelsea then the Goodison club would be relegated for the first time since 1951. But after only six minutes, the tension was punctured in the most unlikely way. Farrelly followed in on his own cross, which had been cleared by Gary Breen under challenge from Duncan Ferguson. The Republic of Ireland Under 21 international, whose only Everton goal had come in the Coca-Cola Cup at Scunthorpe eight months earlier, controlled the ball with his chest and smashed it in off the post on the half volley with his 'wrong' right foot.

The roar from the 40,000-plus crowd that greeted it possibly rivalled the reception for Dixie Dean's record-breaking 60th League goal 70 years to the week earlier, although this one was born of a sense of survival rather than achievement. Strangely, the goal had the effect of making Everton tentative as Coventry took command of the game, led by George Boateng with the home defence having to keep a close patrol on Darren Huckerby.

The mental and physical drain on Everton took its toll as they tired in the second half and Huckerby, Nilsson and Noel Whelan went close to scoring for Coventry. Tension got higher and tempers shorter. Duncan Ferguson then Michael Ball squared up to Paul Telfer and as play was in progress coach Viv Busby raced onto the pitch to tell his players to 'cool it'. A roar went up at the radio news of a 73rd-minute Chelsea goal by Gianluca Vialli - the crowd keeping the players updated - and an even bigger one when referee Paul

Alcock made an astonishing 84th-minute penalty award. Danny Cadamarteri, who had replaced Madar, ran onto Nick Barmby's header but a shooting chance was denied him by a measured, stretching tackle by Paul Williams. Amazingly, the Kent official pointed to the spot. Justice prevailed, though, when Hedman flung himself to his right to produce a superb save.

A minute from the end you could have heard a snail cough, such was the silence that greeted Coventry's equaliser. Ironically, it was Dion Dublin, the player Kendall wanted and resigned over in 1993, who rose to meet a cross from former Everton and Liverpool defender David Burrows and head past Thomas Myhre. Injury time seemed to last forever. But even before Alcock blew the whistle came reports that Chelsea had scored again in the last minute and that Bolton were down. Both they and fourth-from-bottom Everton had 40 points - but Kendall's side stayed up on goal difference.

Goodison rocked to an explosion of sheer, unbounded relief as the pitch was invaded. Tears were shed. Supporters hugged each other before thousands massed in front of the main stand and called for Johnson's head. The chants of 'Johnson Out' reverberated around the streets outside. From the dressing room Dave Watson, who'd fought the closing stages of a relegation battle in cartetaker charge a year earlier, admitted: "We got out of jail but we can't afford to go through that again. I feel drained - not physically but mentally." Kendall reflected: "We had eight players unavailable. We survived and deservedly so. I've had only one season here and I'm not responsible for the other three years when we were in danger of going down. This was a day I do not want to go through again - and this club will not go through another day like this as long as I am manager."

That, as it transpired, would be a brief period. Kendall attended a scheduled board meeting the day after the great escape against Coventry. A month later the board met again and backed Johnson's decision to sack Kendall before the chairman flew to France on holiday. The developments were inevitably leaked to the media and Kendall, in a dignified manner the unworthy circumstances did not deserve, had to field questions about his future while he waited a further three weeks to be told officially of his fate.

Johnson, having been thwarted in attempts to appoint Martin O'Neill and Brian Kidd amongst other candidates to succeed Kendall, managed to lure Walter Smith to Goodison just as he was about to take charge at Sheffield Wednesday. Johnson's hope was that Smith's success at Rangers would translate to football south of the border. It turned out to be an excercise in treading water that spanned almost four years, although Johnson's direct involvement would last only months.

Although the supporters were spared any further last-day emotional cliffhangers during Smith's three full seasons at the helm, Everton finished in the bottom half of the Premiership on each occasion. His last campaign, 2001-02, also saw Everton in the lower reaches of the table and they were one point clear of a relegation place when David Moyes, succeeded him for the final nine games.

Smith brought with him his Rangers assistant Archie Knox and the new regime was launched with a goalless draw at home to Aston Villa, visiting goalkeeper Mark Bosnich saving a ninth-minute John Collins penalty. The team included four debutants: full-back or wing-back Alex Cleland, a Bosman free from Glasgow Rangers arranged by Kendall; midfielder John Collins, £2.5 million from Monaco; midfielder Olivier Dacourt, £3.8 million from Strasbourg and centre-back Marco Materazzi, £2.5 million from Perugia. Smith's first line-up was:

Myhre; Short, Tiler, Materazzi; Cleland, Barmby, Dacourt (Hutchison, 74), Collins, Ball; Ferguson (captain), Spencer (Cadamarteri, 63). Unused substitutes: Gerrard, Watson, Branch.

By the time they had lost 2-0 at Leicester and 1-0 at home to Tottenham they had collected 11 bookings from their first three games and were the only Premiership side without a goal. Even after putting together a 10-game unbeaten run in Premiership and Worthington Cup Everton languished in 15th place by late October.

David Unsworth, who made a £3 million return to the club after a brief stay at Aston Villa, was back in Everton action at Leicester and in September Carl Tiler was sold to Charlton for £700,000. Unsworth was soon followed on Smith's shopping list by Steve Simonsen. The 19-year-old goalkeeper was signed from Tranmere for an initial £500,000 and defender Graham Allen in part exchange - a deal that could have reached £3.3 million depending on appearances. On that basis, Simonsen was labelled Britain's most expensive goalkeeper and most costly teenager but the England Under 21 international had to wait three years for his first Premiership start, made only 37 senior appearances and moved on a free to Stoke in 2004.

Another arrival was Ivory Coast striker Ibrahima Bakayoko - instantly nicknamed by fans as 'Back of the Echo' - who cost £4.5 million from Montpellier. When he faced Liverpool in a goalless Goodison duel in October he became the first Merseyside player to make his debut in a derby since Julian Dicks for Liverpool five years earlier and the first Everton player to do so since Paul Bracewell in 1984.

His first Premiership goal - a 25-yard right-foot spectacular - gave Everton a 1-0 win over Southampton in December when Bakayoko, a Muslim, teamed up in attack with the recalled Mickael Madar, a Jew, to register another first in Everton history. Both of them, however, were soon on their way out. Madar moved on a free to Paris St Germain in January and Bakayoko made a £3.8 million move to Marseille the following June.

But the transfer that dominated Everton's season and proved a watershed in the club's history happened in November. Approaching half-time in a Monday live TV clash with Newcastle - which Everton won 1-0 through a Michael Ball penalty - rumours began to circulate that Duncan Ferguson, ruled out through suspension, was being sold to the north-east club.

Frantic inquiries by the media established that negotiations were in progress as the match was being played. But down on the Everton bench Smith and Knox were blissfully unaware of these dramatic developments. By the final whistle the talk of Ferguson's impending departure had swept the stadium and when it reached Smith's ears he urgently climbed the stairs to the boardroom to ascertain, as one insider put it, "what the hell was going on." He was amazed to discover that Peter Johnson had negotiated and agreed with Newcastle to sell Ferguson for £7 million with a further £1 million tied to appearances. Smith was livid and only the persuasive tongue of Bill Kenwright stopped him resigning on the spot.

Ferguson's move to Newcastle was completed in the next 48 hours to much wailing and gnashing of teeth by the Everton faithful, to whom the towering Scot had become a talismanic figure. All their suspicions and feelings about Johnson, the man whose allegiance was once to Liverpool, bubbled to the surface. Radio phone-in lines were in meltdown with furious supporters, the local newspaper letter pages overflowing with vitriol aimed at Johnson. Nobody, though, was as angry as Smith. His mood was such that unless Johnson went he would walk out of Everton. He felt passionately that any other outcome would undermine his integrity.

A week later, on Monday, November 30, a day when Smith was attending a family funeral in Glasgow and kept in contact by telephone, Everton issued two press releases. The first of them, timed at 12.35pm, said: "In the light of the many comments, some highly speculative, currently being made regarding

Duncan Ferguson's transfer to Newcastle both chairman and manager felt the following statement should be issued on a joint basis.

"After four months in the manager's seat, having spent £20 million on six new players, bringing the squad total to 35, Walter Smith assessed his playing staff and discussed with the chairman his plans for the future. Having seen the manager's report, the chairman emphasised to him the requirement to sell players to return the squad to reasonable proportions.

The club had received a substantial offer for Duncan Ferguson earlier in the season, which was rejected. The chairman and manager agreed that any future offer should be given serious consideration. The club then became aware of Newcastle's interest. Events started to move rapidly last Monday evening. A substantial offer for Duncan Ferguson was received from Newcastle which was discussed with that club's representatives immediately before and during the course of last Monday evening's game.

Their discussions resulted in an agreement being reached at that time. Unfortunately, details of these discussions were not passed to Walter Smith during the course of the game. It is regretted that he learned of the final agreement reached regarding Duncan Ferguson in the manner he did, subsequent to the conclusion of the match."

A second club release, timed at 5.10pm, said: "After 11 years as chairman of a football club, four years with Everton and seven years with Tranmere Rovers, Peter Johnson has decided to step down as chairman of Everton. The role has been particularly difficult to carry out since he moved to Jersey earlier this year and the increased pressure has led to health concerns.

Mr Johnson is delighted that Sir Philip Carter and Bill Kenwright have agreed to take on the roles of chairman and deputy chairman respectively. Mr Johnson is to remain on the board as a non-executive director and over the coming months he will be considering options for his 68 per cent beneficial interest. The decision to step down will not affect the sale of his interest in Tranmere Rovers, which is currently underway."

The deep angst of the Everton fans had been illustrated by a banner at the previous Saturday's 2-1 win at Charlton, by which time Smith had installed Dave Watson as Ferguson's successor as captain. The message was: 'Johnson took us to the cleaners. Well, this one won't wash. Go now.' As Danny Cadamarteri's double was clinching Everton's win, Ferguson was also scoring twice on his Newcastle debut against Wimbledon to compound the Goodison fans' sense of loss.

Now, with Johnson's resignation, the supporters' wish had been granted. Johnson had left - the first recorded occasion of a chairman effectively being sacked by a manager. In his four-and-a-half years as chairman he had overseen almost £105 million of transfer market turnover, with £66.6 million spent on new players and £38.2 million recouped in sales.

At the club's next annual meeting the following October, when Everton reported a record £11.8 million loss on the financial year and a potential £11.3 million bill for outstanding transfer payments, signing-on fees and loyalty bonuses, Johnson was accused by Sir Philip Carter of financially misleading fellow directors. "We had a situation where a multi-millionaire told us in no uncertain terms that he was in charge of finances and talking to the manager", said Sir Philip. "He told the rest of the board to involve themselves in running the rest of the company. We were so concerned that we formed our own financial committee which exposed the problems we have been wrestling with ever since. We asked Peter Johnson about them but were told in no uncertain terms that this was under control and that the bank were more than satisfied with the situation. We then talked to the bank and found out, in fact, that they were extremely concerned about the situation."

Manager Smith earned a standing ovation from shareholders when he told the same meeting: "There has been gross mismanagment. Everyone at the club has to face up to that. It has been mentioned that over the years Everton have spent £100 million on players and on the surface that is OK. But when I came here I realised that selling Duncan Ferguson to satisfy a bank was merely the continuation of an on-going Everton problem. Everton have never had the benefit of buying a player because they buy one and sell two. There is no consistency and no investment on the footballing side of things.

We need new facilities at Bellefield and we are in a ludicrous situation where we cannot complete the building of a youth academy. You look across at Liverpool and the state-of-the-art facilities they have built are a model to everyone else. In my own football career I have previously been involved only with two clubs - Dundee United and Rangers. Both have been extremely well run so when I came to Everton I had a reasonable view of what it takes to make a football club reasonably successful.

I was told by Peter Johnson that this would be his last go at things before he left. I was then to map out exactly how I thought Everton would go forward. I tried to do that. He then backed me in terms of buying a number of players, unbeknown to myself there were no funds to back that, hence the problems we have at the present moment."

And Smith revealed the blow-by-blow account of the amazing night when Ferguson was sold. "The chairman visited the dressing room, as he normally did, in a match at Coventry and said off-the-cuff: 'Walter, I don't think we will ever be a good football team as long as Duncan Ferguson is in it.' I thought that was a strange thing to say. Over a period I received telephone calls telling me there was an effort being made to sell Duncan. He had heard all the rumours as well. I had spoken to him on the morning of the Newcastle game and said I would confront the chairman to find out what was going on.

We proceeded to play the game, which we won 1-0, and I did my usual post-match interview with Sky TV when I was asked about Duncan leaving. I said as far as I was concerned he would be in the team at Charlton that Saturday. I went upstairs to get my wife, who was in the boardroom, and went back downstairs. Duncan was standing there. I said: 'You're going to struggle to get back in the team after that.' He said, adding one or two expletives: 'Yes, I will, because you've just sold me.' My wife and Archie Knox's wife were behind me. They knew because they'd obviously heard it being discussed in the boardroom at half-time. She knew before me that Duncan was being transferred! She saw my surprise.

I got the chairman out of the boardroom and we obviously had words. He said to me: 'Of course you know about it.' He said I must have known. We had one or two other words before a scheduled board meeting the next day, which he did not attend. If your relationship with the chairman breaks down that is it. We had a meeting at London airport before the game against Charlton and I asked him to make a press release stating that he sold Duncan Ferguson without my knowledge. He released that and I was reasonably happy with the situation. But at the next board meeting Bill Kenwright told me he was still telling people I knew about the sale, even though Sir Philip Carter was witness to the fact that he said he didn't tell me."

Johnson's departure was just the start of Bill Kenwright's mission to assume financial control of the club he has loved almost since he could walk. He immediately announced his intention to bid for Johnson's holding, a winding road that took him until the dawn of the new millennium to reach the destination he yearned for - to own his beloved Everton.

Everton were sent hurtling out of the FA Cup with a 4-1 hiding at Newcastle but apart from a welcome 5-0 home drubbing of Middlesbrough, which marked David Weir's debut after his bargain £250,000 move from Hearts, their

Premiership form was poor. After a 1-0 defeat at Leeds they were quoted at 13-8 to be relegated prior to a 1-1 home draw with Wimbledon. Bakayoko conjured two timely goals for a 2-1 win at Blackburn, when Phil Jevons made his debut in place of the injured Barmby. But a 2-0 home crash to Arsenal increased the pressure and also left Don Hutchison facing a three-game ban after his dismissal for elbowing Martin Keown. Danish midfielder or defender Peter Degn, another of Smith's new faces who cost £200,000 from Aarhus, made his debut as a sub in a 3-1 defeat at Manchester United.

The situation was now becoming desperate. Everton were in dire need of a cutting edge, a goalscorer to beat off the club's fifth relegation threat in six seasons. Smith alighted on former Arsenal and Nottingham Forest striker Kevin Campbell, who was playing his trade with Trabzonspor but keen to return to England. He engineered a loan deal for Campbell until the end of the season and, following a couple of false starts, the England 'B' striker flourished after swapping the environs of the Black Sea for the Mersey.

He made his debut along with another new arrival, £200,000 midfielder Scot Gemmill from Nottingham Forest, in a 3-2 Mersey derby defeat at Liverpool where Smith sprang a shock by selecting Michael Branch ahead of Jeffers and Cadamarteri. Olivier Dacourt scored after 42 seconds of his derby debut but Liverpool hit back through two-goal Robbie Fowler - who performed his infamous touchline drug sniffing impersonation after scoring from a penalty - and Patrik Berger. Jeffers was eventually sent on as a late sub and scored on his derby debut, but Liverpool secured their first win in 10 derbies spanning more than five years to deepen the Everton crisis.

Forty-eight hours later, at home to Sheffield Wednesday on Easter Monday, the wheels came off for Everton, who were dumped into the bottom three by a 2-1 defeat. Ahead at the interval for only the fourth time that season they collapsed in the second half when woeful back passes by Materazzi and Unsworth were snapped up each time by Benito Carbone.

With six games to go something special was required to preserve Everton's tenancy in the top flight of English football. As if by magic, it arrived in the form of an explosive scoring burst from Campbell. He scored twice in a 2-0 home win over Coventry, which lifted Everton out of the relegation places but only added to their appalling disciplinary record. Materazzi received his third red card of the season, raising Everton's sendings-off total to eight, while Gemmill's caution was the club's 100th yellow card of the campaign.

Campbell repeated his two-goal act in a 3-1 win at Newcastle where

Gemmill scored the other goal and Thomas Myhre saved an Alan Shearer penalty. For the third game in a row Campbell scored twice, this time in a 4-1 mauling of Charlton with Jeffers and Hutchison joining him on the scoresheet. It was the first time Everton had won three consecutive League games for 15 months and it shot them eight points clear of the drop zone.

Although they lost two of their last three games - 3-1 at Chelsea and 2-0 at Southampton - a Campbell hat-trick in a 6-0 hammering of West Ham helped them to their biggest win since 1996 and guaranteed survival. It took Campbell's goal tally to nine in five outings which blasted away fears of the drop. Six years later he would spearhead an even more remarkable relegation-beating campaign with West Brom. Not surprisingly, Smith paid £3 million to make Campbell's move permanent during the summer when he also brought in defender Richard Gough on a free from Rangers and midfielder Mark Pembridge from Benfica for £800,000.

As well as selling Bakayoko to Marseille, Craig Short to Blackburn for £2.1 million, John Oster to Sunderland for £1.1 million and defender Adam Eaton to Preston for a nominal fee, Smith also sold Dacourt and Materazzi. Dacourt was lured back to France to join Lens for £6.5 million after one season of impressive form and the startling disciplinary tally of 16 yellow cards and one red. Materazzi also returned to his native heath, joining Italian club Perugia for £3 million after snookering Dacourt in the disciplinary stakes with 11 yellows and three reds.

The 1999-2000 season began with Thomas Myhre ruled out after breaking his leg on Norway duty while Jeffers had lodged a transfer demand, the start of a trail that would lead to the young striker making an £8 million departure to Arsenal. Yet there were rosy hopes of European qualification with Everton reaching fifth place in October. But it was a season that ended, once again, in disappointment. They were 10th going into their last match but a 2-0 home defeat by Middlesbrough dropped them into 13th place.

They had opened the season with a 1-1 home draw against Manchester United when Smith paraded an all-British starting 11 - including five Scots - and an all-British substititutes' bench. The line-up, with 37-year-olds Gough and Watson forming the oldest centre-back pairing in the club's history, was:

Gerrard; Weir, Watson (captain), Gough, Unsworth; Ward (Cadamarteri, 69), Gemmill, Collins, Barmby; Hutchison (Phelan, 84), Campbell. Substitutes unused: Ball, Pembridge, Simonsen.

Jaap Stam diverted an 88th-minute Barmby header into his own net to ensure Everton's point after Paul Gerrard had kept the Blues in it with a string of fine saves. But the following midweek, on the day Britain saw the first total eclipse of the sun since Dixie Dean was in his pomp in 1927, Aston Villa totally eclipsed Everton. With a repeat of the previous season's Villa Park result they beat Everton 3-0, a defeat compounded by the dismissal of John Collins for a second bookable offence. Despite two penalties from David Unsworth they lost 3-2 at Tottenham prior to an emphatic first win of the season, beating Southampton 4-1 at Goodison through goals from Gough, an own goal, Jeffers and Campbell.

Campbell and Jeffers were among the scorers again when Everton hit another four, this time without reply, to beat Wimbledon. A 1-0 defeat at Derby saw Richard Dunne sent off but they had a new face in the squad in their 2-0 victory at Sheffield Wednesday. Abel Xavier, a Portugal international full-back or wing-back, made his debut as a substitute at Hillsborough after his £1.5 million signing from PSV Eindhoven .

A 1-0 home win over West Ham sent Everton into the Monday night, September 27 derby at Anfield above Liverpool in the table for the first time in a decade and with confidence high. It was not misplaced. Campbell's fourth-minute goal was enough to give Everton the points in a contest that saw Francis Jeffers and Liverpool duo Sander Westerveld and Steven Gerrard become the eighth, ninth and tenth players to be sent off in the history of Mersey derbies. The win sent Everton climbing to sixth, with Liverpool 12th. A 1-1 home draw with Coventry briefly lifted Smith's side to fifth but they began to slip down the table after a 4-1 hiding at Arsenal, a 4-4 Goodison thriller with leaders Leeds and a 2-1 defeat at Middlesbrough.

With David Moyes before my testimonial match against Bologna, August 2003.

Chapter Sixteen

New Millennium New Horizons

By Christmas 1999, Everton were in mid-table limbo in 11th position but off-the-field major developments were taking place. The approaching 21st century brought with it dire, unjustified warnings to computer and machine users of a millennium bug. Bill Kenwright, though, was feeling a millennium buzz...the conclusion of his quest to buy Peter Johnson's controlling stake in the club. On Boxing Day, as Everton walloped Peter Reid's Sunderland 5-0 to retain their unbeaten home League record, the news was announced that Kenwright's long-awaited goal had been achieved. Johnson had accepted Kenwright's £20.3 million offer for his 67.9 per cent holding at £857 a share. It valued the club at £30 million and ensured that Johnson received £20,520,865 which meant he just about recovered his investment in Everton. It also came as a relief to the football authorities.

Some 14 months earlier the Football Association and the Premier and Football Leagues ordered Johnson to sell either Everton or Tranmere in which he had an 86 per cent holding. The game's rulers admitted, though, that any stringent action could have posed a threat to Tranmere. With a rising club overdraft of £16 million Johnson's agreement to sell did not cure Everton's financial headaches. It was, though, the start of a new Goodison era as the 20th century drew to a close.

Before the end of January the process of due diligence was completed and Kenwright, who invested £6.5 million in the offer package for a 35 per cent stake, officially took control in March with his fellow investors in True Blue Holdings, with Sir Philip Carter remaining as chairman. Kenwright, who also used his home as collateral for a bank loan, declared: "It's taken a long time to sink in that we're finally there. I cried when I heard we'd done it."

Everton's new boardroom group had hardly settled in when a grandiose plan to move the club to a new 55,000-seat state-of-the-art stadium at Kings Dock was mooted. Given its location and costs - originally around £155 million but spiralling towards £200 million - many observers felt the idea was doomed from the start. The saga ran for two-and-a-half years, not only polarising supporters in the 'for' and 'against' camps, but also prompting a rift between Kenwright and Gregg over how to pay for the proposed arena.

Finally, in April 2003, the dream officially died. "It was an exciting vision and I know everybody connected with Everton will be disappointed", said Kenwright. "We intend, however, to use the experience we have gained in this venture to help our ambtions to take Everton forward." Whether that future will be at a revamped Goodison, a new ground or even a stadium shared with Liverpool, only time and money will tell.

On the field, the opening months of the 21st century saw Everton's FA Cup hopes rise and then crash at the sixth-round stage. Earlier in the 1999-2000 season Smith's decision to field an under-strength side in the Worthington Cup rebounded embarrassingly when Everton were knocked out by Oxford. After a 1-1 first-leg draw at Oxford the Second Division side won 1-0 at Goodison to go through 2-1 on aggregate. It was Everton's fifth consecutive exit in this competition to a lower division club - after Millwall, Portsmouth, York and Sunderland - and their eighth in six seasons in both domestic cups.

In the FA Cup they were also made to sweat by Exeter when they met in the third round, staged that season as a one-off in December. The team in the lower reaches of Division Three held Everton to a goalless draw at home and the tie was still goalless with only five minutes of the Goodison replay remaining. Then Nick Barmby spared Everton blushes with a goal that gave them a fourth-round home clash with Birmingham. The Midlands visitors missed early chances before two penalties from David Unsworth in the last 14 minutes took Smith's side through with a 2-0 win.

Unsworth scored Everton's next goal in the competition, a 25-yard free-kick to break the stalemate in the 65th minute of the fifth-round home duel with Preston. Joe-Max Moore, a November signing from New England Revolution, clinched a 2-0 win late on. Moore's arrival co-incided with the end of midfielder Joe Parkinson's two-and-a-half year battle against injury. At 28, knee damage forced him to retire on medical advice. Moore struck again in the sixth round when he hit a 20th-minute equaliser after Steve Stone had put Aston Villa ahead in a televised Sunday tie at Goodison. But Benito Carbone, who was sent off in the last minute, scored again for Villa on the stroke of half-time to end Everton's Cup dreams for another season.

Smith had been active in the transfer market around the turn of the year, selling 1998 last-day hero Gareth Farrelly to Bolton for £400,000, Tony Grant to Manchester City for £450,000 and Michael Branch to Wolves for £500,000. He also gave free transfers to Terry Phelan and John O'Kane, who joined Fulham and Bolton respectively, and sent back striker Tommy Johnson to Celtic after two months of a three-month loan.

Into Goodison came midfielder Stephen Hughes from Arsenal and his namesake but no relation Mark Hughes, the battle-honed former Manchester United striker and acting Wales manager, who was signed on a free from Southampton. The deal for Stephen Hughes was £500,000 down with a £3 million ceiling linked to appearances. In the event he had only 33 outings before being released to Watford in July 2001.

In the League, the new millennium brought an unwanted place in the record books for Dave Watson through the own goal he conceded in the 2-2 home draw with Tottenham in January. When he unintentionally diverted David Ginola's cross into his own net he became the only Everton player to score League goals at Goodison in three different decades! By a remarkable twist of fate it was also the last of his 528 senior appearances for Everton.

Everton were ninth after their 4-0 Goodison hiding of Bradford in mid-April but two defeats and two draws in their last four games saw them finish 13th. Everton were furious, though, that they had to share the spoils with Liverpool afrter a bizarre incident in the Good Friday derby at Goodison. The 162nd League duel of the Mersey rivals was goalless and into stoppage time as Liverpool goalkeeper Sander Westerveld quickly took a free-kick. The ball struck Don Hutchison in the back as he was walking away and bounced into the Liverpool net. Everton fans were ecstatic until their celebrations were doused by referee Graham Poll's ruling that it did not count. The Hertfordshire official said that he had blown for time before the ball hit the net. But 15 seconds of the two extra minutes were left and television film showed Poll's hands by his side as the incident occurred.

In Everton's penultimate outing, three players - Everton's Dunne and Hutchison and Michael Duberry of Leeds - were sent off in a 1-1 live TV duel at Elland Road when Barmby's 10th goal of the season left him two behind 12-goal top scorer Kevin Campbell. The curtain fell on a downbeat note with a 2-0 defeat to Middlesbrough, their win secured by a late dash of Brazilian magic from Juninho, netting after a one-two with Brian Deane.

Smith was highly active in the market to prepare for his third season in charge, with his spending during the summer of 2000 approaching £20 million. Apart from the £3.75 million return of Duncan Ferguson from Newcastle, the signing that captured most people's imagination was his free transfer acquisition of Paul Gascoigne from Middlesbrough.

The former England midfielder, one of the most talented players of his generation and the inspiration of a thousand tabloid headlines, was 33 when he checked into Goodison. Although it was still there in flashes, much of the magic had gone. After making 22 starts, 16 substitute appearances and one goal Gazza joined Burnley on a free in March 2002, later taking his boots to China, Wolves (on trial) and Boston United.

The summer recruits along with Gascoigne and Ferguson were defender Alessandro Pistone (£3 million from Newcastle), versatile Steve Watson (£2.5 million from Aston Villa), midfielder Alex Nyarko (£4.5 million from Lens), midfielder Niclas Alexandersson (£2.2 million from Sheffield Wednesday and midfielder Thomas Gravesen (£2.5 million from Hamburg). In October, Smith added defender Gary Naysmith (£1.75 million from Hearts) and Israeli winger Idan Tal (£700,000 from Maccabi Petah Tikva), taking his spending on players to more than £50 million.

Helping to offset that were the sales of John Collins (£2.25 million to Fulham), Don Hutchison (£2.5 million to Sunderland), Nick Barmby (initial £5 million, rising to £6 million to Liverpool), Mitch Ward (£250,000 to Barnsley), Carl Regan (£20,000 to Barnsley) and the termination of Danny Williamson's contract. They were followed in October by Richard Dunne (£3 million to Manchester City) and Mark Hughes, who moved to Blackburn on a free transfer. It meant that Smith had recouped more than £41 million in sales, giving him a net spend at that stage of around £9 million. The question was: would the wheeling and dealing deliver a side that would bring silverware to Goodison? The answer was in the negative, with the team in closer proximity to the relegation places than the sharp end of the Premiership.

For the season's opener at Leeds, Smith was without eight players - Richard Dunne, who was suspended for the first five games, the banned Gravesen, who had been sent off in a pre-season friendly, and the injured Alexandersson, Pembridge, Gough, Xavier, Cleland and Campbell. His line-up was:

Gerrard; S. Watson, Weir, Unsworth (captain), Pistone; Gemmill (Gascoigne, 74), Nyarko, S. Hughes (Ferguson, 57), Ball; Jeffers, M. Hughes (Moore, 64). Unused substitutes: Simonsen, Cadamarteri.

Everton lost 2-0 to an Alan Smith double but in their second game Ferguson was hailed as the returning hero when he stepped back onto the Goodison stage as a sub against Charlton, and proceeded to secure victory. Jeffers had put Everton ahead early in the second half but Ferguson weighed in with two goals in the final seven minutes to announce his homecoming.

Everton went into the Anfield derby in late October in 14th place to face third-placed Liverpool. Barmby's move across Stanley Park to sign for Gerard Houllier, after rejecting a new Goodison contract worth £28,000 a week, had incensed Evertonians and they were apoplectic when the England man put Liverpool in front with a diving header. Campbell equalised with his second successive goal in front of the Kop but, after Pembridge had missed two great chances, second-half goals from Emile Heskey and a Patrik Berger penalty took Liverpool to a 3-1 win. In the process, Gravesen was sent off for bringing down Vladimir Smicer 14 minutes from the end, the 11th player in more than a century of Mersey derby history to be sent for an early bath.

Everton's Merseyside neighbours Tranmere, fourth-from-bottom of the First Division and ultimately relegated, crossed the river in the fourth round of the FA Cup - which Everton had reached by winning 2-1 at Watford - and gave Walter Smith's side a football lesson. Rovers, forever grateful to Peter Johnson's financial generosity in waiving interest payments, included former Everton striker Paul Rideout in their side and were two-up in 34 minutes through Steve Yates and Jason Koumas. Far from Everton staging a comeback, Tranmere's grip on the game tightened and Yates completed a stunning 3-0 win for John Aldridge's side after 62 minutes to leave Everton in tatters. "They just fell apart", said Rideout. "They didn't show any passion."

Early in the season Everton had bowed out of the other domestic competition, the Worthington Cup, also in embarrassing circumstances by losing on penalties to Second Division Bristol Rovers. But at least they showed some fighting spirit as they dusted themselves down after their traumatic Tranmere experience by twice coming back from behind at home to Middlesbrough to gain a 2-2 draw.

An amazing 164th League derby at Goodison left players and fans breathless...and Everton the losers by the odd goal in five. The goal that won it was distinctly odd, a free-kick more than 40 yards out swept past Paul Gerrard by Gary McAllister three minutes into stoppage time. Emile Heskey had put Liverpool ahead after only four minutes but two minutes before the break Ferguson equalised with his fourth derby goal before Markus Babbel put the visitors back in front after 57 minutes.

After Robbie Fowler thudded a penalty against a post David Unsworth showed how it is done by beating Sander Westerveld with a spot-kick seven minutes from the end. It seemed enough to share the spoils until McAllister's stunning climax to a pulsating battle which saw referee Jeff Winter dish out 12 yellow cards and send off Liverpool's Igor Biscan. Everton's six bookings brought a £25,000 FA fine.

Five days later they had another bad experience at Highbury when they sank 4-1 to Arsenal. In the late stages of the game a barechested Everton fan ran onto the pitch and offered his t-shirt to Alex Nyarko. The Ghanaian midfielder, 27 at the time, responded by walking over to the Everton dug out and asking to be substituted. Two minutes later he was replaced by Tal and after the match announced he was quitting football. Not surprisingly he re-considered that drastic decision and went on a season's loan to Monaco. Subsequently, he returned under a new Goodison regime and made another 14 senior appearances before his work permit was revoked and he quit the club in the summer of 2004.

With that little in-house difficulty still reverberating Everton went into the next match after Arsenal, a home clash with Bradford, still under a lingering threat of relegation. At half-time they were trailing to a third-minute goal from Andy Myers. Although Ferguson equalised almost from the re-start, on his 300th career appearance, Bradford were awarded two penalties in a 10-minute span. The first, taken by Robbie Blake, was saved by Gerrard in the 55th minute and from the second spot-kick Benito Carbone blazed the ball over the bar. Just before that Niclas Alexandersson scored a second goal for Everton to clinch a 2-1 win, ensuring Premiership safety and Bradford's relegation.

The supporters, though, were desperate for a cure for Everton's low-level sickness. When, they asked, would the team break out of the seemingly endless trek around the bottom half of the Premiership as the top flight's great under-achievers? Smith swooped for Alan Stubbs, signing the Kirkby-born former Bolton centre-back, who had beaten cancer while at Celtic, on a Bosman free from Parkhead while Polish-born Canadian international Tomasz Radzinski, arrived from Belgian club Anderlecht for £4.5 million.

However, prolonged contractual wrangles led to two of Goodison's rising young stars leaving. Striker Francis Jeffers, still only 20, joined Arsenal for an initial £8 million rising by a further £2 million after 60 starts. Michael Ball, the 21-year-old defender who had already been capped by England, joined Rangers for £6.5 million. Also on the move out of Goodison were reserve striker Phil Jevons and Danish midfielder Peter Degn. Jevons joined Grimsby for an initial £250,000, rising by a further £100,000 with appearances, while Degn returned to his native land on a free to Brondby.

The treatment room was still well populated when the 2001-2002 campaign opened. New signing Radzinski plus Naysmith, Gascoigne, Xavier and Cadamarteri were all ruled out of the trip to face Charlton when Smith named this line-up:

Gerrard; Watson, Weir, Stubbs, Pistone; Alexandersson (Unsworth, 81), Gemmill, Gravesen, Pembridge; Campbell, Ferguson. Substitutes unused: Simonsen, Tal, Moore, Chadwick.

A season which would see Smith's departure began on an upbeat note. Charlton were beaten 2-1 through goals from Ferguson (penalty) and Weir after Everton had come from behind to register their first opening-day win for eight years. A 1-1 home draw with Tottenham - thanks to another Ferguson penalty - featured a refereeing extravaganza by David Elleray who allowed a Mauricio Taricco foul on Gravesen to go unpunished and left the Dane needing 30 stitches in his leg, ruling him out of the next three matches. Elleray also bizarrely disallowed an Alexandersson 'goal' for a foul on Campbell in the build-up, awarded Everton's highly-dubious penalty for Gary Doherty's tussle with Campbell and sent off Doherty and Gustavo Poyet, stripping Tottenham to nine men for the last 24 minutes.

There were samba dancers at Goodison for the visit of Middlesbrough which ended in a 2-0 home win. A goal from Campbell in the first half and a volley from Gemmill early in the second put Everton top after three games in their best start since 1993-94. The intoxicating rhythm of the samba, however, faded as Everton's fortunes, echoing most seasons over the past decade, began to plunge into an all-too familiar dirge. They lost the next three League games with a run that began with a 4-1 loss at Manchester United, where Everton had taken only one point from the last 27 at stake.

That was followed in midweek by yet another cup exit to lesser bretheren when a 1-1 Worthington Cup second-round draw with First Division Crystal Palace at Goodison ended with them being eliminated on penalties - the 11th time in eight seasons they had been knocked out of a domestic cup by a lower division club. After that they went straight into the Goodison derby with Liverpool, when Merseyside was united in paying their respects to the victims of the 9 /11 attacks on America the previous Tuesday. The Union Flag and the Stars and Stripes were laid in the centre circle as the captains Kevin Campbell and Sami Hyypia placed wreaths prior to the kick-off.

When the match got underway, Campbell put Everton ahead after only five minutes. But Liverpool, whose manager Gerard Houllier said he omitted Nick Barmby from his team to shield him from verbal abuse by Everton fans still angry at his defection, hit back. First derby goals for Steven Gerrard, Michael Owen (penalty) and John Arne Riise fired Liverpool to a deserved 3-1 win to complete Everton's dismal week.

Things got no better in their next match at Blackburn when Gascoigne made his first Premiership start for 10 months and Everton wore their new salmon pink away strip. Their display was somewhat pink, too. Ferguson, who had scored from three penalties already that season, sent another weakly to Brad Friedel's right for the home keeper to save - and the game was won for Blackburn by Corrado Grabbi's only goal in English football.

When Everton lost 1-0 at Middlesbrough on New Year's Day 2002 it was their fifth consecutive Premiership defeat, the last four of them without scoring - a barren run spanning six hours. Although there had been encouraging news off the pitch, that the club's debt had fallen from £25 million in the summer to below £20 million as they urgently sought new investment, funds for Smith to strengthen the team were conspicuous by their absence. His side was now down to 13th in the Premiership and the only new signing since the summer had been Jesper Blomqvist on a free from Manchester United.

Prior to the third round FA Cup trip to Stoke, the opposition and the competition in which Howard Kendall's side secured one of his career-shaping victories in 1984, the Everton board issued a statement backing Smith. Everton duly won 1-0, achieved a similar result at home to Sunderland in the Premiership when Campbell made a shock return after 11 weeks out with a back problem and then drew 1-1 at Tottenham, when Ferguson and Campbell partnered each other for the first time since October.

In January and February, as Abel Xavier made an £800,000 move to Liverpool and Danny Cadamarteri went free to Bradford, three new players did arrive - but they were hardly the cavalry. Sweden international midfielder Tobias Linderoth was signed for £2.5 million from Norwegian club Stabaek, Republic of Ireland midfielder Lee Carsley cost £1.9 million from Coventry and French winger David Ginola on a free from Aston Villa.

Everton's 4-1 defeat of Leyton Orient and 2-1 replay win over Crewe booked them a sixth-round visit to Middlesbrough in a live televised Sunday date. The previous weekend their 1-0 defeat at West Ham left Everton one point above the relegation zone in 15th place after only one win in 13 Premiership games. Ginola had been left on the bench and, his Gallic pride offended, he went home two days before the cup tie.

The events at the Riverside proved too much even for the supportive Bill Kenwright to prolong Smith's tenure. His rudderless side was swamped by three Middlesbrough goals - from Noel Whelan, Szilard Nemeth and Paul Ince - in a seven-minute spell shortly before half-time and lost 3-0. Forty-eight hours later Smith, who had managed remarkably balanced transfer accounts by spending £59.1 million on players and recouping £59.34, met Kenwright in London to be told he was sacked.

So in a situation when perhaps even the combined talents of the Magic Circle might have struggled to make the relegation threat disappear, Kenwright and his colleagues went down the A59 to hand the task to 38-year-old Preston manager David Moyes, who had once played for Walter Smith's Scotland youth team. Moyes had a clause in his contract allowing him to speak to Premiership clubs but the previous summer had rejected the chance to manage West Ham and Southampton and signed a new deal at Deepdale. He had also turned down a coaching role under Sir Alex Ferguson at Manchester United - but the lure of Everton proved irresistible to him.

Born in Glasgow on April 25, 1963 he was a promising defender and played for Scotland's school and youth sides, turning professional with Celtic in 1980. As an 18-year-old he played against Juventus in the European Cup and the highlight of his playing career was winning a Scottish League title medal in 1982. But the following year, at the age of 20, he left Parkhead. "I had to move on to become a more successful player", said Moyes. "It sounds daft to say that I turned down a possible move to Arsenal and went to Cambridge United - but that's what I did."

After playing for Cambridge he joined Bristol City in 1985 and Shrewsbury two years later before moving back to Scotland to join Dunfermline in 1990. After a brief spell at Hamilton he joined Preston on a free transfer in 1993 and the following May captained them when they lost to Wycombe in the Division Three play-off final. Gary Peters succeeded John Beck as manager and in 1995, when Preston finished fifth in the Third Division but lost to Bury in the play-off semi-final, Moyes was appointed player-coach.

In 1996 Preston won the Third Division title and Moyes was appointed assistant to Peters. Two years later, at the age of 34, Moyes was the surprise choice as Preston manager when Peters took over the club's centre of exellence in January 1998. At the end of Moyes' first half season in charge Preston finished 15th in Division Two. The following year they finished fifth, losing to Gillingham in the play-off semi-final, before romping to the Second Division title in 2000 with 95 points.

A year later Moyes led Preston to the brink of the Premiership, finishing fourth in the First Division but losing to Bolton in the play-off final. Then, a year later Everton came knocking, unveiling Moyes as their new manager at Goodison at 7.30pm on Thursday, March 14, 2002. They agreed to pay Preston £1 million to release their prized young manager, who signed a four-year contract and, whether by accident or inspired design, hit the spot with Evertonians in his first words as their fifth manager in a decade.

"This is the people's club in Liverpool," he proclaimed, a phrase that has become part of Everton's new millennium heritage. "The people on the street support Everton and I hope to give them something they can be proud of over the next few years. I would be lying if I said it would be easy but you don't get these jobs when they are easy.

I was brought up amidst Glasgow Celtic and Glasgow Rangers and now I am in a city where football means as much as it does up there. I noticed it as soon as I walked into the building and met the people. I am from a city not unlike Liverpool. When I heard Everton were interested I knew I was privileged to get the opportunity to manage a team that gets 40,000 people supporting it. There aren't many of those." The day before his first game as manager - a home clash with Fulham for which coach Andy Holden picked the team - Paul Gascoigne left on a free to Burnley.

There could not have been a more explosive start to the Moyes era. He had hardly sat down ready to watch his new charges when they scored. Just 27 seconds had gone when Pistone's throw found Gravesen, whose knock-back was sent crashing past Edwin Van Der Sar by David Unsworth's powerful left foot. Ferguson doubled Everton's lead after 13 minutes, the first time they had scored twice in a League game since December, and although Steed Malbranque pulled a goal back and Gravesen was sent off for two bookable offences, the Moyes regime was launched in victory.

A 4-3 win at Derby moved Everton four points above the relegation belt before they came down to earth with a bang at Newcastle on Good Friday. Drawing 2-2 at half-time they crashed 6-2, the first time they had conceded six in the Premiership and the first in any League game since losing by the same score at Aston Villa in November 1989. Two days later they recovered to beat Bolton 3-1 when, with only 19 minutes gone, skipper Ferguson was sent off for the fifth time in his Everton career for punching Fredi Bobic. Costas Constantinidis followed him soon after for two bookable offences on Radzinski, who scored one of the Everton goals. Pistone and Nick Chadwick notched the others - their first for the club. A petulant response from Blomqvist after being replaced by Chadwick was blasted by Moyes, setting down one of the tenets of his management ethos - that he was in charge.

A 3-0 defeat at Chelsea and a 2-2 home draw with Leicester - when Gerrard was recalled for Simonsen for the first time since October - meant that Everton went into their Saturday evening live TV duel at Southampton still not clear of the relegation shadow. But a Steve Watson goal four minutes before the interval secured a 1-0 win and top-flight survival. On the bench, but not involved in the action, was a certain Wayne Rooney. His involvement would not be too long delayed. Everton finished 15th, seven points clear of relegation but having set an unwanted club record of six consecutive finishes in the bottom half of English football's top flight. That sequence would end after Moyes' first full season in charge.

A re-financing of the club with a £25 million loan from investment bank Bear Stearns, linked to season-ticket sales over 20 years, gave Moyes an initial £5 million transfer kitty. His first signing was Nigeria defender Joseph Yobo from Marseille, signed on a year's loan for £1 million with a permanent move concluded for a further £4 million. He also paid £3.5 million - rising to £4.5 million - to Arsenal for goalkeeper Richard Wright and £1.25 million for Juliano Rodrigo from Botafogo, who was fated to snap his cruciate ligament after only four substitute outings and was released the following summer. In addition, as part of Everton's sponsorship deal with Chinese electronics giant Keijan, midfielder Li Tie from Liaoning Bodao and defender Li Weifeng from Shenzhen Pingan joined the club. The latter returned to China after only two senior appearances but Li Tie had 33 first-team outings in his first season. As well as Ginola, Moyes also released Alex Cleland, Jesper Blomqvist, Alex Nyarko - who joined Paris St Germain - and Idan Tal, who moved to Spanish club Rayo Vallecano.

The start of 2002-03, Moyes' first full campaign in charge, co-incided with Everton celebrations of their unique feat in reaching a total of 100 years in the top flight. At their opening game against Tottenham 50 former Everton greats paraded in the Goodison centre circle for the pre-match singing of 'No Other Team'. While the former favourites walked off to the crowd's salute a certain

Wayne Rooney was lining up to become, at 16 years, 298 days, Everton's youngest Premiership player and second only to Joe Royle as their youngest in any senior game. With Yobo, Ferguson, Pistone, Watson, Chadwick, Moore and Gemmill ruled out injured, this was Everton's line-up:

Wright; Hibbert, Weir (captain), Stubbs, Naysmith; Li Tie (Rodrigo, 76), Gravesen, Pembridge; Radzinski (Unsworth, 84), Campbell, Rooney (Alexandersson, 66). Unused substitutes: Simonsen, Linderoth.

Pembridge and Radzinski scored Everton's goals in a 2-2 draw in which Les Ferdinand went on as a substitute and scored his 15th goal in 16 outings against Everton for Tottenham, Newcastle and QPR.

By the time Everton opened their Worthington Cup campaign at Wrexham at the start of October they were lying ninth in the Premiership having already used three goalkeepers. Wright then Simonsen were injured, allowing Gerrard back for two games. Fit-again Wright was back between the posts for the trip to the Racecourse Ground when it was events at the other end that made the headlines. Rooney, sent on as a 64th-minute sub for Radzinski, struck twice in the last seven minutes to give Everton a 3-0 victory. They were his first senior goals for the club at the age of 16 years, 342 days, smashing the Everton record set in 1937 by Tommy Lawton when he was aged 17 years, 132 days.

Rooney was a substitute again in the next match, a remarkable 3-0 defeat at Manchester United when Everton played well but conceded all three goals in the last four minutes. A Ruud van Nistelrooy penalty - for which Weir was sent off after fouling Ole Gunnar Solksjaer - was sandwiched between two goals from Paul Scholes to leave Moyes and his team shaking their heads in disbelief. Three days later Ferguson, who had made only one substitute appearance since the start of the season, underwent back surgery to a sciatic nerve which would keep him out until March. But as the Scot began his long lay-off, young Rooney was about to zoom into national prominence.

The home clash with Arsenal was deadlocked at 1-1, through goals from Radzinski and Freddie Ljungberg, and had reached the last minute when Rooney, an 80th-minute substitute for Radzinski, seized on a Gravesen pass. With merely a glance, he unleashed a vicious 25-yard right-foot shot that flew off the bar and past David Seaman. Arsenal's 30-match unbeaten Premiership run was in tatters. "Remember the name... Wayne Rooney," ITV commentator Clive Tyldesley implored the nation. They could hardly forget it as Rooney's stock and reputation took wing, his face plastered over the tabloids. That goal made him not only Everton's youngest League scorer at 16 years, 360 days but also the Premiership's youngest scorer.

Moyes, though, aware that Rooney still had much to learn and keen to protect his protege, took a step back from all the hype. He used Rooney mainly as a substitute in the Premiership and when he sent him on at Birmingham on Boxing Day to replace Radzinski he was walking off sooner than the Everton manager expected. A two-footed tackle on Steve Vickers was met with a red card by referee David Elleray, thus giving Rooney the unwanted label of being the youngest player to be sent off in the Premiership. Ironically, on the same day as the Everton player's dismissal James Milner's goal for Leeds at Sunderland broke Rooney's two-month old record as the Premiership's youngest scorer. He was aged 16 years. 357 days, three days younger than Rooney.

In the game preceding the trip to Birmingham Everton went to Anfield and came away with a goalless draw which meant that for the first time since 1986 they went into Christmas ahead of Liverpool in the table. They were fourth, a point ahead of their fifth-placed neighbours. It might have been more but for Stephane Henchoz diverting a goal-bound shot from substitute Rooney onto the bar. Moyes, though, handed Rooney his fifth Premiership start in the goalless home clash with Bolton in their last match of the year when he demonstrated the range of his talents and was unlucky not to score. He had five scoring attempts saved by Jussi Jaaskelainen and also hit the bar. It was the first time under Moyes that Everton had failed to score at home in the Premiership. Next time out, against Manchester City at Goodison on New Year's Day, they scored twice through Watson and a stoppage-time strike from Radzinski but were held 2-2 - their fourth consecutive draw. Rooney's booking, though, was his fifth to take him to a one-game suspension which, added to his three-games for being dismissed at Birmingham, meant he would serve a four-game ban. He signed off in the most amazing circumstances with a place in the Everton side that was on the receiving end of the most humiliating result in the club's history, even more stunning than their home FA Cup exit to Tranmere in 2001.

The third-round draw paired Everton with Shrewsbury, seventh-from-bottom of Division Three, at Gay Meadow. Former Everton hero Kevin Ratcliffe, the most successful captain in the club's history, was manager of their opponents who were given two chances by the pundits and the bookies - little and none. Then Nigel Jemson put Shrewsbury in front after 38 minutes, only for his goal to be cancelled out by Alexandersson after 59 minutes. A Goodison replay was looming when Jemson, with two minutes left, beat Richard Wright to score again and clinch a sensational victory. With Everton having won at Wrexham and at Newcastle (on penalties) before losing 4-1 at Chelsea in the Worthington Cup, their shock demise at Shrewsbury meant that for the first time since 1959-60 Everton would not have a single home cup game during the season.

Striker Brian McBride, signed on a three-month loan from American club Columbus Crew following Joe-Max Moore's departure after his work permit expired, scored at Tottenham first-time out. But it was a distinctly unhappy debut for goalkeeper Espen Baardsen, released by Watford and signed short- term by Moyes because of injuries to Gerrard and Simonsen. During the pre-match warm-up at White Hart Lane Wright's knee collapsed under him and Baardsen was plunged into action, the first time Everton had used four keepers in a season since 1926-27. Sadly for the Norwegian he was beaten four times, Robbie Keane collecting a hat-trick after Gustavo Poyet had scored Tottenham's first in their 4-3 win. It was Baardsen's only appearance and he was released after two months with the club.

The defeat at Tottenham still left Everton sixth in the table, a point ahead of Liverpool. Three straight wins - 2-1 at home to Sunderland, 2-1 at Bolton and 2-0 at home to Leeds - put them level on points with fourth-placed Chelsea by February and Europe beckoned. But they were jolted by a 2-1 defeat at Charlton when Rooney returned as a late substitute after his four-game ban a few hours before being named for the first time in the England squad. When he faced Australia as a substitute on Febuary 12 he became England's youngest player at the age of 17 years, 111 days, lowering Michael Owen's record of 18 years, 59 days.

Moyes kept him on the Everton bench until putting him into the starting line-up at Arsenal in March for the first time since New Year's Day and only the seventh time in the Premiership. Lightning did strike twice - Rooney scoring another superb goal. But Arsenal avenged their Goodison defeat with a 2-1 win and it meant that Liverpool went above Everton for the first time since mid-December.

Rooney scored again a week later, heading his fifth Premiership goal in a 2-1 win over Newcastle four days after his first England start and competitive debut against Turkey. Unsworth scored Everton's other goal with a penalty as Moyes' team climbed back above Liverpool and stayed there with a 2-1 win at West Brom to inject even more spice into the Mersey derby at Goodison in mid-April. Illustrating Everton's progress under Moyes was the fact that they were 7-5 favourites to beat Liverpool, who were priced at 8-5. In the event Liverpool came out on top with a 2-1 win, Owen putting them ahead, Unsworth's 25th successful penalty in 28 attempts equalising before Danny Murphy's spectacular 25-yard winner. Everton's misery was compounded by the dismissals of Naysmith and Weir.

A 4-1 crash at Chelsea - the first time they had lost successive League games under Moyes - was another blow to Everton's European hopes. But following a Kevin Campbell goal a stoppage-time left-foot strike by Rooney the day after Moyes' 40th birthday gave them a 2-1 home win over Aston Villa. It kept Everton sixth, three points ahead of Blackburn and still on course for the UEFA Cup. However, a 2-0 defeat at Fulham while Blackburn were drawing with West Brom stretched the Euro battle to the last day. Everton were home to new champions Manchester United while Blackburn, two points behind them, were at Tottenham. Agonisingly for Moyes and his squad after Campbell had put them ahead with his 50th senior Everton goal, United equalised through David Beckham and then won through a highly- disputed penalty as Blackburn were winning 4-0 at White Hart Lane. Referee Mike Riley awarded the penalty for what he judged to be a foul by Alan Stubbs on Ruud van Nistelrooy, a decision that television evidence made even more debatable. The Dutch striker got to his feet and sent the spot-kick beyond Richard Wright to win the match and the Golden Boot with his 25th Premiership goal and 44th overall for the season.

Four defeats in Everton's last five games had been costly. They had missed out on a UEFA Cup ticket by one place after being in the top six since October. Yet they had come a long way in one season under Moyes, who was deservedly named Manager of the Year by the League Managers' Association. Their finishing position of seventh with 59 points and 17 wins represented their best campaign since 1995-96, when they finished sixth with 61 points and 17 wins. It was a far cry from the Japanese water torture style drip-drip of incessant relegation battles which was reflected in Everton's highest average attendance for 25 years, more than 38,000.

Optimism ran high for the following season but with the unpredictabilty that makes football so compelling, if agonising, it was to be an anguished campaign, statistically the worst in Everton history. It was not until September 1, with the season already underway, that Moyes, operating under severe financial constraints, managed to bolster his squad.

Everton opened the season with a 2-1 defeat at Highbury, even though Arsenal had been reduced to 10 men from the 25th minute when Sol Campbell was sent off for bringing down Gravesen. Li Tie was also dismissed after a second booking two minutes from the end. A Thierry Henry penalty and a Robert Pires strike put the home side 2-0 in front before a late reply from Radzinski. Moyes, without the injured Campbell, Gemmill, Carsley, Alexandersson and suspended Ferguson, paraded this side:

Wright; Pistone, Yobo, Stubbs (captain), Unsworth (Li Tie, 67); Watson, Gravesen, Linderoth (Rooney, 57), Pembridge (Naysmith, 67); Radzinski, Chadwick. Unused substitutes: Simonsen, Weir.

They opened their home programme with a 3-1 win over Fulham before a midweek trip to Charlton, the 50th Premiership game under Moyes. A great 72nd-minute goal from Rooney ensured a 2-2 draw, giving the manager half-century figures of 22 wins, 10 draws and 18 defeats. But the limitations of the Everton squad, still hit by a batch of absent casualties, were exposed four days later when they faced Liverpool at Goodison. Wright's knee injury at Charlton meant a recall in goal for Steve Simonsen. It was his first appearance for a year. It would also be his last for Everton before leaving to join Stoke the following summer.

Simonsen saved impressively from Michael Owen and Harry Kewell but was beaten by an Owen penalty late in the first half. Owen added another after the break and the gods conspired against Simonsen late on when he slipped running off his line and from a cross, headed out by Stubbs, Harry Kewell scored his first Liverpool goal in a 3-0 win. It was the biggest margin of derby victory for 20 years and prompted Moyes into urgent action to beat the transfer deadline. He brought in four players for £3.5 million.

England international Nigel Martyn, the 37-year-old Leeds goalkeeper who was allowed to slip through Everton's clutches during the Peter Johnson era, finally arrived for a nominal fee. Republic of Ireland winger Kevin Kilbane, 26, was signed from Sunderland for £1 million, 20-year-old striker James McFadden for £1.25 million from Motherwell and 22-year-old striker Francis Jeffers returned on a £500,000 season's loan from Arsenal. Moyes, who had sold winger Kevin McLeod to QPR for £250,000 a fortnight earlier, recouped a further £500,000 rising to £750,000 by selling Mark Pembridge to Fulham.

As 2004 unfolded Everton's fortunes plummeted. Nine games without a win saw them fall to 16th in the Premiership, three points above relegation, and they bowed out of the FA Cup to Fulham. Jeffers scrambled a replay with a late equaliser in the fourth-round clash at Goodison after Fulham had gone ahead through Sean Davis. The on-loan striker did the same at Craven Cottage to take the second meeting into extra time. But Steed Malbranque's strike in the additional period proved the knock-out blow.

A 3-3 draw at Southampton left Everton with only 26 points from 26 games, their lowest-ever Premiership total at that stage. A headed goal from Ferguson - named captain for the first time in two years in the absence of injured Stubbs - was sandwiched between two from Rooney. But two Southampton goals in the last nine minutes cost Moyes and his team two precious points as the threat of the drop grew menacingly.

They suffered a nightmare finale to the season, comprising four straight defeats. The agony began at Goodison as Blackburn completed the double over Everton with a 1-0 win. They fared no better at relegated Wolves despite an early Leon Osman goal to celebrate his first senior start for the club after returning from a three-month loan at Derby. Osman headed Everton in front early on but they collapsed and lost 2-1 to the doomed Black Country club.

Despite that poor performance and result Everton's Premiership survival was assured the next day when Leeds lost at Bolton, who were Everton's last home foes of the season. Youri Djorkaeff put Bolton in front in the first half when the visitors were dominant. Everton, doubtless responding to some well chosen half-time words from Moyes, improved after the interval and Ferguson equalised, only the second goal scored by an Everton striker in the last seven games. But with three minutes left French star Djorkaeff scored again to give Bolton their first League win at Goodison since 1961.

Worse was to follow a week later when the curtain came down on the season at the City of Manchester Stadium, also known as Eastlands. Badlands would have been a more fitting name as far as humiliated Everton were concerned. They crashed 5-1 to Manchester City, their token goal coming from substitute Campbell on the hour, their heaviest defeat since losing 6-2 at Newcastle more than two years earlier. It completed the worst season statistically in Everton history, applying three-points-for-a-win throughout. A meagre total of 39 points left them in 17th place after a season in which they managed only one away win in all competitions. The one ray of brightness for the club was the fact that Goodison's average Premiership attendance of 38,837 was their highest on record.

But the Goodison figure whose future was in the melting pot was Wayne Rooney, who had made 31 starts in 40 appearances during the season, scoring nine goals and collecting 12 bookings. Overall he had scored 17 goals in 77 Everton outings, receiving 20 yellow cards and one red. During the season he had added the record of England's youngest goalscorer to his burgeoning portfolio after his goal in Macedonia at the age of 17 and 317 days.

Rooney flew out on European Championship duty with Sven-Goran Eriksson's squad as speculation over his future reached feverish proportions. It would stretch through a summer of turmoil and internal convulsion at Everton. Kenwright and the board took the decision not to renew chief executive Michael Dunford's contract. The former Derby secretary and general manager completed 25 years at the Baseball Ground before becoming Everton secretary when chief executive Jim Greenwood retired in November 1994. In May 2000 he was promoted to chief executive by Kenwright in apprecation of his work following Peter Johnson's resignation as chairman.

To succeed Dunford, Everton turned to a man who used to clean Kevin Keegan's boots after becoming Bill Shankly's last signing as Liverpool manager. Trevor Birch became an apprentice at Anfield after leaving Ormskirk Grammar School as a 16-year-old in 1974. At 23 he took the career-changing decision to quit football, joined Southport firm Smith Forshaw and went off to study accountancy at Liverpool Polytechnic, emerging with first class BA Honours. Birch joined Arthur Young, later Ernst & Young, where he was elevated to a partnership. In February 2002 he was appointed successor to Colin Hutchinson as Chelsea managing director.

Despite debts of £97 million at Stamford Bridge he laid the path for the takeover of Roman Abramovich, who funded the biggest spending spree ever seen in British football. Birch quit Chelsea - with a pre-agreed £2.25 million pay-off - after Peter Kenyon's arrival from Manchester United in September 2003. Two months later he moved to Leeds where he rescued the club from the threat of bankruptcy and helped negotiate the £22 million takeover of the club by Gerald Krasner's consortium.

On June 1, 2004 Birch was unveiled as Everton's new chief executive as Kenwright changed title from vice-chairman to chairman, Sir Philip Carter became life president and Keith Tamlin, a director since August 1984, was made deputy life president. The board now consisted of Kenwright, Arthur Abercromby, Jon Woods and Paul Gregg, later supplemented by Anita Gregg. Introducing Birch to the media Kenwright declared: "We have an excellent chief executive who is also a football man - and that isn't common. I want to be his sounding board and I want him to run this club, which is what a chief executive should do. They should dictate the policy of the football club."

Birch's tenure, though, would be brief and stormy at a club with a debt of around £30 million and a 25-year securitisation loan repayable at £2.77 million a year. But just 46 days after arriving Birch quit his £500,000 a year job, with immediate effect, on July 16. The announcement came just an hour before the team began their opening pre-season fixture against Serbian side FK Zeleznik in Austria.

Birch walked out of the club after the board rejected his plans to sell Everton following his blunt warning to the True Blue directors that they may have to sell their shares at a loss to save Everton. His walk-out came only hours after Gregg, who had negotiated the shirt sponsorship deal with Thailand's Chang Beer, had revealed his own plans to restructure the club with the media perceiving a power battle between Gregg and Kenwright and a rift between Birch and Moyes.

Gregg proposed dissolving True Blue's shareholding back into the Everton Football Club Co Ltd and said the aim was to raise £15 million from outside investors and another £15 million from 15,000 fans buying £1,000 worth of shares each. "The constitution of True Blue makes it very difficult for other investors to be part of Everton Football Club because the control is within True Blue", said Gregg. "Shareholders in True Blue should ultimately change their shares for Everton shares. Then there will be a new opportunity to broaden the base for investment and bring new directors onto the board. At the moment investors could put money into the club but still not have a voice in how the club goes forward if they are not part of True Blue."

As Everton went back to square one in their search for a new chief executive, Rooney returned from a valuation-hiking four-goal European Championship display with a broken toe, sustained in England's ill-fated quarter-final against the hosts Portugal. The question of whether he was staying or leaving Everton dominated the media and the thoughts of every Evertonian. Arsene Wenger had no doubts. "He's going to Manchester United," affirmed the Arsenal manager.

Moyes, meanwhile, grew concerned at the lack of new talent. The summer departure of 15 players, ranging from academy youngsters to first teamers, trimmed the wage bill by £5 million and income from transfers pulled in more than £3 million. Yet the only two signings by Moyes were striker Marcus Bent for £450,000 from Ipswich, who had loaned him to Leicester, and midfielder Tim Cahill, a £2 million capture from Millwall, whose Olympics duty with

Australia would mean he would miss the opening three games of the new season. A £2.5 million bid for Robbie Savage was dismissed by Birmingham as 'derisory' while a reported £7 million offer to Leeds for Manchester United-bound Alan Smith proved fruitless.

Departures from Goodison included striker Tomasz Raszinski, who failed to agree contract terms and joined Fulham for £1.75 million, midfielder Tobias Linderoth, signed by FC Copenhagen for £1.5 million, and out-of-contract goalkeepers Steve Simonsen, to Stoke, and Paul Gerrard to Nottingham Forest. David Unsworth, also out of contract, joined Portsmouth, Alex Nyarko had his work permit refused and was released, Francis Jeffers ended his loan spell from Arsenal and joined Charlton for £2.6 million, reserve defender Peter Clarke moved to Blackpool for £150,000 and Scot Gemmill was released and joined Leicester. In addition, Thomas Gravesen refused a new offer to double his wages to £40,000 a week, meaning his exit sooner or later in the final year of his contract was almost inevitable.

Rooney was still injured and out of action along with Chinese midfielder Li Tie when the curtain went up on the new season with a Sunday afternoon live televised home clash with Arsenal. Eight days earlier, at Everton's final pre-season match against Real Sociedad at Goodison, a banner proclaimed: 'From Sir John Moores To Death's Doors! 125 Years.' That mood amongst supporters was deepened by the events of the opening League fixture for which Moyes named this team:

Martyn; Pistone, Yobo, Stubbs (captain), Naysmith; Osman (Ferguson, 71), Gravesen, Carsley, Kilbane; Campbell, McFadden (Bent, 46). Unused substitutes: Wright, Watson, Hibbert.

Everton were dismantled by a superb Arsenal display, the 4-1 scoreline for the Gunners if anything a touch modest for their control of the contest. Dennis Bergkamp and Jose Antonio Reyes put them 2-0 up by half-time, Freddie Ljungberg and Robert Pires scoring in the second half. Everton's reply from Lee Carsley was no more than academic and as the pundits and bookmakers picked over the wreckage of their display, they found evidence to confirm their prediction that Moyes and his side would struggle to avoid the drop.

Statisticians pointed out that Everton's front two against Arsenal, Kevin Campbell and James McFadden, had scored just once in their last combined 46 appearances, with McFadden yet to break his duck. The record books showed, too, that on the last occasion Everton had lost their opening game 4-1 at home - to Tottenham in August 1984 - they went on to win the championship. Cue hollow laughter

But a new Everton was about to emerge, fashioned by a frank forum of opinion involving Moyes and his players during a pre-season trip to the United States and a needs-must tactical response by the manager to the impending loss of Rooney, further depleting a less than bountiful squad. During their stay in America a grand, no-holds-barred stocktaking exercise was held between Moyes and his players. Inquests on the previous dismal season, views on various aspects of the team and its performances and the relationship between Moyes and the players all featured on the open, bonding agenda. From it was forged a new spirit of unity which would prove to be a crucial factor in one of the most remarkably improved performances of the Premiership era, one which mocked all the predictions.

Everton's second game was at Crystal Palace for which Moyes brought in new signing Marcus Bent - who had made his debut as a substitute against Arsenal - and Tony Hibbert for McFadden and Alessandro Pistone. It was the start of the great Everton fightback. Two goals from Gravesen, a first- half penalty and one after the interval, plus a goal from Bent on his first start for the club brought a 3-1 win, ending a run of 12 League and Cup away games without victory since the previous December.

The day before Everton's home clash with West Brom the Rooney saga took another twist. The 18-year-old submitted a transfer request after Everton had turned down three bids for the player from Newcastle and Manchester United, the offers ranging from £20 million to £23.5 million. Only 18 months after being handed his first professional contract, which lifted his weekly wage from £92 to more than £10,000, Rooney had rejected Goodison overtures to sign a new £50,000 a week deal for five years.

While Rooney's pursuers pondered their next move and Moyes declared that it was in the youngster's best interests to stay at Goodison, the team carried on without the still-injured teenager. Two goals from Leon Osman, taking his tally to three in six consecutive starts, gave Everton a 2-1 win over West Brom when a banner aimed at Rooney stated: 'There's only one greedy bastard.' Osman's display was impressive and a triumph for perseverance because the 23-year-old's progress at Goodison had been severely hampered by injuries, including cruciate ligament damage.

Next up for Everton was a Bank Holiday Monday noon kick-off at Manchester United, the day before the August 31 transfer deadline. By now United had made an increased bid of £25 million for Rooney, still short of

Everton's £30 million valuation. Goodison chairman Kenwright and United chief executive David Gill held talks until shortly before kick-off at Old Trafford where Rooney was conspicuous by his absence. It was on this occasion that we had the first glimpse of the re-shaped Everton that would herald a season's performance beyond wildest ambition.

Moyes paraded a formation switching between 4-1-4-1 and 4-5-1 with Tim Cahill making his debut in midfield, Carsley operating between the engine room and back four protection and Bent filling a lone striking role. With a display of character and determination Everton emerged with a goalless draw, the first time in the new millennium they had avoided defeat by United and ending a run of nine straight losses to Sir Alex Ferguson's side. The attendance of 67,803 was the biggest for any Everton away League game and probably nobody in that crowd doubted that Rooney would be arriving at Old Trafford.

A day later the inevitable happened. Rooney joined United in a £27 million transfer that comprised an immediate £10 million payment, a further £10 million due on August 1, 2005 and another £7 million dependent on United's success, a contract renewal and England appearances. Rooney signed a six-year contract until June 30, 2010 on reported terms of £50,000 a week plus extras. United also revealed that the player's agents, Proactive Sports Management Ltd, would receive £1.5 million.

Most Everton fans, who felt stabbed in the back by a lad who not long before had declared undying allegiance to the royal blue of Everton, reacted predictably with the word 'traitor' the most commonly heard on the streets of Merseyside, on radio phone-ins and in letters to newspapers. Moyes, naturally, was sad to lose Rooney's massive young talent, saying: "This a real blow to us. I'm so disappointed because how often in life do you get to work with a genius like Wayne Rooney. I have enjoyed it. I've had a great relationship with Wayne. I think we've had one since we first came together. Obviously I feared that this day might come. If you have an offer on the table that's the biggest contract in the club's history and it isn't signed then the writing is on the wall." Kenwright admitted: "I feel numb but I got the best deal I could for Everton Football Club. Simple as that." Ferguson bubbled: "I'm excited. I think we've got the best young player this country has seen in 30 years. I've known about his potential but the way he's played has been phenomenal. We couldn't afford to miss him, especially after we learned of Newcastle's interest."

Amidst the swirling reverberations of Rooney's departure Everton returned to Manchester the following Saturday and ended a run of three straight defeats at City with a 1-0 win. Cahill showed the scoring flair that would be a feature of his season by collecting the only goal on the hour. Seconds later, though, he was sent off by referee Steve Bennett, who gave the Australian midfielder a second yellow card for lifting his jersey in celebration.

Two days before the win at City the club's new chief executive, 47-year-old Keith Wyness, was unveiled to shareholders who had called an extraordinary general meeting after being alarmed by Everton's turbulent summer. Wyness, who gained a degree in industrial economics at Nottingham University, served three years as chief executive of Aberdeen. He also had experience in the travel industry with British Airways and Radisson and was managing director of Olympic Club, a marketing company at the Sydney Olympics.

The man hired to fill the breach left by Trevor Birch's departure, and who later joined the board, told the 300 shareholders present: "My ambition is to make Everton one of the best managed clubs in the Premiership. We need viability and stability. I will do everything to support the chairman and the board. It is also important to support the manager. Everything the club does off the pitch should be targeted towards that aim. I am here to support the manager and that is the key to how I will be operating."

Kenwright, who warmly shook hands with Paul Gregg, told the EGM that to pave the way for new investment in the club by Fortress Sports Fund they would dissolve True Blue Holdings "as soon as practically possible." He also pledged transfer money for Moyes - "He will have a considerable pot in January and in the summer" - and reported that £700,000 would be spent on improvements at the club's youth academy in Netherton while plans for a new training complex at Halewood would continue.

The proposed Fortress Sports investment would become a soap opera but, back on the pitch and even without the banned Cahill, the players showed that life without Rooney could still be productive with a 1-0 home win over Middlesbrough through a Bent strike. That victory lifted Everton into the unlikely position of third and although the prospect would have been peremptorily dismissed at that early stage, they would remain in the top four for the rest of the season. When they won 3-2 at Norwich it was their best start since 1980-81 when the club also won seven, drew one and lost two of their opening 10 League games. Goals from Kevin Kilbane, Bent and Ferguson, who was now settling into a regular substitute's role, secured Everton's first win at Carrow Road since 1988.

Third-placed Everton went into the season's first Mersey derby in December with their tails up and ahead of Liverpool in the table. Due to increased seating the attendance of 40,552 was the highest ever at Goodison in the Premiership and the biggest since September 1989. Home fans, packed in for the lunchtime kick-off, were yearning for their first win over Liverpool since September 1999, with David Weir the only player remaining from that Everton team.

The 171st league derby, the first for Liverpool's new Spanish manager Rafael Benitez, was into the 68th minute when Liverpool defender Josemi lost possession to Kilbane. The ball was ferried into Carsley's path by Bent some 20 yards out. Although his shot lacked venom it was accurately hit and when it beat unsighted Liverpool goalkeeper Chris Kirkland it sparked an explosion of joy from home supporters.

When referee Steve Bennett blew the final whistle the noise threatened to raise the Goodison roof. Everton had beaten Liverpool at home for the first time since October 1997, ending a nine-game derby sequence without victory, and were now in second place 12 points ahead of their seventh-placed neighbours. It was Everton's biggest lead over their city rivals since winning the title in 1985 and biggest approaching Christmas since 1969. Goalscorer Carsley, who had also curbed the danger of Gerrard, was overjoyed. "It's as if we've won the championship," he beamed. Equally delighted Moyes was moved to utter the memorable phrase: "If you shoot for the moon you sometimes hit the stars."

In the week leading up to the derby Everton's annual general meeting was told that True Blue Holdings, which owned 72 per cent of Everton and comprised Bill Kenwright, Paul and Anita Gregg, Arthur Abercromby and Jon Woods, had been placed into liquidation and that the members had become Everton shareholders. The move was to pave the way for investment by Brunei-based trust Fortress Sports Fund through two new share issues - the first worth around £12.8 million for 29.9 per cent with the option of a second for £17.2 million, giving them a majority shareholding of 50.1 per cent.

Chris Samuelson, the Geneva-based financier behind the consortium, told the meeting: "We are not looking for control of Everton Football Club in any way. Every fund invests for some gain but we want to see a successful football club. I have supported the club all my life and I am delighted to be able to bring money to the table which is useful. We have no planned exit stategy and we are prepared to put money in and keep the club growing."

On the field Everton followed their derby triumph with a goalless draw at Blackburn - unbeaten for the third time in their black away kit - and on Boxing

Day beat Manchester City 2-1 at Goodison. Cahill, who had opened his Everton scoring account with a header at City in September, nodded in another against them. It was his third Everton goal and all headers. Robbie Fowler scored in similar manner late in the first half. It was the former Liverpool striker's seventh career goal against Everton and when he patted his head and ran off the pitch in a bizarre celebration it earned him a booking. City's hopes of a point, however, were crushed by Bent who, not to be outdone, swooped to make it 2-1 to Everton - with a 63rd-minute header.

Everton's Christmas then turned sour with two straight defeats. They went to Charlton and lost to two goals - from Talal El Karkouri and Hermann Hreidarsson - in the last eight minutes. As well as seeing the end of their seven-game unbeaten run they lost injured goalkeeper Nigel Martyn, and had Duncan Ferguson sent off for the seventh time as an Everton player for elbowing Hreidarsson only 10 minutes after replacing Bent late in the second half. The dismissal brought the big Scottish striker a three-match ban and a club fine of two-weeks' wages. Martyn was out even longer. His calf injury, which led to Wright replacing him a minute before the interval, ruled him out of six League and Cup games. It also ended his 54-match unbroken Premiership run spanning 15 months stretching back to his appearance as a substitute for Wright against Newcastle in September 2003. Wright's first League start since then, at Tottenham on New Year's Day, was a nightmare for him and the rest of the team. They crashed 5-2, their heaviest defeat of the season at that stage, as the London club completed the double over them.

Everton kept their fans on tenterhooks three days later against Portsmouth in their first home appearance of 2005. Before kick-off the fans welcomed £6 million new club record signing James Beattie, whose move from Southampton had been completed only hours before the match. But it was a defender who had the supporters on their feet. A rare goal from Alan Stubbs put Everton ahead within the first half-hour. It was his first for Everton at Goodison, where he had scored for Bolton in their FA Cup win 11 years earlier. It was also his first Everton goal home or away for almost three years to the day since scoring in the FA Cup at Stoke in January 2002, a run of 111 senior games. That included a club record for an outfield player of 88 Premiership outings without scoring. But no sooner had the cheering stopped for his welcome goal than Portsmouth went downfield and equalised through Ayegbeni Yakubu's wonder strike.

A share of the spoils seemed certain when the clock showed the scheduled two minutes of stoppage time had overrun by 34 seconds. Then Osman swung his left foot and the ball arrowed beyond Shaka Hislop for his fourth goal of the season. Osman's previous strike had been another late effort, the 88th-minute winner against Southampton at the same Gwladys Street End in October. His latest goal completed Everton's fourth consecutive double over Portsmouth, after achieving it the previous season and in 1987-88 and 1957-58. That last-gasp win meant that Everton were lying fourth with 43 points from 22 games, six points ahead of fifth-placed Liverpool, as they prepared to open their FA Cup campaign at Plymouth.

The trip to Home Park to face the Championship side in an early-evening live TV duel was widely believed to be a tricky one. With Ferguson banned, Moyes handed new capture Beattie his debut as a lone striker with Bent wide on the right. He also rested Gravesen and Cahill. The importance of an early goal in such ties can never be over-stated and one arrived for Everton with only 16 minutes on the clock, courtesy of impressive Osman's first cup goal for the club. He played a one-two with debutant Beattie before lofting his shot over home keeper Romain Larrieu. Two minutes later McFadden doubled their advantage after Kilbane's flick from a Pistone throw. Athough Bjarni Gudjonsson cut the deficit before the interval Nick Chadwick, sent on as a substitute for Bent, seized on a pass from another substitute, Cahill, to fire Everton's third goal.

Moyes used Gravesen as his third substitute and his 12 minutes of action were his last in an Everton jersey. The Dane's rejection of new terms had made his departure almost inevitable with speculation about his future lasting for months. The following Friday Everton accepted Real Madrid's £2.5 million offer and the combative, shaven-headed midfielder was off to join Beckham, Owen, Zidane and company at the Bernabeu.

For the second time in less than five months Moyes had lost a key player. He tried to keep Gravesen but as he would have been a free agent at the end of the season Everton had no option but to sell. Gravesen left expressing his appreciation of Everton fans. "They're amazing", he said. "They used to roar my name. For a foreign player that is special." Also moving through the Goodison departure lounge during the January transfer window was Kevin Campbell. He had made only four starts that season and left for West Brom on a free. His goals after arriving from Turkey in 1999 were instrumental in Everton fending off relegation and, re-invigorated by his move to The Hawthorns, he helped perform another rescue act as West Brom became the first team to survive after being bottom of the Premiership at Christmas.

Cahill's third goal in his last five League outings secured a point against Middlesbrough at the Riverside. But it was hardly Sunday-best behaviour by the players. Four minutes from the end there was a 21-man melee in the Middlesbrough net. Both clubs were charged with failing to control their players and were fined £8,000 by the FA.

Beattie, booked in his first two appearances, made his home debut against Charlton and was denied a goal by the woodwork. But it was a below par Everton display and Charlton's 1-0 win, clinched by Matt Holland's 25-yard spectacular in first-half stoppage time, completed their first League double over the Goodison club since 1950. It was Everton's sixth Premiership defeat, all against London clubs following two reverses against Tottenham and losses against Arsenal and Chelsea.

But a week later Everton had the taste of victory again in the FA Cup with a 3-0 home success against promotion-chasing Championship side Sunderland. Moyes made three changes, bringing in McFadden, Naysmith and Yobo for Bent, Hibbert and Weir. McFadden responded by opening the scoring inside the first 10 minutes, his third goal in four starts. Beattie, somewhat fortuitously, claimed his first Everton goal even though his 27th-minute shot was diverted into the net off Danny Collins. It was Everton's 700th in the FA Cup. Rising star Cahill rounded off the fourth-round victory with his sixth goal of the season and his fourth header. He had now scored four times in his last seven starts.

Before the close of the transfer window Moyes moved for two foreign midfielders. Guillaume Plessis was recruited from French club Lens on a six-month contract while Mikel Arteta was signed from Real Sociedad on a £1 million loan to the end of the season with a view to making the move permanent for a further £1.85 million. Although Plessis sat on the bench for seven games he was destined not to taste first-team football and was released at the end of the season. But the classy touches of Arteta were soon to be evident at the heart of the Everton team.

With Arteta recovering from knee ligament damage neither figured in the home clash with Norwich at the start of February when Nigel Martyn returned in goal and, like his opposite number Robert Green, did not have a save to make in the first half. The keepers were busier after the break but with 12 minutes left, and the game goalless, fate smiled on Everton when two substitutions by Moyes paid dividends. Bent, who had replaced the disappointing Beattie, connected with a McFadden cross. Green beat out his header but as Duncan Ferguson, sent on to replace Weir, stretched for the loose ball it rolled off Gary Doherty's foot into his own net.

Beattie had one of those returns to a former club that players dream of when he scored after only four minutes at Southampton - his first Premiership goal for Everton. The gangling Peter Crouch equalised with a looping header before half-time and Henri Camara put Southampton ahead with a chipped shot over Martyn 10 minutes into the second half, which saw Arteta make his debut as substitute for Stubbs.

Everton were heading for defeat when, deep into stoppage time, second-half substitute Bent exchanged passes with Ferguson, whose entry from the bench chalked up his 200th League appearance for the club. Bent raced wide of Calum Davenport and from an acute angle fired a wonderful equaliser that prompted ecstatic congratulations from his team-mates and a joyful sprint down the touchline by Moyes.

He was far from joyful a week later when Everton hosted runaway leaders Chelsea in a lunchtime kick-off. Just eight minutes had elapsed when Beattie suffered an aberration by bizarrely butting William Gallas in the back of the head and giving referee Mike Riley no option but to show him the red card. Home fans were stunned as Beattie trooped off having received his first red card and the second earliest dismissal in Everton history. Only Sandy Brown was sent off sooner, receiving his marching orders after four minutes against Leeds United at Goodison in November 1964.

Everton's agony was complete when Gallas teed up Eidur Gudjohnsen for the game's only goal in a match that set a new post-war record of 30 League games at Goodison without a penalty for either side. Moyes fined his new signing two-weeks' wages and as 26-year-old Beattie faced the first suspension of his career, his fortunes were to dip even lower. He was hurt in a late-night attack outside a Birmingham nightclub and then suffered medial ligament damage to his left knee, restricting him to just one substitute outing in the next six matches.

Moyes, meanwhile, found himself running out of strikers as he braced himself for a FA Cup fifth-round collision with Manchester United, which heralded Wayne Rooney's first return to Goodison. On top of Beattie's ban and the £250,000 sale of Nick Chadwick to his FA Cup victims Plymouth less than a fortnight earlier, Ferguson was ruled out with a back injury. His plans were rocked, too, by the absence of Cahill, whose foul on Chelsea's Claude

Makelele brought his fifth booking and a one-game suspension.

Moyes settled on a line-up that had Bent as the lone striker, Arteta starting for the first time and forward James Vaughan on the bench at the tender age of 16 years, 220 days. The cup tie was, not surprisingly, selected by the BBC for Saturday live transmission at 5.30pm. In hindsight the decision by the authorities and police to allow such a high-risk match to go ahead at that time was at best unwise and probably downright foolish. Rooney's return, overriding the already fierce rivalry between Manchester and Merseyside, had stoked the build-up to a frenetic level and the evening kick-off allowed potential troublemakers to top-up on alcohol through the day.

The outcome was the most poisonous, frenzied atmosphere I have ever experienced at Goodison. Rooney, now a figure of hate for some Everton followers, was booed and jeered throughout the game and had missiles thrown at him. United, who were convincing winners, were leading through a first-half goal from Quinton Fortune and a second-half strike from Ronaldo when a moment of sheer madness occurred in the 70th minute. A coin, hurled from the Gwladys Street end, hit United goalkeeper Roy Carroll on the head and felled the Northern Ireland international. Fortunately, he was not seriously hurt but the potentially dangerous incident prompted a trawl through closed-circuit television footage to identify the culprit.

After United's 2-0 win there were street disturbances and Merseyside Police made 33 arrests. "We cannot afford to have any repetition of the type of behaviour that took place before, during or after our FA Cup tie against Manchester United", warned Everton chief executive Keith Wyness. "The management, playing staff and everyone associated with Everton FC would urge supporters to ensure that the good name of this club is not jeopardised by the actions of a tiny minority." On a night Everton were second best on the pitch, the most encouraging note for Moyes was the display of Arteta. He produced the pass of the match just before the interval to release Bent, whose shot was blocked by Carroll.

Everton cast off their FA Cup disappointment to produce a fine, fluent display in a 3-1 win at Aston Villa. With Carsley protecting the back four Moyes paraded a midfield of Osman, Cahill, Arteta and Kilbane for the first time. Two goals from Osman and another from Cahill - both of whom could have had hat-tricks - gave Everton their first away win over Villa since April 1987. But when the same quartet came together again in an unchanged side for the live televised home game against Blackburn they failed to reproduce their Villa Park form and sank to a 1-0 defeat, their third in a row at Goodison in League and Cup. Arteta was forced out of the match after only 23 minutes after a tackle from behind by Aaron Mokoena that went unpunished by referee Phil Dowd. Blackburn substitute Jon Stead scored for the second successive season at Goodison to jolt Everton's bid to finish in the top four and grasp a Champions League qualifying ticket.

Their next encounter was at Liverpool the following Sunday, a derby that could prove critical to the European ambitions of both clubs. It was a short but unhappy trip for Moyes and his players. Goals by Steven Gerrard and Luis Garcia gave Liverpool a 2-0 interval lead. Although Everton were far from their best they doggedly forced themselves back into contention after Liverpool's Milan Baros, who had missed two inviting chances, had been sent off for a wild 77th-minute lunge at Stubbs. An 82nd-minute Cahill strike raised Everton hopes although referee Rob Styles doused them when he blew the final whistle after only three minutes stoppage time when, as Moyes complained, seven minutes should have been played. The 2-1 defeat meant that Everton's lead over Liverpool, which soared to 12 points after their derby win in December, was now down to four. Worse was to follow.

The following Sunday, as the world mourned the death the previous night of Pope John Paul II, a 63rd-minute header from Zoltan Gera at The Hawthorns gave West Brom - including Goodison 'old boy' Kevin Campbell - a 1-0 win. It was Everton's third straight Premiership defeat and meant that their lead over Liverpool was now slashed to a single point. They had collected only 11 points from 12 games since Boxing Day and their Champions League quest seemed in dire peril.

Moyes, though, maintained his psychological ploy of keeping any reference to Europe's premier competition off his agenda, insisting: "We have never been thinking about it, only about having the best season we possibly can and at this moment we are close to that. We haven't run out of steam." As if to provide evidence of that his side rammed in four goals without reply at home to Crystal Palace a week later, when young striker James Vaughan wrote his name in the record books. Bent and Ferguson formed a two-man attack and Arteta launched the victory roll with his first Everton goal, flighting a seventh-minute free-kick into the top corner after Palace goalkeeper Gabor Kiraly had handled outside his area.

After Everton had lost skipper Stubbs with a shoulder injury - Steve Watson going on - Arteta's midfield colleague Cahill weighed in with two second- half goals. His first was an eight-yard drive into the roof of the net, the second a header off a Kilbane cross. With 16 minutes left Moyes produced a rabbit from his hat by sending on Vaughan for his debut in place of Naysmith. He was in first-team action for just 13 minutes when he met Kilbane's cross to clinch a 4-0 win and smash three records. At the age of 16 years, 271 days he became Everton's youngest debutant - beating Joe Royle's 39-year record by 11 days - as well as Everton's and the Premiership's youngest scorer.

Everton's comprehensive victory, following Liverpool's defeat at Manchester City the previous day, moved them four points ahead of their local rivals, both after 32 games. Next up, 10 days later, was the live televised visit of Manchester United and Rooney. Thankfully, there was no repeat of the worst excesses of the FA Cup meeting and it was a very different outcome on the field for Moyes' team as a battle-honed warrior turned back the clock.

After a goalless first half Nigel Martyn's great 50th-minute block from Paul Scholes off a fine Rooney pass was the foundation for Everton to strike what proved the winning blow. Five minutes later Ronaldo's foul on resolute emergency left-back Steve Watson, who was an impressive stand-in for the injured Naysmith and Pistone, conceded a free-kick delivered from the left by Arteta. Ferguson, 33-years-old but reminiscent of when he was 23, left Rio Ferdinand a spectator as he met the ball and powered a header past Tim Howard. It had been that same Scottish forehead that had brought Everton's last Premiership win over United more than a decade earlier and at the same Gwladys Street end of Goodison.

Whenever United threatened to cancel out Ferguson's strike they were repulsed by Martyn or their own inaccuracy, although Rooney was not far off target with low shot. The wheels, though, began to come off for United. Their experienced England defender Gary Neville was sent off by referee Phil Dowd for a 72nd-minute act of sheer stupidity in kicking the ball at the crowd. He was the first United player ever dismissed in 152 League games against Everton and in stoppage time there were two, when Scholes received his marching orders with a second booking for kicking at Kilbane.

Everton's win was their first in 21 League and Cup meetings with United, stretching back to the 1995 FA Cup final, and perhaps they had still not come down to earth when Bimingham came to Goodison three days later. Beattie, who had gone on against United as a late substitute for Ferguson, was back in the starting line-up for the lunchtime kick-off, with Bent and Ferguson rested. Everton were chasing the game from the fifth minute, when Emile Heskey put

Birmingham ahead with a superb shot, and Beattie looked ill-suited to the lone striker's role. Home fans gasped in disbelief when he headed wide from six yards off a measured Osman cross and he was replaced after an hour by Bent. But for the second time in three days it was Ferguson who was the hero.

There were four minutes left when Ferguson, who had replaced Carsley, fired the equaliser beyond Maik Taylor after Cahill and Bent had seen opportunities blocked. It was Ferguson's eighth Everton goal as a substitute - equalling Adrian Heath's club record. His delight was obvious and he was booked for jumping into the crowd to celebrate. The value of the point Everton had prised from one of their worst displays of the season increased later that day when Liverpool fell to a shock defeat at Crystal Palace.

Everton were four points ahead with a match in hand and even though they lost 2-0 a week later at Fulham - where their last win was back in 1966 - Liverpool's home draw with Middlesbrough still gave Moyes' side a three-point lead. Now they knew that a win over Newcastle in their final home game would out them within touching distance of clinching fourth place.

David Weir had not scored for three-and-a-half years when he met Mikel Arteta's 43rd-minute free-kick and powered in a far post header. Arteta was there, too, to set up Cahill for a 54th-minute finish that not only secured victory but also the most unlikely fourth place in the modern history of English football. Although at the final whistle Everton still needed one more point to be certain mathematically of fourth spot, Liverpool's defeat at Arsenal the next day guaranteed it.

"To come from 17th to fourth is a big turnaround," said Moyes, with massive understatement, after completing a lap of honour with his players. "When you are in the top four in September and stay there when people are saying you're not good enough and your squad isn't big enough, it is an achievement." Weir, back as skipper for the run-in in the absence of Stubbs, said: "There are no superstars here. We realise it's the collective effort that has got us where we are."

Whether the fact that they had crossed the finishing line to fourth had a mentally negative impact on the squad when they stepped out at Highbury the following Wednesday evening is in the realms of hypothesis. The reality is that they sank to a pride-shredding 7-0 defeat by Arsenal, their heaviest losing margin since an identical result at Portsmouth in the old First Division in September 1949. Arsenal's massive victory was the Premiership's biggest winning margin since Manchester United 8 Nottingham Forest 1 in 1999 and meant that Arsene Wenger's side had put 14 goals past Everton in three League and Cup meetings that season.

"I'm totally embarrassed," admitted a shocked Moyes. Although his side lost their final game of the season 3-2 at Bolton - when top scorer Cahill took his total to 12 and Carsley was also on the mark - some pride had been restored and the season's overall achievement was undimmed. Their fourth place, with 61 points from 38 games, was their highest since 1988 and the first time they had finished above Liverpool, other than as champions, since 1964-65 when they were fourth and their Anfield rivals seventh. Now the unexpected but demanding challenge of Europe beckoned as Moyes, named Manager of the Year by the League Managers' Association for the second time in three seasons, led Everton into a new era.

During the summer he brought in Per Kroldrup (from Udinese for £5 million), Simon Davies (Tottenham, £4 million), Phil Neville (Manchester United, £3.5 million), Nuno Valente (Porto, £1.4 million), Matteo Ferrari (Roma, loan with view to £3.7 million deal), Andy van der Meyde (Inter Milan, £2 million), John Ruddy (Cambridge, £250,000) and completed a permanent £2 million deal for Mikel Arteta from Real Sociedad. Departing Goodison were Steve Watson (West Brom) and Alan Stubbs (Sunderland).

Colin Harvey's football path, after leaving Everton in January 1994 following the arrival of Mike Walker as manager, took him along the highways and byways of the English game, eventually leading back to his spiritual home:

"I definitely wanted to stay in the game but I was in limbo when I left. In fact I wasn't involved in the game for the rest of that 1993-94 season. Then I got a call from Andy King, who was then manager at Mansfield in the old Third Division, asking me if I'd be interested in teaming up with him there as assistant manager. I said I would and that was it.

He'd first of all asked me if I'd help out a bit during the summer and on the August day I arrived at Field Mill, the Mansfield ground, Kingy was leaving to go to visit his mother, who was undergoing a big operation. So I was just left to organise a few days' pre-season training with a load of players I'd never seen or spoken to before. But we got through it and I enjoyed working with Kingy. Obviously we knew each other well from our Everton days and he'd lost none of his bubble and enthusiasm.You never know who will go into management or who will succeed.

But you can judge someone's love for the game right away and he definitely had that. When you looked at him as a player you couldn't have imagined him going into management. He was a bit of a scatterbrain in those days. But he'd changed and having known him for most of his playing career I was glad to help him in management.

Just after I'd agreed to go to Mansfield I got an invitation totally out of the blue from Kenny Dalglish. He rang me and said the reserve-team job was going at Blackburn, where Terry Darracott had gone as youth-team coach. Even though we 'd been managers on Merseyside at the same time and we'd met and chatted on many occasions, as well of course at derby games, I didn't know him well. So that made his call even more flattering. I appreciated it very much. But I was already committed to going to Mansfield so I had to decline Kenny's offer.

I used to travel to Mansfield on a Monday morning, stay in a hotel for a couple of nights, go home on the Wednesday, go back on Thursday morning and go home again on the Saturday night after the match. I used to give a lift to John Doolan, a defender who'd been released by Everton. I got him a trial at Mansfield, they signed him and he turned out to be a good player for them. He was in the team when we completed the Coca-Cola Cup knock-out of Howard Wilkinson's Leeds, which was a fantastic achievement.

We'd beaten Rochdale in the first round and were drawn to play at Elland Road in the first leg of the second round. Nobody gave us a prayer away from home against a Premiership club, especially when we were facing players such as Gordon Strachan, Rod Wallace, Gary McAllister and Gary Speed. But we grabbed all the backpage headlines with a great 1-0 win through an 18th-minute goal from Simon Ireland. 'Stags Party' was one of the memorable newspaper headlines, with a play on Mansfield's nickname.

We still faced a tough job in the return leg but, with Doolan coming into the team, we held out for a goalless draw and went through on aggregate, the greatest feat in the history of the East Midlands club. We lost to Millwall in the next round but I'm sure the memory of knocking out Leeds will last a long time in Mansfield. For me it was wonderful to experience a giant-killing act like that with a small club. The morning after our first leg win at Leeds a special delivery arrived for Kingy and I. We opened it to find a card and a bottle of champagne from Bill Kenwright. The card said: 'Congratulations to two Evertonians.' It was a wonderful gesture.

In November of that season I got a call from Graeme Sharp, who'd been appointed manager of Oldham, offering me the job of his assistant. They were then in the Endsleigh First Division and it was a job I had to take. Kingy understood that perfectly. Graeme had been in temporary charge at Oldham for a week or so following the departure of Joe Royle and Willie Donachie to Everton but once he got the job permanently - their first new manager in 12 years - he asked me to join him and I was delighted to accept. He was one of the great centre-forwards of Everton history and we got on well at Goodison when I was assistant to Howard Kendall and when I became manager. So it was great to team up with him again.

Graeme had gone to Oldham from Everton as a player in 1991 but he'd been having problems with his back, forcing him to think about hanging up his boots. That was a pity because he was Oldham's best player. He played very few games after I'd gone there, which was a massive blow. Even half as good as he was at Everton he'd have been a tremendous asset on the pitch as well as off it. We finished that season 14th in the table and Graeme started only 10 matches before retiring as a player in May 1995. The following year we were 18th which, given the parlous financial situation, was quite an achievement.

In February 1997, with the club bottom-of-the-table after a run of bad results, Graeme tendered his resignation. I'd been alongside side him and I had to go too. I had no complaints about that. It was a situation similar to the one at Everton when Howard quit. So Graeme and I resigned together.

The following month I got a call from a third former Everton player offering me a job! Adrian Heath, who was managing Burnley, asked me if I'd become his assistant at Turf Moor. I accepted and felt very flattered that three ex-players from Goodison had made me job offers. When I joined Burnley, who were in Division Two, it meant that since leaving Everton I'd worked in all three divisions outside the Premiership and it was a tremendous, broadening experience. My time at Burnley, though, was only until the end of that 1996-97 season because I got a call to return to Everton. I didn't even have a contract at Turf Moor.

My old contract at Oldham was running down and I was working for Adrian just for expenses when an associate of Everton chairman Peter Johnson rang me to tell me that they were revamping the entire youth set-up at the club as a forerunner to the setting-up of a youth academy. I was offered the new job of Director of Youth Coaching, which I was delighted to accept. It was my fourth start at Everton, spanning the early 1960s to the late 1990s, and one I took up with relish because helping to develop young footballers is one of the most fulfilling roles in the game. This time It was flattering to be offered the job for a different reason. I hadn't worked for Peter Johnson's regime in the past. I didn't know him. Yet here they were, because of my reputation, bringing me back to Everton.

Before the formalities of my appointment were completed I had a talk with Peter when he told me how interested he was in youth development. The way Manchester United had produced great players from their ranks had made a big impact on him. He said he'd been told I was a good coach, that I was interested in looking after young players and that he was desperate for Everton to win the FA Youth Cup.

At the time I was appointed Everton didn't have a manager. Joe Royle had left in March and Dave Watson had acted as caretaker to the end of the season. When they did appoint someone it turned out to be my long-time friend and colleague Howard Kendall! Now, though, I didn't have a lot of contact with him because I was based at the new youth training complex at Netherton, on the site that was formerly the Littlewooods Sports Ground. Ray Hall was then Head of Youth Development and later Academy Director and I brought former Wales international Andy Holden into the youth set-up, which had seen the departure of John Hurst and Ronnie Goodlass. I'd worked with Andy at Oldham, where he was reserve-team coach. Les Helm moved from first-team physiotherapist to work with the youngsters in a multi-role capacity as fitness and dietary advisor as well as physio. He did it all very thoroughly.

Another man who showed a keen paternal interest in youth development and our work at Netherton was Keith Tamlin, the director with special responsibility for the complex and later elected as Everton's deputy life president. He devoted a great deal of time to it and was also very helpful to me when I returned to the club to take on the youth job. When I started I felt that the self-image of the young players was crucial. I wanted them to think of themselves as budding footballers not schoolboys. That's why I stopped the YTS lads cleaning boots and doing menial jobs. I was well aware it had been going on in the game since the days of Dixie Dean. I had to scrub mud off boots and brush up while Howard Kendall, for instance, once had to paint Preston's ground. But these lads are apprentice footballers and that's what they should be doing - playing football. They have their own playing equipment to look after and they should be treated like responsible footballers. We must do anything that gives them even an extra two per cent to make them better players. Nutrition is also very important, as is lifestyle. We all know they're not going to behave like monks, but if we can teach them to become more responsible earlier it may help.

There is no doubt that investment in a club's youth programme is the way ahead. With telephone number transfer fees as they are it's so important to bring through your own talent. I think it's crucial, too, that in an era of a great influx of foreign players into English football managers give home-produced players their opportunities. I know that in the past some locally-born Merseyside players felt they had a better chance of making it at a club in another part of the country because of a strange in-built bias against locals. That certainly wasn't my experience, but it does provide food-for- thought and something I hope does not escalate into foreign players being preferred to British ones simply because of their nationality.

I was delighted that in my first season back at Everton we achieved Peter Johnson's ambition by winning the FA Youth Cup. It was the sixth time the club had reached the final, having previously won it in 1965 and 1984, and been runners-up in 1961, 1977 and 1983. I have to say that winning the Youth Cup is not an end in itself because I was delighted with our 1979 youth squad which lost in the semi-final but which sent players like Steve McMahon, Kevin Ratcliffe, Brian Borrows, Joe McBride and Paul Lodge on the path to first-team football.

But as I was also youth coach when we'd lost out in the 1977 final to Crystal Palace it was doubly saytisfying to see the lads of 1998 collect the trophy with a 5-3 aggregate success over Blackburn. The squad that season included Richard Dunne, Francis Jeffers, Danny Cadamarteri, Tony Hibbert, Leon Osman and Phil Jevons.

Our 2-2 home draw in the second leg at Goodison came only two days before the first team's critical last match of the season against Coventry, on which Premiership survival hinged. Passions amongst the fans were running high and Peter Johnson was very much a target for their feelings. Yet he turned up for our game flanked in the directors box by three burly police officers with three more in the stand monitoring a group of anti-Johnson hecklers. I really appreciated the fact that he had come in such hostile circumstances to watch the lads. In fact, he had come to most of the games right through our run to the final, even away matches.

At Watford we were losing 2-0 at half-time and ended up winning 3-2, and Peter was beaming when he came into our dressing room. It was the first time I'd ever known a chairman travel that far for a youth game, although later Sir Philip Carter did the same. I know a lot of Everton fans were anti-Johnson from the outset because of his Liverpool affiliation. But he'd put his money into the club and he was desperate for success. I know that from the conversations I had with him. If he'd managed to bring continued success to Everton, all the personal criticism of him would just have faded away and, from the perspective of Malcolm Glazer's takeover of Manchester United, Johnson's previous Anfield link seems small beer indeed.

Although the plans for Everton's state-of-the-art academy set-up didn't materialise, the 1998-99 season saw the launch of a new era in youth football. After years of 'A' and 'B' team football in the old Lancashire Leagues, which gave me my grounding as a player, we joined the new FA Premier Youth Academy, which was devised by Howard Wilkinson in his role as FA Technical Director. It was an exciting initiative and encompassed the best youth set-ups in the country playing each other at under 17 and under 19 levels. It meant that we were now pitting our young players against the best the country had to offer.

We reached the FA Youth Cup final again in 2002 just after David Moyes had succeeded Walter Smith as manager. Walter had taken over from Howard and I was desperately sorry that Howard's third stint as manager lasted only a season. I'm sure he felt bad about it, too. We lost 4-2 on aggregate to Aston Villa in the 2002 Youth Cup final - but we did have a certain Wayne Rooney in our ranks to ease the disappointment!

In 2003 I retired from Everton because of recurring problems with my right hip replacement. I had my left one done in 1984 and I've never had any problems with it. But the trouble I had with my right one, and the pain it caused, led me to call it a day with a year left on my contract. I wasn't enjoying the training anymore. My mobility was affected and it had reached the stage where I was taking out a chair so I could sit down for periods. As far as I was concerned I wasn't doing my job properly so I had a few chats with the club's chief executive Michael Dunford and called it a day. It was a sad decision but one I had to make. The club granted me a testimonial match, in which Everton played Bologna in August 2003, and as I walked out onto the pitch with my first granddaughter Bethany - I now have another, Rebecca - myriad memories came flooding back with the tears.

But I'm still involved in the game. I scout in the North West, mainly outside the Premiership, for my long-time pal Joe Royle at Ipswich. I also do regular Saturday columns in the Liverpool Daily Post during the season, assessing the opposition facing Everton and Liverpool. They contacted me as soon as I left

Everton with the offer of doing columns. I said I didn't want to do a knocking, opinionated column but one geared to player appraisal, tactics and formations. That chimed in with their ideas and so I began. I record all the weekend Premiership games, and any others involving teams due to play Everton or Liverpool. Then on Fridays the sports editor Richard Williamson rings me and from my notes we put the columns together. It's something I take pains over and thoroughly enjoy doing.

I still keep fit and my hip is a lot better because I don't make as many demands on it as I did when I was coaching. But I've always loved training and I still go to a gym every day, although I use a static bike. Everton, of course, will always be in my blood. After all, I began playing for them in the early 1960s and left, after filling various roles, in the new millennium.

I just feel relieved that they seem to have emerged, glimpsing new horizons, from the grim 1990s which was probably the most unstable time in Everton's history with constant relegation battles, frequent changes of managers, takeover issues, boardroom uncertainty and a big debt. I dread to think what might have happened if one of those relegation battles had gone wrong and the club had gone down. Some people even used to say that it was better to be relegated, regroup and come back stronger. I don't go along with that. The Premiership is the place to be. With every passing year it becomes the only place to be - from every conceivable aspect.

I was one of those who throught that wall-to-wall televising of football would have a detrimental affect on attendances. It looks like I was wrong. Premiership football has become the new rock n'roll. People - and that means whole families - can't seem to get enough of it. Stadiums are now comfortable all-seaters and spectators have more and more exotic foreign players paraded in front of them which, as I have indicated previously, carries its own threat to our national game.

The 2004-05 season was phenomenal for Everton and for David Moyes. After the soap opera summer of turmoil off the pitch, losing Wayne Rooney at the start of the season and Thomas Gravesen in the middle of it, to come from relegation candidates to fourth place and the Champions League qualifiers was almost in the realms of fantasy. No wonder Bill Kenwright called it 'a miracle' and the future is challenging to say the least. The Premiership is already several leagues in one - the elite of Chelsea, Arsenal and Manchester United, the next strata of clubs aiming for Europe, a group below that treading water and at the bottom, usually, the promoted clubs scrapping to stay up.

Everton were unlucky to draw Villarreal in the Champions League qualifier. They could hardly have been pitted against more testing opponents than the side that finished third in the Spanish League and they went out on a 4-2 aggregate to drop into the UEFA Cup. The damage was done when they lost the home first leg 2-1, caught by two lethal counter attacks yet the return in Spain was marred by a perverse refereeing display by Pierluigi Collina. The Italian's decisions appeared loaded against Everton from the start and his ruling out of Duncan Ferguson's late strike was utterly baffling.

It reminded me of the European Cup night against Inter Milan at Goodison in 1963 when Roy Vernon had what seemed a perfectly good goal disallowed. Collina said he ruled out Ferguson's header for a foul by Marcus Bent as the corner was delivered. Yet video replays show that Bent was trying to break free from a defender's grasp and they were nowhere near Ferguson. It was an outrageous decision that may well have cost Everton a £15 million bonanza from the group stage. Villarreal were already wobbling after Arteta's equaliser on the night and if Everton had gone 2-1 up with the prospect of extra time, it might have opened the door for Moyes' side. At least it would have given them a chance. Villarreal had been handed a great escape and clinched victory with a last-gasp goal from Diego Forlan.

At one time, Collina was correctly hailed as the best official in the world, but for Everton fans, his performance at the El Madrigal Stadium puts him in the same refereeing hall of infamy as a certain Clive Thomas. Ironically, only a few days later, Collina tendered his resignation after a row with the Italian authorities over his signing of a £600,000 advertising campaign with car firm Opel, who also sponsor AC Milan. It's a great pity it did not happen a week later and Everton might well have been celebrating their passage into the Champions League group stage. Now, though, they must look forward and build on their significant progress.

For Everton to reclaim some of the high ground that many supporters feel is the club's entitlement calls for astute leadership at board and management level. Bill Kenwright unquestionably has Everton's best interests at heart. When his power battle with Peter Johnson was at its height all I genuinely wanted to emerge from it was the best outcome for Everton, regardless of personalities. It went Bill's way and I know whatever decisions he takes will be for the benefit of Everton.

The club went into 2005-06 leading the table of points gained in the top flight of English football with a total of 5,846, applying three-points for a win.

Even if you used two points for a win - 4,223 - they were still out front ahead of Liverpool, Arsenal and the rest. Such is Goodison's rich tradition. I hope it is honed and embellished in years to come and that the motto 'Nothing But The Best' will act as a springboard to new achievement."

Scoring a rare left-footed goal against Middlesbrough in the FA Cup, January 1971.

Chapter Seventeen

The Statistics

Colin Harvey's Playing Record with Everton

	League		FA Cup		FL Cup		Europe		Others		Total	
	Apps	Gls	A	G	A	G	A	G	A	G	A	G
1963-64	2	0	0	0	-	-	1	0	0	0	3	0
1964-65	32	2	4	1	-	-	4	2	-	-	40	5
1965-66	40	1	8	1	-	-	4	0	-	-	52	2
1966-67	42	1	6	0	-	-	4	0	1	0	53	1
1967-68	34	0	4	0	2	0	-	-	-	-	40	0
1968-69	36	4	4	0	4	0	-	-	-	-	44	4
1969-70	35	3	0	0	3	0	-	-	-	-	38	3
1970-71	36	2	5	1	0	0	6	0	1	0	48	3
1971-72	17	3	3	1	0	0	-	-	-	-	20	4
1972-73	24/2	0	0	0	1	0	-	-	-	-	25/2	0
1973-74	15/2	1	0	0	0/1	0	-	-	-	-	15/3	1
1974-75	4	1	0	0	0	0	-	-	-	-	4	1
Career	317/4	18	34	4	10/1	0	19	2	2	0	382/5	24

Colin Harvey's Playing Record with Sheffield Wednesday

	League		FA Cup		FL Cup		Europe		Others		Total	
1974-75	30	2	0	0	0	0	-	-	-	-	30	2
1975-76	15	0	1	0	1	0	-	-	-	-	17	0
Career	45	2	1	0	1	0	-	-	-	-	47	2
Total	362/4	20	35	4	11/1	0	19	2	2	0	429/5	26

Colin Harvey Facts

• Harvey scored three times in 13 reserve-team games in 1962-63 and bagged ten goals in 35 reserve games in 1963-64. His first reserve goal was in a 3-3 draw against Huddersfield in September 1962 and a year later, he scored in a 3-0 defeat of Liverpool three days after his debut in Milan.

• Colin Harvey's debut in the European Cup preliminary round, second leg against Internazionale at the San Siro Stadium, Milan on September 25, 1963 at the age of 18 years, 313 days make him the third youngest player to appear for Everton in European competition.

• His record was lowered by Jimmy Husband, who was 18 years, 32 days old when he played against Ujpest Dozsa in the Inter-Cities Fairs Cup second round, second leg at Goodison Park, November 16, 1965.

• The second youngest player for Everton in Europe was Rob Wakenshaw who was 18 years, 284 days old when he went on as a substitute for Adrian Heath against University College Dublin in the Cup Winners' Cup first round, second leg at Goodison Park on October 2, 1984.

• Harvey is the only Everton player to make his first-team debut in Europe's premier competition, the Champions Cup. Four others also made their debut in Europe; Tommy Wright v Valerengen (Inter-Cities Fairs Cup, 1st round, 2nd leg, October 14, 1964), Imre Varadi as substitute for Peter Eastoe v Feyenoord (Uefa Cup, 1st round, 1st leg, September 19, 1979), Joe McBride v Feyenoord (Uefa Cup, 1st round, 2nd leg, October 3, 1979) and Johnny Morrissey Jnr as substitute for Kevin Sheedy v Inter Bratislava (Cup Winners' Cup, 2nd round, 2nd leg, November 7, 1984).

• Harvey vies with Brian Labone as the Everton player to make most European appearances for the club. They each played 19 times. The pair, along with Gordon West, are the only three players to appear in both Everton's European Cup campaigns of 1963-64 and 1970-71.

• Harvey won 1 full England cap (against Malta, February 1971), made 5 Under 23 appearances and 3 Football League representative appearances.

• Harvey was the only Everton player to be sent off twice in the old First Division - at Fulham in October 1965 and at Leicester City in May 1969.

• Harvey was the first post-war Everton player - and the first since 1929 - to score his first goal for the club at Anfield in a derby match - in the 4-0 win in September 1964. Andrei Kanchelskis emulated Harvey's feat in 1995.

• Three of Harvey's first four away venues of his senior career were, remarkably, the San Siro, Old Trafford and Anfield.

• Liverpool were Colin's most requent opponents of his Everton career. He played in 21 derbies, which stood as a post-war club record when he left the club in 1974. His most regular scoring victims were West Ham (4 goals) and West Brom (3 goals).

• Harvey won 1 full England cap (against Malta, February 1971), made 5 Under 23 appearances and made 3 Football League representative appearances.

• Harvey scored twice for Everton on one occasion - against Chelsea at Goodison in August 1971.

• Harvey, who played for the club in 1964 and 1974, is one of a select group who have appeared for Everton in calendar years a decade apart. Others who have done so, since 1960, are: Brian Labone (1961/1971), John Hurst (1966/1976), Roger Kenyon (1967/1977), Terry Darracott (1968/1978), Howard Kendall (1971/1981), Mick Lyons (1971/1981), David Johnson (1972/1982), Neville Southall (1985/1995), Dave Watson (1990/2000), David Unsworth (1993/2003), Duncan Ferguson (1995/2005).

• Harvey was transferred to Sheffield Wednesday for £70,000 in September 1974, retired as a player through injury in March 1976 and returned to Everton as youth coach in July 1976, becoming reserve-team coach in August 1978 and first-team coach in November 1983.

• Harvey was appointed Everton manager, succeeding Howard Kendall, on June 19, 1987. He was dismissed on October 31, 1990 having been in charge for 175 senior games comprising 75 wins, 52 draws and 48 defeats. In the League only, his record was: Played 126, won 51, drawn 37, lost 38. During his three full seasons at the helm Everton finished 4th, 8th and 6th in the former First Division, reached the FA Cup final in 1989 and won the 1987 Charity Shield.

• Six days after his dismissal as manager Harvey returned to Goodison as assistant to the re-appointed Kendall.

• In January 1994, with Mike Walker having succeeded Kendall, Harvey left Everton, working first as assistant to Andy King at Mansfield Town and later in the year becoming assistant to Oldham Athletic manager Graeme Sharp. The pair resigned in February 1997 and the following month Harvey became assistant to Adrian Heath at Burnley.

• Harvey returned to Everton as Director of Youth Coaching in June 1997 and retired from the club in June 2003, his unique service being recognised by a Goodison testimonial two months later.

Goals against opposition

Name	Games	Goals
AaB Aalborg	2	0
Arsenal	17	0
Aston Villa	6	0
Bedford Town	1	0
Birmingham City	3	1
Blackburn Rovers	6	0
Blackpool	8	0
Borussia Monchengladbach	2	0
Bristol City	1	0
Bristol Rovers	1	0
Burnley	14	0
Carlisle United	1	0
Chelsea	17	2
Colchester United	1	0
Coventry City	12	0
Crystal Palace	9	2
Darlington	1	0
Derby County	9	0
FC Nuremburg	2	0
Fulham	7	0
Huddersfield Town	2	0
IBK Keflavik	2	0
Inter Milan	1	0
Ipswich Town	6	1
Kilmarnock	1	1
Leeds United	18	0
Leicester City	11	0
Liverpool	21	1
Luton Town	1	0
Manchester City	16	0
Manchester United	18	1
Middlesbrough	1	1
Newcastle United	14	0
Northampton Town	2	0
Norwich City	2	0

Goals against opposition

Name	Games	Goals
Nottingham Forest	12	0
Panathinaikos	2	0
Queens Park Rangers	1	1
Real Zaragoza	2	0
Sheffield United	10	0
Sheffield Wednesday	13	1
Southampton	12	1
Southport	1	0
Stoke City	17	1
Sunderland	13	1
Tottenham Hotspur	16	0
Tranmere Rovers	1	0
Ujpest Dozsa	2	0
Valerengen	1	1
Walsall	1	0
West Bromwich Albion	16	3
West Ham United	18	4
Wolverhampton Wanderers	13	1
Total	**387**	**24**

Colin Harvey Everton Appearances and Goals

Season	Date	Opps	Comp	Pos	Venue	Att	F	A	Result	Goals
1963-64	25-Sep-63	Inter Milan	Euro. Cup	8	A	70000	0	1	L	
1963-64	21-Mar-64	Blackburn R	1st Division	10	A	35142	2	1	W	
	27-Mar-64	West Brom	1st Division	10	H	61187	1	1	D	
1964-65	16-Sep-64	Manchester U	1st Division	10	A	50286	1	2	L	
1964-65	19-Sep-64	Liverpool	1st Division	8	A	52619	4	0	W	1
1964-65	23-Sep-64	Valerengen	Fairs Cup	8	A	17952	5	2	W	1
1964-65	26-Sep-64	Birmingham	1st Division	8	A	21240	5	3	W	
1964-65	3-Oct-64	West Ham	1st Division	8	H	45430	1	1	D	
1964-65	5-Oct-64	Aston Villa	1st Division	8	A	23115	2	1	W	
1964-65	10-Oct-64	Sheffield Wed	1st Division	10	H	41911	1	1	D	
1964-65	17-Oct-64	Blackpool	1st Division	8	A	31855	1	1	D	
1964-65	24-Oct-64	Blackburn R	1st Division	10	H	40948	2	3	L	
1964-65	14-Nov-64	Chelsea	1st Division	10	A	30716	1	5	L	
1964-65	23-Nov-64	Kilmarnock	Fairs Cup	10	H	30727	4	1	W	1
1964-65	28-Nov-64	Sunderland	1st Division	10	A	41581	0	4	L	
1964-65	5-Dec-64	Wolves	1st Division	8	H	27533	5	0	W	
1964-65	12-Dec-64	Stoke City	1st Division	8	H	31713	1	1	D	
1964-65	19-Dec-64	Tottenham H	1st Division	6	A	41994	2	2	D	
1964-65	26-Dec-64	West Brom	1st Division	6	H	46719	3	2	W	
1964-65	2-Jan-65	Burnley	1st Division	6	H	42177	2	1	W	
1964-65	9-Jan-65	Sheffield Wed	FA CUP	6	H	44732	2	2	D	
1964-65	13-Jan-65	Sheffield Wed	FA CUP	8	A	50080	3	0	W	1
1964-65	16-Jan-65	Sheffield Utd	1st Division	8	A	21625	0	0	D	
1964-65	20-Jan-65	Manchester U	Fairs Cup	8	A	49075	1	1	D	
1964-65	30-Jan-65	Leeds United	FA CUP	8	A	50051	1	1	D	
1964-65	2-Feb-65	Leeds United	FA CUP	8	H	65940	1	2	L	
1964-65	4-Feb-65	Manchester U	Fairs Cup	8	H	54397	1	2	L	
1964-65	6-Feb-65	Birmingham	1st Division	8	H	34033	1	1	D	1
1964-65	13-Feb-65	West Ham	1st Division	8	A	25163	1	0	W	
1964-65	20-Feb-65	Sheffield Wed	1st Division	8	A	16687	1	0	W	
1964-65	27-Feb-65	Blackpool	1st Division	8	H	35267	0	0	D	
1964-65	6-Mar-65	Blackburn R	1st Division	8	A	15960	2	0	W	
1964-65	13-Mar-65	Aston Villa	1st Division	8	H	32565	3	1	W	
1964-65	20-Mar-65	Leeds United	1st Division	8	A	29701	1	4	L	
1964-65	23-Mar-65	West Brom	1st Division	8	A	12244	0	4	L	
1964-65	31-Mar-65	Chelsea	1st Division	8	H	40385	1	1	D	
1964-65	3-Apr-65	Leicester City	1st Division	8	A	14377	1	2	L	
1964-65	10-Apr-65	Sunderland	1st Division	8	H	29455	1	1	D	
1964-65	12-Apr-65	Liverpool	1st Division	8	H	65402	2	1	W	
1964-65	16-Apr-65	Fulham	1st Division	8	H	38537	2	0	W	
1964-65	17-Apr-65	Wolves	1st Division	8	A	19698	4	2	W	
1964-65	19-Apr-65	Fulham	1st Division	8	A	13323	1	1	D	
1964-65	24-Apr-65	Arsenal	1st Division	8	H	32643	1	0	W	
1965-66	21-Aug-65	Northampton	1st Division	10	H	48489	5	2	W	
1965-66	25-Aug-65	Sheffield Wed	1st Division	10	A	26063	1	3	L	
1965-66	28-Aug-65	Stoke City	1st Division	10	A	30544	1	1	D	
1965-66	31-Aug-65	Sheffield Wed	1st Division	10	H	39640	5	1	W	
1965-66	4-Sep-65	Burnley	1st Division	10	H	44633	1	0	W	
1965-66	7-Sep-65	West Brom	1st Division	10	H	43468	2	3	L	1
1965-66	11-Sep-65	Chelsea	1st Division	10	A	29816	1	3	L	
1965-66	15-Sep-65	West Brom	1st Division	10	A	25513	1	1	D	
1965-66	18-Sep-65	Arsenal	1st Division	10	H	38935	3	1	W	

Colin Harvey Everton Appearances and Goals

Season	Date	Opps	Comp	Pos	Venue	Att	F	A	Result	Goals
1965-66	25-Sep-65	Liverpool	1st Division	10	A	53557	0	5	L	
1965-66	28-Sep-65	Nuremburg	Fairs Cup	10	A	10000	1	1	D	
1965-66	5-Oct-65	Blackburn R	1st Division	8	H	34694	2	2	D	
1965-66	9-Oct-65	Tottenham H	1st Division	8	H	40022	3	1	W	
1965-66	12-Oct-65	Nuremburg	Fairs Cup	8	H	39033	1	0	W	
1965-66	16-Oct-65	Fulham	1st Division	8	A	18110	2	3	L	
1965-66	23-Oct-65	Blackpool	1st Division	8	H	33766	0	0	D	
1965-66	30-Oct-65	Blackburn R	1st Division	8	A	15096	2	1	W	
1965-66	3-Nov-65	Ujpest Dozsa	Fairs Cup	8	A	4000	0	3	L	
1965-66	6-Nov-65	Leicester City	1st Division	8	H	30195	1	2	L	
1965-66	13-Nov-65	Sheffield Utd	1st Division	8	A	16579	0	2	L	
1965-66	16-Nov-65	Ujpest Dozsa	Fairs Cup	4	H	24201	2	1	W	
1965-66	20-Nov-65	Leeds United	1st Division	4	H	36291	0	0	D	
1965-66	27-Nov-65	West Ham	1st Division	4	A	21971	0	3	L	
1965-66	4-Dec-65	Sunderland	1st Division	4	H	25393	2	0	W	
1965-66	11-Dec-65	Aston Villa	1st Division	4	A	18826	2	3	L	
1965-66	15-Dec-65	Manchester U	1st Division	4	A	32896	0	3	L	
1965-66	18-Dec-65	Fulham	1st Division	4	H	20670	2	0	W	
1965-66	27-Dec-65	Nottingham F	1st Division	4	A	34750	0	1	L	
1965-66	1-Jan-66	Tottenham H	1st Division	4	A	34953	2	2	D	
1965-66	8-Jan-66	Aston Villa	1st Division	4	H	34641	2	0	W	
1965-66	11-Jan-66	West Ham	1st Division	4	H	29915	2	2	D	
1965-66	15-Jan-66	Blackpool	1st Division	4	A	14588	0	2	L	
1965-66	22-Jan-66	Sunderland	FA CUP	10	H	47893	3	0	W	
1965-66	29-Jan-66	Northampton	1st Division	10	A	16309	2	0	W	
1965-66	5-Feb-66	Stoke City	1st Division	10	H	38999	2	1	W	
1965-66	12-Feb-66	Bedford Town	FA CUP	10	A	N/A	3	0	W	
1965-66	19-Feb-66	Burnley	1st Division	10	A	19670	1	1	D	
1965-66	26-Feb-66	Chelsea	1st Division	10	H	52752	2	1	W	
1965-66	3-Mar-66	Coventry City	FA CUP	10	H	60350	3	0	W	
1965-66	12-Mar-66	Arsenal	1st Division	10	A	24821	1	0	W	
1965-66	15-Mar-66	Nottingham F	1st Division	10	H	37455	3	0	W	
1965-66	19-Mar-66	Liverpool	1st Division	10	H	62337	0	0	D	
1965-66	26-Mar-66	Manchester C	FA CUP	10	A	63034	0	0	D	
1965-66	29-Mar-66	Manchester C	FA CUP	10	H	60349	0	0	D	
1965-66	5-Apr-66	Manchester C	FA CUP	10	A	27948	2	0	W	
1965-66	8-Apr-66	Newcastle U	1st Division	10	A	30731	0	0	D	
1965-66	9-Apr-66	Sheffield Utd	1st Division	10	H	32720	1	3	L	
1965-66	11-Apr-66	Newcastle U	1st Division	10	H	32598	1	0	W	
1965-66	23-Apr-66	Manchester U	FA CUP	10	N	60000	1	0	W	1
1965-66	30-Apr-66	Sunderland	1st Division	10	A	31147	0	2	L	
1965-66	4-May-66	Leicester City	1st Division	10	A	14504	0	3	L	
1965-66	14-May-66	Sheffield Wed	FA CUP	10	N	100000	3	2	W	
1966-67	13-Aug-66	Liverpool	Charity Shield	10	H	63329	0	1	L	
1966-67	20-Aug-66	Fulham	1st Division	6	A	21634	1	0	W	
1966-67	23-Aug-66	Manchester U	1st Division	6	H	60657	1	2	L	
1966-67	27-Aug-66	Liverpool	1st Division	6	H	64318	3	1	W	
1966-67	31-Aug-66	Manchester U	1st Division	6	A	61114	0	3	L	
1966-67	3-Sep-66	Stoke City	1st Division	6	H	44005	0	1	L	
1966-67	6-Sep-66	Burnley	1st Division	6	H	44063	1	1	D	
1966-67	10-Sep-66	Sheffield Utd	1st Division	6	A	21229	0	0	D	
1966-67	17-Sep-66	West Brom	1st Division	6	H	45165	5	4	W	
1966-67	24-Sep-66	Leeds United	1st Division	6	A	38486	1	1	D	

Colin Harvey Everton Appearances and Goals

Season	Date	Opps	Comp	Pos	Venue	Att	F	A	Result	Goals
1966-67	28-Sep-66	AaB Aalborg	ECW Cup	6	A	13000	0	0	D	
1966-67	1-Oct-66	Newcastle U	1st Division	6	H	38364	1	1	D	
1966-67	8-Oct-66	West Ham	1st Division	6	A	32789	3	2	W	
1966-67	11-Oct-66	AaB Aalborg	ECW Cup	6	H	36628	2	1	W	
1966-67	15-Oct-66	Sheffield Wed	1st Division	6	H	38355	2	1	W	
1966-67	25-Oct-66	Southampton	1st Division	6	A	27179	3	1	W	
1966-67	29-Oct-66	Leicester City	1st Division	6	H	47267	2	0	W	
1966-67	5-Nov-66	Sheffield Wed	1st Division	6	A	27424	2	1	W	
1966-67	9-Nov-66	R. Zaragoza	ECW Cup	6	A	20000	0	2	L	
1966-67	12-Nov-66	Arsenal	1st Division	6	H	45745	0	0	D	
1966-67	19-Nov-66	Manchester C	1st Division	6	A	39572	0	1	L	
1966-67	23-Nov-66	R. Zaragoza	ECW Cup	6	H	56077	1	0	W	
1966-67	26-Nov-66	Blackpool	1st Division	6	H	38127	0	1	L	
1966-67	3-Dec-66	Chelsea	1st Division	6	A	35495	1	1	D	
1966-67	17-Dec-66	Fulham	1st Division	6	H	31396	3	2	W	
1966-67	23-Dec-66	Nottingham F	1st Division	6	H	34084	0	1	L	
1966-67	26-Dec-66	Nottingham F	1st Division	6	A	36227	0	1	L	
1966-67	31-Dec-66	Liverpool	1st Division	6	A	53744	0	0	D	
1966-67	7-Jan-67	Stoke City	1st Division	6	A	27171	1	2	L	
1966-67	14-Jan-67	Sheffield Utd	1st Division	6	H	36722	4	1	W	
1966-67	21-Jan-67	West Brom	1st Division	6	A	26104	0	1	L	
1966-67	28-Jan-67	Burnley	FA CUP	6	A	42482	0	0	D	
1966-67	31-Jan-67	Burnley	FA CUP	6	H	57449	2	1	W	
1966-67	4-Feb-67	Leeds United	1st Division	6	H	48738	2	0	W	
1966-67	11-Feb-67	Newcastle U	1st Division	6	A	31214	3	0	W	
1966-67	18-Feb-67	Wolves	FA CUP	6	A	53439	1	1	D	
1966-67	21-Feb-67	Wolves	FA CUP	6	H	60020	3	1	W	
1966-67	25-Feb-67	West Ham	1st Division	6	H	42504	4	0	W	
1966-67	4-Mar-67	Leicester City	1st Division	6	A	24756	2	2	D	
1966-67	11-Mar-67	Liverpool	FA CUP	6	H	64851	1	0	W	
1966-67	18-Mar-67	Southampton	1st Division	10	H	44997	0	1	L	
1966-67	22-Mar-67	Tottenham H	1st Division	10	H	50108	0	1	L	
1966-67	25-Mar-67	Sunderland	1st Division	10	A	34134	2	0	W	
1966-67	27-Mar-67	Tottenham H	1st Division	6	A	47917	0	2	L	
1966-67	1-Apr-67	Aston Villa	1st Division	6	H	36619	3	1	W	
1966-67	8-Apr-67	Nottingham F	FA CUP	6	A	47510	2	3	L	
1966-67	19-Apr-67	Chelsea	1st Division	10	H	39316	3	1	W	
1966-67	22-Apr-67	Blackpool	1st Division	10	A	13823	1	0	W	
1966-67	25-Apr-67	Arsenal	1st Division	10	A	20567	1	3	L	
1966-67	29-Apr-67	Manchester C	1st Division	10	H	33239	1	1	D	
1966-67	6-May-67	Aston Villa	1st Division	6	A	25302	4	2	W	
1966-67	13-May-67	Burnley	1st Division	6	A	11634	1	1	D	
1966-67	16-May-67	Sunderland	1st Division	6	H	30943	4	1	W	1
1967-68	19-Aug-67	Manchester U	1st Division	6	H	61452	3	1	W	
1967-68	23-Aug-67	Tottenham H	1st Division	6	A	53809	1	1	D	
1967-68	26-Aug-67	Sunderland	1st Division	6	A	37628	0	1	L	
1967-68	29-Aug-67	Tottenham H	1st Division	6	H	57790	0	1	L	
1967-68	2-Sep-67	Wolves	1st Division	6	H	51498	4	2	W	
1967-68	5-Sep-67	West Ham	1st Division	6	H	46762	2	0	W	
1967-68	9-Sep-67	Fulham	1st Division	6	A	25366	1	2	L	
1967-68	13-Sep-67	Bristol City	League Cup	6	A	22054	5	0	W	
1967-68	16-Sep-67	Leeds United	1st Division	6	H	53179	0	1	L	
1967-68	23-Sep-67	Liverpool	1st Division	6	A	54189	0	1	L	

Colin Harvey Everton Appearances and Goals

Season	Date	Opps	Comp	Pos	Venue	Att	F	A	Result	Goals
1967-68	30-Sep-67	Leicester City	1st Division	6	A	22768	2	0	W	
1967-68	7-Oct-67	Southampton	1st Division	6	H	47896	4	2	W	
1967-68	11-Oct-67	Sunderland	League Cup	6	H	39914	2	3	L	
1967-68	14-Oct-67	Chelsea	1st Division	6	A	34206	1	1	D	
1967-68	24-Oct-67	West Brom	1st Division	6	H	44092	2	1	W	
1967-68	28-Oct-67	Newcastle U	1st Division	6	A	34030	0	1	L	
1967-68	4-Nov-67	Manchester C	1st Division	6	H	47144	1	1	D	
1967-68	11-Nov-67	Arsenal	1st Division	6	A	36371	2	2	D	
1967-68	18-Nov-67	Sheffield Utd	1st Division	6	H	37994	1	0	W	
1967-68	25-Nov-67	Coventry City	1st Division	6	A	32330	2	0	W	
1967-68	2-Dec-67	Nottingham F	1st Division	6	H	44765	1	0	W	
1967-68	9-Dec-67	Stoke City	1st Division	6	A	34434	0	1	L	
1967-68	16-Dec-67	Manchester U	1st Division	6	A	57078	1	3	L	
1967-68	23-Dec-67	Sunderland	1st Division	10	H	38216	3	0	W	
1967-68	26-Dec-67	Burnley	1st Division	6	H	54324	2	0	W	
1967-68	30-Dec-67	Burnley	1st Division	6	A	22592	1	2	L	
1967-68	6-Jan-68	Wolves	1st Division	6	A	37802	3	1	W	
1967-68	20-Jan-68	Leeds United	1st Division	6	A	44119	0	2	L	
1967-68	27-Jan-68	Southport	FA CUP	6	A	18795	1	0	W	
1967-68	3-Feb-68	Liverpool	1st Division	6	H	64482	1	0	W	
1967-68	17-Feb-68	Carlisle Utd	FA CUP	6	A	25000	2	0	W	
1967-68	26-Feb-68	Southampton	1st Division	6	A	25860	2	3	L	
1967-68	2-Mar-68	Coventry City	1st Division	6	H	38804	3	1	W	
1967-68	13-Apr-68	Sheffield Utd	1st Division	3	A	25547	1	0	W	
1967-68	20-Apr-68	Chelsea	1st Division	6	H	47370	2	1	W	
1967-68	27-Apr-68	Leeds United	FA CUP	6	N	63000	1	0	W	
1967-68	29-Apr-68	Manchester C	1st Division	6	A	37786	0	2	L	
1967-68	4-May-68	Stoke City	1st Division	6	H	43302	3	0	W	
1967-68	11-May-68	West Ham	1st Division	6	A	28319	1	1	D	
1967-68	18-May-68	West Brom	FA CUP	6	N	99665	0	1	L	
1968-69	10-Aug-68	Manchester U	1st Division	6	A	61311	1	2	L	
1968-69	13-Aug-68	Burnley	1st Division	6	H	48903	3	0	W	
1968-69	17-Aug-68	Tottenham H	1st Division	6	H	56570	0	2	L	
1968-69	19-Aug-68	West Ham	1st Division	6	A	34895	4	1	W	1
1968-69	24-Aug-68	Newcastle U	1st Division	6	A	38851	0	0	D	
1968-69	27-Aug-68	Liverpool	1st Division	6	H	63938	0	0	D	
1968-69	31-Aug-68	Nottingham F	1st Division	6	H	45951	2	1	W	
1968-69	3-Sep-68	Tranmere R	League Cup	6	H	35477	4	0	W	
1968-69	7-Sep-68	Chelsea	1st Division	6	A	42017	1	1	D	
1968-69	14-Sep-68	Sheffield Wed	1st Division	6	H	44517	3	0	W	
1968-69	21-Sep-68	Coventry City	1st Division	6	A	37846	2	2	D	
1968-69	24-Sep-68	Luton Town	League Cup	6	H	30405	5	1	W	
1968-69	28-Sep-68	West Brom	1st Division	6	H	47792	4	0	W	1
1968-69	5-Oct-68	Manchester C	1st Division	6	H	55399	2	0	W	
1968-69	8-Oct-68	Liverpool	1st Division	6	A	54496	1	1	D	
1968-69	12-Oct-68	Southampton	1st Division	6	A	21688	5	2	W	
1968-69	16-Oct-68	Derby County	League Cup	6	H	44705	0	0	D	
1968-69	19-Oct-68	Stoke City	1st Division	6	H	42887	2	1	W	1
1968-69	23-Oct-68	Derby County	League Cup	6	A	34370	0	1	L	
1968-69	26-Oct-68	Wolves	1st Division	6	A	34744	2	1	W	
1968-69	2-Nov-68	Sunderland	1st Division	6	H	40492	2	0	W	
1968-69	9-Nov-68	Ipswich Town	1st Division	6	A	23049	2	2	D	
1968-69	16-Nov-68	QPR	1st Division	6	H	43552	4	0	W	1

Colin Harvey Everton Appearances and Goals

Season	Date	Opps	Comp	Pos	Venue	Att	F	A	Result	Goals
1968-69	23-Nov-68	Leeds United	1st Division	6	A	41716	1	2	L	
1968-69	30-Nov-68	Leicester City	1st Division	6	H	42492	7	1	W	
1968-69	7-Dec-68	Arsenal	1st Division	6	A	40108	1	3	L	
1968-69	14-Dec-68	Southampton	1st Division	6	H	36299	1	0	W	
1968-69	21-Dec-68	Stoke City	1st Division	6	A	20507	0	0	D	
1968-69	26-Dec-68	Manchester C	1st Division	6	A	53549	3	1	W	
1968-69	4-Jan-69	Ipswich Town	FA CUP	6	H	49047	2	1	W	
1968-69	12-Feb-69	Bristol Rovers	FA CUP	6	H	55294	1	0	W	
1968-69	1-Mar-69	Manchester U	FA CUP	6	A	63464	1	0	W	
1968-69	22-Mar-69	Manchester C	FA CUP	6	N	63025	0	1	L	
1968-69	29-Mar-69	Chelsea	1st Division	6	H	42190	1	2	L	
1968-69	1-Apr-69	West Ham	1st Division	6	H	36738	1	0	W	
1968-69	5-Apr-69	West Brom	1st Division	6	A	23156	1	1	D	
1968-69	8-Apr-69	Burnley	1st Division	6	A	17134	2	1	W	
1968-69	12-Apr-69	Coventry City	1st Division	6	H	36165	3	0	W	
1968-69	14-Apr-69	Newcastle U	1st Division	6	H	36035	1	1	D	
1968-69	19-Apr-69	Sheffield Wed	1st Division	6	A	23060	2	2	D	
1968-69	22-Apr-69	Leeds United	1st Division	6	H	59022	0	0	D	
1968-69	25-Apr-69	Nottingham F	1st Division	6	A	26629	0	1	L	
1968-69	29-Apr-69	Arsenal	1st Division	6	H	39689	1	0	W	
1968-69	14-May-69	Leicester City	1st Division	6	A	41130	1	1	D	
1969-70	9-Aug-69	Arsenal	1st Division	6	A	44364	1	0	W	
1969-70	13-Aug-69	Manchester U	1st Division	6	A	57752	2	0	W	
1969-70	16-Aug-69	Crystal Palace	1st Division	6	H	51241	2	1	W	
1969-70	19-Aug-69	Manchester U	1st Division	6	H	53185	3	0	W	
1969-70	23-Aug-69	Manchester C	1st Division	6	A	43366	1	1	D	
1969-70	26-Aug-69	Sheffield Wed	1st Division	6	H	46480	2	1	W	
1969-70	30-Aug-69	Leeds United	1st Division	6	H	53253	3	2	W	
1969-70	3-Sep-69	Darlington	League Cup	6	A	18000	1	0	W	
1969-70	6-Sep-69	Derby County	1st Division	6	A	37708	1	2	L	
1969-70	13-Sep-69	West Ham	1st Division	6	H	49052	2	0	W	
1969-70	17-Sep-69	Newcastle U	1st Division	6	A	37094	2	1	W	
1969-70	20-Sep-69	Ipswich Town	1st Division	6	A	23258	3	0	W	1
1969-70	24-Sep-69	Arsenal	League Cup	6	A	36102	0	0	D	
1969-70	27-Sep-69	Southampton	1st Division	6	H	46942	4	2	W	
1969-70	1-Oct-69	Arsenal	League Cup	6	H	41140	1	0	W	
1969-70	4-Oct-69	Wolves	1st Division	6	A	40838	3	2	W	1
1969-70	8-Oct-69	Crystal Palace	1st Division	6	A	33967	0	0	D	
1969-70	11-Oct-69	Sunderland	1st Division	6	H	47271	3	1	W	
1969-70	18-Oct-69	Stoke City	1st Division	6	H	48663	6	2	W	
1969-70	25-Oct-69	Coventry City	1st Division	6	A	37816	1	0	W	
1969-70	1-Nov-69	Nottingham F	1st Division	6	H	49610	1	0	W	
1969-70	8-Nov-69	West Brom	1st Division	6	A	34298	0	2	L	
1969-70	15-Nov-69	Chelsea	1st Division	6	A	49895	1	1	D	
1969-70	17-Jan-70	Southampton	1st Division	6	A	27156	1	2	L	
1969-70	24-Jan-70	Newcastle U	1st Division	6	H	42845	0	0	D	
1969-70	31-Jan-70	Wolves	1st Division	6	H	45681	1	0	W	
1969-70	14-Feb-70	Arsenal	1st Division	6	H	48564	2	2	D	
1969-70	21-Feb-70	Coventry City	1st Division	6	H	45934	0	0	D	
1969-70	28-Feb-70	Nottingham F	1st Division	6	A	29174	1	1	D	
1969-70	7-Mar-70	Burnley	1st Division	6	A	21114	2	1	W	
1969-70	11-Mar-70	Tottenham H	1st Division	6	A	27764	1	0	W	
1969-70	14-Mar-70	Tottenham H	1st Division	6	H	51533	3	2	W	

Colin Harvey Everton Appearances and Goals

Season	Date	Opps	Comp	Pos	Venue	Att	F	A	Result	Goals
1969-70	21-Mar-70	Liverpool	1st Division	6	A	54496	2	0	W	
1969-70	28-Mar-70	Chelsea	1st Division	6	H	58337	5	2	W	
1969-70	30-Mar-70	Stoke City	1st Division	6	A	33111	1	0	W	
1969-70	1-Apr-70	West Brom	1st Division	6	H	58523	2	0	W	1
1969-70	4-Apr-70	Sheffield Wed	1st Division	6	A	30690	1	0	W	
1969-70	8-Apr-70	Sunderland	1st Division	6	A	28774	0	0	D	
1970-71	8-Aug-70	Chelsea	Charity Shield	6	A	43547	2	1	W	
1970-71	15-Aug-70	Arsenal	1st Division	6	H	50248	2	2	D	
1970-71	18-Aug-70	Burnley	1st Division	6	H	44717	1	1	D	
1970-71	29-Aug-70	Manchester C	1st Division	6	H	50724	0	1	L	
1970-71	2-Sep-70	Manchester U	1st Division	6	A	49599	0	2	L	
1970-71	5-Sep-70	West Ham	1st Division	6	A	29171	2	1	W	
1970-71	12-Sep-70	Ipswich Town	1st Division	6	H	41596	2	0	W	
1970-71	16-Sep-70	IBK Keflavik	European Cup	6	H	28444	6	2	W	
1970-71	19-Sep-70	Blackpool	1st Division	6	A	30705	2	0	W	
1970-71	26-Sep-70	Crystal Palace	1st Division	6	H	43443	3	1	W	1
1970-71	30-Sep-70	IBK Keflavik	European Cup	6	A	9500	3	0	W	
1970-71	3-Oct-70	Coventry City	1st Division	6	A	29212	1	3	L	
1970-71	10-Oct-70	Derby County	1st Division	6	H	46614	1	1	D	
1970-71	17-Oct-70	Arsenal	1st Division	6	A	50053	0	4	L	
1970-71	21-Oct-70	Bor. M'bach	European Cup	6	A	32000	1	1	D	
1970-71	24-Oct-70	Newcastle U	1st Division	6	H	43135	3	1	W	
1970-71	31-Oct-70	West Brom	1st Division	6	A	29628	0	3	L	
1970-71	4-Nov-70	Bor. M'bach	European Cup	6	H	42744	1	1	D	
1970-71	7-Nov-70	Nottingham F	1st Division	6	H	39255	1	0	W	
1970-71	21-Nov-70	Liverpool	1st Division	6	A	53777	2	3	L	
1970-71	28-Nov-70	Tottenham H	1st Division	6	H	44301	0	0	D	
1970-71	5-Dec-70	Huddersfield	1st Division	6	A	27658	1	1	D	
1970-71	12-Dec-70	Southampton	1st Division	6	H	31139	4	1	W	
1970-71	19-Dec-70	Leeds United	1st Division	6	H	47393	0	1	L	
1970-71	26-Dec-70	Wolves	1st Division	6	A	30178	0	2	L	
1970-71	2-Jan-71	Blackburn R	FA CUP	6	H	40471	2	0	W	
1970-71	9-Jan-71	Burnley	1st Division	6	A	17512	2	2	D	
1970-71	16-Jan-71	Chelsea	1st Division	6	H	43628	3	0	W	
1970-71	23-Jan-71	Middlesboro	FA CUP	6	H	54875	3	0	W	1
1970-71	30-Jan-71	Tottenham H	1st Division	6	A	42105	1	2	L	
1970-71	6-Feb-71	Huddersfield	1st Division	6	H	37213	2	1	W	
1970-71	13-Feb-71	Derby County	FA CUP	6	H	53490	1	0	W	
1970-71	16-Feb-71	Southampton	1st Division	6	A	22183	2	2	D	1
1970-71	20-Feb-71	Liverpool	1st Division	6	H	56846	0	0	D	
1970-71	23-Feb-71	Manchester U	1st Division	6	H	52544	1	0	W	
1970-71	27-Feb-71	West Brom	1st Division	6	H	35940	3	3	D	
1970-71	6-Mar-71	Colchester U	FA CUP	6	H	53028	5	0	W	
1970-71	9-Mar-71	Panathinaikos	European Cup	6	H	46047	1	1	D	
1970-71	13-Mar-71	Stoke City	1st Division	6	H	38924	2	0	W	
1970-71	18-Mar-71	Newcastle U	1st Division	6	A	22874	1	2	L	
1970-71	24-Mar-71	Panathinaikos	European Cup	6	A	25000	0	0	D	
1970-71	27-Mar-71	Liverpool	FA CUP	6	N	62144	1	2	L	
1970-71	30-Mar-71	West Ham	1st Division	6	H	29094	0	1	L	
1970-71	10-Apr-71	Wolves	1st Division	6	H	35484	1	2	L	
1970-71	12-Apr-71	Coventry City	1st Division	6	H	24371	3	0	W	
1970-71	17-Apr-71	Derby County	1st Division	6	A	28793	1	3	L	
1970-71	24-Apr-71	Blackpool	1st Division	6	H	26286	0	0	D	

Colin Harvey Everton Appearances and Goals

Season	Date	Opps	Comp	Pos	Venue	Att	F	A	Result	Goals
1970-71	1-May-71	Crystal Palace	1st Division	6	A	21590	0	2	L	
1971-72	24-Aug-71	Chelsea	1st Division	6	H	38854	2	0	W	2
1971-72	28-Aug-71	West Ham	1st Division	6	A	26878	0	1	L	
1971-72	25-Sep-71	Crystal Palace	1st Division	6	A	25619	1	2	L	
1971-72	2-Oct-71	Coventry City	1st Division	6	H	36882	1	2	L	
1971-72	23-Oct-71	Leeds United	1st Division	6	A	34208	2	3	L	
1971-72	30-Oct-71	Newcastle U	1st Division	6	H	38811	1	0	W	
1971-72	6-Nov-71	Tottenham H	1st Division	6	A	40005	0	3	L	
1971-72	13-Nov-71	Liverpool	1st Division	6	H	56293	1	0	W	
1971-72	4-Dec-71	Stoke City	1st Division	6	H	35463	0	0	D	
1971-72	8-Jan-72	West Ham	1st Division	8	H	38482	2	1	W	1
1971-72	15-Jan-72	Crystal Palace	FA CUP	8	A	32331	2	2	D	1
1971-72	18-Jan-72	Crystal Palace	FA CUP	8	H	45408	3	2	W	
1971-72	29-Jan-72	Chelsea	1st Division	6	A	38558	0	4	L	
1971-72	5-Feb-72	Walsall	FA CUP	8	H	45462	2	1	W	
1971-72	12-Feb-72	Leeds United	1st Division	8	H	45935	0	0	D	
1971-72	4-Mar-72	Liverpool	1st Division	6	A	53922	0	4	L	
1971-72	8-Mar-72	Manchester U	1st Division	6	A	38415	0	0	D	
1971-72	11-Mar-72	Manchester C	1st Division	6	H	44649	1	2	L	
1971-72	18-Mar-72	Sheffield Utd	1st Division	6	A	28244	1	1	D	
1971-72	2-May-72	Nottingham F	1st Division	8	H	21513	1	1	D	
1972-73	12-Aug-72	Norwich City	1st Division	10	A	25851	1	1	D	
1972-73	16-Aug-72	Manchester C	1st Division	10	A	38676	1	0	W	
1972-73	19-Aug-72	Manchester U	1st Division	10	H	52348	2	0	W	
1972-73	22-Aug-72	Crystal Palace	1st Division	10	H	38429	1	1	D	
1972-73	26-Aug-72	Stoke City	1st Division	10	A	26360	1	1	D	
1972-73	29-Aug-72	Derby County	1st Division	10	H	39780	1	0	W	
1972-73	2-Sep-72	West Brom	1st Division	10	H	36269	1	0	W	
1972-73	5-Sep-72	Arsenal	League Cup	10	A	35230	0	1	L	
1972-73	9-Sep-72	Leicester City	1st Division	10	A	21080	2	1	W	
1972-73	16-Sep-72	Southampton	1st Division	10	H	37739	0	1	L	
1972-73	23-Sep-72	Birmingham	1st Division	10	A	37133	1	2	L	
1972-73	30-Sep-72	Newcastle U	1st Division	10	H	33028	3	1	W	
1972-73	7-Oct-72	Liverpool	1st Division	10	A	55975	0	1	L	
1972-73	14-Oct-72	Leeds United	1st Division	10	H	47821	1	2	L	
1972-73	21-Oct-72	Sheffield Utd	1st Division	10	A	22946	1	0	W	
1972-73	28-Oct-72	Ipswich Town	1st Division	10	H	30185	2	2	D	
1972-73	4-Nov-72	Crystal Palace	1st Division	10	A	28614	0	1	L	
1972-73	11-Nov-72	Manchester C	1st Division	10	H	32924	2	3	L	
1972-73	18-Nov-72	Arsenal	1st Division	10	A	35738	0	1	L	
1972-73	25-Nov-72	West Ham	1st Division	10	H	27558	1	2	L	
1972-73	2-Dec-72	Coventry City	1st Division	12 (s)	A	22774	0	1	L	
1972-73	9-Dec-72	Wolves	1st Division	10	H	24170	0	1	L	
1972-73	16-Dec-72	Tottenham H	1st Division	12 (s)	H	31129	3	1	W	
1972-73	23-Dec-72	Chelsea	1st Division	10	A	23385	1	1	D	
1972-73	10-Feb-73	Southampton	1st Division	10	A	16756	0	0	D	
1972-73	24-Feb-73	Tottenham H	1st Division	10	A	27427	0	3	L	
1972-73	10-Mar-73	Leeds United	1st Division	6	A	39663	1	2	L	
1973-74	25-Aug-73	Leeds United	1st Division	7	A	39425	1	3	L	
1973-74	28-Aug-73	Leicester City	1st Division	7	H	33139	1	1	D	
1973-74	1-Sep-73	Ipswich Town	1st Division	7	H	32469	3	0	W	

Colin Harvey Everton Appearances and Goals

Season	Date	Opps	Comp	Pos	Venue	Att	F	A	Result	Goals
1973-74	5-Sep-73	Stoke City	1st Division	7	A	22395	0	0	D	
1973-74	8-Sep-73	Derby County	1st Division	7	A	27638	1	2	L	
1973-74	29-Sep-73	Arsenal	1st Division	7	H	31369	1	0	W	
1973-74	30-Oct-73	Norwich City	League Cup	12 (s)	H	22046	0	1	L	
1973-75	8-Dec-73	Liverpool	1st Division	12 (s)	H	56098	0	1	L	
1973-74	2-Feb-74	Sheffield Utd	1st Division	12 (s)	A	19492	1	1	D	
1973-74	9-Feb-74	Wolves	1st Division	7	H	26504	2	1	W	
1973-74	16-Feb-74	West Ham	1st Division	7	A	29374	3	4	L	1
1973-74	23-Feb-74	Coventry City	1st Division	8	H	34762	1	0	W	
1973-74	2-Mar-74	Leicester City	1st Division	7	A	22286	1	2	L	
1973-74	30-Mar-74	Tottenham H	1st Division	7	A	19839	2	0	W	
1973-74	2-Apr-74	Manchester C	1st Division	7	A	22918	1	1	D	
1973-74	6-Apr-74	Newcastle U	1st Division	7	A	45497	1	2	L	
1973-74	20-Apr-74	Liverpool	1st Division	7	A	55848	0	0	D	
1973-74	23-Apr-74	Manchester U	1st Division	7	H	46183	1	0	W	
1974-75	17-Aug-74	Derby County	1st Division	8	H	42293	0	0	D	
1974-75	20-Aug-74	Stoke City	1st Division	8	H	35817	2	1	W	
1974-75	24-Aug-74	West Ham	1st Division	8	A	22486	3	2	W	1
1974-75	28-Aug-74	Stoke City	1st Division	8	A	27954	1	1	D	

* (s) denotes substitute appearance

Bibliography

Ball, Dave and Buckland, Gavin: *Everton - The Ultimate Book Of Stats And Facts*; The Bluecoat Press, 2001.

Corbett, James: *Everton - The School Of Science*; Macmillan, 2003.

Goble, Ray: *Manchester City: A Complete Record*; Breedon Books, 1987.

Inglis, Simon: Soccer In The Dock; Collins Willow, 1985.

Keith, John and Thomas, Peter: *The A-Z Of Mersey Soccer*; Beaverbrook Newspapers, 1973.

Kendall, Howard and Ross, Ian: *Only The Best Is Good Enough - The Howard Kendall Story*; Mainstream Publishing, 1991.

Matthews, Tony: *Who's Who Of Everton*; Mainstream Publishing, 2004.

Platt, Mark: *The Essential History Of Everton*; Headline, 2000.

Radnedge, Keir: *The Ultimate Encyclopedia Of Football*; Carlton Books, 1995.

Roberts, John: *Everton -The Official Centenary History*; Granada, 1978.

Ross, Ian and Smailes, Gordon: *Everton: A Complete Record*; Breedon Books, 1985.

Smailes, Gordon: *The Breedon Book Of Football Records*; Breedon Books, 2000.

West, Gordon: *The Championship In My Keeping*; Souvenir Press, 1970.